Decadent Developmentalism

Brazil has engaged in significant economic and political reforms since the return to democracy in 1985. Yet since the 1980s, the country has also been caught in a low-level equilibrium, marked by lackluster growth and destructive inequality. One cause is the country's enduring commitment to a set of ideas and institutions labeled *developmentalism*. This book argues that developmentalism has endured, despite hyperactive reform, because institutional complementarities across the economic and political spheres drive key actors toward strategies that are individually advantageous, but collectively suboptimal. Although there has been incremental evolution in some institutions, complementarities across institutions sustain a pattern of "decadent developmentalism" that swamps systemic change. Breaking new ground, Taylor shows how macroeconomic and microeconomic institutions are tightly interwoven with patterns of executive-legislative relations, bureaucratic autonomy, and weak control over the beneficiaries of developmental policies. His analysis of institutional complementarities across these five dimensions is relevant not only to Brazil but also to the broader study of comparative political economy.

Matthew M. Taylor is an associate professor at the School of International Service at American University. He is the author or coeditor of books on judicial politics, corruption, and foreign policy in Brazil. He has held fellowships at the Woodrow Wilson Center and the Council on Foreign Relations, and has lived extensively in Brazil, including serving as a faculty member at the University of São Paulo between 2006 and 2011.

Decadent Developmentalism

The Political Economy of Democratic Brazil

MATTHEW M. TAYLOR
American University

CAMBRIDGE
UNIVERSITY PRESS

University Printing House, Cambridge CB2 8BS, United Kingdom

One Liberty Plaza, 20th Floor, New York, NY 10006, USA

477 Williamstown Road, Port Melbourne, VIC 3207, Australia

314–321, 3rd Floor, Plot 3, Splendor Forum, Jasola District Centre,
New Delhi – 110025, India

79 Anson Road, #06–04/06, Singapore 079906

Cambridge University Press is part of the University of Cambridge.

It furthers the University's mission by disseminating knowledge in the pursuit of
education, learning, and research at the highest international levels of excellence.

www.cambridge.org
Information on this title: www.cambridge.org/9781108842280
DOI: 10.1017/9781108900072

© Matthew M. Taylor 2020

This publication is in copyright. Subject to statutory exception
and to the provisions of relevant collective licensing agreements,
no reproduction of any part may take place without the written
permission of Cambridge University Press.

First published 2020

A catalogue record for this publication is available from the British Library.

ISBN 978-1-108-84228-0 Hardback

Cambridge University Press has no responsibility for the persistence or accuracy of
URLs for external or third-party internet websites referred to in this publication
and does not guarantee that any content on such websites is, or will remain,
accurate or appropriate.

For
T.P.T.
and
B.P.T.

Contents

List of Figures	*page* viii
List of Tables	ix
Acknowledgments	x
List of Abbreviations	xiii
1 Introduction	1

PART I COMPLEMENTARITIES IN THE ECONOMIC SPHERE

2 The Macroeconomic Foundations of the Developmental State	35
3 Continuity through Change: Ideas as Ballast for the Developmental State	63
4 The Developmental Hierarchical Market Economy	90

PART II ECONOMIC, LEGAL, AND POLITICAL CONTROL OF THE DEVELOPMENTAL STATE

5 Coalitional Presidentialism and Defensive Parochialism	121
6 Rents, Control, and Reciprocity	157
7 The Autonomous Bureaucracy and Incremental Change	194
8 Conclusion	229
Notes	260
References	304
Index	355

Figures

1.1	Selected countries' per capita income as share of Brazil's, 1985 and 2017	*page* 7
1.2	Institutional complementarities within and across five domains	13
2.1	Gross tax revenue, percentage of GDP	41
3.1	GDP per capita by decade, 1960–2017	78
3.2	Educational backgrounds of senior Brazilian finance ministry and central bank officials, 1995–2015	88
4.1	Brazilian firms by sector, among the top 519 firms	95
4.2	Economic complexity, South Korea and Brazil	110
5.1	Source of donations to federal candidates, 2014 election	143
A	Subway loading at three equilibria	264
B	Reversion to equilibrium	265
C	Shifting preference-incidence curves	265
D	Incremental change under different preference-incidence curves	301

Tables

2.1	Federal expenditures by category	*page* 44
3.1	Economic policy direction and decision-making pattern	76
3.2	Economists among finance ministers, 1960–2015	82
3.3	Volatility of ministerial tenure, 1960–2015	83
4.1	Hierarchical capitalism among Brazil's largest nonfinancial firms	93
4.2	SOEs among the thirty largest companies in Brazil	100
5.1	Comparing the cost of US and Brazilian public election expenditures	139
5.2	Campaign expenditure per vote (in R$ of December 2016)	141
5.3	Tobit regression results for total campaign contributions by largest firms	145
8.1	Incentive alignment across complementary institutions	243

Acknowledgments

Brazil, like other continental nations, is a world onto itself. Despite similarities with other large democracies, it operates in ways that elude facile comparisons. In more than a quarter century of studying Brazil, I have alternated between thinking I had a grip on the country, and then marveling at how little I truly understood anything at all, when the true mechanics were suddenly exposed by a scandal, a shift in policy, or a fascinating journalistic exposé.

In part, the repeated discovery of my ignorance is an outcome of the subjects I have studied: corruption, which is seldom exposed or visible to the naked eye; the judiciary, whose relevance to the path of Brazilian democracy remains underappreciated; and the state bureaucracy, which is vast and has been morphing rapidly, in ways that have significant impacts on policy. My ignorance is also a result of the simple fact that I bring nonnative perspectives and biases to my work. This can be good in that it has allowed me to see Brazil with an outsider's implicitly comparative perspective. But it also means that I continue to be heavily reliant on local interpreters, to whom I am grateful for many conversations that began, "*ô, gringo, não seja ingênuo ...*" or "*conhece a jabuticaba? Pois é ....*" It is a sign of Brazil's complexity that three decades into my study of the country, these conversations remain frustratingly common.

So, first and foremost, many thanks go to the Brazilian friends who have helped me make sense of the country. A book like this comes out of many conversations, and both formally and informally, I have also drawn on the expertise of a wide swath of the actors described in this book: politicians, civil servants, journalists, and executives. In most cases I have avoided

Acknowledgments

citing those interviews directly, but whether cited or not, generous Brazilians have provided the most significant contributions that you will find in the pages ahead.

Because this book is the outcome of a long period of reflection, I have also incurred an obscene volume of academic debts. In Washington, colleagues at American University and at the Woodrow Wilson Center helped me find the time and funding to get the project off the ground. Eric Hershberg, director of American University's Center for Latin American and Latino Studies, has provided wise advice and valuable support over many years. I am grateful to Paulo Sotero for a fellowship at the Brazil Institute at the Woodrow Wilson Center, which provided time and headspace to move the project onto paper. Fernando Limongi made possible a stint at the Fundação Getulio Vargas (FGV) as I worked to finish up the book, as well as providing sage advice as I struggled to pull all the threads together.

Audiences at IPSA, APSA, LASA, Oxford, Princeton, McGill, Cebrap, the FGV, the Federal University of Rio Grande do Sul, and the University of São Paulo have all asked welcome hard questions. At various moments over the course of this project, I received feedback and helpful input from Susan Alberts, Maria Hermínia Tavares de Almeida, Leslie Armijo, Marta Arretche, John Bailey, Manuel Balán, Fábio Bechara, Paulo Castro, Daniel De Bonis, Chris DeSá, Michelle Egan, Ivan Filipe de Almeida Lopes Fernandes, Fernando Filgueiras, Marcio Cunha Filho, David Fleischer, Lilian Furquim, Carlos Grover, Austin Hart, Keith Henderson, Miles Kahler, Diana Kapiszewski, Fábio Kerche, Mark Langevin, Felix Lopez, Maria Rita Loureiro, Moisés Marques, Lindsay Mayka, Al Montero, Shoon Murray, Sidney Nakahodo, Guilherme da Nóbrega, Amâncio Oliveira, Janina Onuki, Roberto Padovani, Gavin Parrish, Tony Pereira, Anna Petherick, John Polga-Hecimovich, Arturo Porzecanski, Tim Power, Sergio Praça, Marcus Rocha, Gilberto Rodrigues, Fábio de Sá e Silva, David Samuels, Marcelo Santos, Ben Ross Schneider, Susan Shepler, Steve Silvia, Sergei Soares, Tony Spanakos, Bruno Speck, Barbara Stallings, Andrew Stein, Matthew Stephenson, Alejandro Angel Tapias, and Laurence Whitehead.

Workshops at the FGV's Center for International Relations and American University's School of International Service saved me much embarrassment: I am grateful to Monica de Bolle, Robert Kaufman, Margaret Keck, Wagner Mancuso, Eduardo Mello, Umberto Mignozetti, Matias Spektor, and David Trubek for all the time and effort they dedicated to reshaping the book, and to Oliver Stuenkel for suggesting the FGV workshop and making it such a fruitful experience, including through insightful comments of his own.

Mario Schapiro, who also participated in the FGV workshop, has been especially encouraging of my exploration of these themes, even as he took me to task. Kathy Hochstetler generously read an earlier undertaking, and her comments on that project spurred me in more productive directions in this one. Lourdes Sola has patiently pushed me forward for more than a decade and a half and encouraged me to think in a more heterodox manner. Kate Bersch went beyond the call of duty and, in addition to sharing from our work together, offered incisive reflections on the book. Luciano Da Ros has been a constant voice in the back of my head, and our conversations are the source of a number of insights in the pages ahead. I hereby exonerate all of the aforementioned of any guilt for errors, omissions, and exaggerations in the text ahead.

Among those I cannot exonerate, but who have saved me from myself, I have been helped by a remarkable group of research assistants in Brazil and the US, including Flávia Bedicks, Natalia Coelho, Tyler Evans, Alex Frances, Eric Franqui, Joice Godoi Garcia, Jorge Miranda, and Matt Timmerman. Valentina Sader jumped in repeatedly to make this book a possibility. The anonymous reviewers were essential to pushing the book over the hump and they did so with generous but hard-nosed encouragement. Throughout the process, Sara Doskow, Cameron Daddis, Robert Judkins, Angela Valente, Raghavi Govindane and the team at Cambridge University Press have been superbly professional and enthusiastic.

I am grateful to everyone mentioned here and to all I have ungraciously overlooked, for encouragement through thick and thin. Of course, my sounding board continues to be my wonderful wife. In so many different ways, this book could never have happened without her. It is dedicated to our greatest joint efforts, T. and B., who have always given me joyful reasons to put my pen down at the end of the day.

Abbreviations

Acronym	Portuguese	Approximate English translation
ABDI	*Agência Brasileira de Desenvolvimento Industrial*	Brazilian Industrial Development Agency
ABEMI	*Associação Brasileira de Engenharia Industrial*	Brazilian Association of Industrial Engineering
ANEEL	*Agência Nacional de Energia Elétrica*	National Electric Energy Agency
ANFIP	*Associação Nacional dos Auditores Fiscais da Receita Federal do Brasil*	National Association of Fiscal Auditors of the Brazilian Federal Revenue Service
ANP	*Agência Nacional de Petróleo, Gas Natural e Biocombustíveis*	National Agency of Petroleum, Natural Gas and Biofuels
ANVISA	*Agência Nacional de Vigilância Sanitária*	National Sanitary Surveillance Agency
BNDES	*Banco Nacional de Desenvolvimento Econômico e Social*	National Bank for Economic and Social Development
CDES	*Conselho de Desenvolvimento Econômico e Social*	Council for Economic and Social Development
CEBES	*Centro Brasileiro de Estudos da Sáude*	Brazilian Center for the Study of Health

List of Abbreviations

CGU	*Controladoría Geral da União*	Federal Comptroller's Office
CIDE	*Contribuição de Intervenção no Domínio Econômico*	Contribution for Intervention in the Economic Domain
CIMA	*Conselho Interministerial de Açúcar e Álcool*	Interministerial Council on Sugar and Alcohol
CLT	*Consolidação das Leis Trabalhistas*	Consolidated Labor Laws
CNDI	*Conselho Nacional de Desenvolvimento Industrial*	National Council of Industrial Development
CNI	*Confederação Nacional da Indústria*	National Confederation of Industry
COAF	*Conselho de Controle de Atividades Financeiras*	Council for the Oversight of Financial Activities
COFINS	*Contribuição para o Financiamento da Seguridade Social*	Contribution for Social Security Financing
CPI	*Comissão Parlamentar de Inquérito*	Congressional Committee of Inquiry
CPMF	*Contribuição Provisória sobre Movimentação Financeira*	Temporary Contribution on Financial Transactions
CSAA	*Câmara Setorial de Açúcar e Álcool*	Sectoral Chamber for Sugar and Alcohol
CVM	*Comissão de Valores Mobiliários*	Securities and Exchange Commission
ENCCLA	*Estratégia Nacional de Combate à Corrupção e à Lavagem de Dinheiro*	National Strategy for Combating Corruption and Money Laundering
FAT	*Fundo de Amparo ao Trabalhador*	Worker Support Fund
FGTS	*Fundo de Garantia do Tempo de Serviço*	Fund Guaranteeing Time of Service
FIESP	*Federação de Indústrias do Estado de São Paulo*	São Paulo Industrial Federation
FINAME	*Agência Especial de Financiamento Industrial*	Special Industrial Financing Agency

List of Abbreviations

FINEP	*Financiadora de Estudos e Projetos*	Financier of Studies and Projects
FSE	*Fundo Social de Emergência*	Emergency Social Fund
IAA	*Instituto do Açúcar e do Álcool*	Sugar and Alcohol Institute
ICMS	*Imposto sobre Circulação de Mercadorias e Serviços*	Tax on the Circulation of Merchandise and Services
INAMPS	*Instituto Nacional de Assistência Médica da Previdência Social*	National Institute of Social Welfare Medical Assistance
INSS	*Instituto Nacional do Seguro Social*	National Social Security Agency
IPEA	*Instituto de Pesquisa Econômica Aplicada*	Institute of Applied Economic Research
IPI	*Imposto sobre Produtos Industrializados*	Tax on Industrial Products
ISEB	*Instituto Superior de Estudos Brasileiros*	Superior Institute of Brazilian Studies
MPF	*Ministério Público Federal*	Federal Prosecutorial Service
PAC	*Programa de Aceleração do Crescimento*	Growth Acceleration Program
PBM	*Plano Brasil Maior*	Greater Brazil Plan
PCdoB	*Partido Comunista do Brasil*	Communist Party of Brazil
PDP	*Política de Desenvolvimento Produtivo*	Productive Development Policy
PDS	*Partido Democrático Social*	Democratic Social Party
PDT	*Partido Democrático Trabalhista*	Democratic Labor Party
PIS	*Programa de Integração Social*	Program for Social Integration
PASEP	*Programa de Formação do Patrimônio do Servidor Público*	Program for Civil Servant Asset Formation

List of Abbreviations

PITCE	*Política Industrial, Tecnológica e de Comércio Exterior*	Industrial, Technological and Trade Policy
PMDB	*Partido do Movimento Democrático Brasileiro*	Brazilian Democratic Movement Party
PP	*Partido Progressista*	Progressive Party
PRN	*Partido da Reconstrução Nacional*	National Reconstruction Party
Proálcool	*Programa Nacional do Álcool*	National Alcohol Program
PROER	*Programa de Estímulo à Reestruturação e ao Fortalecimento do Sistema Financeiro Nacional*	Stimulus Program for the Restructuring and Strengthening of the National Financial System
PROES	*Programa de Incentivo à Redução do Setor Público na Atividade Bancária*	Incentive Program for the Reduction of the Public Sector in Banking
PROEX	*Programa de Financiamento às Exportações*	Export Financing Program
PROINFA	*Programa de Incentivo às Fontes Alternativas de Energia Elétrica*	Program to Incentivize Alternate Forms of Electric Energy
PROMEF	*Programa de Modernização e Expansão da Frota*	Program for the Modernization and Expansion of the Fleet
PRONATEC	*Programa Nacional de Acesso ao Ensino Técnico e Emprego*	National Program for Access to Technical Education and Employment
PSB	*Partido Socialista Brasileiro*	Brazilian Socialist Party
PSDB	*Partido da Social Democracia Brasileira*	Brazilian Social Democracy Party
PSOL	*Partido Socialismo e Liberdade*	Socialism and Liberty Party

List of Abbreviations

PT	*Partido dos Trabalhadores*	Workers' Party
PTB	*Partido Trabalhista Brasileiro*	Brazilian Labor Party
REINTEGRA	*Regime Especial de Reintegração de Valores Tributários para as Empresas Exportadoras*	Brazilian Special Regime for the Reinstatement of Taxes for Exporters
SELIC	*Sistema Especial de Liquidação e Custodia*	Special Clearance and Escrow System
SIAFI	*Sistema Integrado de Administração Financeira do Governo*	Federal Integrated System for the Financial Administration of the Federal Government
STF	*Supremo Tribunal Federal*	Supreme Federal Tribunal
SUFRAMA	*Superintendência da Zona Franca de Manaus*	Superintendency of the Manaus Free Trade Zone
SUMOC	*Superintendência da Moeda e do Crédito*	Superintendency of Money and Credit
SUS	*Sistema Único de Sáude*	Unified Health System
TCU	*Tribunal de Contas da União*	Supreme Audit Court
ZFM	*Zona Franca de Manaus*	Manaus Free Trade Zone

I

Introduction

Brazil has been caught in a low-level economic equilibrium for much of the generation since the return to democracy in 1985. Over three and a half decades, Brazilian per capita income has grown more slowly than citizens' incomes in both wealthier developed nations as well as developing economies. The chaos of the late 2010s – including the worst recession in a century, massive corruption scandals, street demonstrations, and a presidential impeachment drama – underscored demands for change but led to few shifts in the incentives that drive actors toward this suboptimal equilibrium. The potential opportunity offered by these intertwined economic, legal, and political crises also proved insufficient, as of the time of this writing, to significantly remake resilient political and economic structures.

There is considerable agreement about the sources of Brazil's low-level equilibrium. But why does this consensus not translate into action? A long tradition of developmentalism, dating back seven decades, continues to exert enormous influence on the economy, wielded through dominant ideas about policy, reinforced by the institutions of policy implementation, and sustained by the interests that benefit from these institutional frameworks. The empirical argument advanced in this book is that Brazilian developmentalism has staying power, despite its lackluster results, in part because institutional complementarities across the economic and political spheres buttress and sustain the system, and the incentives of political and economic actors drive them toward strategies that are individually first-best, but collectively suboptimal. As a consequence of this self-reinforcing cycle, the Brazilian developmental policy set persists in steady equilibrium.

Introduction

It persists, furthermore, despite the ready availability of other models of economic organization, either of a more effective developmentalist state or of a less *dirigiste* market economy.

The return to democracy in 1985 deepened the institutional complementarities that sustain the Brazilian developmentalist model, complicating reform by introducing a variety of new political demands, new veto players, and new veto points. Although democracy has changed the rhetorical justification for policy, and led to greater emphasis on human development, democracy has not significantly changed many of the standard operating procedures of the developmental state in the economic realm. Despite a general consensus about how to kindle growth, Brazil has settled on economic institutions that privilege regressive social redistribution over growth and that weaken growth drivers by squeezing investment, disincentivizing innovation, and rewarding large (and often oligopolistic) firms over medium and small competitors. Regime change brought new forms of political horse-trading which are significantly more transparent than politics under the military regime, but nonetheless frequently transcend the boundaries between formal and informal, and even between licit and illicit, in ways that benefit incumbent interests over reformers and established firms over newer or smaller competitors. The democratic regime failed, furthermore, to establish the instruments of control that would make the autonomous bureaucracy of the developmental state capable of both engaging firms and steering them effectively in the directions most likely to achieve sustained growth.

Theoretically and methodologically, this book innovates by demonstrating how these institutional complementarities function *within* five economic and political domains, as well as *across* them: the economy, including both 1) the macroeconomy of a middle-income developmental state; and 2) the microeconomy of a particularly Brazilian variant of firm organization that I will call "developmental hierarchical market economy" (or DHME); 3) a political system that can be summarized as "coalitional presidential"; 4) the weak set of control mechanisms this political system sets in place; and somewhat paradoxically, 5) an autonomous bureaucracy that has permitted incremental reform but in consequence, may have moderated demand for more dramatic, paradigmatic reform while also deepening some of the fiscal constraints that impel policymakers to preserve the developmental state apparatus and its fiscally opaque policy toolkit.

A BRIEF SUMMARY OF THE ARGUMENT

In evaluating the causes of Brazil's suboptimal performance since the return to democracy, the book draws upon and contributes to two inter-related scholarly debates in the study of comparative political economy. The first body of work relates to the concept of a developmental state, which argues that the state can serve as a muscular engine of long-term development by consciously altering investment conditions, expanding human capabilities, and tackling the market failures and coordination problems that plague late developing economies (Haggard, 2018). Brazil has long been a prominent case study of a developmental state, but its role has hitherto largely been seen as either a success story or as an intermediate, but not especially problematic, case (Evans, 1992, 1995; Kohli, 2004; Trubek, Garcia, et al., 2013). The pages ahead challenge that perspective, suggesting that the logic, practice, and legacy of developmentalism have sustained political and economic structures that have become growth-constraining and, since the return to democracy, have failed to deliver even on their own decidedly long-term criteria for success. There is scant evidence of convincing improvements since 1985 by any common metrics of development such as industrialization, innovative advancement on the technological frontier, or human capital gains. This is not to say that developmentalism never worked, or that the institutions of development-alism are entirely vitiated or lacking any redeeming value, simply that developmentalism as a set of institutions and policies has failed to deliver during the democratic era. Many of democracy's gains have come about *despite* rather than *because of* developmental policies and institutions.

Second, the "varieties of capitalism" literature provides theoretical leverage to explain the persistence of this relatively ineffectual institutional framework, particularly via the notion that unique national contexts may drive economies into distinct equilibria that are often quite sticky and resistant to change. Pioneering studies of the varieties of capitalism saw a world divided between "liberal market economies" and "coordinated market economies," where complementarities between the structure of labor markets, the organization of firms, and the provision of education created incentives for workers and firms to invest in context-specific institutions, moving actors toward steady equilibria, and thereby limiting the possibilities for convergence between a North Atlantic model and a continental European model (Hall and Soskice, 2001; Hall and Gingerich, 2009). This prevented the convergence toward a common "liberal market economy" that many anticipated with the fall of the

4   *Introduction*

Berlin Wall and the rise of the Washington Consensus and its liberal market-oriented policies in the 1980s and 1990s. This book builds on later works in the varieties of capitalism tradition to draw attention to the unique incentives generated by the pattern of state-firm relations in Brazil, but goes beyond them to focus on the complementarities not just within firm relations, but also within the realms of macroeconomic policy, politics, control mechanisms, and the bureaucracy, as well as across all five domains.

The focus on the incentives generated by institutional complementarities in a developmental state has important analytical consequences. Because they typically study different institutions in isolation – bureaucracy, congress, parties, firms, etc. – scholars have largely missed the ways in which these organizations *jointly* drive diverse actors toward common equilibria. This has often blinded scholars to the fact that different institutional domains are intricately intertwined, nonrandom configurations that provide a contextual logic for economic and political action (Deeg and Jackson, 2007).

A focus on institutional complementarity forces us to expand the lens of analysis of the study of political institutions. Economists have often assumed that all that is needed to get Brazil on a more productive trajectory is political leadership. Political scientists have long emphasized executive-legislative relations to the general neglect of the economy, focusing more on the process of governing than on its content or performance. This has given many social scientists an artificial and perhaps overly optimistic perspective of how well Brazilian politics could function or actually functions, suggesting that all that is needed is stronger leadership, or focused more on narrow measures of legislative production and executive control than on the broader content of this legislation, the murky processes that often produce it, the options that are foregone, or the lackluster long-term performance of the system. Failure to recognize the weakness of control mechanisms, including democratic checks and balances, in constraining the sometimes nefarious interactions between the executive and legislative branches, or between firms and politicians, has permitted overly rosy claims that Brazil is on a path to a new and more virtuous developmental equilibrium. Scholars have also overlooked the almost complete absence of the forms of strategic planning and oversight that would be needed to make the developmental state deliver. The prevailing wisdom further overlooks many of the complementarities that hold together the current institutional framework, including the routinized ties between political incumbents and established private sector firms,

A Brief Summary of the Argument   5

which have important implications for the structure of politics and economic policy.

Failure to incorporate these complementarities into our analysis of Brazil's political economy may have warped our understanding of Brazil's trajectory and contributed to the boom and bust cycle of media reports on Brazil's prospects, which have alternately depicted the country as either taking off into a brilliant future or instead crashing into an inextricable morass. Focusing on institutional complementarities and the equilibrium behaviors they generate enables one to question the triumphalist narrative that took hold in Brazil during the commodity boom of the 2000s. Brazil's heady growth during the 2000s led to a wave of books heralding the important gains the country made since its 1985 transition to democracy, including titles claiming that the country was new, starting over, reversing its fortune, making itself work, and on the rise (Rohter, 2010; Fishlow, 2011; Roett, 2011; Melo and Pereira, 2013; Montero, 2014a). Although many of these works were more nuanced inside their covers than their triumphalist titles suggested, they stood in stark contrast to an alternate perspective that questioned the country's ability to overcome the deadlock generated by multiple veto players, patrimonial politics, party underdevelopment, particularism, and networked capitalism (Cardoso, 1975; Roett, 1978; Mainwaring, 1993, 1995; Ames, 2001; Lazzarini, 2010).

This book falls squarely in the more skeptical camp, but also offers a comprehensive analytical perspective that seeks to weave together various disciplinary perspectives in a way that improves our understanding of Brazil's trajectory and considers new paths forward. It provides a broader understanding of why it is that the political economy of Brazilian democratic institutions has been solid and resilient to shocks, but also unable to bring to fruition the promises of a deeper and more just society. The answer, I will argue, is that many of the economic and political institutions of the new democracy are regressive and inefficient; but more importantly, that complementarities across the political and economic spheres generate incentives that drive actors toward a suboptimal political and economic equilibrium that has become stable over time. This is not to say that change is impossible: the very notion of institutional complementarities suggests that when change occurs in one institutional arena, it may rapidly shift incentive structures in other institutional arenas. Thinking about what shifts are most likely to alter incentives, and thereby generate change, may enable us to consider how best to structure paths toward reform. Understanding how the system functions as a whole may thus help

Introduction

us to better understand the political and economic responses to the crises of the 2010s, as well as the possibilities for change going forward.

EMPIRICAL CONTRIBUTION: COMPLEMENTARITIES THAT STABILIZE INSTITUTIONAL EQUILIBRIA

Brazil's Low-Level Equilibrium

Let us begin with the painful but unsentimental argument that there does not seem to be much objective evidence for a feel-good story about economic development under the democratic regime inaugurated in 1985. Brazil often seems to be ambling leisurely toward a grim future in which an unresponsive political system, an inefficient economic framework, the end of the demographic dividend, and a deeply unjust social structure conspire to rob Brazilian youth of their future. Despite social policy gains since the return to democracy, Brazil's economic performance has been middling. Per capita growth has been unremarkable, averaging 1.2 percent a year between 1985 and 2017, far below the 3.3 percent average for Brazil's upper middle-income country peer group.[1] Indeed, by comparison to many important peer countries and income groups, the country has been steadily losing ground, as Figure 1.1 illustrates. This is true by comparison to BRICs countries such as India and China; to other Latin American economies of various economic policy persuasions, such as Chile and Uruguay[2]; to the upper middle-income nations group, which has doubled its share of Brazilian per capita gross domestic product (GDP) in the past generation, from 37 percent to 76 percent; and to a variety of high-income nations, including the United States, EU countries, and OECD members.[3]

Economists generally agree that one reason for this continued loss of ground is that the factors that might drive Brazilian growth, such as savings and total factor productivity, have remained flat. Although the peak years of the country's demographic dividend were between the late 1990s and 2018,[4] national savings between 1985 and 2017 averaged only 17.6 percent, against a peer group average of 29.8 percent.[5] Total factor productivity at constant prices was 10.5 percent lower in 2014 than it had been in 1985, having declined year-over-year in 14 of those 30 years.[6] Successive governments have proven incapable of getting past emergency fixes and implementing lasting reforms that could put the country on a more fiscally sustainable grounding and permit the investment needed to spur growth.

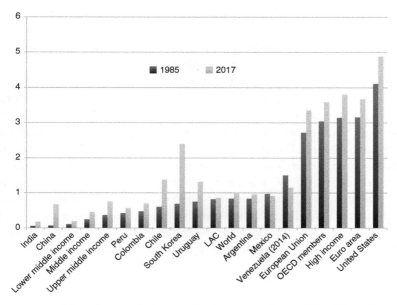

FIGURE 1.1 Selected countries' per capita income as share of Brazil's, 1985 and 2017.
Source: Compiled by author from World Bank World Development Indicators, GDP per capita (constant 2010 US$), accessed September 2018. Shares are calculated as share of Brazil's per capita GDP in 1985 and again in 2017.

Democracy has changed the justifications for policymaking, and forced politicians to adopt more universal programs, leading to improvements in human welfare. Both the *Real* Plan of 1994, which stabilized hyperinflation, and the *Bolsa Família* conditional cash transfer program of 2003, which began to address the severest income inequality, raised hopes for more equitable and durable social policies. By some measures (based on household census data[7]), the country had success in reducing income inequality during the two decades from 1994. But even if these gains prove permanent, rather than yielding to the recession of the mid-2010s, it is important to consider the counterfactual. Brazil did not do better than other large economies in the Latin American region, and in fact, performed worse than its regional and global peers on social matters. Inequality improved notably, by about 12.5 percent in a comparison of the 1985–9 period with the 2010–16 period, but Brazil's gains lagged regional peers (e.g., Chile and Peru, where inequality fell by 15 and 20 percent, respectively), and Brazil's inequality remains higher than all

8 *Introduction*

of its large Latin peers except Colombia. Brazil would have had to double its performance in combatting inequality over this period, in fact, to reach the levels of the other five large Latin economies; it would have needed to triple its gains to reach South Korean levels of inequality.

Something is not working, and Brazilians know it. The long cycle of protests beginning in 2013 demonstrated a palpable frustration with the country's inability to undertake comprehensive reforms that might alter some of the most pernicious incentives present in both the political and economic spheres. The political system is deeply divided, and the 2018 election was the most wide-open since the return to democracy in 1985, in part because the deeply felt desire for change has not been matched by even minimal consensus about the direction of reforms (Kingstone and Power, 2017). But Brazil's stagnation is not simply a problem of political leadership: indeed, virtually all presidents elected since 1989 have run on a promise of reform and change. Something is getting in the way.

The Developmental State

Developmentalism is an academic theory, a set of ideas and ideals, and an array of policies. In all cases, it is motivated by the observation that late developing nations face a unique challenge of competing in a world where relative national wealth results from a skilled work force's ability to produce high value-added goods that are globally competitive and where first movers have already set the terms of competition (Amsden, 2001). Attention to the international context suggests that liberalizing a less-developed economy could be counterproductive, by failing to improve either the stock of human capital or to alter the structure of the economy in ways that move it up the technological frontier, all while worsening the terms of trade (Bairoch, 1972; Haggard, 2018, 11). Indeed, the paradigmatic cases of successful developmental states – such as Japan, South Korea, and Taiwan – turned outward and opened their economies only after first developing indigenous industry and comparative advantages higher up the technological frontier. In developing these capacities, the state played a central role in guiding firms and markets.[8]

Developmentalism thus carries with it a healthy skepticism of open or "free" market prescriptions. One foundational assumption is that the technologies needed to catch up to early industrializers will not be produced naturally by markets in developing nations: market failures, externalities, increasing returns, information asymmetries, and transaction costs may all impede the private sector from moving to fill the gaps or to

Empirical Contribution

invest in overcoming missing synergies that may be impeding development (Reinert, 2007, 36). For a country like Brazil in the 1940s to create an indigenous capacity for steel production required a slew of backward linkages, such as adequate sources of financing, electricity generation, and railroads to move both inputs and outputs. Individual private firms had little incentive to produce any of these, yet without them, not only was steel production unviable, but so too were all the forward linkages that might result from having a steel industry: production of automobiles, white goods, ships, and any variety of other industrial pursuits (Gerschenkron, 1962; Hirschman, 1968, 1987). Second, the human capital consequences were also significant: little demand for skilled labor meant little incentive to invest in education, and few opportunities for the individual skills improvement that would benefit workers and their families. Third, the theory of comparative advantage was misleading: poor countries' lower wages were insufficient to overcome rich countries' higher productivity, and thus any effort to industrialize by specialization in low-technology industries would be unproductive (Amsden, 2001, 5).

Developmentalists argued that the state needed to create incentives to overcome these market failures. At their broadest, these incentives could be summarized in terms of "getting prices wrong": using the state to provide protections, subsidies, rents, and other enticements that would steer the private sector in directions distinct from those dictated by the unfettered market. Such incentives would encourage individual firms to undertake investments they might otherwise avoid, while generating broader gains across the entire structure of industry (Johnson, 1982; Amsden, 1989). Developmental policy goals were ambitious, including reallocating capital, shifting the composition of investment, learning and incorporating foreign technologies, protecting domestic industry, and increasing comparative advantage in strategic industries. The precise toolkit might vary, but it included incentives to large-scale industries, entry regulation, local content requirements, tariffs, preferential financing, and selective liberalization (Khan and Jomo, 2000; Amsden, 2001; Haggard, 2018).

The central balancing act was political. For the developmental state to work in practice required a strong state, capable of both designing policy and pushing firms in the right direction without being captured by a rent-seeking private sector. As Haggard (2018) notes in his masterful review of the developmental state literature, it is "surprisingly hard to find" an integrated statement of the political model that would permit this result, but it seems to demand two characteristics: 1) a strong executive delegating to a capable bureaucracy; as well as 2) political insulation from both the working class and the private sector. The focus on a centralized, internally coherent and politically insulated state was justified by 3) the need to accumulate capital; and 4) to steer investment into "sectors that were dynamically efficient" (Haggard, 2018, 45).

Haggard's political model provides the scaffolding for this book's first argument: namely, that the Brazilian developmental state under democracy has lost the characteristics needed to accomplish this difficult political balancing act. Brazil has a strong executive, able to delegate to a capable bureaucracy. The state's performance as a developmental authority has been clouded by political and private sector influence over the policy process. The insulation of the executive bureaucracy was enforced under authoritarian rule (albeit somewhat capriciously and tenuously) by the coercive power of an executive branch dominated by the military. Under democracy, this coercive power has not been reinstituted, in part because of the president's reliance on a broad coalition for political support, but also because of the corresponding weakness of accountability agencies and the judicial branch as enforcers of the boundaries between state and firm. Lost, too, has been the capacity for strategic planning and strategic control over developmental policies. With regard to the third and fourth components of Haggard's model, the ability of the Brazilian state to accumulate the needed capital and steer it effectively has been severely diminished by fiscal constraints, which are themselves a paradoxical consequence of the growth of the state for much of the past century. Brazil has failed to update the incentive structures of developmentalism which, together with the absence of controls, has led the state into "followership," rather than leadership with regard to the private sector (Wade, 2004). This has limited the state's capacity to effectively "steer" investment and explains many of the country's lackluster results over the past generation, meriting the label "decadent developmentalism."

An Alternate, Neoliberal Path

If Brazil has failed to make the developmental state effective, it has also failed to go down an alternate, more market-oriented path, often referred to as the "neoliberal" path. This is puzzling because these market-oriented options have been available to policymakers for much of the past generation, with a clear and relatively unchanged agenda of suggested reforms.

By way of example, in 1984 the World Bank recommended opening to trade, increasing domestic savings, undertaking fiscal and tax reform as

Empirical Contribution

well as reductions in credit subsidies, expanding public sector investment systematically, improving labor productivity, and paying greater attention to income distribution (World Bank, 1984, xxxii–xxxiv). Fast forward three decades, and the World Bank's list of prescriptions looked little different: trade integration, fiscal policies oriented toward limiting inflation, tax and financial sector reforms, a shift from traditional industrial policy, greater efficiency in public spending, infrastructure investment, and lower regulation (World Bank, 2016, 2017a). A 1995 list of reform recommendations in the *Economist* magazine looks remarkably up to date as a neoliberal "wish list" a quarter century later: social security reform, cutting bureaucracy, limiting civil service benefits, education investment, and privatizations (Economist, 1995).

Although such prescriptions offer a well-meaning roadmap toward an ideal future, their recurrent repetition suggests a belief that achieving growth is simply a matter of technical understanding. Failure to reform is often chalked up to bad faith actors or an abundance of interest groups. Analysts ignore the broader political economy of Brazilian democracy, and the manner by which institutional structures, policy frameworks, and long-standing ideas about development buttress each other in ways that limit the paths of change. Even the keenest observers have often failed to consider the complexities of reform in a system marked by strong complementarities across domains, which have contributed to policy incrementalism, ensured that practices borrowed from abroad function quite differently in Brazil than in their home environments, and led to important gaps between the formal behaviors expected of institutions and their actual performance.[9]

This is not to say that Brazil has not attempted reforms, or that change has been absent. A slew of reforms have been implemented, often at a hyperactive pace. A universal health care system has been created, and an internationally lauded conditional cash transfer program was instituted. A number of agencies, including the autonomous public prosecutor's office, the Federal Police, and the Comptroller General's Office (CGU), have been established or remade, sparking increasingly effective efforts to ensure probity. Famously disorganized fiscal and monetary bodies have been revamped, at all levels of the federation. State-owned companies and state-owned banks have been transformed, undergoing privatization and regulatory reform. More than one hundred constitutional reforms have been passed, and literally tens of thousands of new laws. Further, some of these reforms were "neoliberal" in intent, with the goal of making the economy more "market-friendly" and reducing the role of the state. Indeed, under various presidents, especially in the 1990s under Fernando Collor and Fernando Henrique Cardoso, economic policymakers sought to move toward more "market-friendly" institutions, including through privatization of state-owned utilities, introduction of regulatory agencies, limits on the scope of industrial policies, permission for foreigners to buy into national industry, and opening the economy to trade. But these "neoliberal" reforms did not fully dismantle the developmental state, which has enabled the state apparatus to continue to be used by both market-oriented and developmentally inclined policymakers (Prado et al., 2016; Taylor, 2016; Armijo, 2017).

Brazil has not fit the "modal pattern" seen in the rest of Latin America and portions of East Asia during the past few decades, whereby governments adopted a liberal economic agenda and reformed core social insurance programs (Haggard and Kaufman, 2008, 265). Incredibly, three decades after the democratic constitution was approved, the Bolsonaro economic reform agenda looks astonishingly similar to that of his predecessors, emphasizing inter alia, pension reform, tax reform, and trade opening. As of this writing, at the end of its first eighteen months in office, the Bolsonaro administration has made some parametric progress on the first and third of these, working at a pace that despite its unhurried gait suggests the country is on track to undertake some of the fastest policy reforms of any of the presidential administrations of the post-authoritarian era. Yet it is still a slow and uncertain pace.

All of these phenomena – failure to refurbish the developmental state, failure to reach a new neoliberal equilibrium, and the hyperactivity of reform – have the same source. The institutions of the Brazilian political economy drive toward a common equilibrium that is hard to break, not least because of institutional complementarities across five institutional arenas that jointly explain the country's trajectory since 1985: the resilience of developmentalism as an idea with effects on both policy choices and institutions in the macroeconomic realm; the concentration and segmentation of firm life in the microeconomic realm, DHME; the consensual politics inherent to the coalitional presidential system, which undermine the checks and balances that are frequently assumed to be central to presidential systems; the resulting weakness of the control mechanisms needed to effectively govern the developmental state; and an autonomous bureaucracy that is able to undertake reforms that ensure the developmental state's continued viability but also contribute to its growth-constraining effect by reinforcing the incentive structures set in place by the other institutions. As Figure 1.2 illustrates, *within* three of

Theoretical Contribution

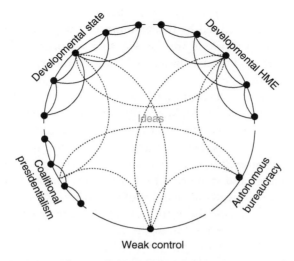

FIGURE 1.2 Institutional complementarities within and across five domains. Source: Author.

these institutional domains, there are important within-domain complementarities, discussed in Chapters 2, 4, and 5. There are also important complementarities *across* domains. These "complementarities as synergy" provide stable and coherent incentive structures to key actors in each domain: business executives, politicians, and civil servants.[10]

THEORETICAL CONTRIBUTION: FROM INSTITUTIONS TO INSTITUTIONAL EQUILIBRIA

Institutions and Institutional Change

Social scientists agree that institutions play a key role in human society by guiding individual and collective behavior. Institutions are "the rules of the game" (North, 1990) and as such, they are reflected in "recurring patterns of behavior" (Huntington, 1968). The behavior reinforces the rule, and the rule constrains the behavior. Given this self-reinforcing cycle, institutions tend to reinforce collective incentives in a particular direction, generating society-wide patterns that are quite predictable over the long haul.[11] Note what institutions are not: they need not be organizations, understood here as a body composed of multiple people working together toward a shared objective, such as a political party, a government agency,

14 *Introduction*

or a firm.[12] They are also not actors. Institutions cannot act, because institutions are constituted by the simultaneous strategic calculations of multiple actors: institutions are the way that we behave given how we anticipate others will behave, based on how they and we have behaved in the past.

A lengthy literature evaluates all the many ways institutions can stay the same or change over time. While this typologizing and taxonomizing has its uses, for now it is sufficient to note that institutions can change in a myriad of ways, just as they can remain the same in a multitude of ways (Thelen, 2003; Streeck and Thelen, 2005). But the causal origin of the process of change and stability is the same: both change and its absence emerge from the strategic calculations of the various actors whose choices generate and revalidate the institution.[13] Because the rule constrains behavior, and behavior reinforces the rule, there is considerable room for continuity. But so, too, a change in behavior can change the rule: failure to apply the rule, failure to comply with the rule, or failure to recognize the rule, for example, might all lead to change.

Let us consider a simple example that illustrates this way of thinking about institutions as dynamic reinforcement of rules by behavior and behavior by rules: the question of how to load a subway car. There are at least three solutions to this question: we might load a subway car by off-loading all passengers on the cars first and only then onboarding passengers, by having off-loading passengers go out one side of a door and simultaneously onloading passengers on the other side, or each passenger could simply try to push through the door come hell or high water. São Paulo, Tokyo, and Washington, DC have each found a distinct solution to this issue. These choices are reinforced through daily use: a tourist visiting any of these metropolitan centers will quickly learn the local rule, and thereby reinforce the local institution. The tourist may occasionally insist on their home-town rule, but after enough glares, chiding, or tramped-on toes, they are likely to fall into line. Oftentimes, the rules are even inscribed in posted guidelines for passengers, and in some cases, made more concrete through the addition of painted arrows and cow gates guiding the expected behavior.

How did these rules emerge? Were they dictated from above by a benevolent stationmaster, or did they simply arise from the daily jostling of commuters beginning the very first day the metro opened? It might be that the first passengers simply followed a rule they had learned elsewhere: stay to the right, ladies first, or first in-last out, for example. Each of the first passengers might have tried their own rule until, after enough days of

Theoretical Contribution   15

meeting sharp elbows, they collectively settled into a recurring pattern. Perhaps some combination of an evolving passenger consensus and a constructive stationmaster drove the choice.

How permanent is our subway car institution? Could it be changed if the benevolent stationmaster so desired, or if passengers employed social coercion, getting on the metro and yelling (as they often do in Washington at rush hour) "let us off before you push on"? Would change be more likely if instituted gradually, say by commuters slowly growing frustrated by the inefficiency and inconvenience of pushing one's way through the crowd every morning? Or would change be more likely if the established institution was suddenly upended by a crisis, such as the crushing of a hapless commuter between the contending boarding and off-loading crowds? It is impossible to say with any *ex ante* certainty, primarily because – again – institutions are at heart the cumulative result of a series of individual strategic decisions, taken in response to what each individual anticipates about others' behavior. A slight change in the composition of those participating in the strategic decisions early in the institutional formation process can seriously alter the rule that gets established.[14] Thus, caprice and happenstance often determine the long-term shape and paths of institutions.

Complementarity between Institutions

Things become a bit more complex when we consider that institutions do not exist in isolation. In the subway example, there may be other institutions simultaneously driving the individual behaviors of the subway passengers as they set about their daily routine of following and thus reestablishing the rules of subway boarding. These simultaneous influences might include rules derived from gender relations ("ladies first"), class (bourgeoisie before workers), or traffic (e.g., we drive on the right, we should board on the right). As a consequence of these overlapping institutions, it may be extraordinarily difficult to establish the rules for any single institution in isolation, because the underlying incentives will not align with the underlying strategies of individual members of society, who are all simultaneously rule-followers and rule-makers in a variety of domains. This leads to the concept of institutional complementarity.

There are multiple conceptualizations of "institutional complementarity." The least demanding sees complementary institutions as being just slightly more than compatible, that is, as having mutual effects on each other.[15] The most demanding conceptualization considers complementary institutions as compensatory, with one making up for the shortcomings of the other (Deeg, 2007; Crouch, 2010). Throughout this book, complementarity is understood as lying near the midpoint of that spectrum between compatibility and compensation, and complementary institutions are understood to be jointly sustaining or reinforcing (Crouch, 2010; Magnin, 2018). One example might be the institutions of driving on the right and boarding subways on the right: the presence of one does not determine the presence of the other, but they do tend to reinforce each other. Said another way, complementary institutions are institutions that guide individual incentives in the same direction and are therefore reinforced by similar strategic choices. This means that they are subject to mutually constitutive processes of institutional reproduction and change (Campbell, 2010). Carrying this through to its logical conclusion, complementarity enables institutional stasis, but it also means that change in one institution is likely to contribute to change in the others.[16]

The concept of institutional complementarity has been used to explain the variety of capitalist forms: in this context, it refers to the idea that "certain institutional forms, when jointly present, reinforce each other and contribute to improving the functioning, coherence, or stability of specific institutional configurations, varieties, or models of capitalism" (Amable, 2016, 79). In the varieties of capitalism literature, institutional complementarity helps explain the emergence of several "families" of capitalism. Initially focusing on the wealthy Organization for Economic Cooperation and Development (OECD) countries in the postwar era, scholars contrasted the liberal market economies of countries such as the United States with coordinated market economies such as Germany. Authors working with Hall and Soskice (2001) identified key distinctions between these two varieties of capitalism with regard to the accumulation of skilled labor, patterns of investment, and the pace of market adaptation. Amable (2003) expanded the taxonomy, identifying five separate varieties of capitalism among twenty-one OECD countries. Other authors have suggested further varieties of capitalism, including a family market and state market variant in Asia, and hierarchical market capitalism, common to Latin America (Schneider, 2013; Carney, 2016).[17] Central to the analysis of all of these forms of capitalism has been the notion that agents' equilibrium strategies in one domain may be shaped by the incentives they face in another domain: for example, the flexibility of hiring practices will shape the patterns of firm investment in training, while firm investment in training may shape the form of the education system and

Theoretical Contribution

firms' willingness to provide employment protection. In sum, "the effects or viability of an institution may depend upon the particular combination of other institutions present within the same political-economic system. These institutional configurations create a particular contextual 'logic' or rationality of economic action" (Deeg and Jackson, 2007).

The literature on institutional complementarities emphasizes the emergent properties of such systems. Complementarities become self-reinforcing across domains, but they typically originate without a central logic or coordinating force (Aoki, 1994; Streeck and Yamamura, 2001; Martin and Swank, 2012; Amable, 2016, 83). Rather, the constant jostling of institutions through daily use leads actors to harmonize their strategies in different domains, which may then settle into self-sustaining patterns whereby one institution's performance shapes and conditions that of other institutions. This often sums up to a set of institutions that looks quite different in one country from its peers (Deeg, 2007). While it may be possible to discuss "families" or "varieties" of capitalism with shared patterns of behavior, institutional convergence is limited by local contexts and historical trajectories, meaning that despite broad similarities within families, actual patterns are often distinct from country to country.

Just as the early "new institutionalist" literature focused on the effects of institutions as static rules of the game, much of the early discussion of institutional complementarity has been criticized for its static nature, which perhaps arose out of the emphasis on institutional configurations as explanations for resistance to the supposedly homogenizing pressures of a globalizing world (Amable, 2016). Institutional complementarity suggests that political leaders do not have a limitless menu of options to choose from; instead, institutions often emerge in response to local conditions and context, in ways that are constrained or conditioned by other institutions. "First-best" institutional models are seldom a realistic choice, as the possibilities for change are limited by the local context. This is path dependence on steroids: not only are particular institutional trajectories constrained by past choices, but they are also constrained by the past trajectories of other, complementary institutions.

In more recent work, scholars have recognized that the emphasis on the path dependence of institutional complementarity may have led to an excessively static depiction of the world. This suggests that institutions would be unable to adapt to changing conditions, such as the rising competitive pressures arising from globalization. But the response of the diverse varieties of capitalism to global pressures such as the rising financialization of the economy, corporate governance reforms, shareholder reforms, privatization, and social welfare system retrenchment demonstrates that the coordinated market economies in Europe and Asia are adjusting and evolving in ways that suggest various paths for change. Globalization has not produced convergence to a single model, but it also has not met an insurmountable barrier in the institutional complementarities that marked non-liberal capitalism (Amable, 2016). In a word, institutional complementarity permits certain adjustments in part because institutions serve as resources for actors, as much as they serve as constraints on actors' strategies (Deeg and Jackson, 2007; Hall and Thelen, 2009; Galvin, 2012). The feedback effects between complementary institutions means that certain paths of change are proscribed, but when changes do take place in a particular domain, they can spark significant changes across other domains. When change happens, it may alter the incentives that undergird complementary institutions, both within and across domains, contributing to an equilibrium shift in the overall system.

Equilibria and Equilibrium Shifts

Throughout this book, I use the term "equilibrium" in the same way a chemist might: a dynamic yet steady state in which a process is constantly recurring, but at rates such that little overall change is taking place. Consider the osmotic rebalancing of salinity levels as fresh Amazon water flows into the salty Atlantic Ocean. Over time, there may be slight variations in the salinity of the water off the coast of Amapá, but in general the salinity of water taken from a particular offshore location on a regular basis is likely to fall within some predictable range. Similarly, an institutional system is at equilibrium when the proportion of rule-followers who hold a particular preference is the same as the proportion who behave according to those preferences. The identity of the individual actors themselves may change from day to day, and there may even be players who do not subscribe to particular rules on occasion (e.g., our out of town subway rider), but the important thing is the overall proportion of those who prefer the rule and follow it.

Note that this understanding of an equilibrium does not entail any sort of functionality: there is no necessity for institutional complementarities to exist, and they do not exist in order to fulfill some basic institutional "need."[18] There is also no judgment about intent: the society does not fall into this equilibrium because its members are

Theoretical Contribution

somehow evil and poorly intentioned or, alternately, angelic and public-regarding (Amable and Palombarini, 2009).[19] Rather the equilibrium exists because key economic and political actors respond to the same incentives over time. This returns to an earlier point: institutions are dynamic in their stability, with the institutional rule guiding behavior, and the resulting behavior reinforcing the rule.[20] Given this cyclical pattern of rulemaking and rule reinforcement, institutions tend to reinforce collective incentives in a particular direction, but if there is change in the underlying behaviors because of a change in actors and their incentives, or beliefs about how others will act, the entire institution may shift. The same is true of complementary institutions: a change in the incentives in one institution is likely to alter incentives in its counterparts. This understanding of equilibrium as a dynamic state implies that complementarities can be as much a source of change as they are a source of stability. Because the equilibrium is dynamic rather than static, it is possible that when incentives begin to change in one realm, they may accumulate in ways that reverberate within that realm and into other institutional realms.

Because institutional complementarities mean that incentives are aligned across more than one institution, it would seemingly be harder to alter any single institution in an institutional system than it would be to alter a hypothetical institution in isolation. Piecemeal reforms in institution A might never find complements in institution B, creating contradictory incentives: if we drive on the left, for example, why would we follow a new rule that asked us to board the subway on the right? Which institution would emerge victorious? Probably not the hierarchically inferior one: flaunting the new subway boarding rules is far less potentially costly than driving on the wrong side of the road.

This raises the question of how the equilibrium of the overall system would ever shift, since the complementarity between institutions – which is really the complementarity between the incentives generated by those institutions – makes the entire system very sticky. How would change occur here?[21] There are several possible paths.[22] The first would be change that doesn't happen: even if the full society is not satisfied with the status quo, it may not be rational to invest efforts in overturning it, or preferences may be so deeply embedded that the need for change simply does not occur to most citizens. In this case, no movement occurs. In the Brazilian case, one example of such a path relates to central bank independence, a case in which institutional complementarities have meant that there has been little meaningful movement away from the extant equilibrium. Former central bank president Pérsio Arida noted that during his tenure (1993–5), the government wished to pass a constitutional amendment establishing central bank independence. However, the uncertainty and even danger posed by the fractious Congress led the government to deliberately forgo such a motion, thereby preserving the status quo.[23] In a world in which central bank independence was the only institution, independence seemed likely; in the real world in which central bank independence needed to be considered in a broader context of coalitional political institutions within a developmental state, a debate about greater independence was a risky possibility that opened a number of other institutional practices up for debate, and was thus a nonstarter.

A second path is change that is reversed or reabsorbed; a shift away from equilibrium happens, but then the institution reasserts itself. An example from Brazil concerns the field of anti-corruption in the mid- to late-2010s, where the incremental accumulation of human capacity and budget resources over the previous generation had offered the promise of change. However, institutional change appears to have been swamped during the Temer and early Bolsonaro presidencies, in large part because although there had been hopeful improvements in transparency and oversight over the course of the previous two decades, weak controls imposed by the judiciary made it very difficult to remove dirty players from the system and thus shift the overall incidence of corrupt behavior, contributing to a reversion of the overall system to the institutional status quo ante (Da Ros and Taylor, 2019a).

A third path is actual change, which might come about either via a big push, or through an accumulation of small changes. In either case, the change would lead to a new equilibrium. The big push might have a variety of causes: for example, a policy package that changes the incidence of particular behaviors, or an influx of immigrants that changes the composition of societal preferences. Small but steady incremental changes could also potentially add up to major equilibrium changes.[24] It is vital to keep this in mind, especially in light of the fact that policy change in Brazil is so frequently incremental: the simple fact of incrementalism does not necessarily imply that sea change is impossible. There are few examples of successful big push institutional changes in Brazil's recent history and a variety of examples of big pushes that failed, including on economic reforms such as stabilization and pension reform. Instead, as Chapter 7 will

Theoretical Contribution

show, incrementalism is the much more common path and its consequences are often more lasting than "big push" reform efforts.

Alternate Conceptualizations of Institutional Stasis and Brazil's Predicament

Before turning back from the theoretical realm to the Brazilian case, it is worth pointing out that the institutional complementarities explanation overlaps with, and – pardon the term – complements at least two other explanations that have been given for institutional stability, both in Brazil and more broadly. A first is path dependence, the notion that once an institutional choice is made, it can be extraordinarily difficult to shift paths, given that it is not possible to simultaneously coordinate all actors in such a way as to permit wholesale change, especially because there may be increasing returns from continuing along that path (e.g., Haydu, 1998; Mahoney, 2000; Pierson, 2000, 2004). Arguments about institutional complementarity are in some respects highly compatible with path dependent arguments: institutional complementarities could be considered, in many ways, the institutionalization of increasing returns. But while institutional complementarity does not in any way obviate most arguments about path dependence, its focus is subtly different, in that a particular historical path is considered to be epiphenomenal to the duration of the institutional framework: that is, the complementarities are more significant than the previous paths taken by a society when it comes to explaining the system's overall durability. Furthermore, the possibility of change is not foreclosed: institutional complementarity approaches are more agnostic about the possibilities for change, recognizing that complementarities could lead to rapid and systemic change off a particular path more quickly than a path dependent approach would suggest. Consider the postwar experiences of many countries, such as Germany, Japan, Korea, or Rwanda, where upended institutions in one domain translated into new ways of organizing political and economic life in other institutional domains. This is not to say that change is somehow seen as easier in the institutional complementarity approach; it is only to reiterate that one implication of institutional complementarity is that when change occurs in one institution, it may trigger a change in preferences that reverberates in other institutions, enabling a significant shift away from previous rules and institutional paths. Analytically, if we think about institutional change as a multistage process, path dependence helps to explain why reforms are proposed (or not) and may even help to explain why changes are approved (or not) because of the feedback effects between institutions and power distributions in society. But it does not do as good a job of describing whether changes are likely to be durable (or not). Here, the logic of institutional equilibrium and institutional complementarity do a better job of framing the issue, by pointing to the possibility of change that reverts to equilibrium or of change that leads to sudden equilibrium shifts, and of the possibility that more than one institution may be influencing the "stickiness" of a particular policy path.

A second explanation for the absence of change is the interest group perspective: the notion that institutions serve the interests of particular actors, and that these actors therefore actively work to prevent change to the prevailing rules and norms that might threaten their interests. The interest-based approach is also not entirely contradictory to the institutional complementarity literature. The interest group literature, with its focus on capture of public policy and on the unique role of veto players in curtailing reform, has a distinguished history in Brazil. Ames (2001) and Stepan (2000), for example, pointed to the plethora of veto players in Brazilian politics, which made almost any change subject to a multitude of potential vetoes and reinforced the incrementalism of the system. Economists, too, have pointed to interest group capture as one of the causes of slow growth under Brazilian democracy, arguing that organized interest groups are able to capture rents which empower them and enable them to block reform (Lisboa and Latif, 2013). But although interest group capture helps to explain patterns of politics, it is somewhat less helpful in explaining why the incremental changes that do take place do not lead to broader systemic reform, especially in the face of massive political mobilization. Interest group capture, then, helps us to understand why change may be stymied or constrained, but it does not help us to understand why it is that change may happen yet have little effect on the overall performance of institutions. Why is it that even when individual interest groups, such as employees of state-owned firms, lose out in reform, as they arguably did in the 1990s, the overarching patterns of political and economic life have not changed, as in the case of state-oriented organization of firm life? Alternately, why is it that even when individual interest groups retain their power, there can be a radical shift in behavior, as in the tightening of fiscal rules since the turn of the century? In sum, both path dependence and interest group perspectives are useful to understanding Brazil's current predicament, but they are made more robust by thinking of the broader context, including the complementarities that hold in place particular institutional equilibria.

SCOPE, METHOD, AND OVERALL CONTRIBUTION: A PRAGMATIC, NATIONAL APPROACH

This book is an unabashed single-country study. The one-country approach is not generally prized in the field of comparative political economy, but a few hedgehogs are needed if we are to say anything meaningful about specific countries, or to provide the detailed analysis that is needed to feed the foxes of multi-country scholarship. Further, the study of institutional complementarity requires a level of attention to detail and context that gives pride of place to country studies, such as the pioneering work of Aoki (1994, 2001) on Japan. A case study can also be helpful to sharpen concepts, create logically consistent theories, evaluate the implications of the theory with empirical observation, and test the validity of our theories (George and Bennett, 2005, 6, 49).

There are also many good reasons to focus on Brazil. It has long been an influential case for the study of development and democracy. Its scale, as the fifth largest nation-state by territory, enables it to serve as a ready-made case for comparison with other continental powers, such as Russia, India, China, and the United States. As one of the world's largest economies – over the past twenty years, it has oscillated between 7th and 10th in the rankings – it is frequently cited in the political economy literature as the primary example of Latin American state-led development. As a member of the upper middle-income set of democracies, it is frequently compared with nations such as Indonesia, South Africa, or Mexico, that are seen as harbingers of democracy's global future. The country has inspired a vast literature – arguably the most vibrant in Latin America – on presidentialism, coalition formation in multiparty systems, executive-legislative relations, judicial politics, and bureaucratic capacity, with an influential impact on the study of comparative politics outside Brazil.

Yet Brazil is idiosyncratic, similar to other countries on the surface but quite different underneath. Although it is a geographical neighbor, Brazil is remarkably distinct from Spanish-speaking Latin America. Although its institutions look classically republican, Brazilian politics is marked by unique institutional combinations that stand apart from other democracies, including other large federal democracies. Although Brazil followed its neighbors through some of the Washington Consensus economic reforms of the 1990s, it ended up in a quite different place, due to considerable "slippage" between the broad agenda of reform and actual policy implementation (Kahler, 1992; Stallings, 1992, 73). Brazil thus offers an intriguing counterpoint to many of the classic understandings

Introduction

of state, democracy, and capitalism. This idiosyncrasy merits comprehensive analysis.

The complexities that make Brazil intriguing as a case study, however, make it difficult to analyze the country at the depth necessary to truly say much of substance about the complex paths it has taken. Throughout this book, therefore, my goal has been to focus on Brazil qua Brazil. Where possible, I have tried to place the country's relative position in context, but the purpose of this project is less to compare Brazil with its peers than to understand the mechanisms that make Brazil function as it does. The primary comparative contribution of this book will be in its intensive focus on institutional complementarities, and particularly on the uniquely developmentalist Brazilian variety of capitalism and democracy, which helps to explain why Brazil has been so historically reticent to follow global and regional trends. Given the complexity of this task, I have left subnational analysis aside, and let my analytical focus rest on the federal government, although many of the patterns described here will have further resonance if analyzed in the future in tandem with state and local governance. The breadth of the material covered here also forces me to set aside many international issues, although Chapters 2 and 7 will touch upon aspects of Brazil's insertion into global markets and the pressures the country faces to conform to international rules. I have largely eschewed a historical approach, although readers with an interest in the historical events described in this text may find useful an online resource developed in tandem with this project.[25]

From the perspective of method, my approach is pragmatic and methodologically plural. The book draws together scholarly pursuits that have labored independently of each other, demonstrating the important links between scholarship on the macroeconomy of a middle-income country, the microeconomy of firm life, the politics of a multiparty system, the links between the bureaucracy and the controls they establish over the economic and political spheres, and the incentives jointly created by these distinct domains of Brazilian society. To accomplish this, the book draws liberally from a broad spectrum of literatures and disciplines, including sociology, law, economics, public administration, and political science. It may be impossible to completely satisfy the disciplinary demands of any single one of these fields, but the goal is to draw lessons from all of them, and in the process, to demonstrate how these individual contributions add up to something greater than the sum of their parts.

This book offers a number of salient contributions to the study of comparative political economy:

Scope, Method, and Overall Contribution

- An in-depth study of a leading middle-income democracy, combining analysis of the macro and micro economy, national politics, and the state bureaucracy.
- A theoretical framework for understanding both the absence of institutional change and the possibilities for change, drawing on existing literature about institutional complementarities and building upon it with a theory of dynamic equilibria.
- An empirical effort to draw together literatures that seldom dialogue with each other (on the macro and micro economies, politics, control over developmental policies, and the state bureaucracy), and to illustrate the importance of addressing both within-domain complementarities and complementarities across these domains.
- An expanded application of the varieties of capitalism literature, beyond its usual focus on firm decisions and the quality of jobs, to incorporate macroeconomic, political, and bureaucratic institutions.

Empirically and theoretically, this book puts meat on the bones of at least three important scholarly literatures that precede it in the study of Brazil and Latin America. With regard to the varieties of capitalism and its application to Latin America, this book seeks to move beyond the central focus on jobs and firms that has guided past work (Schneider, 2013, 19). The book uses the Brazilian case to draw attention to the powerful role of the state in "hierarchical market economies" (HMEs), the overlapping incentives between politicians and firms, and the way in which the absence of control mechanisms contributes to reinforcing economic and political hierarchies. The chapters ahead explore the complementarities between the macro and micro economies, rather than focusing primarily at the micro level on firms and employment. They also offer a few friendly amendments to the HME model from the Brazilian case, highlighting a form of firm life that is more state-centric, in which the financial sector has an influential role, and that has fewer broadly diversified conglomerates than other HMEs in the region.

By drawing attention to the role of political institutions in the developmental state, this book also opens a dialogue with the literature on coalitional presidentialism and its effects on Brazilian development. There is a school of thought that argues that Brazil is on the path to a new development equilibrium, in part because of the increasing strength of checks and balances in the country (Melo and Pereira, 2013; Alston et al., 2016). But a closer look at the incentive structures for key actors in each of

26   *Introduction*

the five institutional domains described here suggests that not only are checks and balances weaker, and oversight mechanisms more tenuous than desirable, but that as a consequence, the path to a new development equilibrium is not in any way preordained, despite the many hopeful incremental improvements of the past generation. The theoretical framing of institutional change and equilibrium shifts described earlier may help us to think more systematically about the possibilities for change and their empirical reflection in Brazilian reality since the return to democracy.

Third, the literature long ago pointed to the existence of a "hyperactive paralysis" in Brazilian politics, whereby there was constant activity but little meaningful change (Lamounier, 1994, 1996). The framework of institutional change laid out above provides a mental map for conceptualizing why this might be the case, but also for evaluating alternate paths by which such hyperactivity might actually cumulate into meaningful change. There are hopeful examples of this third form of change, with a variety of incremental changes adding up to a sea change in particular institutional arenas, described in Chapters 5, 7, and 8. In these cases, hyperactivity has led to the gradual shifting of preferences until a new equilibrium was established; hyperactive incrementalism rather than hyperactive paralysis, in other words.

PLAN OF THE BOOK

The book is divided into two sections of three chapters each. The first section is focused on complementarities in the economic realm, including the macroeconomy, the ideas that sustain economic actors' preferences, and the microeconomy of firm life. The second section turns to the political realm, analyzing the manner by which coalitional presidentialism reinforces hierarchy, the weakness of control mechanisms, and the role of the civil service as a change agent.

Chapter 2 describes the macroeconomic context in which developmentalism has evolved since 1985 and argues that despite enormous changes under democracy, the state remains central to our understanding of how the wider Brazilian political economy functions. The chapter describes the broader macroeconomic, and particularly fiscal, constraints that generate incentives for decisionmakers in both the business and policy realms. Going beyond the focus of many scholars in the varieties of capitalism literature, I argue that macroeconomic complementarities are as much a part of the institutional complementarities that sustain the

Plan of the Book 27

Brazilian developmental state as firm-level complementarities between firms, labor markets, and education provision.

The fiscal imperative that has emerged as a consequence of the economic challenges of the past three and a half decades generates pressures that have altered the landscape of developmentalism, but that also constrain institutional change. The result is a more fiscally-responsible form of developmental state, in which the state is better informed of its size and reach, has centralized oversight of fiscal processes, and adheres to a much harder budget constraint than at any time in the twentieth century, enforced by pressures from investors, bureaucrats, and citizens. Yet the fiscal imperative has also generated pressure for policymakers to resort to the fiscally opaque tools made available to them by the developmental state, such as industrial policies, state lending, cross-shareholding, nontransparent forms of taxation, and selective protections. Resorting to fiscally opaque policy tools has many downstream effects, including obfuscating the true cost of many policy decisions, as well as providing incentives to preserve many developmental institutions, even under reformist presidential administrations. The chapter points to the manner by which five institutional complementarities undergird the patterns of the Brazilian macroeconomy: the scale of the state, the monetary and financial regimes, patterns of state intervention in firm life, the economy's integration into the world system, and the wage-labor nexus. Despite some incursions of "neoliberal" policy under Collor and Cardoso in the 1990s, as well as under Temer and Bolsonaro in the final years covered by this book, policymaking retains state-centric traits in both conceit and practice, even though the collective consequences are unfortunate: regressive social distribution, limited investment, and low growth.

Indeed, continuities are more significant than many scholars assumed after the reformist 1990s. Despite micro- and macroeconomic reforms, much of the scaffolding of the developmental state remains formidable. The Washington Consensus reforms implemented in Latin America during the 1990s washed over Brazil with far lesser effect than in neighboring countries. Although the reforms of that decade consolidated fiscal responsibility, enhanced monetary authority, and enabled price stabilization, they did not represent the structural break seen in other transitioning economies of Latin America or Eastern Europe. As Armijo has noted, "the ubiquitous term 'new developmentalism' may best be used to identify the large degree of consensus on economic policies that has characterized all of Brazil's governments since President Fernando Collor" (Armijo, 2017, 230).[26] Simply put, free market orthodoxy did not triumph in

Brazil, and even reformist presidents tempered change with substantial institutional continuity that enabled their more developmentally inclined successors to adopt developmental policies with little need for prior institutional (re)construction.

Chapter 3 asks why it is that, despite the troubling underperformance of the economic system in the post-transition years, Brazilians still demonstrate substantial support for the basic pillars of the developmental enterprise. While developmentalism may have shifted over time from a "classical" to a "new" version (Bresser-Pereira, 2009, 2016), the common core has informed policy, and developmental ideas provide power resources and policy guidance to policymakers. The chapter looks at both the historical and institutional embeddedness of ideas, as well as the relatively tolerant relationship between developmentalists and what are, at least by Brazilian standards, "liberals" or "neoliberals" in government. This peaceful coexistence has usually reinforced the status quo, allowing policymakers to simultaneously draw on both reformist liberal ideas and the tools made available by developmental institutions. Yet developmentalist ideas also serve as long-term restraints on change: the dominance of developmentalism as an idea points toward particular equilibrium outcomes, prioritizes certain choices between conflicting alternatives, and provides guidance that drives diverse and uncoordinated actors toward particular institutions and policies. Developmentalism has thus served as a ballast for institutions, providing continuity over time.

Chapter 4 moves to the firm level, analyzing the degree to which Brazil fits the model of an "HME," a form of industrial organization prevalent in Latin America that Schneider (2013) has argued is distinct from the liberal, coordinated, and networked forms of capitalist organization found in the European, North American, and Asian contexts. My analysis here is both narrower and broader than that offered in most studies of hierarchical market economies: narrower in the sense that I focus only on the Brazilian case, but broader in the sense that as a result I am able to focus more specifically on what makes the Brazilian case idiosyncratic. Through an analysis of the 519 largest firms and financial institutions in Brazil, the chapter demonstrates that corporate life fits key dimensions of the model of an HME, in ways that replicate patterns found elsewhere in Latin America. But Brazilian capitalism is unique for its home-grown developmentalist model: firms are organized around market principles,

Plan of the Book

although they operate under the unique conditions engendered by the pervasive power of the state; unlisted private sector firms are organized in hierarchical fashion, but appear not to be following the diversification strategies of their regional peers, in part because of the prevalence of state-run finance; and, like HMEs elsewhere, the stratification of firm life means that Brazilian firms dominate in sectors that are commodity-producing, low complexity, and/or labor intensive but not skills-intensive. The one significant exception to this pattern of national dominance in low-skill enterprises is the financial sector, where domestic firms dominate, in large part as a consequence of conscientious long-term state action.

These patterns of firm life mean that Brazil has what I will term a *developmental* HME. One effect of the segmentation of firms is that there is also considerable segmentation of labor markets by firm type – state-owned enterprises (SOEs), multinational, and private sector – with important ramifications for how firms mobilize to demand education and training. A second effect is the degree to which the state is essential to business strategies, especially at domestically owned private sector firms. The chapter evaluates the instruments that the government uses to guide domestic firms, including National Bank for Economic and Social Development (BNDES) lending, share ownership, industrial supports, and sectoral policies. These tools have significant effects in preserving the overall structure of firm life, even as individual firms rise and fall.

If the state is able to wield considerable leverage over the economy, naturally, economic actors will understandably also seek to exert influence over the political system. Chapter 5 points to the fact that the functioning of the political system, at least between 1985 and the election of 2018, was complementary to that of the economic system. Hierarchy in firm life has been matched by hierarchy in political life. The fragmentation of the political system has been somewhat overcome by the toolkit of coalitional presidentialism: the president's agenda-setting powers, cabinet powers, partisan powers, and budgetary authority help to ensure presidential dominance (Chaisty et al., 2018). But these formal powers do not clinch the support needed to ensure effective governance which, as a consequence, is often obtained through informal exchange.

This pattern of political interaction leads to a suboptimal, inefficient equilibrium that drives up the cost of politics, dilutes the coherence of policy initiatives, requires costly side payments, and may diminish public support, by undercutting public confidence in the probity of policy deliberations. But there are many reasons it survives: it provides key interest groups with defenses against policy change, provides executives with support in a fissiparous party system, provides legislative incumbents with powerful resources for political survival, and enables incumbent firms to outcompete their potential rivals.

Chapter 6 seeks to understand why the massive rents mobilized to lofty ends by the developmental state have proven ineffective at moving the country toward a more promising equilibrium. Rents, after all, are a common way of incentivizing economic actors to produce goods or enter new sectors that they might otherwise eschew, and the experience of successful developmental states suggests that rents administered by the public sector have often been a driving force in pushing these countries into higher-income status. The rents made available by the Brazilian state, furthermore, are considerable: in recent years, these have included tax breaks, financial benefits, and credit subsidies that averaged 5.7 percent of GDP between 2013 and 2018, loans from the national development bank that in some years totaled 11 percent of GDP, as well as formidable but less quantifiable market protections, investments by state-affiliated pension funds, and sundry other supports (Lisboa and Latif, 2013; Leal, 2015; Prado et al., 2016; Armijo, 2017; Ministério da Fazenda, 2019).

Yet if rents are to function as a policymaking tool, they must be governed by an effective control mechanism, or "a set of institutions that imposes discipline on economic behavior" (Amsden, 2001). A control mechanism may rely on a principle of reciprocity to ensure that the flow of resources is not a "giveaway," and that recipients are subject to monitorable performance standards, in ways that transform, "the inefficiency and venality associated with government intervention into collective good" (Amsden, 2001, 8). Drawing on four case studies of industrial policies adopted by presidents between the 1990s and 2018, this chapter demonstrates that the nonstrategic bent of Brazilian policymaking is an outcome of the institutional complementarities between the developmental state, the coalitional presidential system, and weak control mechanisms. Despite recognition of the need for administrative and legal controls, and proactive efforts to implement such controls by a variety of presidential administrations, the controls needed to make the use of developmental rents effective are undermined by the difficulty of wielding presidential power in a coalitional system, parochialism and the weakness

Plan of the Book 31

of the upgrading coalition, weak strategic coordination, and lackluster oversight of developmental policies, agencies, and beneficiaries.

The complementarities described so far lead to a distressingly dystopic perspective on the prospects for Brazil's future. Yet important changes have taken place over the past generation. The large number of veto players who can dilute or negotiate any reform halts most heroic, "big bang" reform efforts. But the strength of the executive branch, the scope of the developmental state, and the coalition's need for a stable, functioning state have provided considerable room for the emergence of an autonomous bureaucracy capable of undertaking incremental reforms. Some of the most significant gains in the past generation have come about because of a steady progression of small steps by bureaucrats operating below the radar screen of Congress and out of view of the public. Not all bureaucratic initiatives are positive or laudable, of course. But much of the most significant change in the political economy has come about because of a slow and incremental sequence of iterative problem-solving by autonomous bureaucracies operating across a wide variety of policy arenas, described in Chapter 7. Paradoxically, however, the very success of the bureaucracy in pushing incremental change has in many ways contributed to the institutional equilibrium of the developmental state. The bureaucracy's role as an agent of change reinforces the centrality of the state as an actor, and forestalls private sector or civil society responses, thereby limiting the scope and direction of potential institutional change.

Together, institutional complementarities have undermined the potential effectiveness of the otherwise high-capacity institutions of the Brazilian state to deliver better results. Incremental reforms do not always sum up, or effectively accumulate into an institutional equilibrium shift. Indeed, one of the most interesting facets of the Brazilian political economy over the course of the past generation is the fact that despite hyperactive reform efforts, the country often seems to revert to preferences and behaviors that are not as distant from the status quo ante as hopeful reformers might have envisioned.

If understanding the institutional dynamics that have jointly driven actors toward a relatively stable political economy equilibrium between 1985 and 2018 is the first task of the book ahead, and the second is to consider what this experience says about institutional complementarity and theories of institutional change, the natural way to conclude is by reflecting about whether change is on the way. As of this writing, Brazil appears to be at a crossroads. The final chapter, Chapter 8, describes the new president's search for a new path forward for the economy, and drawing on the experience of his first eighteen months in office, demonstrates that his administration's options remain constrained by institutional complementarities within and across the economic and political systems. There is no denying that the triple economic, political, and legal crises of the second half of the 2010s have begun to alter incentive structures, in ways that may yet accumulate to shift long-standing patterns of political and economic behavior. While the goal of this book is not prognostication, the final chapter concludes with a mix of theoretical and empirical arguments for why change in economic institutions alone is unlikely to lead to improved long-term growth or equity, or a significant move away from the subpar equilibrium that has prevailed for much of the past generation.

PART I

COMPLEMENTARITIES IN THE ECONOMIC SPHERE

2

The Macroeconomic Foundations
of the Developmental State

> Reliance on the mere play of market forces, on foreign private investment
> and on a "hands off" policy on the part of the state, is no solution.
> Raúl Prebisch, 1963

> Inflation is my permanent preoccupation.
> Guido Mantega, 2011[1]

Scholars of the varieties of capitalism understandably invest a great deal of their analytical effort evaluating firm-state relations. Chapters 3 and 4 will turn to firm-state relations, but turning too quickly to firms would mean overlooking the broader macroeconomic, and particularly fiscal, constraints that generate particular patterns of economic policymaking in Brazil. The developmental state goes far beyond the state's role in business alone, after all: the developmental state is not merely, or even centrally, about the degree to which the state owns firms. Rather, it is a system of mutually supportive and long-standing rules and organizations that permit the government to guide economic activity, and thereby shape options across a range of policy arenas. Prices determined by macroeconomic policy are often a central determinant of industrial policy, for example, the exchange rate, interest rates, tax rates, and tariff rates (Amsden, 2001, 9). Macroeconomic policies are therefore an important and largely overlooked part of the story of the institutional complementarities that sustain the Brazilian developmental state.

35

36 *Macroeconomic Foundations of Developmental State*

DEVELOPMENTALISM WITH A FISCAL IMPERATIVE

There have been important changes from the "old" developmentalism of the military regime (1964–85) to the "new" developmentalism of the democratic regime (1985–2018). This section quickly overviews major changes in emphasis, while Chapter 3 discusses changing ideas about developmentalism (for those seeking a more detailed overview of political and economic developments in post-authoritarian Brazil, please see Taylor, 2020).

The democratic regime has been buffeted by a variety of economic forces that created incentives for change in the structures and policies of the developmental state. They included foreign events, such as the 1994 debt crisis in Mexico, emerging markets crises in the late 1990s, and the rise of China in the 2000s; domestic events, such as the return to democracy in 1985, the hyperinflationary crisis of the late 1980s and the pre-salt oil find of the 2000s; and institution-building efforts, whether through the 1988 Constitution or the 2000 Fiscal Responsibility Law (FRL). The resulting changes have been significant: state-owned enterprises (SOEs) have been pruned, a more transparent and rigorous fiscal regime has been implemented, financial institutions have been regulated, the monetary authority was strengthened, and the trade regime has grown less mercantilist and more open to foreign goods.

Three events in particular proved central in shaping the political economy of democratic Brazil: the regime transition and the 1988 Constitution that cemented the rules of the new democracy; the battle against hyperinflation and its fiscal propellants; and, after much turbulence, the emergence of a stable set of macroeconomic policies known as the *tripé*, which has been a cornerstone of policymaking since the turn of the century.

The 1985 regime transition took place in the shadow of the 1982 debt crisis, which contributed to capital scarcity and highly repressed consumption throughout the ensuing decade. The balance of payments crises of the 1970s had already played a substantial role in reshaping import substituting industrialization (ISI) policies in the waning years of the military regime, beginning a process of gradual economic opening that deepened after the transition. The 1988 Constitution was written against this backdrop of political transition and economic crisis, yet it was in many ways a backward-looking document, seeking to retroactively redress the shortcomings of authoritarianism, rather than proactively reenvision the best ways to ensure future governability. The Constitution broke with the authoritarian legacy by expanding civil and

Developmentalism with a Fiscal Imperative

political rights, expanding the social commitments of the political regime, and strengthening the state bureaucracy by establishing merit hiring alongside tenure and wage protections. However progressive the intent, these changes in the political structure greatly exacerbated the already daunting fiscal challenges bequeathed by the dictatorship.

Partly in consequence, hyperinflation would be the central policy challenge of the early years of democracy, from the Cruzado Plan of 1986 through the 1994 Real Plan. The repeated failure of quick and muscular solutions forced governments to invest political capital in building more effective fiscal institutions and curbing the fiscal overreach exacerbated by the Constitution. A variety of fiscal reforms were undertaken after 1988, culminating in the passage of the FRL in 2000, a constitutional amendment which consolidated principles of transparency, placed limits on payroll spending and debt, and together with another statute, established criminal penalties for breach of these rules (Afonso et al., 2016). The failure of the Cruzado Plan, and the chaos that accompanied the five unsuccessful stabilization plans that followed, conclusively demonstrated how deep a hole inflation had dug for the country, and signaled to politicians how great the economic, social, and political gains of stabilization could be.

The successful 1994 Real Plan was thus one of the most significant alterations in the fabric of the Brazilian developmental state in the past thirty years. The political success of the Real Plan meant that inflation became *the* essential driver of macroeconomic policy: because of the high inflation tax on the poor under hyperinflation, and the lifestyle gains engendered by stabilization, keeping inflation low has been central to the political fortunes of every president since 1994. Policymakers' success against hyperinflation, in other words, established macroeconomic stability as a public good (Sola and Kugelmas, 2002, 95–102; Lamounier, 2005, 201). But the survival of various forms of price indexation suggested the need for continued vigilance; recrudescent price increases might spark a revival of the inertial cycle of disastrous hyperinflation. Keeping prices in check thus required a major shift in the state's ability to manage its fiscal accounts and thereby manage economic agents' expectations about spending. Throughout the remainder of the book, I refer to the centrality of fiscal issues to the success of macroeconomic policy as the "fiscal imperative."

The balance of payments crises that pummeled emerging markets throughout the 1990s, from the 1994 Mexican Peso crisis through the Asian crises of the late 1990s, deepened efforts to build a sustainable fiscal

Macroeconomic Foundations of Developmental State

framework. The fiscal imperative thus guided much of the policymaking of the 1990s, providing the justification for the "neoliberal" reforms undertaken by the Collor, Franco, and Cardoso administrations. Economic opening required strong capital inflows to counteract rising current account deficits, explaining the urgency of attracting foreign capital through improvement of fiscal and regulatory conditions. Against the backdrop of the Washington Consensus reforms adopted in much of Latin America during the 1990s, Brazil undertook a privatization program that reshuffled government-firm relations, as well as a series of emergency fiscal reforms that imposed stricter controls on the state. When the dust settled after the devaluation that followed the balance of payments crisis of 1999, Brazil adopted the long-lived and relatively robust policy set known as the *tripé*, or tripod, combining a floating exchange rate, a commitment to fiscal responsibility, and inflation targeting.

Because of its close connection to inflation control, the *tripé* has become a core foundation of economic policy, and when governments have threatened to weaken one of its three legs – especially the fiscal leg – the public din and cry has been significant.[2] The fiscal imperative and its accompanying budget constraint has made much more evident a number of the policy choices implicit in the developmental state of the 1970s, but which had hitherto been obfuscated by the combination of hyperinflation, fiscal profligacy, and an expanding social safety net in the first decade of democracy. The result is a more fiscally responsible form of developmental state, in which the state is better informed of its size and reach, has centralized oversight of fiscal processes, and adheres to a much harder budget constraint than at any time in its first half-century.[3] This constraint is enforced by pressures from investors, economic bureaucrats, and civil society watchdogs. If those "soft" constraints were insufficient, institutions such as the Fiscal Responsibility Law of 2000 also imposed important "hard" consequences for failure to follow the fiscal rules, strengthening government control of its finances and leading to credible threats of punishment for even the most senior policymakers. The fiscal imperative is the essential macroeconomic constraint under which the economy labors.

INSTITUTIONAL COMPLEMENTARITIES

The remainder of this chapter argues that within this context, there are important complementarities across different spheres of the macroeconomy that help to explain patterns of economic performance and the

Institutional Complementarities 39

incentive structures faced by economic actors. Five institutional spheres, in particular, help to determine the performance of Brazil's economic system: the scale of the state, the monetary and financial regimes, patterns of state intervention in industry, the economy's integration into the world system, and the wage-labor nexus.[4] Several stylized facts about the political economy of Brazilian democracy emerge from the interaction between these spheres:

- The fiscal imperative generates incentives for politicians of all ideologies to employ what I term "fiscally opaque" instruments of economic policy that are made possible by the toolkit of the developmental state. These include industrial policies, nontransparent lending, cross-shareholding, regulation, and selective protection of domestic firms.
- The combination of the fiscal imperative and fiscally opaque instruments contributes to the high cost of credit, and low levels of investment, which drive firms to demand state action.
- Brazil's integration into global markets has been a secondary priority after industrial protection and anti-inflation efforts. Partly in consequence, there has been a lasting proclivity toward the protection of domestic producers, at some cost to efficiency and consumers.
- Industrial policy, including regulation and various supports, may reduce overall competition across firms by protecting incumbents, but it serves the purposes of government by providing fiscally opaque tools to meet the needs of domestic firms or guide them toward government objectives.
- The fiscal imperative and the power of interest groups in defending their own "acquired rights" has meant that the burden of balancing the fiscal accounts has fallen disproportionately on the less well-off, through regressive taxes, weak social welfare, and high informality, despite the lofty promises of the 1988 Constitution.
- Ensuing demand for social spending and the squeeze on investment spending generated by the fiscal imperative mean that economic growth, by default, is a residual.
- The one potential alternative source of investment, which might compensate for the weakness of domestic firms and state actors as investors, lies in foreign investment. The longstanding goal of attracting foreign capital, however, has meant that the capital account has been more open than the current account, with the implication that hard stops have been a possibility. Furthermore,

40 *Macroeconomic Foundations of Developmental State*

once inside Brazil's national borders, foreign direct investment often responds to incentives in ways that are similar to domestic capital, producing for the local market behind high protective barriers.[5]

With these patterns in mind, the next section details each of the five institutional spheres in turn.

THE SCALE OF THE STATE

The fiscal imperative, the relative size of the state, and the debt all play a role in sustaining a tax system marked by regressivity and pressure for sectoral relief. The fiscal imperative for sustaining market confidence and economic stabilization means that fiscal constraints are real, with concrete effects on public support for policymakers and politicians who fail to adhere to the basic norms. The relative size of the state is significant: the tax burden rivals Argentina's as the heaviest in Latin America, as do government expenditures as a share of gross domestic product (GDP).[6] The total stock of government debt is less pressing, on the order of 75 percent of GDP, but debt service on outstanding arrears accounted for nearly 74 percent of the nominal federal deficit and the debt rose sharply over the 2010s (Ministério da Fazenda, 2018). The perception of fiscal vulnerability that results from these factors has contributed to i) ongoing efforts to develop tax capacity, ii) record-breaking real interest rates, and iii) incentives for the use of fiscally opaque instruments.

The strength of the Brazilian state is nowhere more evident than in its capacity for taxation. The federal, state, and local governments collect taxes at a rate that rivals that of the wealthier Organization for Economic Cooperation and Development (OECD) nations. Further, as Figure 2.1 shows, total tax revenue has been rising steadily, from 17 percent of GDP at the outset of the military regime in 1964 to nearly twice that – 33.6 percent – in 2018, in what may have been the world's greatest peacetime expansion of taxation (Afonso, 2013, 2).[7] Revenue availability has been essential to the survival of many structures of the developmental state and, in fact, many of the moments of greatest change in the structure of the developmental state have occurred when fiscal tightening was necessary (such as the privatizations needed to make stabilization plans viable in the 1990s or the changes in National Bank for Economic and Social Development [BNDES] lending policies that were implemented after Treasury transfers were curtailed in the 2010s). Tax policy, meanwhile,

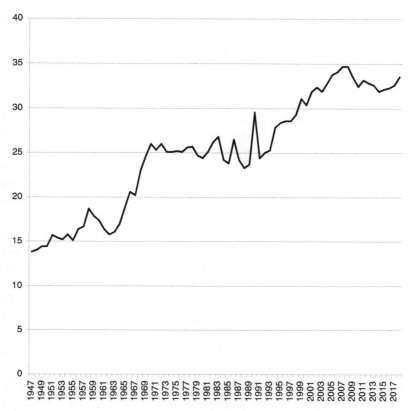

FIGURE 2.1 Gross tax revenue, percentage of GDP.
Source: Compiled by author using data from IBGE for the period 1947–2007, data from the Brazilian Central Bank for the period 2008–10; and data from the National Treasury Secretariat for 2011–18.

has had important repercussions for the persistence of inequality in Brazil. Despite fifteen tax reforms over the quarter century following the 1988 Constitution, there has been little change in the complexity of the tax system – there are currently ninety-two types of taxes nationwide (Sachsida, 2017) – or its regressive nature. Those most hurt by regressive taxation are the least likely to mobilize; the most regressive taxes are among the least transparent to those who pay them; and firms have shown little interest in reform, in part because many have received important compensatory benefits, such as industrial policies designed to offset the competitiveness losses engendered by the high tax burden (Schapiro, 2017).[8]

The regressivity of the tax system is its most distinguishing feature, and income concentration actually worsens after taxation (Rossignolo, 2012, 12; Afonso, 2013, 2). The poorest pay taxes at a proportional rate 86 percent higher than the wealthiest: in the lowest income decile, earning two minimum wages or less, families paid an average rate of 48.9 percent, as compared to 26.3 percent in the upper income decile, of those with household income above thirty minimum wages (Zockun, 2007; Afonso, 2013, 8). The benefits of social policy are largely eaten up by taxes, especially indirect taxes: at most levels of income, net tax to benefit ratios are negative, meaning that citizens pay more in taxes than they receive in benefits. The one exception is the middle income quintile, which concentrates a number of pensioners (Nogueira et al., 2015).[9] The number of poor people who are made poorer through the taxing and spending of government is significant: *Bolsa Família*, for example, does not compensate for what many of the poor pay in consumption taxes (Higgins and Pereira, 2014; Lustig, 2016).

In part, regressivity results from an unwillingness to tax wealthy individuals: capital gains tax exemptions, a maximum income tax rate of 27.5 percent (which is seldom paid, given various exemptions), and low inheritance taxes all reflect the political power of the well-off, and these taxes represent only 18 percent of total revenues (Carvalho, 2018, location 2069). Further, many higher-income wealthy and middle-class professionals are paid not as individuals, but as professional firms, which are taxed at a much lower rate (Afonso et al., 2016).

Regressivity also is a consequence of the emphasis on indirect taxation. The load of indirect taxes is one of the highest in the world, with one-fifth of total national revenue (and 75 percent of state tax revenues; together, this accounts for about half of all revenue nationwide) coming from state value-added taxes on goods and services that are highly regressive, and fall particularly heavily on inputs such as fuel, energy, and communications (Afonso et al., 2016). One consequence is that 50 percent of all tax revenue nationwide is derived from taxes on goods and services, by contrast to an OECD average of 32.4 percent; by contrast taxes on income and assets account for 25.4 percent of tax revenue nationwide, by comparison to 39.6 percent in the OECD countries (Fagnani, 2018, 18). "Social contributions" on wages and salaries, furthermore, are another important tax source, even though they weigh most heavily on the working class (Afonso, 2013, 8; Nogueira et al., 2015, 191). Because they are one of the few taxes that the federal government need not share with state and municipal governments under the terms of the Constitution, however, this helps to explain their enduring appeal.

Tax policy has been one of the most debated aspects of the political economy of the democratic regime. Much of the federal government's fiscal effort over the decades since the initiation of the Real Plan in 1994 has been focused on recapturing revenues transferred to other levels of the federation, so as to meet its fiscal targets. In doing so, it faces an important constraint: the 1988 Constitution handed more revenue over to lower levels of government, including through constitutionally mandated transfers to states and municipalities. Yet in the push to fund constitutional mandates, while also expanding social programs that might enhance politicians' electoral standing, all levels of government have moved in the direction of greater taxation, be it through the creation of new taxes, through managerial improvements in revenue collection, or through "stealth," such as failing to realign income thresholds with inflation (Melo et al., 2014). The result is a complex system that is the most procedurally costly in the world.[10]

Where does all this money go? While absolute government spending has been rising faster than GDP growth since 1991, in real per capita terms the government's share of GDP largely stabilized in the late 1990s. But this may be cold solace in light of the very constrained budget situation and the fact that Brazil's public expenditure is much greater than most countries at a comparable stage of economic development (Schick, 2018). Some fiscal burdens – such as the debt and interest payments that are the single largest component of the budget – predate democracy.[11] Others, such as rising primary expenditures (i.e., spending after interest and debt payments), which have risen from 13.7 percent of GDP in 1991 to nearly one-fifth of GDP (19.69 percent) in 2014, are largely an outcome of the new social contract laid out in the 1988 Constitution (Giambiagi and Castelar Pinheiro, 2012, 19).

Three groups of expenditures were constitutionalized, making them very difficult to alter: transfers to states and municipalities, social security benefits, and personnel spending (rows 2–4 in Table 2.1). Overall, the percentage of "rigid transfers" in the central government budget is the highest in the Latin American peer group: around 92 percent in Brazil, by contrast to 85 percent in Argentina; 82 percent in Mexico and 65 percent in Chile (World Bank, 2017b, 33). Strong rights guarantees enforced by the courts have essentially precluded any wholesale changes to these three spending priorities, except via constitutional amendment (some of which have been struck down by courts; Taylor, 2008). All three expenditures

44 — Macroeconomic Foundations of Developmental State

TABLE 2.1 *Federal expenditures by category*

	Average share of GDP, 1997–2014	Growth of share of GDP, 1997–2014
1. Debt service	3.04%	+0.0%
2. Social security	5.83%	+7.4%
3. Earmarked transfers	4.55%	+2.0%
4. Civil service salaries and benefits	4.73%	+0.1%
5. Other pending liabilities	0.01%	-0.2%
6. *Custeio e investimento*	4.56%	+6.0%
Total	22.73%	+15.3%

Source: National Treasury Secretariat, calculations by author.

have risen more quickly than average annual GDP growth (Giambiagi and Castelar Pinheiro, 2012, 21). Their proportions also have not changed much, even in the wake of parametric reforms to both the civil service and social security systems undertaken under various presidential administrations.

The dirty secret of Brazil's otherwise strong presidency is that once debt payments, other pending liabilities, and these three groups of primary expenditures have been taken into account, only 20 percent of the budget remains as discretionary spending for the supposedly powerful president to allocate to central priorities (the sixth row of Table 2.1; "6. *Custeio e investimento*"). The discretionary portion of the budget, furthermore, is restricted at its outer bound by the high salience of fiscal responsibility, and the fact that the primary fiscal result is the most closely watched indicator of fiscal accounts, so adjustment often must happen within this "discretionary" budget. Even within this discretionary budget, furthermore, there are items that are not entirely discretionary, given that they have built up an ingrained constituency, such as some subsidies (0.3 percent of GDP), the *Bolsa Família* conditional cash transfer program (0.4 percent), and government infrastructure investment programs such as the PAC (0.7 percent).[12]

Together, these constraints on discretionary spending help to explain three phenomena. First, the continued pressure to increase tax revenue, and the upward trend in taxation shown in Figure 2.1.

Second, very low levels of investment, especially in infrastructure, which has been a secondary priority during the post-transition decades.

The Scale of the State

The economy-wide rate of gross fixed capital investment has averaged just under 20 percent of GDP since 1970, falling during recession years (World Bank World Development Indicators [henceforth WDI], various years). Even at its historical average since 1970, this investment rate remains low by international standards (e.g., by comparison to 40 percent in China, and an average of 30 percent among the upper middle-income country group of countries to which Brazil belongs). This limits Brazil's potential noninflationary growth rate. Federal government investment – including by SOEs – has remained between 2.5 percent and 3.0 percent of GDP since the turn of the century,[13] in part because discretionary spending is tilted heavily toward social expenditure.[14] Infrastructure investment since the mid-1990s has been around 2.5 percent of GDP, below the 3 percent a year that is estimated to be needed simply to maintain the capital stock (Pessôa, 2011, 209). Caught between a hard fiscal constraint and expanding social expenditure, the government is clearly limited in its ability to invest, which helps to explain why "neoliberal" governments felt the need to privatize in the 1990s, as did the Workers' Party under its concession programs of the 2000s and 2010s (Paula and Avellar, 2008). Private investment has also been limited, constrained by contextual factors such as recurring exchange rate appreciation that weakens the incentives for investment in industry; rickety infrastructure, which increases the relative cost of investment; and high interest rates, which raise the opportunity costs of investment.

Fiscal pressures have other significant downstream implications. Brazil's debt levels are not so significant as to generate immediate market instability. But the exchange rate is subject both to rapid fluctuation and a secular tendency toward excessive appreciation (Bresser-Pereira, 2017). The volatility is at least in part due to the fact that Brazil's capital account is comparatively more open than its current account, in part because of the need to attract foreign investment to compensate weak domestic investment capacity. The inflationary threat engendered by the fiscal accounts also means that Brazil's interest rates must usually be higher than would be required simply to cover market perceptions of country risk, and Brazilian rates are therefore recurrently among the highest real rates in the world, with two effects. The first is to engender the tendency toward currency appreciation, which hurts exports and competitiveness generally. The second, as noted above, is to diminish private sector investment by driving it to less productive lending (Felipe Salto, author correspondence, 2018).[15]

Finally, constraints on discretionary spending help to explain successive governments' efforts to instead utilize policy tools that have a less direct fiscal impact than outright spending. These "fiscally opaque" tools have an impact on the fiscal accounts that is not immediately visible, and in some cases, is not easily quantified (e.g., the costs of domestic content requirement policies). Under conditions of limited discretionary spending, such fiscally opaque tools are attractive to policymakers as a means of circumventing conventional budget constraints, encouraging economic actors in particular directions, and perhaps rewarding supporters in ways that would not be feasible if policymakers employed mechanisms with a more immediate fiscal impact on the government ledger.[16] Similarly, however, the existence of fiscally opaque tools means that the government is susceptible to pressures from interest groups, such as pressures for trade relief and subsidized credit.

MONETARY AND FINANCIAL REGIMES

Defeating inflation required significant enhancements to the power of the Central Bank during the 1980s and 1990s. This process included elimination of rival centers of monetary policy, the disciplining of both private and public sector banks, and the significant reduction of the central bank's role as an agent of development, including its previous administration of a highly complex set of distinct exchange rate mechanisms and specialized credit programs (Martone, 1993; Sola et al., 1998; Sola and Kugelmas, 2002; Luna and Klein, 2006, 83; Sola and Whitehead, 2006; Taylor, 2009; Schapiro and Taylor, 2020).[17] Yet the Central Bank nonetheless still plays an important role in the sandbox of developmentalism, both indirectly through monetary policy and directly through regulation.

The Central Bank faces a credibility gap, given its continued political subordination to the executive branch, the lingering indexation of prices in the economy, and the fiscal pressures already described.[18] As De Gregorio (2009) and Fraga et al. (2003) have demonstrated, constructing the credibility of monetary authority in emerging markets is a significant challenge, made more difficult by the subordination of monetary policy to fiscal policy, repression of public prices (which leads to fears of resurgent public prices), indexation and the persistence of inertial inflationary pressures, and the possibility of sudden stops in capital inflows. These factors contribute to the inefficacy of monetary policy. Brazil's inflation targets are notably loose: as one banker memorably put it, the inflation targets set by the Central Bank in 2015 (a central target of 4.5 percent, plus or minus

Monetary and Financial Regimes

2 percent) were akin to saying that you will run a mile in thirty minutes, plus or minus ten (Ramos, 2015). Not only is the target relatively unambitious, but the leeway around the target is so significant as to obviate the purpose of targeting. Furthermore, high real interest rates are required to keep prices in check: despite the fact that twelve-month inflation has – with only two brief exceptions[19] – remained in the one-digit range since 1996, real interest rates have consistently remained among the world's highest.

The causes of Brazil's high real interest rates are multiple. A long history of sophisticated indexation of both public and private prices dates back to the 1960s and adds an element of inertia to prices that has not been eliminated: as prices rise in one part of the economy, they often "contaminate" prices elsewhere, quickly ratcheting up inflation across even economically distant sectors.[20] Investors demand inflation-linked bonds, which in turn extend the indexation of the economy, and contribute to inertial inflationary pressures that undermine the effectiveness of monetary policy.[21] Indexation, a long inflationary history, and currency fluctuations all contribute directly to high interest rates paid by the government as well as private sector borrowers (Horch, 2015). Fiscal policy also pressures monetary policy, because if fiscal deficits cannot be financed by public bonds, the fear is that the monetary authority will be "forced to create money and tolerate additional inflation" (Sargent and Wallace, 1981, 2). The size of the public debt, while not enormous by international standards,[22] changes the term structure of interest rates: because of fiscal weakness, government debt is not risk-free and the Central Bank funds rate thus must incorporate a risk premium (Barbosa, 2006).[23] Microeconomic and legal issues play a role: an underdeveloped credit reporting system, the inefficiency of the judiciary in adjudicating insolvency, and a variety of other inadequacies in the legal framework increase the costs of potential default (World Bank, 2018a). The weakness of private lending, itself related to the bifurcation of the banking market between public and private banks and the presence of earmarked loans (below), boosts the cost of credit in the private market.

One consequence is that the channels for monetary policy are clogged: interest rate hikes do not have much influence on the private credit market and directed credit from state-owned banks is unaffected by the Central Bank lending rate. Any effort to control aggregate demand through interest rates therefore requires huge interest rate hikes (Modenesi and Modenesi, 2012; Carvalho, 2018). Such high interest rates have a number of negative consequences, such as their fiscal costs, their effect

48   *Macroeconomic Foundations of Developmental State*

on the exchange rate, the stop and go nature of the economy, and weakened investment (Sicsú, 2002; Afonso et al., 2016; Bresser-Pereira, 2019). These high rates, in turn, create incentives for the "financialization" of the economy. Such financialization has two effects. The first is to turn the economy toward banking: bank earnings made up more than half of the total profits on the São Paulo stock exchange in 2013 and 2014 (Horch, 2015). Second, high rates shift investment decisions, with industrial and commercial firms turning to indexed, high-return public debt as a source of profits that sometimes dwarf the returns from their business operations (Medialdea, 2013). The net effect has been to exacerbate credit scarcity and channel capital out of productive investment, such as infrastructure projects, and into financial assets, such as banking stocks and government debt. Even at the height of government lending through state banks in 2010, 55.5 percent of Brazilian businesses surveyed by the World Bank pointed to finance as a major constraint, with the overall rate of this complaint outpacing all other Latin American economies and comparing extremely poorly with Asian economies such as China (2.9 percent), Korea (12.1 percent), and Indonesia (14.3 percent) (Stallings, 2016, 20).

Two overlapping issues are worth highlighting regarding the direct effects of Central Bank regulation: the bifurcation of financial institutions between public and private banks, and the heavy concentration of the banking sector as a whole.[24]

With regard to the first issue, the Central Bank is a victim of history: public banks have long played a central role in the developmental state. Credit policy, and the various tools available to policymakers through control of the federally owned banks, have been central to government guidance in macroeconomic policy and industrial policy. The historical scarcity of long-term capital in Brazil, together with high levels of inflation,[25] provided incentives for developing systems of government-controlled long-term lending. Public banks still play a very relevant role in public access to finance: although their share of total deposits has fallen from a peak of 59 percent in 1997 to around 40 percent in 2018, public banks still accounted for 48 percent of credit operations in 2018 (Banco Central do Brasil, 2018, 145).

Bank lending is very important in the Brazilian financial system, which is heavily bank-centered, along the lines of the German and Italian economies, rather than capital market-centered, along the lines of the US or UK. In the former, stock market capitalization hovers around 30 percent of GDP, by comparison to 90–110 percent in the latter. This forces firms to look for capital through borrowing and revenue, rather than stock

Monetary and Financial Regimes

market capitalization (Mettenheim, 2005). High spreads and the low availability of private sector credit, however, mean that there is enormous pressure to keep up directed public lending; in chicken-or-egg fashion, the public sector role in banking may crowd out private lenders, generating further pressures for public credit.

The BNDES is the most important long-term lender to large business and plays a role in the provision of credit to small and medium business ventures. Federal banks Banco do Brasil and Caixa Econômica Federal (CEF) also have played a vital role, with longstanding roles in agricultural credit (Banco do Brasil) and housing lending (CEF) (Mettenheim and Lima, 2014). They have been used to provide credit in areas where private banks have long been uninterested or where credit has been scarce, such as agriculture and housing; to provide an alternative to underdeveloped capital markets[26]; to smooth lending countercyclically; to expand access to finance in areas of the country that have been underserved; and even to fulfill social policy objectives.[27] Policymakers in the Rousseff administration also used government banks in a bid to reduce borrowing rates, unilaterally reducing borrowing rates so as to push private sector banks to do the same.[28]

The public banks, however, undermine the Central Bank's role as a monetary authority. The strength and importance of government banks to policymaking helps to explain why central bank independence has been an elusive prospect in Brazil and why some channels of monetary policy have been quite ineffective. Further, earmarked credit offered by public banks has significant fiscal costs and may disrupt "free" or non-directed credit. The funds dedicated to earmarked lending are quite high, accounting for more than 16 percent of GDP.[29] Much earmarked lending has been conducted with implicit subsidies through regulated interest rates; the fiscal cost of these credit interventions reached 2.1 percent of GDP in 2015 (World Bank, 2018a).[30]

The second issue is the concentration of the banking industry as a whole. The loss of inflation-generated profits and the balance of payments crises of the 1990s brought significant consolidation of the banking system that eliminated many of the most high-risk institutions (Almeida and Jayme Jr., 2008). After the mid-1990s, even at moments of enormous stress, systemic financial sector failure has not been a significant risk (Luna and Klein, 2006, 78). Strong regulation of Brazilian banks has meant that the banking system has met and exceeded Basel and Basel II requirements since the late 1990s.[31] Also as a legacy of past crises, the Central Bank has kept reserve requirements for banks comparatively high, so as to ensure

50 *Macroeconomic Foundations of Developmental State*

reserves against a run on banks and control the growth of the money supply.

A stable banking system is an accomplishment. Yet it has come at some cost. Through its regulatory decisions seeking systemic stability, the Central Bank has provided preferential treatment to large Brazilian financial groups. The top ten banks, as measured by total assets, grew their share of banking system assets from 60 percent in 1996 to 82 percent in 2016 (Schapiro and Taylor, 2020).[32] This process resulted in a highly concentrated banking market, where the top five banks – private Brazilian banks Itaú Unibanco and Bradesco, public Brazilian banks Banco do Brasil and CEF, and Spanish-Brazilian hybrid Santander – accounted for the bulk of lending. Although market concentration fell slightly after the 2008 crisis, by 2018, these top five banks accounted for 71 percent of corporate credit, 80 percent of personal loans, and 98 percent of housing loans (Banco Central do Brasil, 2018). This concentration compares unfavorably with other large markets, such as the US (where the top institutions accounted for 20 percent of loans), India (just over 30 percent), and Turkey (just under 30 percent) (Sreeharsha, 2017).

Together with the many factors listed earlier, high regulation and an oligopolistic banking market have meant that lending in Brazil is characterized by high spreads, low availability of financing for medium and long-term investment, and very low lending rates (Luna and Klein, 2006, 99; Almeida and Jayme Jr., 2008; World Bank, 2018a). Lower credit provision hurts investment, since firms have little wherewithal to finance capital improvements, and may as a consequence also reduce productivity. It also helps drive private sector demand for continued public sector-led investment, credit, and industrial policies.

INDUSTRIAL SUPPORTS AND REGULATION

Chapters 4 and 6 delve more deeply into the government role in industrial policy, but it should be apparent that much of the industrial policy set established in the postwar ISI period remains intact, and these "buttons and levers" (Bolle, 2016, 71) have proven shiny and irresistible to policymakers of all stripes trying to navigate complex political and economic terrain. The state has several major levers at its disposal as it develops "open-economy" industrial policies, including tools for allocating credit, guiding business, and providing firm-level and sector-level supports (Schrank and Kurtz, 2005). The BNDES provides low cost credit to firms across a wide range of sectors. The government shapes the economy

Industrial Supports and Regulation

through majority shareholding in state-owned enterprises, as well as cross-shareholding across many of the largest companies in Brazil. Industrial policies have been employed under all presidential administrations, in development plans instituted by presidents of a variety of ideological inclinations.[33] Chapter 4 will describe these tools and their impact on firm life in greater detail. Two aspects of the toolkit, though, are important as we think about the macroeconomic sphere: first, the manner by which the macroeconomic policies described above weaken investment and trigger demand for a state response, and the second, the incumbent- and state-favoring nature of the regulatory bureaucracy.

Public investment has been low and declining over much of the past generation, with public investment falling from an average of 7.8 percent of GDP in the 1970s to 3.2 percent from 2011 to 2017, with much of the difference being spent on the debt service (Bresser-Pereira, 2019). Further, as already noted, infrastructure investment has been particularly hard hit, and it is estimated that inefficiencies in the infrastructure space may reduce GDP by 10–15 percent (Garcia-Escribano et al., 2015). The World Economic Forum (WEF) ranking of infrastructure routinely places Brazilian roads, railroads, airports, electricity, and ports in the lower third of all countries surveyed. The government's inability to fund investment has driven it to a variety of remedies, including privatization of infrastructure sectors, private-public partnerships, and the targeting of public investment toward perceived infrastructure bottlenecks.

In developing these alternatives to public sector investment, the state has turned to a new regulatory bureaucracy. There are two essential types of regulatory bureaucracies in the Brazilian federal government: autonomous regulatory agencies, which regulate public services through the application of area-specific legislation; and executive agencies, which follow government guidelines and policies to regulate specific sectors (Salgado, 2003, 32; Paula and Avellar, 2008). The line between them has become less clear than it was initially designed to be, in part because the independence of many of the regulatory agencies has been constrained through budgetary inducements and partisan appointments, as well as the efforts of "old-style" technocrats to "pour the old wine of state developmentalism into the new bottle of the regulatory state" (Correa et al., 2008; De Bonis, 2016; Sá e Silva and Trubek, 2018, 920). This has meant that despite their ostensible autonomy, regulatory agencies have somewhat ironically emerged as a further tool for government guidance of the private sector.[34]

There is considerable variance in the frameworks of each of the regulatory agencies, in part because the ministry in each sector was assigned the task of designing their own regulatory agencies' structure (Correa et al., 2008). Sectoral politics and the degree of ministerial expertise thereby played a significant role in shaping regulatory agency design (Prado, 2008). In some sectors, the dominance of particular firms also meant limited agency autonomy from the industry that it is supposed to regulate. This is especially the case for the National Petroleum Agency (ANP), which must regulate an oil market dominated in its upstream, middle stream, and downstream[35] by a single firm, which is also the largest state-owned enterprise: Petrobras.[36] In other sectors, such as telecommunications, constitutional prohibitions meant that the regulatory body was subordinated to a ministry and reliant upon it for writing laws (Sá e Silva and Trubek, 2018, 924). Finally, there are also coordination problems and turf wars between the regulatory agencies and associated state bureaucracies, as for example, in environmental regulation, where there is considerable friction between the electric regulator (ANEEL), the petrol regulator (ANP), the water regulator (ANA), and the environmental protection agency (IBAMA) (Paula and Avellar, 2008). The consequence of these political aspects of regulatory governance is that the system of regulatory bodies has shifted, but not eliminated, government influence in the infrastructure sector (Paula and Avellar, 2008, 251).

In addition to these regulatory bodies, there are also a variety of executive branch agencies with regulatory powers. Among the most important is the Administrative Council for Economic Defense (CADE), an antitrust body which was created in the early 1960s but gained autonomy from the Ministry of Justice under a 1994 reform law. Like its counterparts in the US and the UK,[37] the CADE is charged with preventing the abuse of economic power in the marketplace and has the power to levy heavy fines against companies found to have engaged in monopolistic or predatory behavior. Within particular sectors, there are also a variety of executive agencies that may enhance government control over economic activities. For example, within the healthcare and pharmaceutical sector, Vashisth et al. (2012) describe a series of interlocking agencies within the national system of sanitary surveillance, including not only the ANVISA agency, but also the Oswaldo Cruz Foundation (FIOCRUZ), the National Institute for Quality Control in Health (INCQS), and a variety of others. Together, the standards they impose are "costly and time consuming" by comparison with the other BRICS (Brazil, Russia, India, China, South Africa) countries, but they serve an important policy

Integration in the Global Economy

function by putting pressure on providers to improve local production, limit the participation of foreign producers, and impose controls on drug prices (Vashisth et al., 2012). On the flip side, of course, these many regulatory hurdles may reduce competition by keeping new firms out of the market (Soares, 2016, 17).

It is ironic that the regulatory framework established to facilitate the privatization of a variety of firms in a number of sectors has been repurposed over time to serve as a tool of government control over the economy. The federal government has used regulation and regulatory agencies to control a variety of prices, whether it was by halting electricity rate increases during the 2000s or controlling gasoline prices during the 2010s. As Prado (2008) points out, the use of regulatory agencies to achieve the government's macroeconomic objectives runs counter to their statutory mission. At the extreme, in fact, the combination of altered regulatory oversight and government shareholding in SOEs has enabled the government to regulate prices, even at the cost of diminished profitability, amounting to a "license to expropriate minority shareholders" and use SOEs "for social and political purposes" (Musacchio and Lazzarini, 2014, 192). Regulation, in other words, is tempered by the interests of the central stakeholder, the government. Regulatory agencies are often used more as tools of proactive policy control than to enhance arms' length market competition.[38]

INTEGRATION IN THE GLOBAL ECONOMY

Brazil's economy has opened considerably since the military regime, but it has done so slowly and remains remarkably closed both with regard to trade and, to a lesser degree, investment. Although Brazil's economy has oscillated between the seventh and tenth largest in the world, it is only the twenty-fifth largest exporter, and its share of global exports is less than half its share of the global economy. The share of imports in the economy is the third smallest in the world, behind only Nigeria and Sudan (Bacha, 2016). Despite strong pressure to attract foreign investment, Brazil preserves a number of regulations discouraging foreign ownership. While many large countries are able to build economies of scale that reduce the relative weight of trade in the economy, size alone does not explain Brazil's predicament: Brazil's trade is about three times smaller than would be expected even by comparison with other large countries (Canuto et al., 2015). Further, Brazil has actually grown more protectionist since the last major trade liberalization episode in the late 1980s and early 1990s, with nontariff barriers increasing in the interim (Oliveira et al., 2019, 7). The perceived centrality of manufacturers to development and the vulnerability of macroeconomic policy to external shocks have contributed to the inward bias of integration, with the consequence that government guidance of firms is often used to manage ensuing inefficiencies and provide ongoing protections.

Partly, this is a consequence of external constraints. During the twenty-first century, the rising sophistication of Brazil's agroexport industry led Brazil to push for the opening of specific sectors of developed markets, whether through the Cairns Group of agricultural exporters or through its insistence that the Doha Round include agricultural trade concessions. The government played an active role in promoting trade, using export promotion through APEX, the export financing program PROEX, and loans to a variety of hand-picked firms (Pereira da Costa and da Motta Veiga, 2011; Porzecanski, 2015). Success has been mixed, however, in part because Brazil is truly disadvantaged in global trade by high tariff rates on its agricultural exports, which face more unfavorable access to international markets than Brazil's regional or income-level cohorts. Given that agricultural exports (including both raw goods, such as unprocessed coffee beans, and manufactured goods, such as processed soy) have accounted for nearly one-third of Brazilian exports since the turn of the century, easing market access has become a vital but unsatisfied policy objective that limits Brazilian integration into global markets (Hornbeck, 2006; Soares de Lima and Hirst, 2006; Oliveira, 2011, 174).

The conditions by which economic opening took place also explain the relatively low insertion of Brazil in global markets: a frequently over-appreciated currency, economic volatility, and trade policy's subordinate role to macroeconomic stabilization, foreign policy, and industrial policy have all contributed to a rough climate for firms seeking out export markets (Bonomo, 2012). Many noncommodity producers had a hard time adjusting to globalized competition, especially in the wake of China's rise, leading them to prefer to hunker down behind the protective barrier provided by the state and to actively push the state for further protections.

But Brazil's trade underperformance is by no means solely an external imposition or just a consequence of bad luck. Brazil has long been protective of business, and import protections, antidumping initiatives, domestic content requirements, and exchange rate management have been implemented by governments of all stripes (Gómez Mera, 2007; Montero, 2014b). Much has changed in the past thirty years: the overall trend has been toward lower tariffs under the

Integration in the Global Economy

General Agreement on Tariffs and Trade (GATT) and World Trade Organization (WTO) agreements, and Brazil has been extraordinarily active in building the legal capacity to take on major powers in trade disputes in the WTO (Shaffer and Badin, in press).[39] Yet despite these changes, comparatively speaking, Brazil still has among the highest median nominal tariffs in the world (Moreira, 2009, 4; Villela, 2015; Canuto, 2018; World Bank, 2018b). Although the maximum tariff rate of 35 percent is historically low, the most-favored nation (MFN) applied simple tariff average of 12.2 percent is high by comparison with Brazil's regional peers.[40] While Brazil performs worse than the OECD average on almost every measure of product market regulation, its worst score is on tariff barriers, which are more than 2,300 percent greater than the OECD mean. Nontariff barriers are another cause of trade underperformance, and the Overall Trade Restrictiveness Index measure for Brazil is 20 percent, as opposed to 12 percent in Latin America, and 12 percent among Brazil's peers in the upper-middle-income country group.[41] Other measures – such as the number of days for imports and exports to clear customs, and the average industrial tariff, are similarly high by comparative standards (Soares, 2016, 14). Domestic content requirements have become increasingly relevant as tariffs have declined (Abreu, 2015). While some companies such as Embraer produce a large portion of their content outside Brazil (Bonomo, 2012), Brazil ranks third in the world in terms of the prevalence of local content requirements, after only the US and Indonesia (Stone et al., 2015). Much of the development of the pre-salt oil finds has been conducted under strenuous local content guidelines, and tax incentives are often structured around the proportionality of local content.

Even at moments of trade liberalization, the overall bias has remained inward looking. In the 1980s, reforms were undertaken in response to balance of payments constraints, and in some cases, also in consequence of conditionalities imposed by international financial institutions (Trubek, 2013, 8; Campello, 2015). Policymakers faced an unpalatable choice between immiserating isolation from the world economy or opening an economy long shielded from competitive pressures. Policymakers chose a middle route, adopting a liberalizing approach, but seeking to control the timing and depth of opening to support larger strategic goals, and in the process, maintained many developmentalist policy tools in trade (Sikkink, 1991; Boschi, 2011; Ban, 2013; Hochstetler and Montero, 2013; Montero, 2014b). Under the Sarney and Cardoso presidencies, trade liberalization was undertaken as an expediency, but given the strong, pent-up demand for consumer goods and the bundling of trade opening with other desirable policies, economic opening found broad support. Consumers were provided huge lifestyle gains from access to imports after decades of living with few ties to foreign markets, and industrialists tolerated the potential costs because of the broader economic gains (Kingstone, 2001; Baker, 2003). Trade opening served a central purpose, of keeping domestic prices in check, albeit tempered by continued protections and supports for domestic producers.[42] But particularly "once the Real Plan was put at risk by a succession of international crises, pro-liberalization technocrats in the Ministry of Finance and the Central Bank prioritized stabilization, leaving industrial and commercial policy to protectionist elements in the administration . . . " (Villela, 2015, 174; see also Bonomo, 2012).

The recurrent appreciation of the exchange rate has only deepened this inward-looking trend in trade. In part, this is again because of the subordination of trade to other policy objectives, such as controlling inflation, attracting foreign capital, and increasing investment. An overvalued exchange rate hurts the competitiveness of manufacturers and exporters, of course, but this does not often drive them into overt opposition.[43] One reason is that the number of exporting firms in Brazil is really quite low – roughly the same number as Norway – and exports are highly concentrated in a small number of firms (the top 1 percent of firms generate 59 percent of total exports; Canuto et al., 2015), allowing the state to provide a variety of compensatory policies for affected firms. The productivity of many agricultural exporters is such that they remain globally competitive even under an appreciated exchange rate. Roughly half of Brazil's industrial exports are produced by subsidiaries of multinational companies, who may be able to play offsetting currency trades in other locales. The fact that much of Brazilian production is only marginally integrated into global production chains may diminish pressure for policy relief (Baumann, 2009, 7; Baumann, 2012; Canuto et al., 2013; Canuto, 2018). Finally, the ties between firms' business interests and their longstanding relations with government agencies and policymakers may blunt opposition to inward-looking government policies: firms that might otherwise lobby against inward-looking policies may decide that their interests in other areas of the economy, and their ties to other firms, might be damaged by staking out too vehement an oppositional stance (Lazzarini, 2010; Bonomo, 2012; Musacchio and Lazzarini,

Integration in the Global Economy

2014). Given that the preponderance of large firms in Brazil are not export-oriented, such concerns with maintaining good relations mean that the balance of policy activism naturally falls on the side of an inward-looking business orientation.

Brazil has long been a target for significant foreign investment although, as skeptics point out, this may be in part because foreign firms hope to benefit from oligopolistic command of markets behind protective barriers (Abreu, 2015). The 1988 Constitution lays out a number of constraints on foreign investment: although foreign and national capital are considered equal, and must be taxed equally, a number of protections remain, for example banning foreign ownership in newspaper and broadcasting, transportation (although restrictions on airline ownership were definitively lifted in 2018), healthcare, nuclear energy, and postal services (Smith and Bernardes, 2013). Although a number of reforms have been undertaken in the past two decades, there is still room for considerable ambiguity and petulance in the application of these multilayered legal rules. Even as they have opened the economy, governments have placed restrictions on investments in the gas and oil industry, limited foreign ownership of rural land, and otherwise established hurdles for foreign capital.

In sum, the state seeks to "benefit from participation in the global economy while avoiding the dangers of free-trade fundamentalism" (Trubek, 2013, 4). Brazilian policymakers have favored policies that curb international pressures for economic reform, constrain the developed countries' push for trade liberalization, and simultaneously expand opportunities for Brazilian exports. Brazil has invested in trade deals that reinforce these tendencies: during the 1990s, the creation of Mercosur was an inherently political – rather than solely trade-oriented – initiative, aimed initially at overcoming historical animosity between Argentina and Brazil. Subsequently, it served as a useful counterweight to US efforts to expand its trade influence in the region, such as the Clinton and Bush era Free Trade Area of the Americas (FTAA). The Mercosur customs union has been particularly useful in allowing Brazil to liberalize at its own speed, "using the advantages of being a regional hegemon in a minilateral strategy" to control the pace and process of trade liberalization along "neo-mercantilist" lines (Aggarwal and Espach, 2004, 31). Given its competitiveness advantages relative to its partners, Brazilian exports to Latin America are more manufacture-intensive than exports to the rest of the world, which is seen as "good trade" by many developmentalist economists (Oliveira, 2011, 189; Armijo, 2017).

LABOR MARKETS AND SOCIAL POLICY

One of the most remarkable facets of the Brazilian economy is the coexistence of a very strong system of labor protections, dating to the codification of the Consolidation of Labor Laws (CLT) in 1943, alongside high levels of labor market informality, affecting somewhere between 20 and 40 percent of the employed population (Barbosa Filho, 2012). Given that participation in the formal labor market is a prerequisite for obtaining a variety of social benefits, including social security payments and wage protections, it is hard to discuss the effectiveness of social policy and macroeconomic policies on development without reference to labor policy and its rather lopsided application.

The centrality of the formal labor market is enhanced by the role of the minimum wage as a political tool: annual minimum wage increases have been de rigueur during the democratic period, and since the Real Plan was implemented in 1994, these increases have often represented real wage hikes. Furthermore, many social programs are explicitly tied to the minimum wage, most notably social security benefits. As a consequence of real wage increases and growing eligibility, federal social expenditures have been growing at about 0.35 percent a year, for over two decades (Pessôa, 2015).

The duality of the labor market – split between formal and informal – is heightened by two phenomena. First, the most common type of worker – who is black, young, male and has not completed primary education – earns only about one-third of the minimum wage (Pessôa, 2011, 208). Second, as Chapter 4 will discuss, the bifurcation of firms is replicated in the bifurcation of education markets as well as low added value in most Brazilian exports (Almeida, 2009). Third, inequality in labor earnings is further exacerbated once workers retire. Social insurance coverage, including pension coverage, is higher in Brazil than any other Latin American nation as a share of GDP (McGuire, 2012, 201). But not only do very few workers earn pensions at the level of the full minimum wage, but social security goes overwhelmingly to higher-income workers: poor and extremely poor individuals represent 26.3 percent of the population, but only 5.3 percent of social security beneficiaries (Giambiagi and Castelar Pinheiro, 2012, 40). Said another way, 35 percent of benefits go to the 20 percent richest, and civil servants earn about 67 percent more in pensions than their private sector counterparts (Medeiros and Souza, 2013). Brazil spends three times as much with public and private pensions as demographically similar countries, according to Pessôa (2011), who concludes that, given that programs linked to the minimum wage are expanding faster than GDP, and the only way to finance this is by raising taxes, Brazil's implicit social contract essentially treats economic growth as a "residual."

Indeed, Pessôa (2011, 207) offers one of the most cogent political economy interpretations of social policy's role, arguing that the implicit social contract of the democratic regime is one in which high income inequality and high inequalities of human capital lead the majority of the population to demand the expansion of social programs. Partly in consequence, however, social spending has more than doubled over two decades (Afonso et al., 2016). Implicit in this demand, however, is that slow growth with redistribution is preferable to faster growth without redistribution, meaning that the central trends of the past few decades have been low growth, tax revenue increases, and expanding income transfers (Pessôa, 2011, 210). Low growth is virtually guaranteed because the demand for social transfers reduces domestic savings, just as Brazil has reached the end of its demographic boom years, when the country should theoretically have saved the most.

As we have seen, the fiscal imperative constrains the unbridled growth of spending, but within these budget constraints, social spending crowds out growth-enhancing investment and tends to reinforce the regressive nature of budgets. It also weakens savings, in part because the state's high spending on the economically well-off means that they need not set aside money in private pensions for the future, but also because major public budget programs such as social security are pay-as-you-go, meaning that there is no pension savings in the present.

THE REINFORCING NATURE OF COMPLEMENTARITIES

Chapter 1 laid out one of this book's guiding theoretical arguments: institutional complementarities provide incentives that drive actors toward a particular equilibrium. They provide compatible incentives across diverse areas of the economy, and thereby reinforce strategic choices by firms, managers, and workers (Deeg, 2007), as well as policy-makers and politicians. Change is not impossible, but because of the joint incentives they provide, the complementarities across institutions help to provide a certain collective resilience. Not all incentives affect all actors in the society equally, of course: some institutional arrangements will have strong effects on the incentives of some groups, but not for all, as for example, in the distinction between Multinational Corporations (MNCs) and domestic firms, or between larger and smaller firms (Deeg, 2007; Hall and Gingerich, 2009).

The complementarities between the five institutional spheres of the Brazilian macro-economy have a number of consequences. Among the most important to understanding the history of the past thirty years are fiscal policy, demands for social spending, and low domestic savings and investment. Fiscal policy is constrained because the debt crisis of the 1980s and the hyperinflation of the next decade placed a strong premium on avoiding policies that might frighten away foreign investment or threaten a resurgence of inflation. In a context in which the size of the fiscal pie has been constrained, the trade-offs between the low discretionary budget, high demands for social spending, and as a consequence, limited domestic savings, have pushed policymakers to rely heavily on opaque policy instruments that have little immediately observable fiscal impact, such as lending by the BNDES, credit policies managed through federally-owned banks, minority shareholding of large corporations, credit policy, regulation, and sectoral industrial policies, such as tariff protections, export subsidies, tax incentives, and domestic content requirements. In good times and bad, revenues from social funds (such as the FGTS, PIS-PASEP, and FAT) serve as useful, fiscally opaque tools to policymakers, enabling them to offer low-cost credit to particular sectors or projects in ways that are not immediately visible and may thus explain their continuity, despite the distortions they produce. Further, taxes are hidden in a variety of ways, leading to a "fiscal illusion" that has complicated rational discussion of tax policy and its costs and benefits (Nogueira et al., 2015).

The complex social policy framework is marked by regressive taxation, unbalanced labor protections, and generous pension provisions for the upper-income brackets. In a tight discretionary budget, meanwhile, social transfers and their very central role in the democratic social contract limit domestic investment and therefore increase the relative importance of foreign investment to growth, further enhancing the importance of building international confidence through fiscal responsibility and strong oversight of domestic financial institutions. Foreign capital is needed if Brazil is to grow above the dwindling levels permitted by low domestic investment by the private and public sectors. One of the reasons fiscal reforms and privatization have been such a constant subject of policymaking is that reluctant reformers know that they must convince foreign investors of their good intentions so as to ensure continued capital flows. Indeed,

The Reinforcing Nature of Complementarities 61

Bolsonaro's economy minister, Paulo Guedes, has argued repeatedly that pension reform is required precisely to regenerate investor confidence and spur foreign investment. Yet this pressure is perhaps less change-inducing than in some other leading Latin economies: Campello (2015) suggests that Brazil is subject to some disciplining by foreign capital, but not so much as to completely obliterate policy discretion. Her analysis demonstrates that Brazil comes under strong pressure from international capital markets to follow macroeconomic orthodoxy but may be permitted a less orthodox microeconomic policy set, including industrial policies and other developmental measures. Meanwhile, although the constraints imposed by international institutions such as the WTO may limit the most radical policies, they still provide considerable latitude for national preferences, domestic content requirements, preferential lending, and even trade barriers that help the developmental policy set to retain its relevance (Wade, 2018). The floating exchange rate in place since 1999 weakens the direct pressure of markets in favor of reform. So, the leverage of foreign capital and foreign rules in sparking change is middling, at best.

These institutional complementarities, however, have costly implications. Among those touched upon here: the regressivity of taxation and social benefits in an already unequal society; the natural limits to the inexorable expansion of tax collections; the particularism of sectoral policies; the costs to consumers of living in a relatively closed economy; the duality of labor markets; the stop and start nature of growth generated by ineffective monetary policy; and the low levels of growth that accrue from lasting patterns of low investment. This regressive framework in a country already marked by high inequality has, paradoxically, driven the further expansion of social programs, lowered savings, and reduced potential growth in favor of redistribution.

This all begs the question of why firms, consumers, and taxpayers tolerate the system. Two possible answers are that reform may pose a classic collective action problem – reform costs too much for any individual actor to invest in change – or that special interests hold sway. But it could also be that the very breadth of the state's role across multiple dimensions of the economy has helped to sustain the developmental state against challengers, creating incentives that drive sectors of business, civil servants, labor, and the public at large into recurring behaviors that reinforce the underlying rules of the game. This coalition is buttressed by organizations that in many cases predate democracy, such as many state-owned enterprises and banks. Though the structure has come under immense pressure at various moments – such as the debt crisis of 1982, the hyperinflation of the late 1980s and early 1990s, the balance of payments crises of the late 1990s, the fiscal crisis of the 2010s, and the Rousseff impeachment in 2016 – its basic contours remain remarkably stable.

The next two chapters further explore the basic ideational and policy fabric of the system. Chapter 3 evaluates the ballast that stabilizes the relationship between five components of the equilibrium described here: the idea of developmentalism. Chapter 4 then turns to the firm level to evaluate the industrial organization of the Brazilian economy and the toolbox of incentives the state uses to guide firms.

3

Continuity through Change: Ideas as Ballast for the Developmental State

... barbarism is privatizing the Vale do Rio Doce, privatizing telecoms, handing over our petroleum reserves to foreign capital.

Congressman Jair Bolsonaro, 1999[1]

We are bound by prejudice. The word "privatization," in Brazil, is a curse word.

President Fernando Henrique Cardoso, 2010[2]

The starting point for exploring the relevance of ideas is the observation that the Washington Consensus reforms implemented in Brazil represented far less of a break than they did in other transitioning economies of Latin America or Eastern Europe. With the possible exception of Collor, none of the presidents in office between the late 1980s and 2016 were deeply committed to free market orthodoxy. Although Franco, Cardoso, Lula, and Rousseff tolerated and even supported "neoliberals" on their economic teams, they tempered the most extreme policies and balanced reformers against developmentalist true believers. Meanwhile, important political allies – including the cabal of senators around Franco, the PSDB Party around Cardoso, and the "new" developmentalists of the Workers' Party (Partido dos Trabalhadores, PT) years – were at best ambivalent about economic liberalism and the diminution of state power and indigenous industry inherent in so-called "neoliberal" reforms.

Further, many of the policies adopted by Brazil's reformers were adopted only as emergency responses to crisis. These policies were adopted pragmatically, in response to complex contingencies, rather than as part of a neoliberal strategy that was conscientious or to any

64 *Ideas as Ballast for the Developmental State*

extent planned. Even the Real Plan, developed by a brain trust of market-oriented economists from Rio's Catholic University (PUC-Rio), was heterodox, failed to receive International Monetary Fund (IMF) imprimatur, and followed Franco and Cardoso's clear directives that any stabilization plan must be gradual and transparent to the public. Together, the unwillingness of key policymakers to adopt radical neoliberal prescriptions, the pragmatism of many leaders, and the turbulent external conditions of the period meant that even as Brazil in the 1990s moved toward reform, many facets of the developmental state remained in place. This is not to say that the "neoliberal" 1990s did not change Brazil, but they did not always move the country toward prevailing global economic orthodoxy, and the changes at times even reinforced a commitment to developmentalist economic thought and practice.

As Chapter 2 noted, inflation stabilization and the fiscal imperative engendered one of the most significant course corrections of the past half century in the role of the government in the economy. But it was a partial shift, leading to a layering of policy that was clearly no longer the import substituting industrialization (ISI) of the 1960s, but also was a step removed from the "free market" sought in other Latin American countries. Notably, this shift also failed to dismantle the institutions of the developmental state. Tariffs were reduced, but many nontariff barriers and national preferences were preserved. Privatization occurred, but alongside a considerable effort to maintain state influence across a range of sectors, as well as to constrain the worst market impulses through regulation. Industrial policy was pruned, but sectoral policies were maintained, and in some cases, expanded, as in Cardoso's automotive regime or Rousseff's *Plano Brasil Maior*. Financial reforms led to the consolidation of the banking sector but gave pride of place to domestic institutions and preserved behemoth federal banks. Social policy began to shift but retained the structures and middle-class bias of the military regime. One factor that helps to explain Brazil's continuity through change is the influential hold that developmentalist ideas retained over political and economic elites.

DEVELOPMENTALISM, BRAZILIAN-STYLE

The ideas shared by intellectual, cultural, and political elites often have a significant effect on public policy. Institutional stability derives from a continuous process of sustaining and reproducing patterns of behavior and expectations (Thelen, 1999, 399; Carey, 2000, 754). As Chapter 1

Developmentalism, Brazilian-Style

argued, institutional complementarities may contribute to this process, by ensuring that incentives across diverse institutions reinforce each other. But especially in moments of uncertainty, when multiple institutional equilibria are possible, ideas can provide the justification for moving toward one equilibrium rather than another, while the availability and prevalence of particular ideas may reinforce commitment to one particular equilibrium over another (Cohen et al., 1972; Goldstein and Keohane, 1993, 12; Finnemore, 1996, 11; Wedeen, 2002, 718). Ideas create roadmaps that guide otherwise unconnected members of large and complex organizations toward common objectives, serving as a coordination mechanism (Goldstein, 1993, 3; Goldstein and Keohane, 1993; Blyth, 2003). Ideas create cognitive frameworks for understanding and accumulating knowledge and may also be used to legitimate interests and the rules embodied in organizations (Pareto, 1972 [1906], 94–5; Portes, 2012). Ideas serve as a means of mobilizing support, by providing "a 'project' that captivates and inspires people" and otherwise holds together disparate coalitions (Sikkink, 1991, 17). Ideas leave institutional vestiges that carry on in time, as state organizations continue to function according to legislation laid down by previous generations of policymakers, and their members internalize norms and shared rules associated with those ideas.[3]

Developmentalism – understood as the notion that underdevelopment can be overcome "through capitalist industrialization, planned and supported by the state" (Bielschowsky, 1988, 431) – has played all of these roles in Brazil.[4] Developmentalist ideas serve as long-term constraints within institutions: the dominance of developmentalism points toward particular equilibrium outcomes, enables prioritization between conflicting alternatives, and provides guidance that drives diverse and uncoordinated actors toward particular preferences and behaviors. Developmentalism has thus served as a kind of ballast for policy and institutions, providing continuity over time. Patterns of economic behavior engendered by developmentalist thought, and by the institutions and policies that have grown up around them over seven decades, provide supports for, and constraints upon, policymaking. The combination of developmentalist ideas and the institutional complementarities described in Chapter 2 has shaped the tenor of policymaking: even under the most reformist of governments, Brazilian policymaking has been of a shade that is far more gradual, inward-looking, and accepting of an active role for the state in regulating and shaping markets than its large Latin American peers. What then are those ideas, and what evidence is there for their role in Brazil, especially in the democratic era?

66   *Ideas as Ballast for the Developmental State*

The common theoretical core of Brazilian developmentalist ideas include elements of Keynesianism, structuralism, and suspicion of liberal economic orthodoxy (Bresser-Pereira, 2011, 113, 122). The 1930s represented a key "turning point" across Latin America, including Brazil (Diaz-Alejandro, 1984, 17). The Depression, in particular, forced sharp policy shifts toward import-substitution and nascent industry protection. Trade volumes shrank, terms of trade worsened,[5] and capital outflows increased, pushing governments into import-substituting policies:

> The Great Depression backed many Latin American countries into an ISI strategy by default. The drop in international commodity prices left Latin Americans with little foreign exchange to spend on imports, forcing them to produce substitutes for imported essentials. This is not to imply that the crash stimulated growth in the region; real incomes plummeted with lower export earnings. However, political agitation in urban areas prompted governments to finance new industrial projects to create employment. Protectionist barriers were also erected to cope with balance of payments problems and protect local jobs. (Cardoso and Helwege, 2000 [1992], 155)

Many of the policies adopted by Latin American governments during this period looked Keynesian in their implicit assumption that markets on their own would not lead to productive allocation of savings, investment, and consumption. But Keynesianism was not a cause of the adoption of muscular government-led policies: in the 1930s Keynes was relatively unknown in the region; his *General Theory* only went to print in February 1936 (Skidmore, 1999, 99). The experience of the war years and the Depression, though, prepared the ground for a general receptivity to Keynesianism, to a robust government role in the economy, and especially for a special subset of economics directed only at the problems of developing nations (Hirschman, 1989, 358).[6] By the 1950s, some Latin American governments "sought to recoup the former economic stature of their countries by instigating programs of intensive industrialization, usually predicated on nationalism" (Baerresen et al., 1965, 29). Incipient industrialization required capital reallocation, and by the late 1930s, governments were becoming more intensely involved in management of trade and exchange controls to stabilize the balance of payments and reallocate capital internally (Love, 1996, 221; Kingstone, 2011, 19–44).

The postwar situation, coupled with rising nationalism and fear of popular unrest, set the stage for structural theories of growth, which would eventually be "embraced as a virtual official ideology by many governments" across Latin America (Gootenberg, 2004, 241; see also,

Developmentalism, Brazilian-Style

Hirschman, 1981). Policies that had been adopted on an ad hoc basis, in response to specific economic stimuli of the 1930s and 1940s, slowly coalesced into national policy paradigms that sought to resolve both the Depression-War conditions and the issue of social unrest. From there, they would develop into structuralist theory that sought to distinguish the experience of developing nations from others and provide a framework for many of the policies that had already been adopted. The structuralist argument found several expressions, most notably in the works of Raúl Prebisch (1949), Hans Singer (1950), and the Economic Commission for Latin America (CEPAL), which argued that the structure of the global economy established unique challenges for Latin American economies.[7]

Structuralists argued that capitalism on the "periphery" of the global order was historically unique, rejecting the notion that poorer countries were merely in an early stage of capitalist development, from which their economies would naturally progress. The functioning of the world economy was such that poor countries would not simply overcome under-development through "patience and the passing of time" (Ficker, 2005, 146). Peripheral development, according to the structuralists, was marked by syndromes of low productivity and excessive consumption, contributing to unemployment, secular deterioration in the terms of trade, balance of payments disequilibria, and structurally induced inflation. Peripheral nations that specialized in commodity exports, such as Brazil, would be particularly vulnerable to deteriorating terms of trade, given that industrial production was constantly advancing technologically, contributing to improving worker productivity in the wealthy countries, while commodities showed negligible productivity gains, contributing to a long-term downward trend in the terms of trade between primary products and manufactures (Toye and Toye, 2003, 437; Ficker, 2005; Love, 2005, 201). This view is well-encapsulated by Singer:

... the specialization of underdeveloped countries on export of food and raw materials to industrialized countries, largely as a result of investment by the latter, has been unfortunate for the underdeveloped countries for two reasons: (a) because it removed most of the secondary and cumulative effects of investment from the country in which the investment took place to the investing country; and (b) because it diverted the underdeveloped countries into types of activity offering less scope for technical progress, internal and external economies taken by themselves, and withheld from the course of their economic history a central factor of dynamic radiation which has revolutionized society in the industrialized countries. But there is a third factor of perhaps even greater importance which has reduced the benefits to underdeveloped countries of foreign trade-cum-investment based on export specialization on food and raw materials. This third factor relates to terms of trade. It is a matter of historical fact that ever since the [eighteen] seventies the trend of prices has been heavily against sellers of food and raw materials and in favor of the sellers of manufactured articles. (Singer, 1950, 477)

According to this view, manufacturing exports provided developed nations with increasing returns in terms of technology and knowledge, an advantage only deepened by the declining terms of trade in favor of manufactured goods. What manufacturing industries exist in developing countries, Singer noted, were often foreign-owned, not deeply embedded in those countries' economic firmament, and therefore brought few of the technological gains that might otherwise accrue to the local economy. To make matters worse, technical gains in manufacturing tended to be distributed to producers in the form of higher incomes, while any gains from technical progress in commodities tended to be distributed to consumers via lower prices, rather than accruing to home-country producers (Singer, 1950, 479; Toye and Toye, 2003, 461).[8] When commodity prices were on the rise, there was little incentive to actively develop homegrown industry, as the prices of manufactured imports were relatively low. When the relative prices of manufactured goods were rising, however, the desire for industrialization rose, but the wherewithal to finance it went missing (Singer, 1950, 482). Similarly, Prebisch argued that even if workers at the periphery were able to raise prices on primary goods, this would lead to the contraction of industrial production, and ultimately cut demand (and thus prices) for commodities (Toye and Toye, 2003, 460).[9]

Structuralists proceeded from this observation to argue that government action was needed to channel investments that would enable nascent industry to develop, to improve the composition of trade and the production of manufactures, and to reallocate savings to change the structure of the economy. The influence of the structuralist approach would dominate Latin American economics for a generation.[10] Preeminent Brazilian economist Celso Furtado, who served as a CEPAL staffer in the 1950s, was heavily influenced by these views and in turn influenced others through his textbook, *The Economic Development of Latin America* (which might be the "most widely circulating Latin American social science text of the times, at least until overcome by the best-selling 'dependency theorists'" [Gootenberg, 2004, 241]). Furtado's work highlights the fact that growing world demand for raw materials in the 1920s actually had the perverse effect of simultaneously and more than proportionately increasing raw materials exporters' demand for manufactured goods (Furtado, 1978, 100). Furtado concluded forcefully, in a Prebischian vein, that further state action was needed to move to the next stage of development and, in particular, to foment the intensive domestic use of productive capacity and expanded demand for intermediate products and equipment.

The take-up of structuralist-inspired developmentalist ideas was also facilitated by Brazil's long history of critical interaction with classical liberal thought, which preserved developmentalism against a potential rival set of economic policies. Even before developmentalism had emerged as a coherent set of ideas in the postwar period, liberalism in both its political and economic guises was derided in Brazil for its failures to achieve universalism or achieve either effective representation or equality during the First Republic (Maia and Taylor, 2015, 40).

The practice of liberalism was particularly criticized for failing to overcome the "institutional fetishism" of early twentieth century liberals such as Rui Barbosa and their belief that simply copying liberal institutions and bringing them to Brazil would resolve what ailed the country (Santos, 1978; Brandão, 2001, 33; Ricupero, 2007, 37). This adoption of formal liberal political institutions without attention to their effect in the "real" world had often "grotesque and tragicomic" results in the early twentieth century (Love, 2009, 308). Another criticism was of liberalism's association with the most privileged in an extremely unequal society: many of the leading liberal reformers at the turn of the twentieth century were representative of an oligarchic provincial elite with tenuous claims to democratic legitimacy. Prominent intellectuals continue to refer to liberalism as practiced in Brazil as an "out of place" idea (Schwarz, 1973) and a "second class ideology" (Ricupero, 2007, 40). Central to this skepticism is the fact that liberalism as a set of coherent ideas has been debased by the experience of *liberalism as practiced* in Brazil, limiting its appeal. These failures of liberalism have concrete consequences, in part because each failure of liberal reforms has deepened the commitment to developmental institutions, and increased the costs of a move in a more classically liberal direction.[11] Yet many foreigners' prescriptions for Brazil suggest a series of liberal reforms, without recognizing this deep domestic resistance to liberalism.

These historical experiences caused many Brazilians in the second half of the twentieth century to be suspicious of the naiveté of implementing liberal institutions in a country marked by extreme inequalities and power disparities. Partly in consequence of the perceived failures of liberal policies in the interwar period, Brazil took a different tack both politically and economically in the wake of the Great Depression. Getúlio Vargas' "top-down" incorporation of the citizenry in the 1930s, as part of his larger effort to confront regional power brokers and centralize power, provided citizens with social rights long before they had either civil or political rights.[12] This history has had important knock-on effects, as in the popularity of long-surviving labor market protections and pensions for those with formal employment. It also positioned the state as the guarantor of rights against rapacious elites: institutional fetishism was suspect to critics who placed great weight on the importance of the state as an arbiter in an unequal society (Bresser-Pereira, 2017).

Ideas over time build up their own constituencies which help to propagate and support them. The developmentalist model had strong support from postwar political coalitions between the urban bourgeoisie, the state bureaucracy, and industry (Malan, 1986). The list of its beneficiaries has remained remarkably constant over time, even as the mode of production has changed: many of the coffee producers of the early twentieth century, for example, would become the industrialists of the second half of the twentieth century (Abreu, 2007, 2015; Villela, 2015). As developmentalism unleashed industrial growth, these new industrialists became increasingly powerful in policy formation, particularly within the porous developmentalist state of the 1950–80 period. Prebisch, Furtado, and their acolytes did much to actively court Brazilian industry, and to influence industrialists' thinking through the National Confederation of Industries (CNI) and other associations (Sikkink, 1991; Love, 2005, 117). Bureaucrats were supported by industrialists in their internal debates, and bureaucrats in turn supported industrialists arguing that strong state planning was required to achieve development. Meanwhile, nationalists in the military found much to cheer in the notion of preserving strategic sectors, while politicians were pleased with a policy framework that simultaneously permitted large investment projects and tolerated a soft budget constraint (Guimarães, 2005, 537).

This is not to say that there were not challenges to developmentalist policies: the catastrophic experience of the 1970s and 1980s threatened both its material and ideational foundations. The struggles with the macroeconomic chaos of the "lost decade" that followed the debt crisis of 1982 eroded the legitimacy of the import-substitution policies that were followed by developmentalist policymakers (Kingstone, 2011, 45). The developmentalist alliance was weakened, in part because it was associated with low growth, fiscal profligacy, and high inflation.

From Old to New Developmentalism in Brazil 71

Simultaneously, intellectual justification for overtly market-friendly policies became more rigorous, premised in the works of scholars ranging from Milton Friedman through Anne Krueger, and implemented by politicians as diverse as Pinochet, Thatcher, and Reagan. At their core lay the belief that the private sector could more effectively resolve many problems of market coordination than the public sector, which was prone to capture, inefficiency, and unproductive allocation decisions (Krueger, 1974). Explanations for the rapid emergence of the Asian "tigers," correctly or not, put emphasis on their outward trade orientation. Ricardian models of free trade, with their emphasis on gains from specialization and gains from exchange, once again found powerful proponents (e.g., World Bank, 1987), just as the mantra of globalization – be it of capital, trade, services, or ideas – exploded in popular culture (e.g., Friedman, 1999). The Washington Consensus provided a general zeitgeist in favor of reform, alongside a strong intellectual backlash against ISI, protectionism of all stripes, and managed trade (Blyth and Spruyt, 2003). The increased leverage of multilateral financial institutions over policymaking played a role in propagating these ideas. Chile's early success, albeit sometimes exaggerated, served as an influential role model for wavering policymakers in other Latin American nations, suggesting that freer markets might bring other policy benefits, such as greater creditworthiness and more foreign direct investment (Rodrik, 1996; Biglaiser and DeRouen, 2006).[13]

FROM OLD TO NEW DEVELOPMENTALISM IN BRAZIL

Brazil's response to these international currents was different from its peers. The reforms of the 1990s and the commodity boom of the 2000s led to an important rethinking of the content of developmentalism. Many old theoretical influences remained highly influential, including the ideas of Gunnar Myrdal, Arthur Lewis, Prebisch, Singer, Hirschman and Furtado. But so too, global experience since the 1980s shaped the local zeitgeist, with the works of Chalmers Johnson, Alice Amsden, and Robert Wade on the Asian experience, and of Ha-Joon Chang, Eric Reinert, and Joseph Stiglitz on the historical and global role of the state in development, greatly influencing developmentalist thinking about the proper mix of state and market (Diniz, 2011; Bresser-Pereira, 2016). Within Brazil, a growing number of academics began rethinking developmentalism for the Washington Consensus and post-Washington Consensus era, including Luiz Carlos Bresser-Pereira, João Sicsú, Luiz Fernando de Paula, Luiz

72   *Ideas as Ballast for the Developmental State*

Gonzaga Belluzzo, and Daniela Prates, with the generally evolving consensus by these and other authors leading to the elaboration of "Ten Theses on New Developmentalism" by a Ford Foundation-funded group of academics in 2010 (Diniz, 2011; Ten Theses, 2011).

Charting the meaning of this new developmentalism is not always easy, because in some cases the presentation of the concept is explicitly theoretical, while in others it is premised on the new developmentalism "as practiced," a consensus on economic policies that has characterized all of the post-Collor presidencies (Armijo, 2017). So, there are stricter and looser understandings, and more idealistic as well as more realistic renderings. Furthermore, because there was never a sharp break with the past, many of the features that distinguish the "old" developmentalism of the 1960s and 1970s from the newer developmentalism of the 2010s have evolved piecemeal, making it hard to draw a clear line between the two. But with the benefit of hindsight, it is possible to argue that there are two major continuities and four key differences between old and new.

The continuities center around the centrality of the state and industry. Strong states are able to "maximize growth because of the way they can deliberately get the prices 'wrong' in an effort to spark rapid industrialization and the creation of new comparative advantages, while at the same time shaping and constraining the activities of powerful economic agents in ways that prevent inefficiency and rent-seeking" (Kurtz, 2013, 4, drawing on Amsden, 1991, 284). In this regard, new developmentalist logic retains the state-centric ideas of the postwar period: development on the periphery requires an active effort to coordinate investment; without state action, market forces will not invest in competitiveness-enhancing industrial processes and the terms of trade will continue their secular deterioration; comparative advantage can be created; and the state is the only actor capable of effectively coordinating and carrying forward the project of national self-discovery (Amsden, 1989, 2001; Wade, 1990; Rodrik, 2004, 2007; Almeida, 2009). The state can take development further than would be possible under free markets, solving coordination problems, resolving market failures, and helping to overcome the problems of regulating certain natural monopolies (Musacchio and Lazzarini, 2014, 28–9). Building domestic industry is the central objective of state action, because industry generates spillover effects throughout the economy, encouraging development over a much wider swathe of economic activity, and with much more advanced use of human capital, than would be possible in the production of primary goods (Suzigan and Furtado, 2006). Industry is far

From Old to New Developmentalism in Brazil 73

more likely to increase the sophistication of production and move labor from low to high income production (Bresser-Pereira, 2016).

The alterations in the overall focus of developmentalism were motivated by the earlier failures of the "old" developmentalism, and thus also by the neoliberal challenge posed by the debt crisis and the Washington Consensus. As a consequence, they assimilated some elements of the neoliberal policy set (Ban, 2013). The resulting changes shifted the new developmentalism in a more outward direction, emphasized macroeconomic stability, sought to avoid the social regressivity of the "old" developmentalism, and reconsidered the role of the state as the chief driver of growth (Armijo, 2017).

A new emphasis on outward-looking growth sought to avoid the inefficiencies of an overly closed economy. Despite this shift in emphasis, however, counter-developmentalist forces in Brazil have been less institutionally powerful than in many other Latin countries: Brazil has long been marked by the "absence of active social forces advocating trade liberalization, industrial deregulation, and privatization" (Sola, 1994, 157). As consequence, the new developmentalism has been "selective" in its outward orientation, with more openness to trade but simultaneous willingness to use industrial policy to help firms to become more competitive internationally, to temper trade liberalization through the use of export subsidies and capital controls, and to preserve domestic preferences. This emphasis on building a strong domestic market has a foundation in the notion that nation states compete with each other through their firms, and therefore has been permissive with regard to state control over industrial champions, restricted access for foreign bidders, and the continued presence of state-owned enterprises (SOEs) and public banks.

A more significant break came through increased attention to macroeconomic stability, particularly inflation. In theory, the new developmentalism aims to get five macroeconomic prices right: profits, the exchange rate, the interest rate, the wage rate, and the inflation rate. As Bresser-Pereira (2016) argues,

"Right" prices do not mean prices defined by full competition, but prices that make sense economically and politically: (a) the profit rate must be high enough to support investment by business; (b) the exchange rate must make business enterprises competitive; (c) the level of the interest rate should be as low as possible; (d) the wage rate should increase with productivity, and be consistent with a satisfactory profit rate; and (e) the inflation rate should be low.[14]

In recent years, this wish list has been largely met only with regard to inflation, and, to a somewhat lesser degree, the associated task of maintaining fiscal balance (Datz, 2013; Amann and Barrientos, 2016; Armijo, 2017). As a commodity producer, Brazil has had far greater difficulty adjusting the exchange rate to avoid volatility and an overvalued currency; use of the exchange rate to keep domestic prices in check has also tended to lead toward excessive appreciation, and domestic savings shortages have implied a reliance on foreign savings that exacerbate the problem. As Chapter 2 also noted, there are numerous pressures that have raised interest rates to world record levels. Finally, profits have been raised by government action, but not in a manner that has been conducive to greater investment.

Perhaps because it has developed under democracy, new developmentalism recognizes the importance of improving social equity. This manifests in at least three ways. The first has been the focus on overcoming the regressive effects of inflation on the real incomes of the poor (Amann and Barrientos, 2016). Second, a significant expansion in social protection, including through redistribution via conditional cash transfer programs (Arbix and Martin, 2010). Third, a theoretical interest in overcoming the tendency of wages to increase below the growth of productivity, engendered by the existence of an ample supply of labor (Ten Theses, 2011). Policymakers have tried to implement these changes through expansionary minimum wage increases, designed to keep the minimum wage rising above inflation (Bresser-Pereira, 2011; Milanez and Santos, 2015).

Finally, the role of the state in the new developmentalism has shifted in significant if subtle ways. Arbix and Martin (2010) note that the new developmentalism is marked by a new state activism that is "market adjusting" rather than "market dominating." The state nudges firms to improve technological sophistication, building competitiveness through innovation policies; and productive transformation through private research and development (Rojas, 2013; Trubek, 2013). This entails a diverse set of new priorities: innovation policies to enhance competitiveness, credit to improve productive capacity, regulatory oversight of markets, and public-private sector dialogue (Boschi, 2011, 13; Morais and Saad-Filho, 2012, 791).[15]

In sum, despite rising world trade, changing geopolitics, the increasing global hegemony of neoclassical economics, rising Asian competition, and the challenges imposed by the debt crisis of the 1980s, Brazil remained heavily inclined to developmentalist ideas, while revising them to tackle a new context and incorporate shifting theoretical conceits. To demonstrate how ideas influenced Brazil's take-up of neoliberal reform, the next section turns to a comparison with two other large middle-income South

Embeddedness of Ideas in Comparative Perspective 75

American economies, Argentina and Chile. I focus on the evidence that developmentalist ideas are embedded quite differently among Brazil's policy elites than in its peer countries, and as a consequence, that there has been more space for the conscientious implementation of developmentalist policies from the postwar period through the Temer administration.

THE EMBEDDEDNESS OF IDEAS IN COMPARATIVE PERSPECTIVE

By the 1990s, Argentina, Brazil, and Chile had all adopted policies aimed at trade liberalization, economic stabilization, and shrinking the role of the state. But there has been considerable cross-national and temporal variation in policy adoption, which can be compared on two dimensions. First, the direction of policy change, and whether it was toward more market-oriented or more state-oriented strategies. Second, the relative volatility of those changes, and particularly, the degree to which policy-making is "resolute" or "decisive." Cox and McCubbins (2001) note that government institutions cannot be simultaneously decisive and resolute. That is, a presidency invested with the powers to take quick decisions is likely to do so, and this decisiveness may lead to considerable policy volatility over time, especially if the society is polarized between two political forces with distinct policy preferences. Similarly, policymaking by a president whose autonomy is constrained is unlikely to change rapidly; policy paths are likely to be resolute, or unwavering over time.[16]

A postage stamp summary of the historical record suggests that there has been far greater decisiveness in the Argentine case, which when combined with the divergent interests and ideas of rural and urban elites, drove significant volatility in economic policy. This volatility was especially pronounced by comparison to the resoluteness shown in both Chile and Brazil, which plodded forward consistently, albeit in two very different directions: Chile's resoluteness led it to emerge as the poster child of the steady adoption of neoliberalism, especially after its crisis of the early 1980s, while Brazil's resoluteness manifested in the direction of much more state-focused, inward-looking reforms (Table 3.1).

In Argentina, the political system is highly decisive, allowing for rapid policy reversals. Presidents are the central players, and ministers are oftentimes less important to economic policymaking than the President or powerful secretariats (Butler, 2012). The combination of strong federal government leverage over states who depend on federal transfers, a weak federal legislature and judiciary, and a strong executive have meant that

Ideas as Ballast for the Developmental State

TABLE 3.1 *Economic policy direction and decision-making pattern*

	Resolute	Decisive
Market-oriented	Chile	↑
		Argentina
State-oriented	Brazil	↓

Source: Author.

political power is "concentrated to an enormous degree, in the hands of a single individual," the president (Snow and Wynia, 1990, 161–2). Economic policy lacks deep institutionalization or a broader, polity-wide commitment to an ongoing strategy that extends beyond a single presidency, and instead tends to be "erratic" (Agosín, 2012), "ad hoc" (Bouzas, 2012; Butler, 2012), and unstable. As a consequence, policy has been pendular, swinging from one extreme to another as presidents come and go, with a degree of volatility that is significantly greater than in Chile or Brazil (Lengyel, 2012; Doyle, 2014, 10–11).

Historically, Argentine industry has been influential with policymakers, especially because geographical proximity to the government permitted industrial leaders in Buenos Aires to collectively push revenue-seeking policymakers to focus their revenue-seeking efforts on more dispersed and less organized agricultural producers, via export taxes and import tariffs. But there is not usually a deeper theoretical strategy driving these demands, and such policies are periodically overturned when the level of taxation on agricultural production becomes intolerable (Sturzenegger, 1990). The depth of developmentalism's roots in both broader public ideas and government agencies has long been shallower than it was in Brazil. As Sikkink (1991) pointed out, debates over economic policy in the immediate postwar focused on the alternatives of liberalism and populism, leaving little space for developmentalism. The introduction of developmentalism was therefore less successful politically than in Brazil, with Frondizi's reforms plagued by his weak legitimacy and policy reversals, as well as a significant difficulty in expanding the developmentalist constituency to preexisting ideological camps. The amplitude of the Argentine political system's pendular swing appears to have diminished in the past two decades, as democracy and multilateral

Embeddedness of Ideas in Comparative Perspective   77

commitments reduced the amount of leeway for radicalism. But the pendular tendency persists: witness the swings from Menem to the Kirchners to Macri to Fernández. Policies, with few exceptions, continue to be debated primarily between individual firms and government, without ongoing, broad-based sectoral or popular participation, and without a clear national commitment to a lasting set of ideas.

In Brazil, economic policymaking has been resolute. The overall strategy from the 1950s to the 1980s remained dirigiste and inward-focused, and even reforms, such as the export incentive program undertaken by the military regime in the late 1960s, sought only to modify this strategy at the margin. The crisis-driven reforms of the late 1980s and early 1990s were largely focused on addressing the dire fiscal situation but did not significantly challenge the developmentalist strategy or dismantle its strongest institutions. While trade opening did occur (largely because of international pressure, the need to rebuild capital stocks, and as an instrument of the fight against inflation), trade remains below the levels that would be expected even of a large nation and the beneficiaries of both inward-looking and outward-looking trade policies have frequently been the same (Veiga and Ventura-Dias, 2004, 102).[17] State-guided industrial policies have continued to be used to enhance investment, and with a few notable exceptions (Collor's trade opening in one direction and Guido Mantega's fiscally expansionist policies in the other) there has been very little radical movement away from the general consensus around a heterodox and pragmatic policy set that permits a forceful role for the state.

Chilean policymaking since the late 1970s has also been marked by a high degree of resoluteness, but policy was driven in a completely different direction than Brazil's, toward openness and a limited state role in the economy. There was relatively little conflict over the general economic strategy between the 1980s and the mid-2010s, and policy was much more universal than in its peer countries: decisions applied to the full economy, with little room for sector-specific policies. On trade strategy, there were very few countries in the world that could implement lower tariffs with only a single vote of legislative opposition, as in Chile (Aninat, 2012). As trade deepened in the post-Pinochet decades, it weakened the hand of any inward-looking holdouts and forced them to adapt to the new market, thus deepening consensus even among those who might not have welcomed the overall strategy under other conditions. As one specialist told me, economic opening has been converted into "a public good, with almost no marginal cost …. Sir, this is a blessing from

God" (Aninat, 2012). There was a widespread belief that small countries like Chile need "fair, transparent, and non-discriminatory rules that limit unilateral measures among trade partners as much as possible ..." (Rosales, 2004, 19). Agreement was facilitated by the fact that Chile's economy was much smaller and less diverse than its counterparts, without as many divergent and powerful industrial, agricultural and labor groups as Brazil or Argentina (Aggarwal and Espach, 2004, 15). Further, beginning in the 1970s policymakers and business groups had reached the conclusion that uniform trade rules were better than sector-by-sector exemptions and tariff rates (Sáez, 2007). The democratic government that took office in 1990 saw no reason to reopen that particular Pandora's box, and as one economist told me, "the Chilean ethos or mindset is such that Brazilian-type policies would not be feasible in Chile.... We don't have anything like the BNDES" (Agosín, 2012).

What explains the hold that different ideas seem to have in these three nations?

A first answer is relative success. As policies are successfully implemented, they may generate feedback loops that cement their core ideas in place: as the introduction framed this point, incidence reinforces preference, and vice versa. Once in place, successful policies may generate support for ideas: the "scant support for liberalism" in Brazil (Villela, 2015, 171–2), for example, has as much to do with periods of growth under developmental policies as anything else. As Figure 3.1 demonstrates, Chile saw the greatest gains most clearly under neoliberal export-oriented policies in the late 1980s and throughout the 1990s.

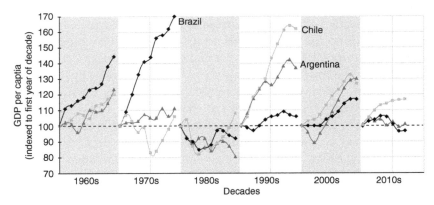

FIGURE 3.1 GDP per capita by decade, 1960–2017. Source: Feenstra et al. (2015); indexation by author.

Embeddedness of Ideas in Comparative Perspective 79

Furthermore, the trauma of the Unidad Popular government in the early 1970s scarred many of that generation, contributing to a strong consensus among Chilean economists and political leaders of a certain age (Tironi, 2012).[18] These experiences have influenced policymakers' perceptions of the effectiveness of policy paths, as well as public beliefs about the likely gains from reform.

In Brazil, by contrast, until the commodity boom of the 2000s, Brazil's largest and still most significant economic expansion came under developmental policies during the 1960s and 1970s. The classical developmental period of Brazilian history, between 1931 and 1980, was marked by enormous gains: Brazil grew faster in nominal terms than any other country in the world, with the economy expanding by 6.6 percent a year; in per capita terms, Brazil was second only to Korea, with 4.0 percent annual growth (Bresser-Pereira, 2017). The widespread perception of the successes of the import-substitution model of this period contribute to making relative protectionism a "common sense" idea among policy makers and the bureaucracy (Oliveira et al., 2019, 34). Industrial policy and growth were mistaken for each other during half a century when both were strong, "producing a diversified and integrated industrial system ... and extremely high GDP, income and employment growth" (Suzigan and Furtado, 2006, 176, translation by author). The period between 2003 and 2010, the pinnacle of what has been dubbed the "new developmentalist" era, likewise brought strong performance, culminating in 7.5 percent nominal annual growth in 2010, alongside enormous strides in inequality and poverty reduction, and "[c]orrectly or not, this growth spurt was credited to the neo-developmentalist agenda ...." (Porzecanski, 2015, 151).

Periods in which liberal, market-oriented economic policies have been ascendant in Brazil since World War II have been relatively circumscribed, and account for only about three years in every ten during this seven decades: 1945–7; 1954–5; 1964–7; 1990–1; 1994–2002; and perhaps 2016–18 (Oliveira, 2012).[19] Whether as cause or consequence of this erratic history, liberal policies have had rather a lackluster performance. The stop-and-start pattern of economic activity in the crisis-prone "neoliberal" 1990s may have also provided some vindication for a more state-centric development strategy. It does not help matters that many of the deepest neoliberal reform efforts took place under governments whose political legitimacy was also suspect, such as Presidents Fernando Collor, impeached in 1992, and Michel Temer, the most unpopular president of the post-authoritarian period. Nor have liberals been particularly well-supported politically: from Eugenio Gudin in the 1950s to Joaquim Levy

Ideas as Ballast for the Developmental State

in 2016, there are numerous examples of orthodox policymakers being forced from office by the unpopularity of their austerity policies.

It is also worth noting that the impacts of the debt crisis were far less severe in Brazil than in other countries in the region: the country faced lower pressure on its current account, had relatively low capital flight, and continued to grow amidst the crisis, especially by comparison to its peers. Although the fiscal crisis contributed to hyperinflation, debt accounted for only 38.5 percent of Brazilian gross domestic product (GDP) in 1982, compared to 50.3 percent in Argentina and 71.3 percent in Chile (Montero, 2014b, citing Frieden, 1991). This may have lowered the leverage of international actors over domestic policymakers (Stallings, 1992, 55). Even when reform came, furthermore, businesses were compensated using the institutional tools of developmentalism. Exporters were given considerable subsidies and cheap credit under the military regime's export push of the late 1960s and early 1970s, as well as access to government technology agencies and their resources. So too, firms hurt by the opening of the economy in the 1990s were provided with National Bank for Economic and Social Development (BNDES) financing for restructuring, and the privatization of the 1990s favored national buyers through BNDES financing (Kingstone, 1999, 79; Montero, 2014b; Lyne, 2015). The beneficiaries remained similar, even when this seemed not to jive with the rationale of creating national champions or export giants (Markwald, 2005; Oliveira, 2011). Business elites who in other countries might be expected to advocate for liberal projects have often been a part of the coalitions backing developmentally inspired policies, whether it was the predominance of São Paulo industrial interests in the PSDB and the PT governing coalitions of the 1990s and 2000s, or the economic liberals who participated in the conservative coalition that backed the military regime in the 1960s and 1970s (Fiori, 1992, 174; Villela, 2015, 180, note 21).

In the post-privatization period, furthermore, a key support for developmental practice has emerged: while outright state ownership of enterprise has declined significantly, a web of cross-shareholding has created a strong network of ties between large private sector firms and state-controlled shareholders, providing the state with considerable leverage over the private sector (Lazzarini, 2010; Musacchio and Lazzarini, 2014; next chapter, Chapter 4). Ironically, the neoliberal reforms of the 1990s may even have enabled the state to better address the weaknesses of the developmental policy set without revising the entire framework. For example, the Brazilian state was virtually unaware of the fiscal situation of its state-owned enterprises before the debt crisis – and may not even

Embeddedness of Ideas in Comparative Perspective 81

have known in the 1970s how many SOEs it controlled – but in response to internal fiscal demands and external pressure from markets and multilateral bodies such as the IMF, developed better fiscal controls over its companies in the 1980s and 1990s (Werneck, 1987; Musacchio and Lazzarini, 2014, 90).

Although developmentalism as an idea has been particularly embedded among Brazilian state elites, its relative success has had an influence on public attitudes, too. Polls consistently demonstrate widespread public support for state-owned enterprises. Support for privatization increased slightly at the outset of the Collor administration, in 1992, and again in 1995, in the wake of the successful Real Plan. But negative feelings about privatization and many other market reforms were quick to resurface after the failure of Collor's stabilization plans and reappeared again during the Cardoso years, especially after the crisis and devaluation of 1998–9. Nearly a decade after that trauma, a 2007 Ibope poll showed that an overwhelming majority of Brazilians thought privatization had been a net negative (62 percent, versus 25 percent in favor), disapproved of Cardoso's selling off of state companies, and thought that privatization hurt national development objectives (51 percent) (Garcia and Gastaldi Filho, 2007; IPSOS Public Affairs, 2007). Polling by IPSOS since 2005 has regularly asked about privatization and found only weak support, from less than one-fifth of the population (IPSOS Public Affairs, 2007).[20] A Datafolha poll in December 2017 showed that 70 percent of voters were against privatization, with majorities on both the right and left of the political spectrum coming out against the sale of public firms (Folha, 2017c). Fewer than three of ten Brazilians polled in 2018 wanted to see Petrobras privatized, echoing the sentiments of newly elected president Jair Bolsonaro (Latin News, 2018); a 2019 poll found that a majority (53.2 percent) of Brazilians thought foreign firms should not be allowed to compete with Petrobras in the petroleum sector, while only 35.5 percent thought they should (Jota, 2019).

Not all market-friendly policies are so negatively evaluated: Baker (2003, 2009) has convincingly demonstrated that trade opening, for example, generated consumer gains that, at least in the short-term, were wildly popular. But public opinion has been largely supportive of the institutions of the developmental state, and reluctant to dismantle state-owned enterprises such as Petrobras or the BNDES: in the 2010 election, for example, the Rousseff campaign relied heavily on messaging that played on fears of privatization; nearly a decade later, a 2019 Datafolha poll showed that only 25 percent of Brazilians were in favor of privatizations, while 67 percent were opposed (Folha, 2019b). IPSOS polling in 2015 suggests that by comparison to their peers elsewhere in the hemisphere, Brazilians have the highest demand for government control of major industry and reticence toward foreign firms (IPSOS Public Affairs, 2015, 12). A poll conducted by Datafolha in 2017 shows that Brazilians are socially conservative and economically statist (Folha, 2017a); fully three-quarters (76 percent) of Brazilians believe that the government should be held responsible for generating prosperity.[21]

A second answer to the hold that different ideas have in these three countries relates to the extent to which ideas are embedded in state agencies. In all three countries, networks of economists and economic policy bureaucrats are vital to explaining how new ideas were taken up, and old ideas defended against challenges (see, e.g., Klüger, 2018 on networks in the BNDES and Olivieri, 2007 on the Central Bank). In all three countries, one key conduit since the 1950s has been academia, with its goal of training technocrats who could govern "scientifically," applying specialized knowledge to the complex tasks of developing national economies. Training increased the public stock of economists, giving them an aura of technocratic wizardry that has catapulted them past the previously dominant Latin American elite, lawyers, at the head of many public bureaucracies (Dezalay and Garth, 2002). Over the past generation, across Latin America, doctoral degrees have increasingly become a necessary qualification for joining the administrative leadership cadre, especially in economic policy. In all three countries, Table 3.2, column 1 shows that economists accounted for around seven out of every ten days that finance ministers held office between 1960 and 2015.

Foreign training, in particular, has brought an air of refined knowledge, especially as the core of economics moved in a more mathematical

TABLE 3.2 *Economists among finance ministers, 1960–2015*

	(1) Days economists ran ministry	(2) Days home-trained economists ran ministry	(3) Days US-trained economists ran ministry	(4) Difference
Argentina	69%	42%	26%	-16%
Brazil	76%	45%	31%	-14%
Chile	75%	1%	74%	+73%

Source: Author.

Embeddedness of Ideas in Comparative Perspective

direction, as well as toward the so-called neoclassical synthesis in the United States during the 1980s and 1990s. Such foreign-trained officials were "important carriers of neoclassical ideas, forming the core of transnational policy coalitions favoring liberalizing reform" (Haggard and Kaufman, 1992, 13). The technical sophistication of this training, the reputations of those who returned from highly selective programs abroad, and the association of many such economists with the tenets of the neoliberal wave mean that training in US academic programs serves as a crude proxy for the acceptance of neoliberal, rather than developmentalist, ideas. The postage stamp summary of the three countries' trajectories plays out in the origins of the ministers described in columns 2 through 4. In Argentina and Brazil, home-trained economists have dominated, accounting for more than half of economists' tenures. By contrast, in Chile, academic training at US universities has been a virtual *sine qua non* for ministers, especially since the 1980s.

TABLE 3.3 *Volatility of ministerial tenure, 1960–2015 (indexed to Chilean average, 737 days = 1)*

	(1) Average tenure (n)	(2) Noneconomist tenure (n)	(3) Economist tenure (n)	(4) US-trained economist tenure (n)
Argentina	0.51 (54)	0.37 (23)	0.61 (31)	1.03 (7)
Brazil	0.95 (29)	0.37 (18)	1.89 (11)	2.82 (4)
Chile	1.00 (29)	0.59 (12)	1.29 (17)	1.35 (16)

Source: Author.

Note: calculated using the total days each minister spent in office. Economists is defined as anyone with a BA, MA, or PhD in economics, an MBA, or an accounting degree.[22] The totals ignore the "interim" designation in Brazil, on the assumption that the acting minister is likely following instructions from the minister on leave. Argentine and Brazilian ministers have been counted from January 1, 1960 through December 2015, when both the Argentine and Brazilian ministers stepped down. The Chilean set includes the full term of Minister Rodrigo Valdés, who served through 2017.

84 *Ideas as Ballast for the Developmental State*

Table 3.3 demonstrates how these educational characteristics and the ideas they roughly represent become embedded in state institutions. Given policy volatility in Buenos Aires, it is perhaps unsurprising that ministerial tenures in Argentina have been about half those of Brazil and Chile (column 1). This makes it harder for particular policies to gain traction, and presumably also complicates the task of embedding particular ideas about economic policy in state institutions. In all three countries, columns 2 and 3 show that economists have significantly longer tenures than noneconomists: 62 percent longer in Argentina, twice as long in Chile, and more than four times as long in Brazil. Comparing columns 3 and 4 shows that US-trained economists have had significantly longer-than-average tenures than domestically trained economists, ranging from 5 percent longer in Chile to 69 percent longer in Argentina. The reasons for this may be manifold, but especially in the wake of the Cold War, one plausible hypothesis has been that foreign schooling might – other things equal – enhance a minister's market credibility in a world of international capital flows (Haggard and Kaufman, 1992, 13; Stallings, 1992, 48). Comparison of column 1 and 4 suggests some evidence for this hypothesis: in Argentina, a US-trained economist's tenure as minister is twice as long as the national average; in Chile, 35 percent longer; and in Brazil, nearly three times as long.

The relative absence or presence of US-trained economists leads to a third answer to the question of the hold ideas have over these three countries: the career options available to policymakers who hold distinct ideas. This goes to a larger issue of the density of epistemic communities, the group of individuals who share common ideational frameworks and propagate them within organizations and across society (Haas, 1992; Jacobsen, 1995; Santana, 2011). A number of factors have shaped epistemic communities in the three countries: the attractiveness of academic or think-tank careers that could sustain economists even when government positions were unavailable; the tradition of technocracy in each country and the prestige of technocrats; and the degree to which there has been space for dissenting viewpoints in academia and civil society (Montecinos and Markoff, 2009).

In the case of Argentina, as Biglaiser (2009) points out, the attractiveness of alternate careers for economists no longer in government has been especially low, given that academic salaries were pitiful until the advent of private universities in the 1980s; the military was intolerant of dissenters; and there was not much of a technocratic tradition within government. It is not surprising that with a few prominent exceptions, networks of

Embeddedness of Ideas in Comparative Perspective 85

Argentine economists in international financial institutions have been far stronger than within the national state bureaucracy itself. To the extent that domestic epistemic communities existed, they tended to revolve around various think tanks of specific political leanings, such as the *CEMA* (whose members included ministers Martínez de Hoz, Fernández, and Pou), *Fundación Mediterránea* (which employed Domingo Cavallo before he became minister) (Schvarzer, 2004, 18–19), *Fundación Nuevo Milénio* (which employed Cavallo after he left the Menem administration) and on the left, *Asociación de Economía para el Desarrollo de la Argentina* (AEDA; headed by a former director of Banco Nación) and *La graN maKro* (associated with minister Amado Boudou), both associated with *Kirchnerista* economics.[23] Careers in academia have been unattractive, particularly for liberals. Efforts in the 1960s by the University of Chicago to establish a partnership with the Universidad de Buenos Aires (UBA), similar to its Chilean partnership with the Universidad Católica, were rejected, and UBA's curriculum remained heavily Cepalino (Sikkink, 1988, 110; Biglaiser, 2009, 71).

In Chile, the dominance of neoliberal thought has been strengthened by the availability of well-paid and prestigious academic and business positions for scholars with US degrees; by the military regime's strong support for neoliberal policies; by the *Concertación* parties' eagerness to illustrate their policy conversion by hiring neoliberal economists of their own; and by the strong technocratic tradition of the civil service, dating back to the 1920s. Especially since the economic revolution begun by the Chicago boys in the 1970s, however, there has been little room for more heterodox perspectives on economics, and the three most prominent Chilean universities are heavily dominated by US-trained liberal economists (Montecinos et al., 2009, 20–1).

Despite a growing number of foreign-trained economists, Brazil's universities have relatively few US-trained economists, with only four out of nineteen major universities having a majority of the faculty with US degrees (Montecinos et al., 2009, 20–1). Of these, only two Rio de Janeiro-based schools, the Fundação Getulio Vargas (FGV-Rio) and the Catholic University (PUC-Rio), are considered to adhere to liberal economic training (Codato and Cavalieri, 2015).[24] This has meant that Brazilian academia has been less permeated by the neoclassical theory that is the focus of training in most US economics departments. More importantly from the perspective of the circulation of ideas, it also means that Brazilian universities are more open to heterodox thought and

86 *Ideas as Ballast for the Developmental State*

practice. The large scale of Brazilian academia means that it is harder to conquer all of the academic high ground, especially by comparison with other Latin American countries.

Partly as a consequence, by contrast to much of the rest of Latin America, neoliberal thought has never been dominant within academia, even when it was ascendant (Maia and Taylor, 2015). There has been considerable tolerance for dissent: as one economist with long experience in Brasília told me, "Brazil never had the radicalism [of Argentina or Chile] ... texts by the opposition are not so emotional, not so violent *[nem vêm do fígado, nem são tão violentos]*" (Baumann, 2012). Taken together with a long-standing technocracy, and a very vibrant academic community that is several orders of magnitude larger than most of its regional peers, this has meant considerable space for economists of many persuasions. There have been two academic poles since the return to democracy: on the one end, UNICAMP and UFRJ put more emphasis on developmentalist theory and the structuralism of the CEPAL, housing leading developmentalists such as Luiz Gonzaga Belluzzo and Márcio Pochmann (Unicamp), and Maria da Conceição Tavares and Carlos Lessa (UFRJ). At the other, PUC-Rio has a far more liberal, formal, mathematical, and US-oriented curriculum (Loureiro, 2009, 119), and has housed leading reformers, such as Marcelo Abreu, Edmar Bacha, and Gustavo Franco.[25] But in the messy middle, there is considerable room for debate, and many departments house members of both factions. As a result, neoliberal or neoclassical economic theory "has never held complete hegemony in Brazil" (Loureiro, 2009, 133).

Despite their sometimes bitter policy disputes, these groups were ultimately fluid and largely conciliatory: one illustrative historical example is that leading liberal Bulhões helped leading developmentalist Furtado get his job at the CEPAL in the 1950s (Loureiro, 1997, 45). Each ideational current settled into distinct perches within specific bureaucracies and universities, with the "right entrenched in organs such as BNDE, SUMOC and FGV, and the left in Vargas' Economic Advisory Board, in CEPAL and in ISEB" (Loureiro, 2009, 113). With the arrival of the military regime, these perches did not change significantly (with the important caveat that Furtado and other left-of-center economists were exiled by the military). The remaining economists continued to rise and fall depending on which general was in power, but the military was strongly "developmentalist" at its core, even as it tolerated liberals like Bulhões in positions of great power.[26]

Embeddedness of Ideas in Comparative Perspective   87

Brazil's federal bureaucracy was quite capable of implementing developmentalist policies, in part because the economic ministries (Planning and Finance) and autarkies (BNDE, Banco Central do Brasil, and Superintendência da Moeda e do Crédito [SUMOC]), were exceptional pockets of efficiency, provided with extraordinary presidential support during most years, and exempted from the patronage politics that were a constant in other arenas (Geddes, 1994, 43–82). As Schneider (1999, 285) notes, drawing on Leff (1968), the military resorted to the already extant "modernizing nationalist ideology" of developmentalism, effectively nixing all other alternatives. Furthermore, there was strong continuity in the policymakers and *técnicos* who would implement policy. This was a very different scenario from that seen in Chile and Argentina, where "the composition of government elites, in particular that of the economic teams, suffered a radical and irreversible change" under military rule (Sola, 1998, 32). In other words, there was no radical discontinuity between the policymakers and bureaucrats of the pre-1964 period and those of the postcoup moment.[27]

This heterogeneity was also apparent during the democratic period. Even at the heyday of the Washington Consensus during the 1990s, the mainstream in Brazil has been much less wed to neoliberal prescriptions than its counterparts in Chile, Argentina, or Mexico. There has also been considerable cohabitation within government: under a variety of administrations since the 1990s, for example, the Central Bank[28] and Finance Ministry were reliably more neoliberal, while the Planning Ministry and BNDES were run by more developmentalist policymakers (Montero, 1998, 37–8; Montero, 2014b).[29] There was thus a certain "hybridity" of policymaking, across both agencies and top officials.[30] Among top secretaries in the Finance Ministry and directors in the Central Bank, from 1985 onward, only 27.7 percent of these high officials held foreign Ph.D. diplomas (including from non-US universities); 17 percent held doctorates from Brazilian universities, and 55 percent of the entire sample had no doctoral diploma. Figure 3.2 demonstrates the educational heterogeneity of the top economic policymakers serving in the Finance Ministry and Central Bank between 1995 and 2015, during the PSDB and PT administrations, under the tenures of the three prominent finance ministers of this period: Pedro Malan, Antonio Palocci, and Guido Mantega.[31]

Figure 3.2 shows some of the patterns to be expected: a far greater proportion of foreign degrees in reformer Malan's economic team than in Mantega's, for example; a relatively high proportion in the pragmatic Palocci's team; and then the predominance – but by no means hegemony –

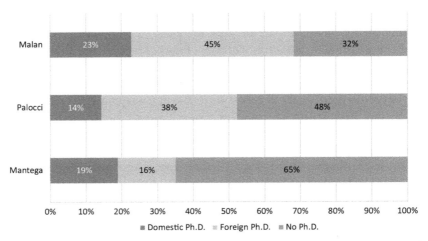

FIGURE 3.2 Educational backgrounds of senior Brazilian finance ministry and central bank officials, 1995–2015. Source: Compilation by author from database of Finance Ministry and Central Bank officials compiled by De Bonis (2016), courtesy of Daniel De Bonis.

of Brazilian trained economists under neo-developmentalist Mantega. Even under reformers such as Pedro Malan, however, a sizeable number of officials held degrees from Brazilian schools, including institutions which are considered centers of developmentalist thought. Conversely, a sizeable share of officials under the governments of the Workers' Party held degrees from foreign universities considered to represent mainstream liberal economic thought, even under the "neo-developmentalist" Guido Mantega.

The hybridity of policymaking may have contributed to the lasting influence of developmentalism. Montero (2014b), for example, notes that developmentalists and neoliberals have shared concern with domestic industrial competitiveness, and the inability to capture all of the academic or think-tank high ground may have contributed to a tradition of compromise in Brazil's diverse business community. Perhaps as a result of this hybridity, Brazilian "neoliberals" have been more pragmatic than their orthodox peers in other South American nations. As one Brazilian official noted, "our liberals are not so liberal after all" (Oliveira, 2012). Policy has followed a heterodox route: the conceptualization of inertial inflation that lay behind the Real Plan, for example, was written by what were, by Brazilian standards, "neoliberals" from the PUC-RJ, but the plan never received the blessing of the IMF, and evolved in a much more gradual fashion than the shock therapies adopted elsewhere. Such pragmatism has meant that in the twenty-first century, developmentalism has not merely been an artifact of the Workers' Party's thirteen years in office (2003–16), but in fact was tolerated even during the supposedly neoliberal 1990s (Tavares de Almeida, 1996; Montero, 2014b). This inertial influence of heterodox thought occurs partly because of scale, which makes Brazil less susceptible to the conditionalities imposed by international institutions; but also because a larger academic community means it is harder to conquer all of the academic high ground. The result is a tendency for ideas to fall into the messy middle; sometimes closer to the left, and sometimes further to the right, but seldom moving away from a pragmatic middle ground that tends to preserve extant developmental institutions and the policy sets that they make possible.

FINAL IDEAS

It is difficult to demonstrate a specific causal path by which ideas have an effect on policy (Hirschman, 1989). Yet ideas help to constitute actors' interests and identities and, indeed, if nothing else, ideas frequently serve as a "catalyst or binding agent" that determine the composition of economic and political institutions, while shifting key players' very perceptions of their interests (Hall, 1989, 367–83; Tannenwald and Wohlforth, 2005, 7). This is as much the case for developmentalism as it is for neoclassical economic liberalism.

This chapter has sought to triangulate between various types of evidence that suggest the variety of ways by which Brazil's ideational foundations differ from its peers, as well as ways by which ideas about the relative merits and demerits of developmentalism may have become embedded in policymaking. For a variety of historically contingent reasons, ideas about the merits of developmentalism have helped to catalyze state elites' beliefs about the proper role of the state in driving the Brazilian economy.

In this way, ideas have become an important ballast that has helped to ensure the resoluteness of Brazilian economic policies, and of the institutional structures of the developmental state. Of course, the causal arrow points in both directions, and institutions themselves also help to form and sustain common expectations about behavior. Chapter 4 turns to the question of how the institutions of the developmental state are used to shape and sustain firm-level behaviors.

4

The Developmental Hierarchical Market Economy

The costs may even be a little bit higher, but since it is national production, jobs and taxes will be generated here.

Minister Edson Lobão, discussing national preferences[1]

Fuck the market.

President Luis Inácio Lula da Silva, upon canceling a round of oil field auctions[2]

This chapter continues the pursuit of institutional complementarities, moving now to the firm-level organization of the economy, and seeking to better understand the particular political economy of relations between firms, labor, and the developmental state. The chapter begins by looking at more than 500 leading firms and financial institutions, to evaluate how well corporate life fits into a Latin American pattern of institutional complementarities that Schneider (2013) has termed "hierarchical market capitalism." In analyzing Brazil's fit to this particular form of capitalism, five institutional characteristics stand out: the segmented firm structure; the muscular influence of developmentalist policy tools on firms; the segmentation of labor markets; the segmentation of skills; and the segmentation of social policy provision. I argue that while Brazil adheres to the general characteristics of the hierarchical market economy (HME), it differs on important dimensions, especially the role of the developmental state in firm life, the non-diversification of large businesses, and the tight relationship between segmentation of labor, skills, and social policy. These differences establish important institutional complementarities unique to the Brazilian case, which as a result might best be termed a *developmental* hierarchical market economy (DHME).

A SEGMENTED MODEL OF FIRM ORGANIZATION

The "varieties of capitalism" literature emphasizes the manner by which institutional complementarities span the entire economy, generating institutions and incentives in one realm of the economy that may have strong influence in other realms (Crouch, 2010; Schneider, 2013, 17). Chapter 2 has already demonstrated the relationship between five facets of higher-level macroeconomic organization; this chapter focuses at the firm level, building on the insight that the way in which firms are structured is influenced by the availability of credit and finance, and that firm structure is both shaped by and formative of labor market structure, and through it, of social outcomes and productivity incentives.

Schneider (2013) has argued that Latin America has a "variety" of capitalism that does not fit into established research on varieties of capitalism, as it is distinct from the liberal, coordinated, and networked forms of capitalist organization previously analyzed in the European, North American, and Asian contexts. He argues that the Latin American "hierarchical" variety of market economy has been marked by four characteristics. First, multinational corporations (MNCs) dominate higher technology manufacturing, alongside domestically owned diversified business groups which predominate across the remainder of the economy. Second, in the absence of deep equity and credit markets in HMEs, domestic groups and MNCs "have been the main private institutions for mobilizing large-scale investment" (Schneider, 2013, 43). Alongside the predominance of MNCs and diversified domestic business groups have come low levels of education and vocational skills, in a "low-skill equilibrium" with high labor turnover. These economic factors are reinforced by, fourth, political structures that reinforce the power of insiders and buttress the core economic institutions that favor their interests.

Schneider's general model is designed to apply to most of Latin America and does a remarkable job of capturing patterns of firm-level organization across the region's diverse macroeconomic settings. But Brazil, as noted in Chapters 2 and 3, has an institutional and ideational commitment to developmentalist thinking and institutions that in many ways makes it a distinct version of the HME. This means that although Schneider's larger point about complementarities holds, these complementarities are quite different from those seen in HMEs elsewhere in the region, with important differences in macroeconomic orientation of the economy, in the state's role in firm life, and as Chapters 5–7 will show, in the political system.

92 · *The Developmental Hierarchical Market Economy*

In evaluating Brazil's fit to the HME model, a first question is whether we should even consider Brazil to be a market economy, or whether it might better be considered a state-run economy, given the role of the state in guiding and shaping economic activity. Certainly, the common use of terms like "state capitalism" to describe the Brazilian economy suggest this possibility. But defining Brazil in this manner would suggest that the state is more important than private firms in determining the shape of the political economy. This does not seem to be the case: central government final consumption expenditure was 19.7 percent of gross domestic product (GDP) in 2018, about one-fifth higher than the 16.2 percent Latin American average, but not so large as to suggest that the state dominates the full economy (World Bank World Development Indicators, various years).[3] The state is powerful, but it is not able to do much more than shape the incentives of private firms, although it has greater power and greater autonomy in some sectors than others. Brazil is a curious case in which the "market" component of "market economy" has a deep vein of state action, but in this it is less the exception to the rule than simply a particularly intense exemplar of the state's role in contemporary market economies.[4] The remaining state-owned enterprises (SOEs) present in Brazilian corporate life are of course a partial anomaly, but their acceptance of non-state minority shareholders, their subservience to many of the same regulatory rules as private firms, and their increasing reliance on private partners all suggest that the state is committed to allowing market forces to operate, albeit susceptible to frequent policy nudges.

Moving on, the first dimension of Schneider's HME concept concerns the existence of hierarchically structured business groups. Among the 519 leading firms and financial institutions in Brazil in 2014,[5] large business empires are readily apparent: the JBS meatpacking firm and its constellation of acquired subsidiaries; the Itaú Unibanco group, with its various financial, credit, and insurance businesses; and the Odebrecht construction behemoth, with its multiple subsidiaries. All are marked by family control and intra-firm hierarchy.[6] They are not, however, marked by significant diversification across sectors: each tends to remain focused on its particular segment of the economy, rather than expanding across very divergent spheres of economic activity (on this point, see also Khanna and Yafeh, 2007; Xavier et al., 2014). Later, this chapter will note one of the prominent forms of diversification in Brazilian business – cross-shareholding through minority stakes – but such cross-shareholding does not appear to follow the logic of a diversification strategy, except in isolated cases. With only a few exceptions, Brazilian firms do not

A Segmented Model of Firm Organization

demonstrate the degree of diversification across spheres of economic activity that is seen, for example, in the traditional Chilean *grupos*.[7]

The relative non-diversification of Brazilian firms may be in part a consequence of Brazil's credit and equity markets, which are large by regional standards, and the easy availability of state credit, especially for large firms. This may obviate the need for intragroup financing that is one of the driving forces for horizontal group diversification in other Latin economies. On the credit side, the state remains an important source of funding: the National Bank for Economic and Social Development (BNDES) provided preferential loans to fully 31 percent of the largest firms between 2013 and mid-2015, including 24 percent of leading multinationals and 36 percent of large Brazilian companies. Although it is relatively small by comparison to the scale of the economy,[8] the BM&F Bovespa stock market (renamed the B3 – Brasil Bolsa Balcão S.A. in 2017) trades shares of 37 percent of the largest domestically owned firms.[9] In other words, there may be less need for large Brazilian firms to diversify across sectors so as to guarantee access to capital and mobilize large-scale investment than is the case in much of the rest of Latin America.

Brazil does, however, share some other superficial characteristics of HMEs. Table 4.1 demonstrates that the pattern of MNC and domestic firm dominance characteristic of HMEs is present in Brazil: together, listed and unlisted foreign firms and unlisted private Brazilian firms accounted for fully 78 percent of the top nonfinancial firms in Brazil in 2016. However, in terms of firm scale as measured by net worth, the picture is a bit less clear-cut. Foreign firms (listed and unlisted) accounted

TABLE 4.1 *Hierarchical capitalism among Brazil's largest nonfinancial firms*

	Adjusted net worth (R$ million)	%	Number of firms	%
Foreign, unlisted	512,154	52%	159	32%
Brazilian state, listed	145,455	15%	14	3%
Brazilian private, listed	125,462	13%	68	13%
Brazilian private, unlisted	95,021	10%	203	40%
Foreign, listed	65,795	7%	30	6%
Brazilian state, unlisted	38,766	4%	30	6%
Total	982,652	100%	504	100%

Source: Calculated by author using data from *Revista Exame* (2016).[10]

94   *The Developmental Hierarchical Market Economy*

for a majority share of leading firms' net worth (59 percent), but unlisted private Brazilian companies account for a mere 10 percent. Brazil is indeed reliant on MNCs, but the remainder of business life was roughly equally divided between public and private-sector firms (19 percent[11] and 23 percent of total net worth, respectively), and in the private sector, between listed and unlisted Brazilian companies (13 percent and 10 percent).

In net worth terms, then, although Brazil meets the first standard of HMEs – the dominance of MNCs – it is less clearly hierarchical with regard to domestic firms. On the private-sector side, Brazil's firms are less dominated by large, vertically integrated private firms akin to Chile's *grupos*. More important, the state's role as a business actor introduces a different sort of hierarchy that justifies the use of the term "developmental state" to describe the organization of the economy. SOEs play an outsized role (small in number, 9 percent of total, but large in net worth, at 19 percent), and there is a relatively small niche (23 percent of net worth) for private firms between their state-owned and MNC peers. Firm life is marked by a significant role of the state, both as a majority shareholder in large SOEs and, as will be discussed shortly, as a minority shareholder in select firms. Brazil still fits the larger argument about HMEs, which is that domestic groups and MNCs play an important role in allocating investment, but it has the substantial wrinkle of active state banks, such as the Banco do Brasil and the BNDES national development bank, discussed below.

HMEs tend to have a competitive advantage in commodities production, and local firms in these economies tend to specialize in these areas, leaving higher technology sectors in the hands of multinationals (Schneider, 2013, 64–8). Here the evidence from Brazil's leading firms is unequivocal in favor of the HME model, as shown in Figure 4.1, which demonstrates that Brazilian firms tend to dominate among the largest firms in sectors that are commodity-producing, low complexity, and/or labor intensive but not skills intensive (sectors on the right side of the 50 percent line in Figure 4.1). The one exception is banking, where the Brazilian financial sector has been very effective in staving off foreign competition, even while employing relatively high-level human capital and engaging in often high-complexity, high-tech ventures.[12]

Brazil may differ from other HMEs in Latin America because its economy is larger and more regionalized. So, although certain firms dominate large segments of particular markets (e.g., beer, cement, or frozen foods) (Schneider, 2013, 69) or geographical areas (e.g., construction firms in a particular region of the country), there is nationwide

A Segmented Model of Firm Organization

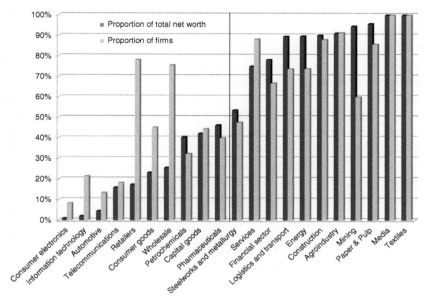

FIGURE 4.1 Brazilian firms by sector, among the top 519 firms.
Source: Author, using data from *Revista Exame* (2016).

competition within sectors. But despite these differences of scale by comparison to the rest of Latin America, there is a strong pattern of concentration among the 519 largest firms: concentration among the largest firms in most sectors is below 0.25, which is usually considered the threshold for excessive concentration, but nearly half of the sectors have indices above 0.15, which are considerable.[13] In four sectors, furthermore, concentration among the largest firms exceeds 0.25: mining; energy; capital goods; and paper and pulp. This relative concentration will be very important to the later discussion of the cross-domain complementarities between the economic and political spheres.

In sum, like HMEs elsewhere in Latin America, firm structure tends to be bifurcated between foreign and domestic, and Brazilian firms dominate in sectors which are low complexity, commodity-oriented, and labor-intensive, where ownership also tends to be highly concentrated. The hierarchical model is present in firm life through the rather significant degrees of sectoral concentration, MNC participation, protection of dominant shareholders' control, and segmented labor markets. Brazilian firm life differs from other HMEs in the region, however, due to significant levels of state activity, the presence of large but relatively undiversified business groups, and credit and equity markets with a large dose of state participation that may enable firms to behave and organize in ways that differ from their regional peers. Firm life is less dominated by large vertically integrated private firms than the prototypical HME, and more dominated by the state, as both a participant in business life and a regulator of it. This is in many ways a replication of the long-standing pattern established during the military regime, with the state dominating in infrastructure, foreign capital dominating in dynamic industries, and national firms dominating in traditional industry and select segments of dynamic industry (Suzigan and Furtado, 2006, 170). A complementarity between the macro- and microeconomic domains arises from the legacy of market protections provided to both foreign and domestic firms, which has incentivized product imitation for the domestic market, rather than innovation for export, and diminished demand for skilled labor in a significant, nationally dominated segment of the labor market.

THE TOOL KIT OF DEVELOPMENTAL STATE INFLUENCE

The state's role in the economy is perhaps the most significant difference accounting for the distinction between Brazilian firm structure and HMEs elsewhere in Latin America. The state's discretion in managing the economy has very deep legal foundations, which give the state enormous latitude in guiding economic activity (Parglender, 2016). This section evaluates various tools available to the state should it choose to employ them, as well as some of the objectives that might guide state use of these tools. The government role in industrial policy is significant, including lending, share ownership, and industrial policies, as well as regulation, which together permit the state to function as "regulator, inducer, and coordinator" of economic activity (Diniz, 2010, 22). Two aspects of this government role are particularly important: first, much of the state's role is autonomous, requiring no political approvals beyond the bureaucracy itself; and second, the overall tendency has been to deepen the use of these state tools in response to economic crises, ensuring their continuity throughout the democratic regime (Lisboa and Latif, 2013, 3, 18).

BNDES LENDING

The BNDES has long been one of the most important institutions of the Brazilian developmental state, in part because of its insulation from

BNDES Lending

political pressures, its recognized competency, and its ability to allocate low-cost credit to firms across the economy. The BNDES has been employed and repurposed in a variety of ways: lending to public projects in the 1950s, financing private companies in the 1960s, serving as an essential tool of industrial consolidation in the Second National Development Plan (PND II) in the 1970s, helping to develop domestic industry in the wake of the oil shock of 1979, aiding in restructuring after the 1982 debt crisis, enabling privatization and serving as a minority shareholder in the 1990s, and since the turn of the century, providing financing that would be used in part to enable overseas expansion and mergers and acquisitions for the creation of national champions (Hermann, 2010; Hochstetler, 2011, 35; Musacchio and Lazzarini, 2014, 244–7).

In light of recurrent fiscal limitations, it is perhaps not surprising that policymakers have sought to use the fiscally opaque tools at their disposal. The forced savings and investment profits that finance the BNDES, augmented in good times by subsidized government loans, have provided policymakers with a relatively low-cost, powerful and fiscally opaque instrument that they can use to push their particular policy priorities.[14] The BNDES has an outsized role in credit provision, and in its heyday in 2010, accounted for 70 percent of bank loans of greater than three years' duration and supplied more than 30 percent of investment in industry and infrastructure (Colby, 2013, 1). It is financed through a combination of funds from mandatory paycheck deductions (the *Fundo de Amparo ao Trabalhador*, FAT, and a public sector analog, PIS-PASEP), profits from past credit operations, bond issues, and loans from the federal government, often at very low base interest rates.[15] These sources of funds have permitted the BNDES to expand its loan portfolio considerably over the years, often lending at "concessional" interest rates (Porzecanski, 2015).[16] The loan portfolio averaged nearly US$65 billion in loan disbursements annually in the decade from 2006 to 2015, during which it nearly quadrupled in size (Leahy, 2015), with assets three times those of the Inter-American Development Bank and nearly equivalent to those of the World Bank (Coutinho, 2010; Armijo, 2017). The run-up in BNDES lending was especially pronounced between 2009 and 2014, during which time Finance Minister Guido Mantega sought to stimulate economic activity to counteract the effects of the global financial crisis. The implicit Treasury subsidy to these loans was estimated to be on the order of R$184 billion, although critics argue that this lending had little effect on the overall rate of investment in the economy as a whole (Versiani and Amora, 2015).

The low cost and long duration of BNDES loans, especially as compared to private-sector lenders, has made it the best source of long-term finance in Brazil (Santana, 2011; Montero, 2014b). It is an especially important funder of Brazil's 519 leading firms: between 2012 and 2015, nearly one in four leading foreign firms in my dataset received BNDES loans (23.7 percent), and fully one in three leading Brazilian firms received them (36 percent).[17] Many of the recipients of this BNDES credit are in fact the same "champions" who received financing in the period between the end of World War II and the end of the authoritarian regime four decades later. The fact that these firms have not been weaned off the BNDES' credit portfolio is explained away by defenders as the logical next step in expanding the global penetration of these firms (Coutinho, 2010, 29; Hochstetler and Montero, 2013). Yet, it also leads to significant concentration of lending: the five largest construction firms, for example, received nearly US$12 billion in loans for foreign expansion. This was further concentrated within this elite group, with 58 percent going to Odebrecht and 24 percent to Andrade Gutierrez (Carrasco and Pinho de Mello, 2015).

As a consequence of its oversized role in the economy, the BNDES became "more central to the development model of democratic Brazil" in the 2010s than it was even during the statist period, with its share of gross fixed capital formation – the net flow of fixed capital acquisitions in the economy – doubling from 10 percent in 1979, at the height of the military's national development plan, to 20 percent in 2010 (Montero, 2014b, 1). Critics noted, however, that there were substantial costs to this role, including adverse selection problems in credit markets (lending to the best borrowers, who could probably obtain credit elsewhere), as well as undermining monetary policy, by indirectly increasing government borrowing, which exacerbated fiscal pressures and drove up interest rates (Bolle, 2015). Until the beginning of the Bolsonaro administration, the BNDES offered loans at a low, subsidized rate known as the long-term interest rate (*Taxa de Juros de Longo Prazo*, TJLP), which was often about half the interest rate at which the government itself borrowed money, the SELIC rate (*Sistema Especial de Liquidação e Custodia*). The costs were significant: one study found that in more than 500 loans to the construction sector between 2007 and 2015, totaling US$12 billion, the total BNDES subsidy to borrowers was more than US$4 billion (Carrasco and Pinho de Mello, 2015). Loans from the BNDES reached 11 percent of GDP by late 2012, with an implicit credit subsidy of around US$10 billion (Lisboa and Latif, 2013, 30; Armijo, 2017). The fifty largest

BNDES clients received nearly half a trillion *reais* in loans in the decade and a half leading up to 2019; with Petrobras, Embraer, Norte Energia, Vale, and Odebrecht leading the list of borrowers (G1, 2019b). Further, it is worth recalling from Chapter 2 that in addition to the BNDES, other state-owned banking institutions are also granting credit; non-BNDES preferential subsidized earmarked loans for specific government programs accounted for roughly another one-fifth of outstanding credit in 2012 (Lisboa and Latif, 2013, 30).

SHARE OWNERSHIP

As of 2017, the Brazilian government held a stake in a variety of business interests as both a majority and a minority shareholder. It was the majority shareholder of 141 SOEs, clustered around five leading SOEs: Petrobras, the state oil company; Eletrobras, the electricity generator and distributor; Correios, the postal service; Banco do Brasil, the largest federal bank; and the CEF, a federal savings bank.[18]

The state's role in business has shifted to adjust to fiscal realities, but it remains central to much "private-sector" activity. In the wake of the 1982 debt crisis, losses from state-owned companies weighed heavily on fiscal results, and rising borrowing costs ratcheted up the fiscal burden of state-owned firms (Frieden, 1991; Musacchio and Lazzarini, 2014, 91).[19] This led to the first privatizations of firms, under military rule, as well as tighter scrutiny by the government, including – only in the late 1970s! – the first census of state-owned firms (Trebat, 1983; Werneck, 1987; Musacchio and Lazzarini, 2014, 88, 90). In consequence, the total number of companies wholly owned by the Brazilian federal government has fallen, from 251 in 1979 (Trebat, 1983, 36) to a total of 141 of much smaller size in 2014 (Ministério do Planejamento, 2014).

This is not to say, however, that the government's role in the economy was reduced to insignificance. Despite the privatization of more than $100 billion in assets between 1981 and 2002, the state remained a major player in business. Although the number of Brazil's thirty largest companies under government ownership peaked at twenty-eight in 1979, a large number of behemoths of capitalism in Brazil remained majority-owned by the state, as shown in Table 4.2. The value of these SOEs that remain in state hands reached US$756.8 billion in 2009 (Musacchio and Lazzarini, 2014, 99), the high point of SOEs' value under the Workers' Party governments.[20] In 2014, before the Lava Jato investigation went into high gear, the investment budget of Petrobras' supply directorate

The Developmental Hierarchical Market Economy

TABLE 4.2 *SOEs among the thirty largest companies in Brazil*

	1962	1979	1995	2000	2010
Number	12	28	14	11	9
Percent	40%	93%	47%	37%	30%

Source: Compiled by author from the following sources: 1962 and 1979, Bulmer-Thomas 1994, 356–8; 2000 and 2010, *Revista Exame*, based on "patrimônio líquido ajustado"; 1995, based on "patrimônio líquido legal."

alone was R$18 billion, larger than the executed budget at all but eight of the twenty-seven ministries in the federal government (Dallagnol, 2017, 112).

Minority shareholding offers another avenue by which the state can exercise control. Musacchio and Lazzarini (2014) note the significant alteration in the role of the state in business since the 1970s, with the "Leviathan as majority investor" model shifting to a "Leviathan as minority investor" model. Rather than outright ownership of SOEs, governments use "pyramidal ownership structures or state-owned holding companies to manage their ownership in a large number of firms" (2014, 51). The costs of minority shareholding may be negligible, in light of the potential returns: for example, mining giant Vale paid nearly $1.4 billion in royalties to the government each year, on top of nearly that amount in taxes (Musacchio and Lazzarini, 2014, 224). Total royalties paid to the federal government summed to $8 billion in 2014, or 0.5 percent of GDP, in addition to another 0.3 percent of GDP in dividends (Secretaria do Tesouro Nacional, 2015). Through its direct shareholding of both majority and minority stakes, the federal government was the tenth largest shareholder in the equity market in 2019 (Abreu, 2019).

Crucially, even after privatization, the government continued to control significant portions of Brazilian corporate life through minority shareholding, held in place using a combination of the BNDES' investment arm, BNDESPar; the pension funds of SOEs[21]; and cross-shareholdings by SOEs. Although it owned majority shares in only nine of the top thirty companies, the government in 2010 owned minority shares of the remaining twenty-one top private sector companies through the BNDESPar and the top three public-sector pension funds,[22] valued at $17 billion and accounting for nearly 9 percent of their total adjusted net worth.[23]

Share Ownership

In 2015, BNDESPar held equity stakes in seventy-four private firms, as well as seventy-one publicly traded corporations accounting for nearly 60 percent of Brazil's total market capitalization (Parglender, 2016). Estimates suggest that at the peak of the economic boom in the 2000s, the federal government, through BNDESPar and pension funds, controlled over one-fifth of the value of the São Paulo stock exchange and held stakes in nearly 200 Brazilian companies (Romero, 2012; Ban, 2013; Montero, 2014b). The government also held golden shares that gave it outsized influence over many of the largest firms (Schneider, 2009; Hochstetler and Montero, 2013, 1486). Leverage provided by debentures and other debt instruments further augmented the state's influence over firms that it did not control outright, suggesting that as many as 600 or more firms were under the influence of the state (Brey et al., 2014). The structure of corporate law, meanwhile, and the state's role as both player and referee in the marketplace, permitted the state to shape the law to fit its shareholder interests. The law was written to benefit the state as shareholder, the state has not been hesitant to change the law when needed,[24] and courts and regulators have been largely acquiescent in these changes (Parglender, 2016).

This web of instruments led to "collusion" among state-related actors to reinforce the government's control (Lazzarini, 2010; Mussachio and Lazzarini, 2014, 218). Minority shareholding and cross-shareholding across a variety of firms enabled the government to selectively wield pressure on companies. Sometimes, this was designed to favor local industrial consolidation: Collor used BNDES funds to block foreign bids for Siderbrás, and to favor Brazil's Gerdau; under Cardoso, private sector firm Vicunha received public funding to buy Companhia Vale do Rio Doce (Abu-El-Haj, 2016). Under the Cardoso administration, cross-shareholding was strategically deployed during the privatization process to preserve government leverage in the hopes of avoiding oligopolistic concentration, and more broadly, to shape particular sectors to the new regulatory frameworks that were being created. Prior to privatization, the firms up for sale went through productive restructuring, often with credit and a range of supports from government agencies (Montero, 1998; Hochstetler and Montero, 2013, 1486). The BNDES helped finance buyers in the privatization process, which permitted it to influence which buyers were successful, and BNDESPar permitted the government to preserve influential minority shareholdings.

Cross-ownership and interlocking boards of directors have also been very important to maintaining government control, in a system that

Lazzarini (2010) described as *"capitalismo de laços,"* roughly translated as capitalism of shared ties, or networked capitalism. Interlocking boards are those in which board seats are occupied by directors also serving on the boards of other companies: in the 2000s, nearly three-quarters of the companies traded on the stock exchange had interlocking boards (Santos et al., 2012). Complex interwoven ownership structures protect companies from direct competition, and also permit the government to guide firms in the directions it finds most productive for accomplishing its broader macroeconomic and developmental goals. Minority shareholding and cross-shareholding across a variety of firms has enabled the government to selectively wield pressure on private companies.[25] The pension fund Previ, for example, had the power to nominate 285 board members across a range of industries in 2009 (Dieguez, 2014, 113). Early in the Lula administration, the Previ pension fund blocked the more than 100 companies in which it held shares from doing business with Banco Opportunity; this decision was followed by other pension funds, who also stopped doing business with Citibank, which had an association with Opportunity's owner, Daniel Dantas (Dieguez, 2014, 69–71). The motive for this state boycott was an effort by Dantas to block a government-led consolidation of the cellular telephony market.

Cross-shareholding ties can be enormously complex. In 2013, the mining giant Vale ostensibly had only eight major shareholders, which included the major pension funds, private banks and firms, and BNDESPar. But a 2016 analysis of the shareholders behind those shareholders, conducted by the online "Eles Mandam" project at Repórter Brasil[26] investigated the shareholdings of Brazil's one hundred largest companies, its fifty largest conglomerates, and its ten largest pension funds. The study revealed that behind the eight major shareholders were nearly three and a half dozen significant cross-shareholdings by large firms. This complex structure helps to explain one of the most dramatic episodes of state influence brokering that is a part of the lore of the Workers' Party's time in office: in 2011, the CEO of Vale – an ostensibly private company – was dumped at government urging, after undertaking a particularly aggressive series of cost-cutting measures, including layoffs, at a time when the government sought to ameliorate the effects of the global financial crisis on the economy.[27] Although the government was no longer a majority shareholder in Vale, which had been privatized in 1997, cross-shareholding in a variety of other stakeholders permitted it to exercise its leverage and fire the offending executive. Other examples abound: for example, the government used minority shareholding to push back

Share Ownership 103

against the unwelcome hostile takeover of Vale by private sector tycoon Eike Batista in 2010 as well as the buyout of Sadia, a major food producer, by foreign firms (Dieguez, 2014; Gaspar, 2014).

Industrial Supports and Sectoral Policies

Industrial policy has been a constant of democratic Brazil. At its broadest, this has meant wide scale programs for industrial development: an alphabet soup of sixteen unique national programs were implemented between 1985 and 2013, under six ideologically diverse presidential administrations. Together, they have in common the goal of improving the competitiveness of Brazilian-sited firms, especially after the opening of the economy during the late 1980s and early 1990s (Trubek, Coutinho, et al., 2013, 49). These programs have included a combination of "horizontal" measures intended to improve efficiency across the economy, as well as "vertical" measures such as tax incentives and market protections intended to support specific sectors.

Industrial policy has routinely been targeted "vertically," providing particular industries with tariff protections, export subsidies, tax incentives, and domestic content requirements. In spite of the trade liberalizations of the late 1980s and early 1990s, tariff policy remains an important component of industrial policy: Veiga (2009) notes that although tariffs fell, many sectors maintained high effective levels of protection, especially in manufacturing. As Chapter 2 noted, this led to a variety of tariff peaks that were high by comparison with Brazil's global peers; moreover, frequent changes in the tariff schedule introduced uncertainty for importers. Export financing through FINAME, supplier credits through BNDES-EXIM and export tax exemptions were also frequently used, for example, through the 2011 *Reintegra* program, which provided exporters with a tax credit equivalent to 3 percent of their export value and exempted nearly US$47bn in exports from certain taxes (USTR, 2013).

Tax incentives have been routinely readjusted to take into account changing sectoral conditions and boost the competitiveness of those sectors, reflecting the reality that multiple taxes on manufactures and imports may nearly double their cost. Both state and federal governments have used tax incentives, such as exemption from the ICMS tax on the movement of goods and services, to attract relocating firms. Extant firms have frequently been able to benefit from temporary reductions in the IPI industrial production tax. The threat of layoffs has led to recurrent IPI reductions in sensitive sectors such as white goods and automotive production, under governments of all ideological stripes. The Federal Accounting Tribunal (TCU) estimated that all told, federal tax exemptions in 2012, including BNDES credit benefits, amounted to 5 percent of GDP (Lisboa and Latif, 2013, 26–7).

Domestic content requirements are another lever that has been utilized, often in combination with tax incentives, such that firms reaching a certain threshold of domestic content are taxed at a lower rate than their importing competitors. In the 2000s, domestic content requirements were introduced in a variety of industries in an explicit bid to increase local technological development, such as solar and wind energy, oil and gas production, and information technology.[28] Most notably, local content requirements were introduced for the pre-salt oilfields discovered off Brazil's southern coast in 2007, and the government pushed for petroleum exploration to be carried out using domestically built ships. Even more ubiquitous, however, are local content requirements in a variety of fields in which government procurement plays a role. Notable is health care, where the universal healthcare system (*Sistema Único de Saúde*, SUS) allowed regulatory bodies to play an influential role in procurement of pharmaceuticals and medical equipment, and led to rules granting preferential treatment to domestic producers in public tenders.[29] Similar requirements are also present in other fields, including the information technology sector and entertainment, where cable and TV programming are controlled to ensure minimum domestic content. FINAME provides export financing, but only to firms which exceed 60 percent local content by value or weight.

Associated with the domestic content issue are the somewhat ambiguous rules concerning foreign ownership. Under the military regime, the government pursued a policy permitting foreign firms to participate in the local market, provided they followed the same laws governing domestic firms. Simultaneously, however, it closed certain sectors entirely to foreign-owned production. One result was that foreign companies dominated the automotive sector, even as the computer industry was completely closed to foreign investment through an Informatics Law that preserved the market for Brazilian firms until the 1990s. This ambiguity carried over into the 1988 Constitution, which included two definitions of "national firm": one based on having an office in-country, and a second, more restrictive one, based on ownership by individuals residing in-country (Almeida, 2009). While the article defining national capital was removed from the constitution in 1995, and the need for foreign investment has tempered discriminatory inclinations, a lingering preference for national

Share Ownership 105

firms persists, as do restrictions on foreign ownership of land and certain sectors.[30] As recently as 2011, Brazil's attorney general required foreign firms to receive authorization from the Ministry of Rural Development or the Ministry of Development and Foreign Trade before purchasing land; they were not forbidden from doing so, but the process required jumping hurdles that domestic firms were not subject to (Judd, 2011, 20).

A guiding force behind all of these policies has been the developmentalist belief that the local siting of industry is central to economic development, even if the companies are not Brazilian: this has meant the country "has served as a platform" for multinational producers to "satisfy the needs of the large (and relatively protected) domestic market" (Porzecanski, 2015). In most sectors, this has permitted foreign firms to benefit from all of the market protections provided by law, and many of the benefits of developmentalist policies, without necessarily leading to the development of indigenous firm capacity. Under Dilma Rousseff, new laws were established that provided a 30 percent reduction in IPI tax on automotive firms that produced using 65 percent local content. But this was not unique to the Workers' Party: under the Cardoso administration, too, automotive manufacturers were given their own special automotive regime, complete with tariff protections, fiscal incentives, BNDES support, and even attractive siting agreements for newly arrived Asian and European firms (Almeida, 2009, 37). Nor was the auto industry the only beneficiary of industrial policy under the ostensibly neoliberal Cardoso administration: sixteen sectoral funds were charged with incentivizing innovation and competitiveness (Trubek, Coutinho, et al., 2013).

The particular political economy ecosystem that results from the tool kit of developmentalism ensures that, despite the enormous privatizations of the 1980s and 1990s, the government has retained influence over private-sector actors, through strong tools to manage price levels, aggregate supply, and aggregate demand. Over the past two decades, the Brazilian government has demonstrated a willingness to use its powerful policy instruments to a variety of ends. Sometimes, control of firms has been used to meet immediate political needs. The Rousseff administration used its control of the petroleum sector to freeze gasoline prices when inflation began to rise, and it used the Banco do Brasil to drive down interest rates when policymakers felt that these had risen too high. SOEs were also used to further foreign policy objectives, whether it was in the use of Petrobras in a joint venture with Venezuela's PDVSA to build the Abreu e Lima refinery or the use of BNDES funding to refurbish the Mariel port in Cuba.

The Developmental Hierarchical Market Economy

Using both direct share ownership, as well as indirect shareholding through intermediary companies, the state has exerted its leverage to its own benefit as a shareholder: to increase the government's voting power (e.g., Petrobras' public offering in 2012); to elect minority board members who are sympathetic to the government (e.g., the selection of Jorge Gerdau Johannpeter, a close confidante of Lula, and Josué Gomes da Silva, the vice president's son, to sit on the Petrobras board); or to replace private sector executives who are insufficiently sympathetic to government goals (e.g., the removal of Vale's CEO in 2009).

These tools have also been employed to achieve strategic economic goals. Share ownership and leverage from lending have been used to encourage Brazilian purchases of privatized firms (e.g., Tele Norte Leste); force mergers (e.g., the creation of Brazil Foods); and recapitalize firms facing liquidity troubles (e.g., JBS and Net). These instruments permitted the government to actively select state champions in particular sectors and work to encourage consolidation of firms into global giants, such as Brazil Foods (a merger of Sadia and Perdigão), Banco Itaú Unibanco (a merger of the two largest private banks), Fibria (made possible when Aracruz was purchased by Votorantim with government support), and the Oi telecommunications firm (a merger of Telemar and Brasil Telecom). Brazil Foods is a particularly good example of the phenomenon: Perdigão was rescued from bankruptcy in 1994 by nine state pension funds. When its biggest competitor, Sadia, got into financial trouble in 2009, it was rescued with nearly R$1 billion in emergency loans from the Banco do Brasil and then, with capital from state pension funds, merged with Perdigão, making it not just the largest food processing firm in Brazil and Latin America, but also an essentially state-controlled firm (Dieguez, 2014, 157–63).

These tools also have provided supports to firms expanding abroad, as in the meatpacker JBS' purchase of a variety of firms in the United States, including Swift and Pilgrim's Pride. The expansion of national companies through foreign acquisitions was justified by the government in the belief that doing so would lead to technology and productivity gains that would eventually return home (Abu-El-Haj, 2016). Industrial policies have been used to develop local industry, such as through the use of domestic content rules in Petrobras refinery equipment purchases and tanker purchases.

The various components have not always emanated from or followed a single master plan or blueprint, and tend to have evolved piecemeal, over time, as the result of close co-development and incidental repurposing.[31] One consequence is that such programs can be quite costly: as the TCU

Segmented Labor Markets

noted in its evaluation of the government's 2016 fiscal accounts, the R$378 billion in tax incentives implemented that year exceeded the budget deficit (Fleischer, 2017). Historically, use of these tools has not always demanded a counterpart commitment by firms to meet clear goals of productivity or competitiveness, nor to commit to improve the quality of their labor force (Fiori, 1992, 181). Even when such counterpart commitments are firmly established, industry has not always complied with their obligations (e.g., Wiziack and Prado, 2017).[32] Nor is efficiency usually a central objective: previous scholars, for example, have found that SOEs tend to be slower to lay off personnel in the wake of a crisis and to stray from maximizing returns (Musacchio and Lazzarini, 2014, 145–63). There is also ample evidence, described in Chapters 5 and 6, of political influence in the deployment of these tools of the developmental state. In sum, state policies in the democratic era have tended to be more effective in preserving employment than in achieving higher-order development objectives, such as moving Brazilian industry or the labor force up the technology frontier. Before turning to the central issue of productivity, though, it will be useful to consider the segmentation of the labor market that is a defining feature of Brazil's HME.

SEGMENTED LABOR MARKETS

Despite some reforms over the past quarter century, there has been considerable continuity in labor policy over the past three-quarters of a century.[33] Overall, the corporatist labor pact established by Getúlio Vargas' *Estado Novo* has tended to bifurcate labor between formal and informal sectors, with the state playing the key role as an arbiter of labor conflict in the formal sector. This pact deepened one characteristic of HMEs: the existence of "segmented" labor markets, which tend to be marked by high levels of regulation, rapid turnover, high levels of informality, and low union density. During the period covered by this book, Brazil fit the first three elements of the HME portrait neatly: its *varguista* labor code was in many ways strengthened by the provisions of the 1988 Constitution, helping to make it one of the more rigid labor markets among the developing countries, at least superficially (Ban, 2013).[34] For formal sector workers, there was a very extensive body of legislation, protected by dedicated labor courts. Multinationals and many large firms were largely unable to escape these laws, and governments could not easily limit civil servants' formal rights. However, the laws' grip was uneven, with many laws not faithfully executed and recent reforms opening up exceptions for smaller firms, leading to de facto flexibility and a two-tiered labor market (Coslovsky et al., 2017). Further, smaller domestic firms were allowed a variety of techniques to sidestep regulations, including outsourcing, which accounted for around a quarter of formal employment, temporary contracts, and self-employment of workers (Costa et al., 2015).

Brazil during this period was distinct from the HME model of labor, however, in the degree of union density. Public sector unions were strong. Private sector unions were numerically broad-reaching, and until the Temer administration, had expanded considerably in response to perverse incentives in the law: many unions were formed in part to garner the compulsory labor tax that, until reform took place in 2018, were the exclusive right of unions who represented a particular segment of industry. Labor taxes helped fund a variety of labor and patronal associations, with around 10,000 such bodies sharing "labor contributions" of approximately R$3 billion annually (Batista and Berta, 2015). Unions could not compete with each other in the same geographical region, but they could create smaller unions for more specific categories of workers. The availability of the labor contribution and this possibility of splitting incentivized the unruly growth of unions while undermining their overall strength. But unions tended to be far from representative, and most private formal sector workers paid one day's wages a year in union fees without expecting much in return or ever mobilizing for collective union goals.

The segmentation of labor markets followed some of the segmentation of firms: in labor intensive sectors, such as construction or food processing, employees tended to have predominantly primary educations; in capital intensive firms, such as mining, they tended to have secondary education; and in services such as banking or telecommunications, employees showed higher levels of tertiary education (Schneider, 2013, 118). An associated phenomenon was a split between three segments of the labor market: informal, formal but with high turnover (and therefore low skill), and highly regulated, long-tenure segments, which include both formal private firms and government and state-owned firm employees (Schneider, 2013, 190). Turnover rates in the labor market have consistently been above 40 percent, and most employment situations last less than one year (Costa et al., 2015). The distinction between MNCs and Brazilian firms also is relevant here: relatively few private domestic firms offer stable and long-term employment relations, while MNCs have little

Segmented Labor Markets

option but to do so, lest they fall afoul of stringent labor laws or fail to retain skilled employees needed in the sectors they dominate.

Within the major metropolitan regions, formal employment accounted for 48 percent of the economically active population (excluding domestic workers). Government employees (at all levels of government) accounted for a further 30 percent of the economically active population, meaning that informal workers represented 22 percent (IBGE, "Pesquisa mensal de emprego"). This figure was likely unrepresentative nationally, however, given that the informal sector workers may not self-identify as economically active, and these figures report only data from the six largest metropolitan regions, where formal sector employment is likely greater than elsewhere. But segmentation is also evident in the broader but less precise national estimates, which put the number of formal sector workers at around 40 percent of the economically active population, in addition to a further 10–12 percent of public sector workers, who were covered by their own formal labor legislation (Folha, 2016b).

The prevalence of a large informal labor sector reflected a long-standing neglect of the development of a high-productivity labor force. The decision to rotate through a low skills workforce represented "a choice of a kind of Taylorism, without Fordism" (Fiori, 1992, 178); that is, an effort to make workforce production more efficient but without empowering workers as consumers. Low wages were aggravated by the existence of a huge pool of underemployed workers (Trubek, Coutinho, et al., 2013, 48). Because access to the formal labor market had direct consequences for workers' ability to access basic social services such as pensions, the segmentation of the labor market likely fed back into inequality. Meanwhile, the existence of a large pool of low-skilled reserve labor meant that firms had little incentive to invest in labor force productivity, or to organize collectively in favor of better educational standards and performance. Further, even reforms intended to increase formalization of small firms (such as the Simples regime of simplified taxation) did not have the desired effect, for the simple reason that although the gains from formalization may be important, such as becoming integrated into the social security system, the costs are even greater, such as becoming visible to the state and therefore to tax collectors (Cardoso, 2016). In sum, the existence of a large informal mass of workers that represented somewhere between a fifth and half of the economically active population generated incentives that exacerbated the cycle of informality, low productivity, and inequality.

SKILLS DEVELOPMENT AND WORKER PRODUCTIVITY

Although there are some sectors (and firms) where production may have caught up with or even set world standards – such as aviation (e.g., Embraer), deep sea oil exploration (Petrobras), agribusiness (J&F), automotives (Marco Polo), and mining (Vale) – there are many sectors where the country remains far from the technological frontier. This is especially the case in the knowledge economy.[35] The MIT economic complexity index of the economy, a measure of the knowledge intensity of the products it exports, places Brazil mid-range in the global economy, but it has fallen relative to other countries, especially with the commodities boom of the 2000s (see Figure 4.2 for comparison with South Korea). Brazil is a laggard in patents, as well as in value added to exports.[36] There are few opportunities for the labor force, even well-educated workers, to work in more knowledge-based, complex industries, which undermines educational demand and supply in those fields (Hartmann et al., 2016).

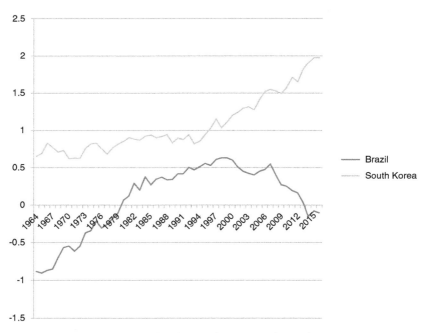

FIGURE 4.2 Economic complexity, South Korea and Brazil.
Source: Author, compiled from data at https://atlas.media.mit.edu/en/rankings/country/eci/, accessed April 2018.

Skills Development and Worker Productivity

Productivity is a central challenge across the economy, with low productivity associated with physical capital shortcomings, human capital deficiencies, and the inefficiencies associated with the architecture of the developmental state (Newman, 2016; Soares, 2016, 2017). Soares (2016, 2017) notes that Brazilian GDP growth has been driven in recent decades largely by growth in the size of the labor force. The second potential engine of growth, labor force productivity, has increased at only 0.7 percent a year on average since 1980, after growing 3.3 percent a year between 1950 and 1980. Labor productivity has grown more slowly since 1980 than in any of the large Latin American economies, save Argentina and Mexico. With labor force growth declining, and expected to enter negative territory by 2030, these low rates of labor productivity growth mean that economic growth will likely become even slower once the labor force stops expanding.

The factors that might improve matters are unlikely to improve in the short or medium term. Increased capital investment is unlikely: national savings and investment rates have remained in the 20 percent ballpark since the 1990s. As Chapter 2 demonstrated, Brazil saves less than its Latin American peers, in part because it has run a persistent nominal government deficit and is therefore "drawing resources from savers and ploughing them into its consumption and transfers" (Soares, 2016, 9). In the private sector, low competition tends to create few incentives for investment; in the public sector, as already shown, post-debt public spending is heavily tilted toward consumption.

A second way to increase overall productivity would be through improved educational attainment. But human capital development has been woeful, with Brazilian students performing very poorly on student skills (Bezerra and Cavalcanti, 2009, 83–4), and 29 percent of the population considered functionally illiterate (twice the global rate).[37] Although Brazil has made huge strides in increasing schooling since 1990, there are at least three persistent problems. Education performance has been improving in part because of a very low starting point: among the largest Latin American economies, Brazil had the lowest average years of schooling in 1990, so it was playing catch-up. In part, this was due to the fact that for nearly a century, illiterate citizens could not vote; with the expansion of suffrage to illiterates in 1985, demand for basic education spiked (Abrucio, 2018). Second, and in part in consequence of the structure of business life, human capital improvements transfer only partially to labor productivity (Soares, 2016). Third is the fact that educational improvement has largely occurred via improved access to schooling, but the quality of that schooling in many cases remains abysmal.

Although enrollments have exploded across the board since the return to democracy, the quality of education has long been far below what would be anticipated, given per capita income or spending as a share of GDP (Amann and Baer, 2009, 40). Public spending on education is high, at 5.4 percent of GDP (for primary to tertiary education), by contrast to an OECD average of 4.8 percent and Argentina's 4.9 percent (OECD, 2017a, 5). Yet spending per student is relatively low, especially at earlier levels of education. Primary education ranks in the lowest decile of the World Economic Forum (WEF) Global Competitiveness Index. Fewer than three-quarters of those fifteen to twenty-four-year-olds have completed primary education, placing Brazil in the bottom three countries of Latin America, alongside Nicaragua and El Salvador (Paes de Barros and Coutinho, 2014).

Over half of the economically active population has not completed secondary education, more than double the OECD average of 22 percent (OECD, 2017a, 3). Brazil has a long tradition of vocational training through the network of semi-public training institutions supported by the "S system" (Senai, etc.), which is allocated nearly 0.3 percent of GDP (Afonso et al., 2013; Lisboa and Latif, 2013; Balbachevsky and Sampaio, 2017, 157). But vocational training levels for secondary students are only slightly more than 9 percent of students enrolled, far below the 25 percent average for Latin American countries with data, or the 46 percent average among OECD countries. Brazilian vocational training, furthermore, is largely targeted at getting into university, rather than building skills for the labor market, perhaps because Brazilians are accustomed to treating bachelors' degrees as professional degrees, and there is strong regulation of the labor market on the basis of professional degrees (Balbachevsky and Sampaio, 2017, 156).[38] Secondary attainment rates rose to 64 percent of adult population in 2015, but only 57 percent of students complete secondary education within five years of entry, and student teacher ratios are high, reducing quality (OECD, 2017a, 3). Although tertiary education leads to a "notably higher earnings advantage" than among other OECD countries, and increases employability, college remains a luxury available to only 15 percent of twenty-five to sixty-four-year-olds, below the remainder of Latin America and the OECD average of 37 percent (OECD, 2017a, 5).

Education outcomes are lackluster. Brazil's scores in cross-national Programme for International Student Assessment (PISA) testing place it far below average in math, reading, and science (it fared no better than fifty-fourth out of sixty-five countries; OECD, 2016). Although access to education has increased at all levels of the educational system since the return to democracy, spending continues to privilege higher education, whose beneficiaries are wealthier than average.[39] Even under the leftist governments of the PT, many of the largest budget education policies remained focused on higher education: ProUni scholarship and FIES student loan programs to expand access; REUNI to restructure federal universities, and Science without Frontiers to send promising Brazilian college students abroad to study at world universities. Total undergraduate enrollments rose rapidly under the PT, from 2.7 million students in 2000 to 8 million in 2015 (Balbachevsky and Sampaio, 2017, 155).[40] Many public universities, which charge no tuition fees, serve primarily those who have been able to afford elite, private secondary schools. Given that university graduates earn 2.5 times the salary of a high school graduate (OECD, 2017a), entrepreneurs have moved to fill the void by creating private universities. Such for-profit schools now enroll about three-quarters of all students, providing tuition-based higher education to those willing to pay. The consequence is a "sharply stratified" system, with tuition-free public universities at the top, serving about 24 percent of the student population, and low-quality tuition-based institutions at the bottom. Government efforts to regulate the private schools backfired, by creating a large regulatory burden that drove many of the smaller schools to sell out to investment firms and global higher education providers, leading to the consolidation of the market in a few large education firms (Balbachevsky and Sampaio, 2017, 157, 160).

This combination of free public higher education, paid private college, and relatively low investment in vocational skills training exacerbates inequality while diminishing the collective action needed to improve education across the board, for at least three reasons. The first is a form of "low productivity trap": employers see little need to invest in vocational training either because they can afford the premium on better educated workers (e.g., the public sector and MNCs) or because they rely on a high turnover, low-skilled labor force and therefore the investment in demanding better trained workers could not be recouped (e.g., private firms). A second is the "unsqueaky wheel": the middle and upper class who might be expected to complain about substandard education do not do so, in part because they can opt into better private education and as a consequence, may perform better than public school graduates in the competition for tertiary education. Third, there is the opportunity cost of education in a poor society: for many of the poorest students in the worst secondary and vocational schools, a job – even in the informal sector – may provide benefits that far outweigh the opportunity cost of continuing in a low-quality education with uncertain return on investment. All of these reasons sap the collective action needed to engender meaningful educational change.

Finally, productivity is hemmed in by institutional complementarities. Soares (2016), for example, argues that reforms to state institutions would increase productivity by increasing competition: economic openness and a change in the autarkic policies that protect national producers from competition; reductions to a self-preserving bureaucracy whose regulation keeps potential competitors out of the market; and overhaul of an inefficient tax system that unduly burdens firms seeking competitiveness improvements. But these pillars of the developmental state are held in place by a variety of interlocking institutional complementarities. Reconstructing longstanding pillars of the developmental state is an uphill battle, especially in favor of the uncertain, long-term and amorphous collective goal of improving society-wide productivity.

SEGMENTED SOCIAL POLICY

Segmentation in firm life and in the labor market, and segmentation in skills development, all intersect to increase inequality. Much of this inequality, though, is mirrored in social policies. Chapter 2 discussed the macrolevel regressivity of the tax structure and how it is exacerbated by the regressivity of government spending: when all is said and done, the progressivity of social policy and social assistance programs is annulled by regressive transfers. The progressiveness of the policy commitments the 1988 Constitution set in motion is legion: universal health care and nearly universal pension coverage, for example. Associated with this package, however, are a series of rights that exacerbate the divisions listed above: strong labor protections, strong civil service tenure protections, and pension guarantees. The result is segmented social protection, which has tended to benefit most those who are best able to organize collectively to demand their rights: first and foremost, civil servants, concentrated as they are in a few urban areas and with a choke hold on policy; second, formal private sector workers who are able to organize on a sectoral basis; and dead last, the large mass of informal sector workers.

Social spending has risen throughout the democratic era and is higher than in any of Brazil's Latin American peers. Per capita social spending

Segmented Social Policy

more than doubled in real terms in the two decades after 1990, and non-pension social spending quadrupled to 2.1 percent of GDP in the first decade of the twenty-first century alone (Melo et al., 2014). But the system remains hugely regressive, on net. Social insurance spending (old age, disability, illness, and unemployment) accounted for about three-quarters of total social spending, and the wealthiest quintile benefited in a 7:1 ratio by comparison to the lowest quintile (McGuire, 2010). A comprehensive study of the effect of government transfers on family income found that the only two categories of government policy that swing in a slightly progressive direction are direct taxes (which reduce inequality in household income by about 14 percent) and social assistance programs (which reduce it by 0.6 percent) (Medeiros and Souza, 2013). Even the much-lauded *Bolsa Família* program is "a drop" of progressiveness in "a sea of regressive state" policies: although it had praiseworthy side effects such as increasing average years of schooling and life expectancy, the less than 1 percent of family income from social assistance pales by comparison to the 20 percent provided by pensions (Medeiros and Souza, 2013, 26).

Many scholars enthusiastically heralded the new social contract that emerged in Brazil in the 2000s. But this celebration was premature. As Nogueira et al. (2015, 192) demonstrate, there is scant evidence for a meaningful change in overall government social policies, once all transfers are netted out: "... the net effect of the government budget on inequality in Brazil can hardly be said to be a reflection of an effective social contract for redistribution. ... the equalizing effect of the tax-transfer system improved only slightly between 2003 and 2012." Their calculations suggest that the poorest two quintiles of the population receive 15 percent of total cash transfers, hold 12 percent of gross income, and pay 15 percent of taxes; the corresponding shares for the wealthiest quintile are 49 percent, 56 percent, and 55 percent, reproducing social inequality (Nogueira et al., 2015, 194). Most social policies still follow old corporatist patterns, with spending captured either by civil servants or formal sector workers covered by labor protections. One-third of inequality in family incomes is directly related to payments made by the state to these sectors, 95 percent of which are related to the pension system and civil service salaries (Medeiros and Souza, 2013). This significant effect does not even take into account regressive indirect taxes on consumption, whose effects on family incomes are hard to quantify, but which clearly swamp the slight progressivity of direct taxes. Although reforms to the social security system have been ongoing since the 1990s, even these very modest marginal changes have only been made possible by grandfathering in current civil servants, meaning that the regressive effect of pensions will persist for at least another generation (and probably longer, given the incrementalism of reform).[41] In sum, it is no surprise that even after all the important changes in social policy during the 1990s and 2000s, there is scant evidence of a significant improvement in income inequality: fully three-fifths of income gains went to the wealthiest income decile, while the poorest half of the population received less than one-fifth of the gains (Medeiros et al., 2015; Morgan, 2017).

THE REINFORCING NATURE OF COMPLEMENTARITIES IN FIRM LIFE

The developmental state contributes in a variety of ways to the patterns of firm structure, labor market segmentation, productivity challenges, and social inequality described in this chapter. Two effects are particularly evident: the fiscal effect, and the firm segmentation effect, which both have downstream implications for labor, productivity, and inequality. The developmentalist tool kit both necessitates a strong and large public sector and constrains the share of the budget that can be dedicated to social policy. The fiscal imperative increases the temptation to use fiscally oblique developmental policies that further exacerbate this tendency.

On the firm side, the use of the tool kit of developmentalism, with the priority given to nationally sited state and private firms, contributes to concentrating the market, especially for domestic firms, and segmenting it between foreign and domestic producers. Over time, firm-level segmentation has contributed to a clear delineation of firm characteristics, with large private-sector firms focused more on product imitation than innovation or focused on low-skill commodity exports; clusters of SOEs congregated in a few key strategic areas; and MNCs specializing in the most value added and skills-intensive fields. Segmentation in firm life has also carried over into segmentation in labor markets, with the market divided between a large pool of low-skilled, low-productivity informal workers and more highly educated civil servants and formal private sector laborers. The relationship between labor market segmentation, productivity patterns and inequality has been mutually formative: for example, inequalities in educational opportunities carry over to lower productivity and lower competitiveness in labor markets; lower competitiveness in

Complementarities in Firm Life

labor markets in turn feeds back into a lesser ability to mobilize collectively for the improvement in educational performance that might overcome labor market segmentation.

It is worth recalling that there are also important complementarities between the firm-level characteristics described in this chapter, the macro-economic variables described in Chapter 2, and the ideas used to justify public policy choices in Chapter 3. The consequences of these within-domain and cross-domain complementarities are significant. A variety of authors have described the implications of HMEs. A high concentration of corporate control is widely understood to lead to the distortion of public policies regarding innovation, capital markets, and property rights (Morck et al., 2005; Salles et al., 2017). The bifurcation of firms between MNCs in high value added industries and national oligopolies in primary production depresses research and development spending (Schneider, 2009). The returns from investing in improved human resources are insufficient, given that most national firms rely on low-skill labor and most MNCs see little to be gained from engaging in reform, since they can poach talent, and in any case, often seek to avoid the public attention that comes from mobilizing for change. Altogether, this leads to a "low-skill trap" which is very difficult to break out of (Schneider and Karcher, 2010; Doner and Schneider, 2016; Salles et al., 2017).

The most marked complementarity between the macro and micro domains is the relationship between the fiscal imperative, the absence of private credit, and the recurrent recourse to the fiscally opaque tools of the state. These consequences are all the deeper in Brazil because of the unique role of the state in what I have termed the *developmental* HME (DHME). The many levers of state control pose a potential threat to corporations; at the same time, the combination of market profits with state protections provides a number of lucrative opportunities from interaction with the state.

This places politics at the center of many business decisions.

With this in mind, Chapters 5, 6, and 7 ask: how it is that Brazilian politics structure the forms of economic organization? Why do firms acquiesce in the use of the developmentalist tool kit and even mobilize to demand state action? To what degree is the state able to perform autonomously, preserving its ability to guide firms and the economy along particular strategic paths? What explains the weakness of the Brazilian state in asserting leadership over firms rather than followership, as it seeks out its developmental goals? Alternately, what keeps the Brazilian state from discarding developmentalism altogether and moving in the direction of a neoliberal market economy? The answer, I will argue, lies in the collusive ties between political and economic elites, and the difficulty of establishing control over development strategy in a system that is democratic, and therefore subject to multiple overlapping vetoes from a variety of choke points, but lacks conventional checks and balances that might ensure a more equitable and effective use of public resources.

PART II

ECONOMIC, LEGAL, AND POLITICAL CONTROL OF THE DEVELOPMENTAL STATE

5

Coalitional Presidentialism and Defensive Parochialism

> Brazil is a country full of promises and possibilities, but it was taken by assault by interest groups that knew how to take advantage of the state for their own benefit. And they still take advantage. These groups protect themselves from competition, in an effort that tends to close the economy and inhibit efficiency.
>
> Douglass North, 2006[1]

> But Vale is a world . . .[2]
> Senator Aécio Neves, in wiretapped conversation with Joesley Batista

Incentives within the political system drive toward an equilibrium that is supportive of an ineffective developmental state and make exceedingly difficult a shift toward either a more effective developmentalism or a more liberal market economy (LME). Among the political institutions that are relevant to understanding this equilibrium, four stand out. The 1) electoral system tends to fragment political party representation. The strategy for overcoming party fragmentation has been 2) coalitional presidentialism, whereby a strong president uses a variety of tools to build coalitions that achieve a modicum of governability. Many of the 3) tools of coalition formation available to the president are derived from or facilitated by the developmental state apparatus, including appointments and fiscally opaque instruments. The fragmentation of party life, alongside the many veto players engendered by coalitional presidential system, has enabled 4) the emergence of both pluralist and corporatist forms of interest representation. The consequences of the complementarities between these four institutions are concrete: a resolute political system, in which change tends

122 *Coalitional Presidentialism*

to be slow and incremental, marked by long-term reciprocal relations between private firms and public actors, defensive parochialism, weak checks and balances generally, and more specifically, the weakness of controls on the use of the developmental state apparatus.

Together, the complementarities between these four political institutions lead to an institutional equilibrium in the political domain which I will collectively label "coalitional presidentialism." This chapter proceeds in four sections. The first offers a brief overview of the shape of federal politics, noting its fragmentation, the reliance on the developmental state to solve coalition bargaining problems, and the defensive parochialism of firm involvement in politics. The next three sections evaluate firms' participation in associational life, campaign finance donations, and illicit relations between firms and political actors, all of which contribute to reinforcing Brazil's developmental hierarchical market economy (DHME).

THE STRUCTURE OF POLITICS

The most significant trait of federal politics in democratic Brazil has been the resoluteness of policy, noted in Chapter 3. This trait has both positive and negative consequences: on the one hand, it has been hard for presidents to change policy direction quickly to resolve pressing issues decisively, yet on the other, the political system has also avoided the volatility that has plagued other countries in the region. This is not to say that nothing gets done: the high number of constitutional amendments (99), complementary laws (164), and ordinary laws (6,112) approved between the 1988 Constitution and the end of 2018 do not suggest significant institutional impasse.[3] But change tends to be incremental: the large number of potential veto players in the coalitional system has meant that even though the executive branch often gets its way, reform efforts are often diluted during proposition, in deliberation, or in execution. Further, there are certain aspects of policy that are very difficult to change: reforms to the judiciary or to the social security system have been parametric rather than paradigmatic, and certain policy arenas have proven nearly impervious to wholesale reform. In consequence, many of the most momentous changes in policymaking have been highly reactive to short-term crisis resolution rather than guided by longer-term strategy (Kingstone, 2000).

Chapter 3 suggested that political and economic elites may have little ideational motivation to substantially reform the structures of the

The Structure of Politics

developmental state. But even assuming that they should wish change, the collective action problem faced by reformers everywhere is exacerbated in the Brazilian case by at least three phenomena. The first is the fragmentation of the party system, which complicates all collective action that is not driven forward by an executive branch that has all too often been distracted by crisis management. The second is the fact that many of the tools that enable the coalitional presidential system to function are in fact reliant on the structures of the developmental state, and there is little incentive for executives who have limited tactical options for addressing the pressing demands of governance to burn their own tool kit. Finally, the equilibrium incentives for firms are far more defensive than offensive, meaning that it is far easier for firms to engage in politics to prevent change than to push a massive reform project uphill against institutional gravity.

Fragmentation and the Tool Kit of Coalition Management

Brazilian democracy's party system is recognized as one of the most fragmented anywhere, largely as a result of the use of open-list proportional representation (OLPR) in elections to the Chamber of Deputies, high district magnitudes, and coalition representation rules that preserve small parties.[4] The number of parties represented in Congress jumped from two under the military regime to eleven in 1985, fluctuated between seventeen and twenty throughout the 1990s, and then rose to twenty-eight at the 2014 election.[5] The largest party in Congress in 2016 had a mere 13 percent of all seats; and the effective number of parties in Congress was the world's highest (Melo, 2016, 65, note 14; Nicolau, 2017).[6] As of the end of 2018, the effective number of legislative parties (calculated by the Laakso-Taagepera method) stood at 16.5, up from 6.6 at the turn of the century (Almeida, 2018).

These fissiparous tendencies are partially overcome by "coalitional presidentialism," a "strategy of directly elected minority presidents to build stable majority support in fragmented legislatures" (Chaisty et al., 2018, 14). The tools of coalitional management used by minority presidents worldwide include agenda-setting powers, cabinet powers, partisan powers, budgetary authority, and informal institutions of executive-legislative exchange (Chaisty et al., 2018).

Brazil has one of the most powerful presidents in the region, especially with regard to the first three of these tools (Shugart and Carey, 1992; Payne et al., 2007, 97–8; Bonvecchi and Scartascini, 2014; Melo et al., 2014).[7]

The president's strong legislative agenda-setting powers include the ability to request accelerated deliberation of key laws, through *"urgência"* and *"urgência urgentíssima"* consideration. She may issue provisional measures, decrees that have immediate effect, and are only voted on after sixty days, which ensures that the Congress is voting on laws after they have already had an impact on the status quo that may improve their chances of approval (Figueiredo and Limongi, 1999, 2002).[8] Partly in consequence of presidential agenda power, members of Congress were responsible for drafting only about one in five laws produced between 1988 and 2010. The president's cabinet powers are also significant, with presidents typically appointing upwards of twenty ministers (reaching as many as thirty-seven under Rousseff, in addition to thousands of subministerial appointees).

The president's partisan powers are also formidable. Although parties are fairly weak in the electoral arena, fragmentation of parties in the legislative branch is partially overcome by the centralization of decision-making. The few disincentives to party-switching that existed until a court decision in 2007, and the many incentives for the creation of new parties since then, suggest that parties should be fragile and unable to faithfully represent a core set of interests.[9] The executive branch should need to bargain individually with each of the 513 deputies and 81 senators, meeting their personal needs rather than parties' broader programmatic or ideological goals. Further, the high levels of electoral competition and the weakness of parties should push legislators to try to take home budget "pork" to their constituents (Ames, 2001; Pereira and Rennó, 2001; Pereira and Mueller, 2002). Yet these worst-case scenarios did not come to pass, in part because congressional rules handed enormous power to party leaders, including the power to set and control the congressional agenda, the ability to take some votes on behalf of the entire party, and the power to decide which votes will be nominal.

These powers tend to neutralize the otherwise centrifugal incentives generated in the electoral arena, and the congressional party leader's position is therefore usually a good indicator of party members' votes (Figueiredo and Limongi, 1999, 2002).[10] Provided the president keeps the party leader onside, obtaining legislative support is not as complex as it might otherwise seem. A congressman who wishes to effectively challenge the president can only do so if he has the support of his party. Party discipline in the legislative branch has been impressive (Figueiredo and Limongi, 1999; Lima Jr., 2000; Lyne, 2005; Melo, 2006; Santos and Vilarouca, 2008; Limongi and Cortez, 2010; Rennó and Cabello, 2010;

The Structure of Politics

Braga and Pimentel Jr., 2011; Marenco and Da Ros, 2017). Legislators appear to have a core set of ideological beliefs that are relatively consistent over time and that express themselves in party voting behavior, while the party system as a whole has grown more institutionalized than it was in the 1980s (Power and Zucco, 2008, 2011; Hagopian et al., 2009; Melo and Câmara, 2012; Mainwaring et al., 2017). Congressional votes tend to follow party lines, and party alignments have proven more important than state loyalties permitting, for example, approval of difficult fiscal reforms that brought revenue back to the federal government (Almeida, 2005; Arretche, 2009; Marenco and Da Ros, 2017).

The fiscal imperative constrains the executive's ability to use budgetary authority as a central tool in coalition-building. As a consequence, although the president's budgetary authority is significant, particularly relative to Congress, executive power has tended to be used defensively, to protect against congressional profligacy, rather than offensively, to build reform coalitions (one exception is when political survival is in doubt, as in Temer's wild disbursement of budget amendments during his troubled term of office). Nonetheless, presidential budgetary powers are significant. The president is the only actor who can initiate budget or tax legislation. In practice, legislators are only able to amend the investment section of the budget law, which generally accounts for no more than 5 percent of the annual budget and is one of the few areas of discretionary executive power (Figueiredo and Limongi, 2002, 314; Praça, 2013). The executive branch actively controls the size and timing of budget outlays, and – until a 2019 constitutional amendment (see Chapter 8) – had the power to withhold outlays at will, as Congress could only authorize spending but not mandate it. Partly as a consequence of executive power, individual legislators' pursuit of pork via individual budget amendments has been less significant than feared (Figueiredo and Limongi, 2002; Vasselai and Mignozzetti, 2014).[11]

Together, these four powers help to explain Brazilian presidents' success. Presidents since 1985 have generally been able to construct legislative majorities that exceed three-fifths, and in some cases, are as high as four-fifths of Congress. The executive branch was able to obtain the support of Congress on average for four out of five legislative proposals it put forward during this period (by comparison with an average success rate near 60 percent in a sample of all existing presidential democracies between 1945 and 1999) (Cheibub et al., 2004). Because any individual legislators' action is unlikely to lead to policy change, participating in the presidential coalition is often the most effective way to further a political career. It has also enabled presidents to draw together "A to Z coalitions," incorporating parties that run the ideological gamut (Nobre, 2010). For legislators, the biggest worry may be exclusion from the currencies that make their electoral survival more likely. But this process is not a one-way street, and while a legislator who wants to change public policy must perforce participate in government, once they are in the coalition, legislators also have significant leverage over the content of legislation and policy.

Said another way, the first four tools fail to eliminate uncertainty in coalition bargaining. The president's agenda-setting powers ensure that the president controls the content of the agenda under deliberation, but this only gives the executive branch control over the topics under discussion, not the content of amendments or the ultimate disposition of reform. The complex legislative process, with its various arenas of deliberation and multiple choke holds on proposals, combined with the Congress' "appetite for amending proposals," means that "executive proposals do not pass unscarred by Congress" or without "arduous" bargaining (Hiroi and Rennó, 2016). The president's cabinet powers help to ensure that allies are committed to the overall success of the coalition, but it does not necessarily guarantee their commitment to programmatic objectives. The president's partisan powers are strong when voting takes place, but these powers do not permit the president to control the amendments that are offered and there is always space for holdouts to bargain for last-minute leverage, often to disastrous effect. The combination of the fiscal imperative and the fissiparous party system, which could lead to costly bargaining, means that the president has been reluctant to use budgetary authority as a regular coalition management tool.

The uncertainty that therefore remains even after the first four tools have been used has pushed both executive and legislative actors to resort to informal, unwritten mechanisms of exchange as the solution to the problem of coalitional coordination.[12] Brazil is a textbook case of the exchange of favors necessitated by larger and more fragmented coalitions. Longtime congressman Roberto Cardoso Alves was once asked why he supported the Sarney government's quest to extend the presidential term to five years. He replied, "*é dando que se recebe*," or roughly, "it's by giving that one receives" (Folha, 1996). Proving the point, Alves went on to become a minister in the Sarney administration, and the phrase has remained in the popular lexicon as shorthand for the horse-trading that helps to explain how coalition politics works. Surveys of Brazilian legislators conducted by Chaisty et al. (2018) show that over 90 percent of

The Structure of Politics

legislators agree with the statement that "coalitional presidentialism leads to a style of politics based on the exchange of favors," the highest result of the ten coalitional presidential systems surveyed and three times higher than Chile.[13] Evidence from congressional votes suggest that the spoils of executive power are at least as relevant as ideology in determining roll call behavior (Zucco and Lauderdale, 2011, 365).

The phenomenon of favor-exchange is perhaps best captured by the fact that for much of the past generation one of Brazil's largest parties, and the third pole between the PT and the PSDB in the partisan balance that prevailed from 1994 to 2018, was the amorphous and hydra-headed Party of the Brazilian Democratic Movement (PMDB). The PMDB and some other supporting parties position themselves strategically in the ideological middle, united more than anything else by a willingness to participate in the government of the day (Melo and Câmara, 2012, 73).[14] The ideological malleability of these center parties – the PMDB has found a way to participate in governments run by presidents of the right and left, without exception – led Nobre (2010) to argue that Brazilian politics is marked by PMDB-ization (*pemedebização*), driven by the guiding principle of obtaining coalition goods. Individual legislators have a very hard time obtaining public attention as proactive agenda-setters, since they cannot push legislation through Congress without the tools of coalition management available to the president. Many thus prefer to join the executive branch coalition and use some combination of the individual favors noted here to advance their careers. The notion of *pemedebização* captures a recurring theme of political life: the possibility that crucial players may be motivated less by ideology than by avarice and enabled by executives' willingness to exchange favors for programmatic legislative reforms.

These patterns also mean that checks and balances between the executive and legislative branches are weaker than needed to make the exchange of favors efficient and effective. For at their most basic, the incentives in the system are such that legislators have little electoral reason to call for more effective oversight, and executives seldom desire greater transparency about their bargains with legislators. Later sections of this chapter and Chapter 6 will detail how the interwoven alliances inherent to the Brazilian coalitional presidential system tend to undermine or dilute incipient efforts at control and oversight that are key to improving development outcomes. For now, it is enough to simply flag an argument that underlies much of the next two chapters: checks and balances are weak in Brazil. This position, of course, runs directly counter to the influential works of Melo and Pereira (2013) and Alston et al. (2016), who suggest that the trajectory established by the 1988 Constitution strengthened both the beliefs undergirding democratic inclusiveness, and the institutions of checks and balances themselves. The implication that they derive is that this trajectory is contributing to a critical transition toward economic and political openness and to the emergence of a new and more sustainable development path (Alston et al., 2016, 7, 173). While this argument is normatively attractive, and there is no reason to disagree with them that organizations such as Congress and the courts have gained budgetary and human capacity since 1988, there is simply not much evidence to sustain the view that checks and balances have functioned as desired, much less that lackluster interbranch oversight is driving an equilibrium shift or a move to a new development trajectory. Indeed, the evidence instead points to the possibility that checks and balances have remained weak, at least in part because strong checks and balances would not align easily with the preferences and behaviors of key actors in the other complementary institutional realms detailed in this book.

Executive dominance combined with the ideological diversity of presidential coalitions and the internal heterogeneity of major parties tends to move conflict inside the government. Much of the drama in federal politics over the past generation has played out not so much between incumbents and opposition, or between the executive and legislative branches, as between warring factions within the incumbent administration. A central reason for this intramural instability is well summarized by the expression "*criando dificuldades para vender facilidades*," roughly "creating difficulties so as to be able to sell solutions." Coalition members have everything to be gained by staying in the coalition, but nothing to be gained by appearing too committed to it. The jealousies that arise as a consequence mean that internecine bickering is usually more important than external oversight; as Balán (2011) has shown, many corruption scandals emerge less from checks from outside the coalition than from denunciation from within the coalition.[15]

If horizontal checks and balances are weak, vertical accountability by voters offers little compensating accountability, undermined as it is by the combination of large, state-wide electoral districts and OLPR. Together, these electoral rules generate an immense number of candidates from an expanding number of parties, while undermining the possibility of oversight. Most deputies are elected on the coattails of celebrity politicians: fewer than 10 percent of deputies are elected with enough votes of their own to fulfill the electoral quotient.[16] This undermines voter recall –

The Structure of Politics

surveys show that very few voters recall their choice of deputy – only 12.5 percent of voters surveyed in the 1990s remembered who they had voted for in the previous election (Nicolau, 2002) – and dilutes the responsiveness of politicians to any particular electoral constituency, a process that may have accelerated in the 2010s (Hagopian, 2016). There is considerable path dependency to these complementary rules: presidents have little desire to shift patterns of coalition management that may have permitted them to overcome the fissiparous party system, and members of Congress have little desire to change the electoral rules that got them elected or the informal coalition bargaining that may help them get reelected.

Coalitional Presidentialism and the Developmental Tool Kit

Coalitional presidential systems typically use four currencies for the exchange of favors: election-related funds, privileged treatment for legislators' businesses, slush funds, and appointment to influential positions (Chaisty et al., 2018, 191–2). All four are used extensively in Brazil. Election-related funds, including both official and unofficial campaign donations, may be channeled by party leaders and brokers within the executive branch. Many legislators represent particular sectoral interests and advocate for them directly in Congress, allowing presidents to provide privileged treatment to particular business sectors. Slush funds make repeated appearances in recent Brazilian history, including the alleged payments used to obtain support for Cardoso's reelection amendment as well as the payments that apparently kept Lula's small-party allies onboard during the *mensalão* scheme. Finally, the appointment power of the president is ample, covering at least 7,000 positions and extending to influence over promotions and nominations in more than 22,000 federal executive branch positions, as well as state-owned firms and banks (Bersch et al., 2017a, 2017b).

The fiscal opaqueness of the developmental state both makes the use of these currencies possible and is sustained by them. In a context of limited investment budgets, which make it difficult for presidents to build infrastructure projects in key legislators' districts, and a demanding fiscal imperative, which does not permit significant budgetary outlays to benefit particular legislators, presidents have resorted to these four currencies to attract supporters. State companies' pension funds, state-owned enterprises (SOEs), and state banks help bind together the coalition, by providing the president access to fiscally opaque policy tools that are not available in the very small proportion of the budget that is discretionary. Loans to particular sectors, or privileged tax treatment, are some of the more legitimate opaque tools made possible by the developmental state. Slush funds may also be funded out of either illicit activities in SOEs or murkily channeled public procurement. The wide range of possible appointments is a source of both licit gains for politicians – e.g., the goodwill from having an ally's friend nominated to a prestigious agency – as well as illicit income, such as bribes passed up the bureaucratic ladder (e.g., the Correios scandal that triggered the *mensalão*).

An example may illustrate how the weakness of checks and balances, and the importance of the developmental tool kit to coalition formation, drive Brazil toward an equilibrium that makes little sense from the perspective of conventional understandings of how the three independent branches of government should function. In May 2017, wiretaps were released by prosecutors seeking the suspension of Senator Aécio Neves from the Senate. The wiretaps detailed a conversation two months earlier between the head of the JBS meatpacking behemoth, Joesley Batista, and Senator Neves, of the PSDB party. The two men discuss the appointment of the president of Vale, the ostensibly private-sector mining conglomerate, with Batista asking Neves to nominate his desired candidate, Aldemir Bendine, the former president of Banco do Brasil and Petrobras, who had been accused of corruption by plea bargaining Odebrecht executives. Neves responds that he unfortunately cannot meet Batista's wishes, since he has already put forward a candidate to be Vale's new president, but that he could find Bendine a position as a director of Vale. After all, as he noted in the epigraph at the outset of the chapter, Vale "is a world," presumably referring to the world of possible appointments the firm can provide.

There are so many strange things about this conversation that make no sense without reference to the intertwined logic of coalitional presidentialism in a developmental state. Why is a private-sector meatpacking billionaire interested in the appointment of a former public bank president to head a private sector mineral firm? Why would it make sense for him to approach, and pay bribes to, a senator to accomplish this? Why would a PSDB senator ever acquiesce to appoint Bendine, who, in addition to facing credible charges of corruption, also had headed up the state-owned Banco do Brasil under the presidential administration of the PSDB's archrival, the Workers' Party?

This pattern of politics makes a nonsense of conventional understandings of checks and balances. It is also exemplary of a suboptimal,

Government Relations in Brazil

inefficient equilibrium that drives up the cost of politics; dilutes policy initiatives; requires costly side payments; obfuscates the real justifications for policy choices; and may diminish public support for democracy, by undercutting public confidence in the probity of policy deliberations. But there are many reasons it survives: the system provides key interest groups with defenses against policy change; provides executives with support in a fissiparous party system; provides legislative incumbents with powerful resources for political survival; and enables incumbent firms to outcompete their rivals or potential rivals. The remainder of this chapter fleshes out the dynamics of the interaction between the economic and political spheres, which is carried out through government relations, campaign finance, and illicit transactions.

GOVERNMENT RELATIONS IN BRAZIL

There are many motivations that drive firms into the messy business of politics: pursuit of firm-specific advantage and profit; neutralizing or containing harmful government policies; obtaining information that might provide a competitive edge; or improving national conditions and the overall business environment. All of these efforts can be subsumed under the overall category of "lobbying" or "government relations."[17] The segmented nature of Brazilian firm life means that firms of different sorts – privately held Brazilian firms, MNCs, and SOEs – are all involved in the political effort, with a plethora of motivations and strategic calculations across the menagerie of corporate life. However, the segmentation of firm life in a context of significant party fragmentation also suggests that firms are able to use their influence in a primarily defensive manner to preserve their parochial or sectoral interests against threatening legislation.

There are two broad schools of thought on firms' role in Brazilian politics. The first sets out from Schmitter's highly influential analysis of Brazil's state corporatism (Schmitter, 1971) to argue that collective action by businesses in Brazil is likely to be anemic.[18] As Schneider (2013) notes, economy-wide peak associations in Brazil are extremely weak by comparison to their peers elsewhere in the region, such as the very strong national associations in Mexico and Chile. Longstanding corporatist structures ensure the continuity of stodgy old industry associations such as the nationwide industrial confederation, CNI (*Confederação Nacional da Indústria*). Over time, the overrepresentation of both small states and small firms within the CNI – mandated by corporatist statutes – undermined the CNI's ability to represent core segments of industry and to effectively intermediate member interests (Kingstone, 1999, 130; Schneider, 2004, 16, 94–5). Yet the CNI received significant public funding through compulsory worker contributions, which ensured its staying power despite its rather weak representativeness.[19] Such support enabled corporatist-inspired organizations that had been created in the 1940s to impede efforts to build alternative institutional spaces (Kingstone, 1999; Schneider, 2004, 96–7, 125). While the Federação das Indústrias do Estado de São Paulo (FIESP) emerged as a powerful alternative institution by the 1980s, it too suffered from corporatist distortions, such as the overrepresentation of small and medium firms (Kingstone, 1999, 130; Schneider, 2004, 95). Meanwhile, the porosity of the government bureaucracy to business and policymakers' willingness to include business representatives on government coordinating bodies meant that there were few incentives for businesspeople to invest in developing collective organizations, particularly peak associations (Cardoso, 1975; Schneider, 2004, 96; 2013, 16).

A second school of thought emphasizes industry's effectiveness in achieving its parochial objectives, as well as its ability to move beyond individual firm interests to actually push a collective agenda (Mancuso and Oliveira, 2006; Kasahara, 2011). The increased openness of the Brazilian economy since the late 1980s brought in new multinational actors, loosened the dominance of SOEs, and also incentivized some associations to push for sectoral relief. Drawing on the experience of the business response to trade opening in the 1990s, for example, Mancuso (2007) discusses the creation of the *Coalizão Empresarial Brasileira* (CEB), centered around improving the competitiveness of the business environment and pushing a broad agenda focused on reducing the so-called "*custo Brasil*" (the cost of doing business in Brazil). Diniz (2010, 108) emphasizes business' willingness to exert influence on Congress in favor of reform, while Mancuso (2004, 516) notes the huge investment that even the CNI has made in monitoring government actions, including by building an office in Brasília that can accompany congressional initiatives, analyze legislation, adopt policy strategies, and orient and pressure legislators. Partly as a consequence of this effort, Mancuso (2004, 526, 530) argues that industry has had enormous sway over legislation, helped along by its strong ties to the executive branch.[20]

Synthesizing the two schools' perspectives suggests that since the return to democracy, Brazil has been marked by the existence of a hybrid two-track system of "modified corporatism," whereby firms are able to access

Government Relations in Brazil 133

government both via corporatist structures and more pluralist paths (Diniz and Boschi, 2000; Thomas, 2009, 19–22; Gozetto and Thomas, 2014, 223).[21] Firms have not been entirely incapable of collective action, but such collective action has largely been focused on addressing the *custo Brasil* or on narrow sectoral matters.

Business actors have become savvy about using both extant corporatist channels as well as new, more plural associations in tandem. Kasahara (2011) provides a vivid example of this phenomenon, describing how financial institutions banded together during the military regime to create an alternative to the stodgy old corporatist association in banking, Fenaban. In the transition period, Fenaban and the new voluntary association, Febraban, merged. But small banks and international banks felt marginalized, and a broader National Confederation of Financial Institutions (CNF) was formed to represent the entire sector during the debate over the 1988 Constitution, operating as an arm of the industrial federation CNI. Big Brazilian banks could thus employ either the somewhat more parochial Febraban or the broader, but more reactive, CNF to lobby Congress. In the late 1980s, however, the STF refused to hear constitutional challenges from the banks, arguing that neither the Febraban nor the CNF had standing as nationwide associations (a requirement for filing a constitutionality suit known as a Direct Action of Unconstitutionality, or ADIn). A National Confederation of the Financial System (CONSIF) was hastily created – sharing the mailing address of the CNF – and obtained standing in the STF, enabling it to file more than twenty constitutional suits against state and federal laws affecting the banking sector in the ensuing two decades (Kasahara, 2011, 212). In sum, old state-created corporatist structures were replaced by newer voluntary associations, which then reorganized themselves in neo-corporatist fashion to access the courts, which provided them with a defensive veto point within the political system.

The complex landscape provides a wide menu of venue shopping possibilities for banks to influence policymakers. In the wake of the Real Plan, banks lost their seats on the state National Monetary Council (CMN). But they have been effective at building close relationships with individual bureaucrats within the CMN, the Central Bank, and the Comissão de Valores Mobiliários (CVM), Brazil's securities and exchange commission. They have been able to offer collective opinions when these agencies hold sporadic public consultations on impending policy changes. Banks may also lobby Congress either via pluralist associations such as Febraban[22] or corporatist associations like CNI and may be able to utilize their neo-corporatist representative body CONSIF to bring constitutional cases before the STF. Banks acting individually are also large campaign contributors, with the ability to influence individual politicians, and several prominent bankers have run for legislative office in recent years.

"Modified corporatism" thus takes advantage of the diverse venues available to firms in the more pluralistic world of the democratic regime to create multiple paths for either firm-level or collective-sectoral action. Multiple studies show the capacity of firms to use access to veto points across the three branches of government to neuter or dilute regulatory oversight by agencies such as ANVISA, ANEEL, ANAC, ANS, and banking authorities (e.g., Kasahara, 2011; Baird, 2012; Batista, 2012; Baird and Fernandes, 2014; Scheffer and Bahia, 2015; Schapiro and Taylor, 2020). Firms often pick and choose from among a variety of strategies that incorporate narrow firm interests as well as broader sectoral concerns. The first category includes the set of tools most akin to the rent-seeking (but not necessarily illegal) behaviors North described in the epigraph, focused on building individual connections between firm leaders and policymakers to achieve the narrowest and most parochial of objectives, through private lobbying and campaign finance contributions.

The second category includes efforts to nominate sectoral leaders to ministries, participation in pluralist private sector associations or their corporatist counterparts, organization of parliamentary fronts, and other efforts to build relationships with particular political leaders. The so-called parliamentary fronts (*frentes parlamentares*) are "lobbies constituted institutionally within Congress," which register any group that can bring together 195 legislators, and they are often more powerful than individual political parties on specific sectoral issues (Santos, 2007, 338). For example, the rural grouping, known informally as the *bancada ruralista*, has a lock on the agriculture and rural policy committee in the Chamber, and has often played an important role in selecting personnel in the Agriculture Ministry, as well as pushing for policies such as agricultural debt renegotiations (Santos, 2007, 338–45).[23] Because of its power, the *bancada* is able to attract campaign donations that maintain influential members in office; it also has ensured that the bancada could rewrite the Forestry Law in a self-serving fashion, against and over the objections of some members of the executive branch (Cunha and Mello-Théry, 2017). Another One of the largest bancadas, traditionally, has been the *bancada empresarial*, of deputies acting on behalf of business (DIAP, 2011).[24]

Sectoral influence is often advanced through efforts to build relationships with congressional leaders, such as committee chairs and party leaders, so as to ensure that policy change is not detrimental to firm interests. Schneider (2013, 144; citing surveys by Yadav 2011) argues that businesses in Brazil are far more likely to seek to influence individual legislators than their peers in India, who prefer to lobby party leaders. The fragmentation of the party system in the proportional representative system provides many avenues for access to legislative influence, including from individual legislators who may be able to wield veto power individually, or provide access to information about proposals that may be of interest to firms. Yet my analysis of campaign finance data from 2014 (later in this chapter) shows that congressional leaders were also the recipients of a disproportionate share of donations (more than ten times the average), suggesting that firms strategically court congressional leaders, knowing that either through control of party votes or through control of committees, they may be able to control the legislative agenda (see also Santos, 2007).[25]

Models of hierarchical capitalism suggest that different firms will have different incentive structures, with the consequence that they face distinct constraints and therefore may choose different mixes of the options and venues described above. MNCs, for example, have internal constraints that influence their government relations strategies. Organizationally, for example, many MNCs have their top government affairs officials in Brasília report to corporate officers in the headquarters country rather than to the chief operating officer in Brazil.[26] In terms of their external relations with government, MNCs are often treated differently by policymakers, either because of legal rules or simply because of policymakers' innate preference for domestic firms. As a Brazilian executive at an MNC told me, when an MNC officer meets with Brazilian government officials, "you are received differently." Multinationals thus engage in a great deal of effort to "mimic" local firms, pointing to their decades of work in Brazil, the number of jobs they produce in the country, the amount they contribute to Brazilian exports, and so forth. But at heart, the central difference may be a difference in trust: by their very nature, executives in MNCs turn over frequently, and there is no single point of contact who remains in the job for decades and can therefore provide personal credibility to long-term arrangements with political figures (although corporate lawyers and other local staff may partially fulfill that function). On the demand side, too, MNCs tend to be bad collective actors, since they are globally mobile, and may not see much gain from lobbying for broader collective goals in any given market (Doner and Schneider, 2016). As the president of one leading multinational commodity producer responded when I asked whether he was concerned about the overvalued exchange rate at the time, "as long as all my competitors [in Brazil] are facing the same rate, why should I worry?"

Brazilian firms (particularly family-held firms) are led by top executives who may have decades-long ties to Brasília, and thereby develop "symbiotic" relations with the government that may be shaped by a shared ideology as well as shared social ties. Together, these ties help to build trust about long-term exchanges, allow for "give and take" in their relations, and generate a willingness to tolerate some short-term losses imposed by the government in exchange for longer-term gains.[27] Also relevant is the fact that global issues outside Brazil are less relevant to most Brazilian firms than in-country issues. Over time, this may lead Brazilian firms to side with the government on many policy issues and otherwise seek to build goodwill in reciprocal, long-term relations; sometimes this manifests as a desire not to "rock the boat," even if this means passively swallowing policy choices by the state that undermine the firm's short-term interests.

Institutionally, these different incentives also mean very different possibilities for government relations. MNCs will face unique constraints – for example, the prospect of Foreign Corrupt Practices Act (FCPA) enforcement actions in the United States in response to their dealings in Brasília[28] – but they will also be able to engage in a "multipronged approach" to lobbying, bringing pressure to bear in both foreign jurisdictions as well as Brazil (Judd, 2011, 24). One powerful example is Advamed, an association of medical device manufacturers based in Washington, which responded to increasingly worrisome regulations in Brazil by pressuring the US government for succor. This led the US Department of Commerce to convene a conference in Brasília in 2009 to discuss trade issues, even as Advamed worked through Brazilian associations so as to present a "Brazilian face" (Judd, 2011).

Associational life is also very different for distinct types of firms. In many sectors, there are associations of foreign firms, which have an interest in intellectual property and harmonizing legislation across cross-jurisdictional boundaries, or simply increasing bilateral trade with a particular country (e.g., the Brazilian-American Chamber of Commerce). Similarly, there are many associations of national firms, such as the FIESP and CNI. Many multinationals may participate in both domestic and foreign associations but, generally speaking, their role in domestic industry associations is often limited. Meanwhile, their participation in associations of foreign firms tends to be limited to very specific sectoral issues (e.g., trade regulation) that do little to change broader patterns of economic policymaking in the Brazilian economy. Finally, as the next section illustrates, campaign finance contributions by foreign firms are limited by law.

Together, these factors mean that the overall ability and willingness of MNCs to effect change through associational lobbying is more limited than that of domestic firms. The long-term horizons of large national firms, meanwhile, may make them less willing to rock the boat in their relations with government officials, especially on issues of national salience, exacerbating the tendency away from collective action and toward the reactive defense of parochial firm interests.

CAMPAIGN FINANCE

As in many democracies, another way to ensure that firm interests are heard is through corporate campaign finance. The significance of this tool is well illustrated by the meatpacking giant JBS, which donated more than R$300 million during the 2014 campaign (US$112 million at the year-end exchange rate). Its co-owner, Joesley Batista, noted that donations brought the "empathy" of politicians when it came time to resolve the firm's problems. Batista's perks included unscheduled meetings with the president, weekly meetings with ministers, and the approval of laws helpful to JBS' interests (Rizzo and Velasco, 2018, 197). Corporate donations were permitted up until 2015, when the STF banned them.[29]

Campaign finance donations may be driven by pragmatic motivation to support parties, the risk of policy change, and ideological commitment (McMenamin, 2012). In Brazil, firms have high levels of pragmatic motivation. Although ideological commitments are generally low, the combination of pragmatic motivation to support particular politicians and fear of prejudicial policy change have contributed to comparatively high levels of political contributions by international standards. Campaign finance donations may serve business by providing a useful hedge against policy volatility, and potentially even offer important economic gains. But politicians also provide a number of services beyond simply vetoing inconvenient initiatives or providing access to public contracts. Donations may enable firms to more closely accompany hearings in the political sphere, discuss rule changes with key legislators, find advocates during public hearings, and provide support to particular appointees (Scheffer and Bahia, 2011).

Campaign finance everywhere suffers from the problem of credible commitment: nothing guarantees that a donation today will be reciprocated in future, especially because the tacit bargain underlying a donation cannot be legally registered as a contract, and both sides may have different understandings of what the other seeks to gain, which cannot be recorded or clarified without placing both sides in legal jeopardy (Wood, 2001; Iversen, 2005; McMenamin, 2012). This has been partially addressed in Brazil through two mechanisms. On the donor side, privately owned firms may be able to develop long-term relationships with particular politicians. On the party side, it is frequent around the world to have senior members of the government who may be able to convince firms that they are "involved in a stable and mutually beneficial reciprocal exchange" (McMenamin, 2012, 27). Such senior brokers have loomed large in Brazil, including P.C. Farias under Collor, Sérgio Motta under Cardoso, and José Dirceu and Antonio Palocci under Lula and Rousseff. There have been important brokers within smaller parties as well, such as José Janene in the PP and Roberto Jefferson in the PTB, who may serve a "fiduciary role," guaranteeing to donors that somebody is communicating their contributions and needs to the relevant powers that be (Abranches, 2016).

There is little question that campaign finance has been an integral tool of government affairs between 1985 and 2018. In the 2014 elections, nine in ten *reais* donated for pursuit of federal office came from corporate donations. These donations were in addition to public funding of parties (*Fundo Partidário*), free airtime for campaign advertisements (*horário gratuito de propaganda eleitoral*, HGPE), and individual donations. All of these expenditures together meant that in comparative terms, even if when we restrict our focus only to legal contributions – which are only part of the overall picture – Brazilian elections have been quite expensive.

The comparison in Table 5.1 is not intended in any way to suggest that the United States should be a benchmark for Brazil on electoral law and campaign finance regulation: in many ways, Brazil's electoral system is far more uniform nationally, better able to address voting fraud allegations, and more transparent when dealing with reported official donations than the fragmented and impenetrable US system. But it is illustrative that Brazil's expenditures have exceeded those of a democracy that is far richer and a third more populous.

Campaign Finance

TABLE 5.1 *Comparing the cost of US and Brazilian public election expenditures*

	Brazil[30]	US[31]	% difference
Free airtime (HGPE)	R$25.9 billion	-	-
Campaign expenditures (national)	R$4.7–R$5.9 billion	US$8.6 billion	-
Fundo Partidário	R$1.2 billion	-	-
Total in local currency	R$32.4 billion	US$8.6 billion	-
At year-end exchange rates[32]	US$15 billion	US$8.6 billion	+74%
At purchasing power parity	US$24.1 billion	US$8.6 billion	+180%

Source: Author, with data on the United States courtesy of Anna Petherick.

A second telling data point from Table 5.1 is the extent to which the Brazilian state has been a primary financier of party politics – contributing more than 80 percent of the cost of campaigns through the HGPE and *Fundo Partidário*. This proportion may have been even higher, given that the state provided fiscal incentives, such as tax breaks to parties, that are very difficult to quantify (Campos, 2009). Naturally, parties write the laws on electoral finance, which may explain why public funding is as significant as it is. This tends to reinforce the power of extant parties, but it also has generated incentives (especially after a court decision blocking party switching), for politicians to start new parties, further fragmenting the party system. At the end of the day, though, because the public funds are provided on relatively even conditions across all parties, private donations are often the key to obtaining a competitive edge over other parties or over candidates from one's own party.

Supply and Demand in Campaign Finance

What drives Brazil's comparatively large campaign expenditure? On the demand side, politicians in Brazil are motivated by a number of factors. Weak parties, which are riven by intraparty competition under OLPR and historically have been further weakened in the electoral realm by the possibility of party switching, have meant that the party brand requires extensive reinforcement and candidates are driven to augment their personal vote (Samuels, 2002; Boas et al., 2014). There are strong incentives to nationalize parties early in their existence to ensure access to the free airtime that is only available to parties with congressional candidates; doing so requires money (Speck and Campos, 2014). Free airtime may drive candidates to produce expensively produced campaign jingles and materials that stand out in a crowded field. Public funds are allocated to parties, rather than candidates, encouraging individual candidates to boost their own individual collections in order to compete with internal rivals (Speck, 2013, 52).

The huge magnitude of electoral districts in congressional races, where the district is the entire state and each party may field 1.5 times as many candidates as there are positions to fill, discourages parties from significantly limiting the number of candidates, driving up campaign costs (Samuels, 2001). Given flexible rules on intraparty transfers, candidates may build goodwill by transferring campaign funds to other candidates and their party apparatus, encouraging them to over-collect (Mancuso and Speck, 2014, 138). Political finance rules were designed under the authoritarian regime, for a context of limited political competition (Speck, 2013, 47). Although they have been considerably strengthened since the impeachment of Fernando Collor for flaunting then-existing bans on corporate finance (Speck, 2010),[33] the sky was virtually the limit on corporate contributions until the 2015 high court decision banning them. While campaigns must set their own ceiling on campaign expenditures, as Speck (2010) notes, this was akin to each driver setting their own speed limit. Further, although firm donations were capped at 2 percent of gross revenue and individuals are still capped at 10 percent of income, these limits were not terribly constraining for large firms or wealthy individuals. Critically, politicians believe that higher campaign expenditures affect the vote, and there is solid evidence that the more money a candidate collects, the better their chances of election (Speck, 2010); candidates elected in the 2002 and 2006 elections spent nearly five times as much as those who were not elected (Lemos et al., 2010, 388). In sum, candidates who wish to win office know that they must find money to make it possible. One consequence has been an "arms race" in campaign spending, as Avelino et al. (2017) have demonstrated by comparing the campaign expenditures per vote in elections since the turn of the century (Table 5.2).

On the supply side, there are two dimensions useful for characterizing donations. Are donors behaving ideologically, seeking public goods, or are they acting pragmatically, in pursuit of private goods? Second, do donors seek reciprocal exchanges, in which donor contributions and government actions are "separately performed and the terms are unstated

Campaign Finance

TABLE 5.2 *Campaign expenditure per vote (in R$ of December 2016)*

Position	2002	2006	2010	2014	Change 2002–14
Deputy	6.65	9.59	17.98	18.20	174%
Senator	2.22	3.53	5.19	6.95	213%
President	1.25	3.58	4.80	9.52	661%

Source: Author, from data in Avelino et al. (2017).

and uncertain," or discrete exchanges, which are "explicit and simultaneous" (McMenamin, 2012, 7)?

Although there is a widespread assumption that campaign finance violations have been widespread in Brazil, the electoral courts and some other accountability institutions work sufficiently well that in most cases of official donations (*caixa um*), actors would be foolhardy to seek discrete rather than reciprocal exchanges. The story may be quite different when it comes to illegal donations (*caixa dois*), but in the legal market for donations, most signs point to reciprocity, in the absence of direct evidence of discrete exchange.

However, the evidence also suggests that there is a substantial link between contributions in one particular electoral cycle and subsequent government behavior. The relevance of the government in providing corporate finance, in particular, may enhance the gravitational pull of the political realm on corporate leaders. Scholars have found that campaign contributions are associated with cheaper loans; that BNDES loans are correlated with betting on the right candidate; that investments financed by BNDES loans tend to be allocated to municipalities run by coalition allies; and that donations do not determine whether firms get preferential loans from the BNDES, but donations to winning candidates do increase the amount of loans received and donations to winners have been found to increase government contracts, with returns fourteen to thirty-nine times the average contribution (Claessens et al., 2008; Boas et al., 2014; Musacchio and Lazzarini, 2014, 271; Bandeira-de-Mello, 2015; Lazzarini et al., 2015). There is also some evidence of a correlation between donations and tax benefits, although it is difficult to establish causality (Gonçalves, 2012).

Without any demerit to the impressive scholarship cited, it is important to note that many reciprocal exchanges may have been quite long-term, extending beyond a single electoral cycle.[34] The relationship between construction firms and politicians, for example, dates back to the early days of the military regime, and perhaps even to the Kubitschek's construction of Brasília in the 1950s (Pedreira Campos, 2014). A particular political comparative advantage of private domestic firms is that they may have the ability to "bear an extended and consequential grudge" over the long-term and commit credibly to hurting those who cross them (Schneider, 2013, 148). More positively, their long horizons may allow them to invest in particular politicians' long-term career success in ways that pay diffuse but potentially significant dividends. The result is that there has been a certain endogeneity to campaign finance, because it is so historically embedded. For example, firms may give to parties that have controlled particular ministries responsible for public spending in their sectors; knowing this, parties may seek out those ministries during coalition negotiations over appointments.

Who Donates?

As for the pursuit of public versus private goods, donor characteristics provide some clues. The 2014 elections are a particularly critical case because they were the first since 2002 in which the Workers' Party's hold on the presidency was in serious question. A year before the election, two-thirds of voters expressed a desire for Rousseff to change policy direction, and although she continued to lead in the polls, there were signs that the election would go to a second round that would be too close to call (O Estado de S. Paulo, 2013; Rodrigues, 2013).[35] The election thus provides a good case of the logic of campaign donations under significant competition, both at the presidential level, as well as in the congressional and senatorial races that would determine the composition of the governing coalition. The competitiveness of the election is perhaps best seen in the scale of spending in the presidential race, which almost doubled from 2010 to 2014 in real terms (Table 5.2).

The election was also significant because it took place against the backdrop of the most consequential investigation of corruption since the return to democracy, the Lava Jato case, which, beginning early in 2014, began to air significant allegations of corruption and campaign finance violations. The shock of the investigation may have led firms who were behaving illegally (and thus aware that the allegations had merit) to move donations from illegal channels back into formal electoral channels that could be tracked.

Many of the patterns in campaign donations seen during 2014 confirm those of past elections. Figure 5.1 demonstrates that private firms were the

Campaign Finance

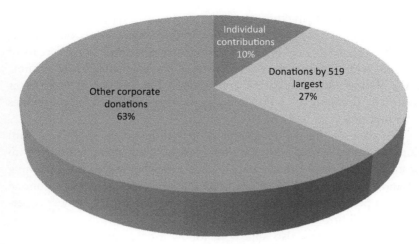

FIGURE 5.1 Source of donations to federal candidates, 2014 election.
Source: TSE data, compiled by author.

primary source of funding in the 2014 elections (Mancuso and Speck, 2014, 2015; Mancuso, 2015). However, most of Brazil's largest firms did not actually contribute: of the 519 largest firms and banks analyzed in Chapter 4, 71 percent, or 370 firms, did not register any donations with the TSE.

Despite this relatively low official participation rate, large firm donors still accounted for a remarkably high percentage of total private electoral finance. Large firms made up less than 3 percent of the donor pool, but they accounted for 27 percent of total contributions, and each of their single contributions was more than fifteen times greater than the average contributions made by other corporate donors. Large firm donations were also more fungible, since they gave predominantly to parties and campaign committees (72 percent of the total value of their contributions, as opposed to 36 percent from smaller donors), which permitted the parties to reallocate revenues as needed to support competitive candidates.

Who were these large donors? Given the high share of MNCs among the top firms in Brazil, and limits on donations by foreigners, it is perhaps not surprising that so few large firms donated to elections.[36] Meanwhile, 36 percent of the 325 Brazilian-controlled large firms donated. Among large firm donors, fully 73 percent were privately held, and only 27 percent were publicly traded firms. This suggests that private firms may be particularly interested in seeking influence and access, or less beholden to shareholders when making campaign donations. When they donated, however, publicly held firms gave nearly three times more, on average, than their privately held peers, suggesting strategic aims. Three sectors of business with strong sectoral concentration had particularly high proportions of large firm donations: construction (68 percent of large firms recorded donations), pulp and paper (71 percent), and textiles (100 percent).

The data on formal campaign contributions show that large firm donors had a strongly pro-incumbent bias, confirming findings from past elections (Lemos et al., 2010). Their contributions to the governing PT and its allies in the PMDB were higher than those by small firm donors: while 32 percent of donations by large firms went to the PT, only 19.5 percent of small firm donors gave to the PT.

The contributions also appear to follow a defensive logic of incumbency. Principal component analysis of donations from the largest firms demonstrates that donations were clustered in four groups:

1) *core parties* were heavily financed, accounting for two-thirds (67.3 percent) of the total value of contributions by large firms. Not surprisingly, the three core parties in this cluster held the presidency iteratively, with only one interruption, between 1985 and 2018: the PMDB, the PSDB, and the PT. It is important to note that the PSDB was out of office in 2014, so donations to it were likely seeking a hedge against change;

2) *supporting parties* were the second most well-financed, accounting for 19 percent of contributions. All four supporting parties were important allies to incumbents throughout the democratic period, although they come from different segments of the ideological spectrum: DEM on the right, PSB on the center-left, and PP and PSD at center. Interestingly, many of the donors to these supporting parties were also donating to the core parties, suggesting a hedging strategy;

3) *satellite parties*, which were usually part of larger congressional blocs because they were individually quite small, even though they had some ideological consistency. These parties vary from the PCdoB on the left to the PRB on the right, and accounted for 9.9 percent of donations; and

4) *nano-parties*, which had far fewer contributions – only 0.3 percent of large firm contributions by value – perhaps because they are either had little or no track record (PRP) or appealed to a very narrow ideological segment of the population (PSTU).

Overall contributions seemed to follow a pragmatic strategy. Firms gave to parties across the political spectrum, but privileged the three most central parties and, then, their midsized coalition allies. The pragmatism of the approach, though, is complemented by hedging that may be aimed at ensuring access to alternate veto players. On average, firms spread their donations among candidates for federal deputy and to parties more than they did in campaigns for the Senate and presidency. Using a Herfindahl-Hirschman index, where 1 would represent a firm giving all of its money to a single candidate, the firm average concentration was deputies (0.55), parties (0.64), senators (0.82), and president (0.93). This seems to be in line with the strong pro-incumbent bias present in Brazil's majoritarian elections, and the likelihood that there will be fewer candidates in majoritarian contests. It also may reflect much greater uncertainty in OLPR races, which may encourage donors to spread contributions more widely.

As noted earlier, the relationship between firms and politicians is more long-term and enduring than a single election cycle, reducing the likelihood that any single election represents the totality of exchanges between firms and politicians. Nonetheless, regressing firm characteristics and ties to the government on campaign donations in 2014 suggests a certain

TABLE 5.3 *Tobit regression results for total campaign contributions by largest firms*

	Model 1	Model 2	Model 3
CDES membership	6,215,292*	6,068,382*	4,143,963
BNDES loan value	−0.00197	–	−0.00132
Presence of BNDES loan	–	−1,430,507	–
State pension fund	5,911,757*	5,217,049*	4,813,352
Firm size	96.08	53.28	54.97
Brazilianness of sector	12,900,000**	13,000,000**	8,126,480*
Sector concentration	−18,400,000**	−19,700,000**	−3,824,099
Constant	−15,800,000**	−15,400,000**	−16,100,000**
Construction sector	–	–	18,000,000**
Consumer goods sector	–	–	4,718,305*
Banking sector	–	–	7,565,391
Steelworks sector	–	–	6,534,232*
Pseudo R2	0.0063	0.0059	0.0135
N	509	509	509

Note: See footnote[37] for description of core variables. **p>0.05; *p>0.1.

reinforcement of hierarchy across a variety of model specifications. Firms in sectors dominated by Brazilian companies ("Brazilianness of sector") donate more than those in sectors dominated by foreign companies. Although firms participate in campaign finance more in sectors with high ownership concentration ("Sector concentration"), per firm donations are lower in such sectors, suggesting that as competition within the sector declines, there may be less reason to invest heavily in politics. There was also a link between proximity to the government and donations. Firms that had received investments from the three big state-affiliated pension funds (Previ, Petros, and Funcef; "State pension fund") showed a tendency to invest more in campaigns, and firms that had executives on the CDES ("CDES membership") also tended to donate more (albeit in both cases statistical significance never surpasses p>0.1). The size of the firm is consistently unimportant to the size of the donation, although this may be an artifact of the fact that the firms in the model are all among the country's largest. A firm's sector is extremely relevant and including dummies for the four highest donating sectors in the regression shows important sector-specific effects even when holding other variables constant; different sectors have different inclinations to participate in politics. The construction, consumer goods, and steelmaking sectors together accounted for 82 percent of total donations in the sample and participation in those sectors was associated with higher average contributions, other things equal. In sum, the results of the licit market for influence suggests that the firms who benefit most directly from DHME were more actively involved in campaign finance than their peers.

These results confirm previous studies suggesting that campaign donors were an elite and highly concentrated group (Mancuso, 2015; Mancuso et al., 2016). Money has been essential to electoral success, and perhaps more influential than the goods politicians deliver to voters (Samuels, 2002, 852; Mancuso, 2015, 159). As Reis pointed out, the large number of candidates competing for power juxtaposed with the small number of large donors, created conditions for especially effective "rent-seeking" (Reis, 2018, 72).

Donations were fairly pragmatic, going to parties across the political spectrum, but favoring those most likely to wield power. Donations tended to benefit incumbents and business-oriented candidates tended to perform particularly well in this system (Bourdoukan, 2009; Araújo et al., 2015; Mancuso et al., 2016). Firms subject to government regulation were particularly active in campaign finance (Samuels, 2001; Bandeira-de-Mello et al., 2008; Mancuso, 2015), with the top funders representing

Illicit Influence 147

large firms in meatpacking (JBS), drinks (Ambev), mining (Vale), construction (OAS, Andrade Gutierrez, UTC, Queiroz Galvão, and Odebrecht), and banking (Bradesco and BTG Pactual).

ILLICIT INFLUENCE

The Lava Jato case that emerged in 2014 opened a window on the role of illicit finance in the political system.[38] Despite a number of problems with the prosecutions, the preponderance of the evidence from the investigations provides concrete evidence of an important institutional complementarity that was not previously appreciated: corruption and impunity link the tool kit of the developmental state and that of coalitional presidentialism, creating incentives to preserve the former, while enabling the latter, under governments of all stripes.[39]

The Lava Jato case erupted in public in March 2014, when an investigation into money laundering found evidence of links between money launderer Alberto Youssef and Petrobras executive Paulo Roberto Costa. Costa's bombshell testimony was central to the case. During more than 100 separate depositions, Costa detailed how political appointments within Petrobras were distributed, how a cartel of construction firms was built to win Petrobras contracts, how bribes were paid to political parties, and how a congressional investigation into Petrobras was sidetracked through bribes to influential congressmen. Costa's testimony ultimately implicated more than three dozen political figures, including ministers in the Lula and Rousseff administrations, governors, presidential candidates, party leaders from the PT and PP, and a former president of the PSDB opposition party; as well as two dozen different firms, including leaders in the construction and shipping industries. Several of the depositions also suggested that similar cartel-and-bribe schemes were underway in the energy, port, and airport sectors.

The system Lava Jato unveiled linked coalitional presidentialism, campaign finance, and the developmental state. With regard to the first of these, Petrobras directorates were allocated within the coalition. Costa, who had been a Petrobras employee since 1977, noted that nobody at any of the SOEs rose from a career position to an appointed position without a political "godparent" (*"padrinho"*). He recognized that his appointment as a director, between 2004 and 2012, only came about because of the sponsorship of José Janene, the president of the PP, to whom he thereby owed certain favors (Macedo and Brandt, 2015). As a Petrobras director, he had to meet certain monetary demands from the PP, and also on occasion from politicians from other parties (including the PP's allies in the PMDB and the PT, as well as the opposition PSDB).[40] Failing to meet those demands, he claimed, would lead to his immediate replacement (Polícia Federal, 2014a, 291). The remarkable thing about this system was that politicians colluded with each other to hide the system, even when they were electoral opponents. Members of the same coalition did not rat each other out. More surprisingly, even when they had evidence of wrongdoing, few opposition politicians took a strong stance against their opponents' corruption, perhaps fearful of losing access to a lucrative cash cow when they came to office, or of having their own malfeasance revealed.

With regard to campaign finance, Costa testified that it is a "big fallacy" to affirm that there are campaign donations in Brazil, when in fact they are actually only "loans to be redeemed later at high interest" from incumbents (Polícia Federal, 2014a, 289). Payments to political parties were widespread across the Petrobras directorates. Costa estimated that officially declared campaign contributions corresponded to only about a third of what was declared, with the remainder coming from illicit or undeclared funds, such as those provided by overpricing in public tenders at Petrobras. Of this, a significant chunk went to political parties: up to 3 percent on top of any contract with Petrobras, with two-thirds of that payment going to the incumbent PT, and the remaining third to the party that nominated that area's director. Of that remaining third, Costa estimated that 60 cents of every *real* would be allocated to the party, 20 cents to pay for overheads, and 20 cents to the director personally (Polícia Federal, 2014a, 291). Estimates derived from the values brought to light by Lava Jato suggest that somewhere between 6 percent and 46 percent of all campaign finance was illegal (CEPESP, 2019).

Third, with reference to the developmental state: in an oil sector dominated by state-owned Petrobras, on the one hand, and sectorally concentrated private national firms, on the other, there were few firms with the technical capacity and scale to take on the types of projects that Petrobras required, especially the large-scale projects envisioned after the pre-salt discoveries of 2006. The small number of firms helps to explain the ease with which private sector firms came together to form a cartel for public contracts in this area. In a low accountability environment, these private firms engaged in egregious price-fixing, holding meetings at the Rio offices of their sectoral association (*Associação Brasileira de Engenharia Industrial*, ABEMI) where they openly colluded to set prices for public contracts, determine bribe percentages,

Illicit Influence 149

and determine ahead of time which firms would win public bids. The success of this arrangement was epitomized by the fact that there was no overt meddling in the bidding process. There was no need, since the cartel determined winners ahead of time, and the bidding process itself was therefore, strictly speaking, carried out within the formal limits of the law (Polícia Federal, 2014a, 290). Meanwhile, Petrobras was not the only element of the developmental state involved: Lava Jato expanded to include investigations into the energy sector, the Planning Ministry, the federally owned Caixa Econômica Federal (CEF) and Banco do Brasil, and the Correios postal service.

Political leaders, Costa noted, seldom privileged Petrobras' interests over those of its majority stakeholder, the government. He detailed political nominations under both Cardoso and Lula, and noted that the logic for keeping some directorates running (such as the International Affairs directorate) had much more to do with politics than good business practices.[41] Costa argued that board members appointed by the government – such as Rousseff and Guido Mantega – held the administration's interests above the interests of Petrobras and that the private sector members of the board who might have served as a check on these interests remained largely passive for fear of damaging their access to government and SOE contracts (Polícia Federal, 2014b, 558–9). In sum, the links between parties, the private sector, and the developmental state were focused more on achieving the political interests of the government than on economic objectives, and SOEs like Petrobras served political ends first and foremost, rather than efficiency or profitability goals. Developmentalist rhetoric, however, helped to justify some of these business decisions and inefficiencies, offering a plausible rebuttal to those who criticized the suspiciously high costs of the system.

The case moved quickly on from Costa's testimony, in phases that were organized by the Lava Jato task force to take down specific groups of core conspirators. Charges were brought against more than 100 politicians from 14 different parties, including the former speaker of the house Eduardo Cunha, of the PMDB, former president Lula, of the PT, and former opposition presidential candidate Aécio Neves, of the PSDB.[42] More than 200 defendants were convicted in trial court, but only a single case against a sitting politician whose case was heard under the original jurisdiction of the high court (the STF) led to conviction as of 2019.

Lava Jato replicated several patterns visible in previous scandals dating back to the 1980s. It found ample evidence of cooperation between four types of actors that we might otherwise expect would have little legitimate reason to cooperate: politicians from diverse parties; prominent private sector businessmen; public employees at state-owned firms; and a variety of shady external "operators," who made the scheme function, whether by helping to launder payments within Brazil, by making offshore payments, or by negotiating bribes on behalf of private sector firms. The trial court conviction of President Lula for receiving bribes from the OAS construction firm noted that payments in exchange for Petrobras contracts were a "market rule." Sometimes these payments were direct quid pro quos (in the OAS case, for example, a "current account" of bribes were paid out from specific public sector contracts). In other cases, the terms of the relationship were much more "indeterminate," without a clear exchange of a particular bribe for a particular service; more of a long-term gentleman's agreement than a one-off discrete transaction.[43]

The politicians involved were not always close to the presidential incumbent: some were reticent members of the PT coalition, but surprisingly, some cases also involved members of the opposition, like Aécio Neves. These cross-cutting types of corruption may help to explain the frustratingly passive acceptance by political actors of each other's wrongdoing, as well as the general weakness of legislative or partisan checks and balances. In previous scandals, such as the Banestado money laundering case at the beginning of the century, the PT may have been more passive in opposition than it otherwise would have been, because it feared the investigation might reach its mayors; similarly, the PSDB may have been more acquiescent as a member of the opposition during the Lava Jato investigation because several of its most prominent members were also potential targets.

Many of the players in these scandals were repeat actors, appearing across widely different cases and thereby demonstrating the real costs of practical impunity. Brazil had 1,499 discrete federal officeholders from the 2002 to the 2014 elections, holding 2,349 distinct electoral slots in the Chamber, Senate and state gubernatorial mansions, as well as ministerial postings in the presidential cabinet.[44] While the high degree of impunity means that data on judicial convictions is almost nonexistent, I have created a rough proxy for criminality by compiling legal cases that have been brought against these federal officeholders.[45] Although false claims against politicians are of course possible, the proxy is a realistic if imperfect indicator of criminal behavior, in part because the strength of defamation provisions and the relative power of officeholders vis-à-vis police and prosecutors suggests that few charges would be brought without significant evidence. Of the nearly 1,500 politicians in office during this period, 28 percent faced an investigation or indictment in federal courts for any type of crime, ranging from tax evasion to homicide.[46] Corruption cases – including the closely related crimes of administrative responsibility and *peculato* (when a public servant abuses their office to personal ends) – are by far the most prevalent of these cases. Nearly 13 percent of the politicians in the sample were being investigated or had been indicted in one of five major corruption cases between 2002 and 2018.[47]

The levels of alleged corruption and crime indicated by this data are very high. Roughly three of every ten politicians was under a cloud of suspicion, including a number who had been fixtures of public life for much, if not all, of the decade and a half between 2002 and 2017. Accountability has been very low: of the nearly 1,500 officials, and of the 423 who are under investigation or indictment, fewer than two dozen have ever been convicted.

These very low levels of accountability suggest that the checks and balances from the legislative or judicial branches are nowhere near sufficient to alter the patterns of business-state relations. Especially with regard to the corruption by political figures, critics argue that the judicial system may in fact *be designed* to generate impunity, rather than somehow lacking the capacity or wherewithal to do so (Dallagnol, 2017; Pontes and Anselmo, 2019). This argument finds empirical confirmation in the shockingly passive and permissive role the two high courts – the STJ and STF – have played in ensuring the impunity of elites. But in a system in which the executive and legislative branches are deeply intertwined, is it all that unusual that the judiciary would play an ambiguous and even neutered role when it comes to the oversight and punishment of powerful political players? As Mello and Spektor (2018) note, the shared interests of the executive and legislative branches give them an incentive to limit the actions of watchdog institutions. It is hard to avoid the clear implication that the high courts – which hear all cases against sitting politicians – know that their preservation against the elected branches hinges on a certain tolerance for prevailing patterns of executive-legislative relations, licit and illicit.

Finally, in analyzing the leading companies involved in the scheme, there is considerable evidence of links between SOEs, private sector firms, and executives. The leading companies involved in the scheme – as measured by my Eigenvalue centrality measures based on the number of alleged ties mentioned in indictments – are J&F (the parent company of JBS), Odebrecht, Braskem, OAS, Santander, El Dorado (a J&F subsidiary),

152   *Coalitional Presidentialism*

Bradesco Asset, Furnas, and Mendes Júnior. With the exception of the banks, these are classic hierarchical firms, dominated by family ties in a highly concentrated sector.[48]

Too frequently, the focus of social scientists studying Brazilian politics has been on legislative process and policy outcomes, which have often led to quite positive conclusions about how the system functions, rather than on the low quality of representation, the high costs of the "exchange mechanisms" required, or the middling governance outcomes that result. In a variety of scandals since the turn of the century, state entities appear frequently and recurrently: pension funds, Correios, Banco do Brasil, CEF, TCU, Petrobras, Planning Ministry, and of course, Congress. Political appointments and the logic of godparents (*padrinhos*) is widespread, aimed at sustaining the coalition. While there are instances of transactional quid pro quo corruption (bribes paid to individual public employees), a more pernicious relationship is also evident: powerful private sector companies use long-term, reciprocal corrupt exchanges as a quotidian element of their business strategies, to influence access to public contracts and public works, ensure privileged regulatory treatment, and engage in defensive influence peddling to preserve their interests. They are helped in this task by a phalanx of facilitators, such as *doleiros* linked to politicians, criminal defense lawyers ready to sow doubt and ensure delay in the court, and high courts that are tolerant of politicians' foibles.

This is an expensive system, and Lava Jato revealed a great deal about the economic costs of corruption in the coalitional presidential system. The direct costs were obvious: individual convicted defendants returned more than US$3.1 billion in ill-gotten gains; Petrobras in April 2015 took a write down to its audited accounts of R$50.8 billion (US$16.8 billion), of which R$6.2 billion (US$2.05 billion) were directly attributed to corruption (Reuters, 2015); in November 2015, Eletrobras took an impairment of R$4.01 billion (US$1.06 billion) related to its corruption-stricken Angra 3 nuclear plant (Stauffer and Blount, 2015); in a December 2016 settlement by the Odebrecht construction firm and its petrochemical subsidiary Braskem (partially owned by Petrobras), the two firms agreed to pay at least $3.5 billion to authorities, the largest global corruption settlement in history; and a September 2018 settlement under the US FCPA was the largest single-company FCPA settlement ever to date, with Petrobras agreeing to penalties and disgorgement totaling US$1.78 billion (Cassin, 2018). Between its peak in May 2008 and the trough in February 2016, the market capitalization of Petrobras fell more than 90 percent, from $260 billion to under $22 billion.

Illicit Influence 153

Indirect economic costs, meanwhile, included foregone competition in the construction sector, the promotion of firms that were competitive only by virtue of their corruption, the costs of unnecessary or inefficient projects that served only as a pipeline for bribes, and the enormous costs of a recession that was greatly exacerbated by political paralysis and investor uncertainty around the case. The public policy distortions caused by the scheme have also been significant. A number of legislative changes appear to have been driven primarily by the need to satisfy the businesses at the heart of the scandal. Odebrecht alone admitted to buying passage of nine provisional measures (Schwartsman, 2017). The policy distortions also run in the opposite direction, from Congress to firms, with some deputies holding unrelated legislation hostage in exchange for nominations to SOEs. For example, according to Cerveró's plea bargain, one group of about fifty deputies suggested that they would only vote for the CPMF tax if they could nominate the head of the Petrobras international directorate.

The prisoners' dilemma of campaign finance in Brazil meant that almost all long-term politicians had an incentive to use off-books contributions to fund expensive campaigns, because in a context of high competition, on-books contributions might be an insufficient guarantee of a win. The scale of the subsequent illicit donations was significant. For example, Odebrecht was among the most important legal campaign contributors to candidates for federal office in 2014. Plea bargains by leading executives at the firm suggested that the ratio of illicit to licit contributions by the firm was eight to one (Odebrecht's legal contributions to federal elections from 2002 to 2014 totaled $80 million, or only 13 percent of the $599 million in bribes it admits to having paid to politicians in Brazil in the same period).[49] Because of the high cost of campaigns, even some of the wealthiest politicians were accused of having received illicit funding. But this led to a suboptimal equilibrium because everyone was worse off than they would have been if they did not have to chase extra money and engage in illegal activities to fund politics. In an effort to temper some of the downside, politicians appeared to have reached a tacit agreement to compete electorally but collude corruptly: politicians on opposite sides of the aisle were aware of their peers' wrongdoing but remained mum for fear of upsetting their collusive arrangement.

Because the links between SOEs, firms, and politicians are ongoing and reciprocal, rather than discrete, even otherwise clean politicians face enormous opportunity costs if they advocate for breaking up corrupt networks. An otherwise clean politician may rationally come to the conclusion that breaking up such networks is a thankless endeavor. The willingness of clean politicians to fight corruption may be undercut by the fact that inter-coalitional financial transfers can be significant, so calling out wrongdoing by coalition allies may undermine a candidate's own campaign finance prospects. The normalization of illegality means that many otherwise clean politicians remain passive, employing a free-rider strategy, rather than trying to spark the collective action that would be needed to combat corruption.[50] On the flip side, a rational but corrupt politician knows that acting opportunistically to break up the network would mean foregoing future returns from years of past exchanges, and that the risk of detection and punishment is minimal, in any case.

One final consequence of this prisoners' dilemma is that all too often opposition has been a farce, and because political opponents are unable or unwilling to criticize incumbents for wrongdoing, checks and balances by the political branches are weak. Congressional investigatory committees (CPIs) seldom result in meaningful outcomes. The leadership of the congressional oversight body known as the *Tribunal de Contas da União* (TCU) is populated by the old boys' network of politicians, and not surprisingly, many TCU ministers over the years have been accused of complicity with corrupt networks. At best, the implicit gentleman's agreement between opposition and government parties means that there has been little political instability as a result of scandal: why act vociferously in opposition if it would only lead to revelation of my own wrongdoing? At worst, though, it means that there has been little removal of corrupt political elites from the political system, despite verifiable evidence of brazen corruption.[51]

In sum, political corruption at the federal level in Brazil between 1985 and 2018 appears to have followed a logic that was closely attuned to local conditions of campaign finance and coalitional presidentialism, and facilitated by weak accountability and the impunity it permits. Even though these corrupt networks solved some of the problems imposed by the political system – such as the high cost of elections and the difficulty of holding coalitions together – they simultaneously sapped the meaning from that system. While the political system "works," in the sense of permitting some basic governability, it has done so in ways that undermined its own democratic legitimacy and prevented the system from reforming itself in the face of changing national and global conditions. As this chapter demonstrated, seldom is corruption a direct quid pro quo. Rather, over time, running debts circulate through the system, and as they circulate, they help to maintain the loyalty of actors to the overall network (Cartier-Bresson, 1997, 58). This logic contributes to a perverse cycle that

Final Thoughts 155

reproduces itself over time, deepening the links between the role of the state in the economy, coalitional presidentialism, and weak oversight of the developmental state, described in Chapter 6.[52]

FINAL THOUGHTS

Hierarchy at its political core is expressed in the steady reinforcement of advantage. Certain firms are protected, their interests are privileged over other organizations in society, and their power is institutionalized through rules and regulations. The top firms in Brazil benefit from more government-backed loans, more subsidies, and more access to policymakers than smaller firms. Hierarchical structure is also be reflected in institutional rules. Stock markets in Brazil, for example, have permitted firms to issue as much as two-thirds of their shares as nonvoting, allowing shareholders to continue to maintain dominance even after they open their firms to outside investors. Regulatory structures benefit SOEs, as in the case of ANP and Petrobras, or are captured by private firms in the regulated industry. Hierarchy is also reflected in control over the commanding heights of the state apparatus: rural elites have an effective lock on nominations in agriculture-related agencies, banks have deep ties to many top economic policymakers and regulators, and traditional industrialists are heavily represented on consultative bodies and the boards of SOEs.

The political system provides many venues that reinforce the DHME. The complex governance demands imposed by coalitional presidentialism incentivize the use of the developmental state apparatus, not always to developmental ends. The breadth of the state and the fragmentation of party life offer multiple venues for accessing policymaking and decision makers. Leading firms and politicians have developed intricate systems for using these political institutions in tandem to achieve their aims. Large firms can be called upon by policymakers seeking particular goals of employment, investment, or corporate reorganization; policymakers may be asked to repay the favor when firms are in need of credit, subsidies, or general succor from market conditions. In light of these complementarities, reform coalitions will find the path hard going: even at moments when the executive branch evinced an intense desire for change – such as during the Collor, Cardoso, and Temer years – most such change happened only when business and government interests could be aligned, and even then, change happened in a much more incremental and parametric manner than in most of the rest of Latin America.

In part because at the commanding heights of the economy, successful business empires have either been built through close ties with government or have benefited from government backing, there may be little incentive among large domestic firms for overhauling the institutions of the developmental state. Big Brazilian corporate names with long histories of influence on and ties to politics abound; consider Globo, Camargo Corrêa, Brazil Foods, Fibria, JBS, OAS, Odebrecht, Iguatemi, Gerdau, and the Maggi agrobusiness empire. Furthermore, the public sector exerts a gravitational pull, even on new private sector entrepreneurs. Eike Batista, an Icarus-like figure who was briefly the seventh richest man in the world, epitomizes the phenomenon. Even as he portrayed himself as the innovative and creative face of a new and emergent Brazil during the late 2000s, Batista eagerly sought out government contacts and sought to become "Lula's businessman" (Gaspar, 2014).[53]

Once in place, these ties to politics tend to be self-reinforcing, since many firms that have invested heavily over the years to develop reciprocal long-term relations with political incumbents with long careers see little to be gained from rocking the boat and contesting political and economic institutions that may be suboptimal in the aggregate but have been generally beneficial to their interests over the long haul.

6

Rents, Control, and Reciprocity

Where one cow passes, a herd will soon follow.
Congressman Arnaldo Faria de Sá, 2011

The sum of desires is not always compatible with revenues.
Former Finance Minister Pedro Malan, 2019[1]

The central balancing act of a developmental state is political. Evans (1995) famously noted that developmental states require "embedded autonomy": sufficient autonomy to design strategies, develop policies, and implement them, while simultaneously remaining sufficiently embedded in society and markets to understand where the political and economic bottlenecks to growth lie, in ways that permit learning and recalibration. Central to this balancing act is strategic oversight by states, to ensure that as national development plans are implemented, they are achieving the desired objectives, that long-term strategy predominates over short-term needs, and that the process of moving the economy to a higher plateau is not captured by bureaucrats or business people. I refer to this strategic oversight, constant reevaluation and readjustment as "control."

One reason that control is so important is that the twenty-first century developmental state is operating in a world context of far greater global competition than its twentieth century predecessors. Some former lower-income countries such as South Korea and Japan have already moved into the upper-income bracket, and others, like China, are pushing hard to get there. As a consequence, "... middle-income countries are caught in a developmental nutcracker, 'unable to compete with low-income ..., low-wage economies in manufactured exports and unable to compete with advanced economies in high-skill innovations'" (Gill and Kharas, 2007; Doner and Schneider, 2013, 609, citing Kharas and Kohli, 2011, 282; Wade, 2018). Because the goalposts have moved, emerging from the middle-income trap requires not just the relatively straightforward development of basic industry, but also a much more complex effort to increase productivity growth through greater savings, higher investment, better infrastructure, better education, and more innovation and R&D (Doner and Schneider, 2016, 609). In the Brazilian case, these challenges must also be faced in a democratic context, where the demands for state action are wide-ranging, where electoral pressures are significant, and where the many veto points in the political system provide economic and political actors with strong defensive instruments against change, as noted in Chapter 5. Without strategic control, the typical policies of developmentalism are unlikely to be effective, especially those that rely on providing extraordinary incentives, or rents, that coax firms in the particular directions sought by policymakers.

The focus of this chapter is on the instruments of control that permit strategic guidance and implementation of policy, to ensure that the bureaucracy is fulfilling mandates, that the process of creating mandates for firms effectively drives the economy forward, and to guarantee that policy is being implemented without corruption or capture. The first section describes the purposes of control in developmental states. The second examines the Rousseff government's development plan to illustrate how controls functioned, noting that even when policymakers were fully committed to the developmental enterprise and fully cognizant of the need for controls, as they were under the developmentalist policymakers of the PT administration, old practices swamped those mechanisms. The third briefly summarizes three other policy arenas to illustrate, first, that the absence of control was not solely a problem of the PT, and second, that the inadequate implementation of controls tends to lead industry back to equilibrium behaviors that are collectively suboptimal for growth. The final section concludes with an overview of the causes of weak control and their implications for the effectiveness of the developmental enterprise.

CONTROL AND THE DEVELOPMENTAL STATE

Political mechanisms of control range from narrow administrative controls up through broad checks and balances across branches of government. Any economic policy set (e.g., developmental, social democratic,

Control and the Developmental State 159

neoclassical) establishes a central overall strategy, then determines the tactical objectives needed to achieve it. By virtue of its central objective – moving the economy to higher value-added production – a developmentalist strategy focuses heavily on the incentives needed to bring firms to the table and ensure that their production incentives are different from those in a world without policy. State organizations are vitally important, providing the capacity and the resources to guide firms and economic actors: strategic planning, consultative mechanisms, counterpart reciprocity, and evaluation and readjustment.[2]

Many neoclassical economists and public choice scholars assume that interventionist economic policies will devolve into rent-seeking, as interest groups seize the machinery of government in self-interested ways (e.g., Buchanan and Tullock, 1962; Krueger, 1974, 1990; Bhagwati, 1982). Economists of a more heterodox, developmentalist persuasion also share concern about the perverse incentives set in place by intervention, and the possibility that policies will be only loosely implemented, failing to achieve their broader developmental objectives. The central concern for developmentalists, though, is not the presence of the rents themselves, but the degree to which rents are generating the incentives needed to accomplish the ends of policy.

This point bears explanation, if only because public discussion, heavily influenced by neoclassical economics, often assumes that rents are always and everywhere a bad thing. Developmental economists, by contrast, suggest that rents are at their most basic simply the "excess income" over and above what an individual or firm might earn in the next-best opportunity (Khan, 2000a, 21). Rents are widespread in economic life, and may be either inefficient and growth-retarding, or instead serve as incentives to development. For late developing countries, resource concentration such as inequality of land or capital provides substantial rents that increase the opportunity costs of making a shift into manufacturing (Amsden, 2001, 291). The voyage of developmental discovery is about generating the correct incentives for developing, investing in, and copying technologies: creating rents that would draw comfortable coffee growers, for example, off their *fazendas* and into industrial ventures.

Rents, therefore, are not seen by developmentalists as uniformly pernicious to development. Indeed, producing new technology, ensuring property rights, training labor in new fields, and providing know-how across industrial sectors often requires rents that elicit productive firm behavior (Chang, 1994; Haggard, 2018). There are of course rents that are less preferable, such as returns from monopoly, or from ownership of scarce natural resources. But positive rents are commonplace the world over: rents rewarding innovation, learning, efficiency, and good management. Even neoclassical economists recognize this implicitly, for example, in their defense of intellectual property rights, and the profits and royalties many intellectual property regimes use to encourage and reward innovation.

From a developmentalist perspective, the central question is whether rents have been implemented in strategic ways and with appropriate controls to drive economic actors in societally beneficial directions. As a consequence, an overarching strategy is needed to guide both the choice of metric as well as the incentives provided to firms. The political challenge is to "construct and reconstruct institutions and politics in developing countries to sustain developmental rents and rent-seeking while attacking value-reducing rents and rent-seeking" (Khan, 2000b, 141). Rents must be strategically informed and adjusted to local challenges. Policymakers should establish metrics for evaluating whether rents are functioning as desired, and when the social costs of a rent outweigh their social benefits. When rents are not producing the correct results, there must be a clear measurement strategy to demonstrate this and government must be autonomous enough to withdraw benefits. None of this is easy, but it must also be done while protecting against active rent-seeking, "the expenditure of resources and effort in creating, maintaining, or transferring rents" (Khan, 2000b, 70).

There are a variety of possible institutional configurations that might achieve the effective application of rents. Schapiro (2016) offers a useful heuristic model for thinking about the structure of controls in a democracy like Brazil's, focused on how much control is imposed, how well, and what sort of coordination there is in the application of that control.[3] Drawing on the influential work of David Trubek, Guillermo O'Donnell, Jerry Mashaw, and Susan Rose-Ackerman, he distinguishes between two intertwined motives for control: regulatory governance for economic development, and administrative governance for policymaking in democracy.

The instruments of control in the economic sphere include many of those already discussed in this book, such as fiscal inducements and rules imposed by regulatory agencies, while in the political sphere of administrative control, they include vertical controls such as elections, media coverage, and citizen oversight, as well as horizontal controls, such as both internal controls within government and external controls by Congress, the TCU accounting tribunal, and the courts. One of

Control and the Developmental State 161

Schapiro's core contributions is to draw attention to the difficult balancing act of imposing control: too little control may generate a temptation to use the tools to meet short-term policy objectives; too much may generate bureaucratic paralysis. Across a variety of different sectors and policy arenas, he finds that both problems occur simultaneously: for example, the BNDES has too little control over the impact of its lending, but simultaneously suffers from an immobilizing focus on the probity of its staff.

There are at least three other concrete challenges that Brazilian policymakers have faced in seeking to impose controls: 1) the difficulty of maintaining an overall strategic direction for developmental policy in the face of the many economic crises that have buffeted Brazil between the 1982 debt crisis and the 2008 global financial crisis; 2) the problem of institutional multiplicity (Jenkins, 1991; Abers and Keck, 2013; Carson and Prado, 2016) and particularly, the difficulty of coordinating developmental regulatory and administrative governance across the wide range of institutions of the developmental state; and 3) the challenge of constantly reevaluating and recalibrating the effects of the rents being offered and the controls imposed to ensure that they set neither too lenient nor too rigorous a standard for targeted actors.

Without attention to all three of these, institutional complementarities across the economic and political spheres will tend to generate incentives that push actors back into their regular patterns of behavior, failing to generate any significant shift in the development equilibrium. Control may use both carrots and sticks to avoid such problems. It may include soft controls such as reciprocity, as in agreements that suggest a firm should accomplish a particular metric by a particular date, in exchange for a particular incentive or rent. It may also include harder controls, such as the possibility of CEO removal, bankruptcy, or even judicial sanction for failure to meet objective targets. Central to the notion of control is that there is a metric or benchmark that firms are being measured against.

Yet the complementarities described in the previous four chapters have militated against effective control of developmental policies in democratic Brazil. Although these will be discussed in greater detail in the final section of this chapter, a few sentences demonstrate the issue. The impetus to rely on fiscally opaque tools may militate against effective administrative oversight of the costs and benefits of policy. Regulation is complicated in a context of executive dominance, firms' political influence over the regulatory apparatus, and multiple veto points. Control over property rights and more generally, the legal governance of the state's role as an economic agent, are susceptible to multiple pressures, most notably from the demands of coalition formation and from short-term economic contingency management. One consequence is considerable regulatory uncertainty (Amann et al., 2016). Governance of policy is complicated by the weakness of accountability described in a preliminary fashion in Chapter 5: control over policymaking is focused more on command and control than on impact analysis; control over performance is focused more on the administrative probity of the process than actual policy outcomes; and protection of rights – especially property rights – is weakened, as later sections of this chapter will argue, by the hydra-headed and irresolute functioning of the judicial system.

In sum, the institutional complementarities between the developmental state, the coalitional presidential system, and the judicial system effectively dilute strategic control. The consequence is that the use of rents has been costly and had little discernible effect, even when policymakers have been attentive to the need for strategic controls. By way of example, let us turn to the story of one massive developmental program, announced in 2011, which exemplifies many of the issues that have been raised here.

PLANO BRASIL MAIOR

The *Plano Brasil Maior* (Greater Brazil Plan, PBM), announced in 2011, aimed to increase innovation and improve the technological composition of industrial production. The justification for the program was a mix of immediate crisis measures and longer-term developmental objectives: address exchange rate overvaluation, lower unit labor costs, increase competitiveness, drive infrastructure investment, and increase workforce technical skills. To benchmark progress, the PBM included a series of quantitative goals: increasing fixed investment, R&D ratios, human resource qualifications, the percentage of industrial production in total production, etc.

The scale of the PBM was massive, mobilizing more than a half trillion *reais* over three years as well as staff across a wide range of federal agencies. The plan was designed as an extension of two previous development plans under PT governments, the *Política Industrial, Tecnológica e de Comércio Exterior* (PITCE) (2003–07) and the *Política de Desenvolvimento Produtivo* (PDP) (2008–10). Its management structure cut across a variety of agencies; it was headed by the CNDI (*Conselho Nacional de Desenvolvimento Industrial*), a committee with representatives of both government and the private sector, managed by the Ministry

Plano Brasil Maior 163

of Industrial Development and Trade (MDIC), with support from the presidential chief of staff's office (Casa Civil), the Finance Ministry, Ministry of Science and Technology, the Planning Ministry, BNDES, and FINEP. Below that managerial committee, nineteen executive committees and councils specialized in sectoral matters. The Brazilian Agency for Industrial Development (ABDI), an autonomous agency operating outside the federal budget, was given the role of program coordinator, with the ministers of MDIC and Science and Technology alternating yearly as presidents (Salerno and Daher, 2006; Stein and Herrlein Júnior, 2016; Arbix et al., 2017).[4]

The PBM encompassed nearly 300 distinct policies, initially 19 different sectors, in 3 distinct groups: tax and tariff reductions, credit and financial stimuli, and institutional reforms (Stein and Herrlein Júnior, 2016; Arbix et al., 2017). Tax relief included reductions in the tax on industrial goods (IPI) to incentivize machinery purchases, refunds of taxes on revenue for pensions and labor,[5] special tax regimes for small and micro businesses, tax benefits for technology investments, and trade protections. An alternative payroll tax was instituted, allowing firms in specific sectors to choose between paying a 20 percent payroll pension tax per employee or instead paying 1–2 percent of gross revenue, a significant cost savings for many labor-intensive firms. Credit stimulus included efforts to streamline lending procedures, targeted lending for R&D and innovation programs, and the extension of lending programs aimed at investment and export promotion. Statutory reform built on the legal frameworks established in the PITCE and PDP, while also setting public procurement preferences of up to 25 percent for national firms and establishing a new National Program for Access to Technical Learning and Employment (PRONATEC), aimed at increasing technical training at the secondary level.

Despite its ambitious mobilization of resources and policy, as well as policymakers' awareness of the need for control, a number of factors undermined the effectiveness of the PBM, including a poorly designed strategic process, inadequate content and weak targeting, high and expanding costs, little strategic evaluation and recalibration, and the absence of reciprocity by benefited firms. All contributed to the overall weakness of control in the drafting, implementation, oversight, and reappraisal of the program.

The strategic match between the grand objectives of the PBM and the policies used to implement it was weak. Many of the plan's declared strategic priorities resembled a hastily compiled listing of work that ministries were already engaged in, rather than an innovative new strategy for development (Mattos, 2013). The drafting of the strategy was heavily influenced by a 2011 seminar that brought together FIESP and labor unions, with the consequence that many of the measures were aimed at reducing the tax burden on beneficiaries, rather than on pushing beneficiaries to develop new technologies or move into new fields (Carvalho, 2018). Overall, development of the plan was marked by a certain "improvisation" (Stein and Herrlein Júnior, 2016). The government's strategic formulation of the plan followed firms, rather than leading them.

As a consequence, the content of the plan has been criticized for failing to adequately target developmental objectives. Several of the sectoral programs were nothing more than old programs in new clothing. On the left, critics saw the plan as a sop to business (e.g., Leal, 2015) while on the right, conservative media pilloried the plan for failing to adequately target benefits on a firm-by-firm basis (e.g., O Estado de S. Paulo, 2011). Many of the protectionist measures were open-ended, with no sunset date (Almeida, 2013a; Canêdo-Pinheiro, 2013). There was little emphasis on developing human capital beyond PRONATEC (Baldocchi, 2014). The sectors selected to participate did not always seem like good prospects for technological gains. Some benefited sectors were already doing well before PBM: fully 24 percent of the measures benefited agroindustry, and another nearly 10 percent were aimed at the aviation industry, both sectors which were already globally competitive (Mattos, 2013). Other beneficiaries seemed like bad prospects for industrial policy, like retailers and service providers. Despite an overall emphasis on innovation – highlighted in the plan's motto of "innovate to compete, compete to grow" ("*inovar para competir, competir para crescer*"), only a third of the measures were focused on innovation, per se. Many of the least innovative sectors were among the most benefited, in part because the government was at least as concerned with short-term employment as it was with long-term development of industrial innovation. This led Glauco Arbix, an influential formulator of the Workers' Party's early innovation policies, to conclude alongside his coauthors that "even if the PBM declared innovation and increased competitiveness as solutions to accelerate economic growth, the measures it defined more resemble anticyclical policy than an effective industrial policy ..." (Arbix et al., 2017).

The lack of a targeted, strategic core did not reduce the plan's cost. The MDIC's budgeting for the first two years of PBM forecast direct costs of R\$20.7bn from tax breaks alone (Máximo, 2011; Leal, 2015). Between 2011 and 2014, the BNDES lent R\$ 466 billion to firms in the PBM,

Plano Brasil Maior 165

roughly 80 percent of the bank's total lending (Stein and Herrlein Júnior, 2016). Indirect costs are hard to estimate, but they were significant, whether it was through the distortions generated by trade measures and sectoral incentives, or the effective transfer of funds out of the pension system to firms, implicit in the alternative payroll tax.

Furthermore, these costs grew over time. By way of example, between 2011, when the plan was announced, and 2014, when it was slated to end, the number of sectors that benefited from a single measure in the PBM – the alternative payroll tax – expanded fourteen-fold.[6] Payroll tax relief was initially granted to four sectors: textiles, shoe wear, furniture, and software, with the goal to "incentivize the installation and modernization of firms through the reduction of production costs."[7] When Congress was deliberating on whether to convert the original provisional measure on payroll taxes into law, Deputy Arnaldo Faria de Sá (PTB) presciently made the statement in the first epigraph of this chapter, that "where one cow passes, a herd will soon follow" (Câmara dos Deputados, 2011, 58827).[8] Two years later, a combination of new provisional measures and congressional amendments drafted by coalition partners had vastly expanded the payroll tax measures, from four to fifty-six sectors. The APT was no longer a temporary measure but had become permanent tax legislation. The National Association of Fiscal Auditors of the Revenue Service (ANFIP) estimated the total revenue loss from the alternative payroll tax at R$19 billion in 2013, just under 10 percent of the R$218 billion in tax breaks provided that year.[9] ANFIP estimated that the cost of the alternative payroll tax expanded to $34.8 billion in 2015, with all tax breaks having reached 4.76 percent of GDP in 2014 (Leal, 2015).[10]

There was little strategic evaluation of the plan's effects or recalibration to make them more effective. Critics noted that the measures were expanded constantly with little reflection on their costs and even less analysis of their effects. One magazine's efforts to evaluate the cost of the plan discovered that the ABDI, which was responsible for overseeing the plan, did not even maintain up-to-date data regarding progress toward meeting the plan's ten central objectives (Baldocchi, 2014). The broad nature of the government's stated objectives – e.g., increasing investment, trade, and value-added by industry – was not conducive to effective prioritization or recalibration, since too many contextual factors could get in the way of these goals, making it impossible to ascertain whether the plan was failing because of its own shortcomings or because of a difficult macroeconomic environment.[11]

Reciprocity was almost nonexistent: as one critic noted, the PBM was all about carrots, with very few sticks (Mattos, 2013). A 2015 analysis by *Valor Econômico*, for example, found that companies benefited by the APT were firing more than they were hiring (Leal, 2015). In 2018, a postmortem by the government think tank IPEA (*Instituto de Pesquisa Econômica Aplicada*) compared sectors that had benefited from the alternative payroll tax with those who had not, and found that despite its high cost, the tax relief had no discernible effect on formal employment (Garcia et al., 2018). However, the government itself did not analyze these factors or in any way penalize firms for their labor choices, and there was no counterpart commitment that the government demanded from recipient firms (De Toni, 2014). Strategic appraisal of the plan's performance was conducted only with regard to aggregate measures, without any systematic evaluation of the performance of individual firm beneficiaries (Baldocchi, 2014; Botelho, 2015). The principal stick the government relied upon to motivate firms was competition (Guerriero, 2012; 165; Stein and Herrlein Júnior, 2016). But in a fairly closed economy with strong sectoral concentration (especially in industry) and with policies designed vertically, to benefit entire sectors, inter-firm competition was unlikely to do much to discipline firms and ensure that rents were driving them in a developmentally sound direction.

As a consequence of all of these factors, the *Plano Brasil Maior* essentially privileged incumbent firms. A variety of industries were benefited, ranging from low-technology sectors like footwear and leather goods, through high-tech sectors like oil and gas. But for all of the emphasis on innovation and technology, the list of beneficiaries included most of the usual suspects – such as truck and car makers, parts manufacturers, agroindustry, and mining concerns – and a group of industries whose likely benefit from technology policy was minimal, like mining, metallurgy, paper and pulp, textile, and agrobusiness. The end result was to preserve the structure of the developmental hierarchical market economy (DHME), defending extant firms against external competition, while enhancing incumbent power in the domestic economy (Stein and Herrlein Júnior, 2016).

Nor was the PBM an outlier in terms of its ineffectiveness as an industrial policy or a developmental plan. There was a clear decline in the quality and effectiveness of industrial policy over the course of the Workers' Party governments. The PITCE had achieved some important institutional changes, including statutory changes such as an innovation law and a law providing incentives for research and development (*Lei do*

Bem), as well as the creation of new financing programs for innovation, like FINEP (Salerno and Daher, 2006; Almeida et al., 2012; Schapiro, 2013a; Stein and Herrlein Júnior, 2016; Arbix et al., 2017). If PITCE was neo-Schumpeterian and innovation-seeking, however, subsequent programs were less so. PDP and PBM seemed more focused on providing sectoral rents, trade protections against "unjust and predatory competition," and countercyclical measures (Canêdo-Pinheiro, 2013; Botelho, 2015). Further, even though industry's share of GDP fell fairly consistently over the course of the three plans, from 17.8 percent in 2004 to 12 percent in 2015 – there was little effort to recalibrate policy or the strategic objectives themselves (O Globo, 2018b).[12]

ECONOMIC RENTS AND CONTROLS IN BRAZIL

It could be argued that the failures of the PBM were idiosyncratic, explained by President Rousseff's policymaking predilections, the response to the global financial crisis, or the political pressures engendered by the slowdown of GDP growth, which peaked in the first quarter of 2014, the final year of the PBM, and declined almost incessantly for the next eleven quarters, through 2017.[13] But the haphazard application of controls seen in the PBM was not unique to Rousseff, to the economic moment, or to moments of recessionary pressure. Rousseff's ambition and commitment to the tools of the developmental tool kit may have been more significant than some of her peers, as was her administration's vocal recognition of the need for controls and reciprocity. But many examples can be offered of the only haphazard controls imposed on developmentalist policies by presidents of various stripes. Three are sufficient to illustrate the issue and the manner by which it transcends individual presidencies.

Zona Franca de Manaus

The Manaus Free Trade Zone (*Zona Franca de Manaus*, ZFM) may be the iconic example of haphazard controls on developmental policies, from Sarney through Bolsonaro. Created by the military regime in 1967 with the goal of populating the Amazon region, the ZFM's declared motivations have shifted subtly over time, but with the essential constant of providing heavy subsidies to manufacturing in Manaus, the capital of the state of Amazonas (Possebom, 2017). The ZFM is in essence a free trade zone, with tax reductions and tariff exemptions provided in exchange for job creation and R&D investments of 5 percent of annual earnings in the Amazon region.[14]

The ZFM has been the source of a significant proportion of most consumer electronics sold in Brazil, including more than a third of Brazil's cell phones, as well as many computer and IT products (Michaud, 2015). In 2018, it housed nearly 500 firms, employing roughly 80,000 workers. It was home to several MNCs, including Gillette's largest South American plant, Harley Davidson's only factory outside the United States, and one of Honda's largest plants outside Japan (Bekerman and Dulcich, 2017).

The ZFM's tax exemptions were renewed on multiple occasions in the half century since it was created, under intense pressure from firms and politicians, and it has been continually renewed since its intended expiration in 1997. Most recently, in 2013, the fiscal incentives that established the ZFM were extended through 2073. A study by the Fundação Getulio Vargas (FGV), financed by many of the manufacturers and associations present in the ZFM, showed that Manaus had grown far faster than other cities since 1960, both in population and in terms of the economy (Holland et al., 2019). But the question for developmental policy is whether this populational effect – a consequence of increasing manufacturing in a northern city far from the rest of Brazil's industrial hubs – is offset by the costs of fiscal incentives and protections needed to artificially stimulate production in the Amazon.

The direct cost of the tax rebates offered by the ZFM were around R$26 billion in 2018, an unexceptional year (Folha, 2018a). In terms of its benefits, the local effects were mixed, while the national effects were inexpressive. Using the synthetic control method to compare Manaus to other cities in the north and northeast, Possebom (2017) found "ambiguous" effects of the ZFM on the local municipal economy: there was no evidence of an effect on manufactures relative to the counterfactual, suggesting that the ZFM had failed to meet the criteria for its creation; meanwhile, the ZFM drove down local agricultural production by as much as 10 percent. On the positive side, the ZFM did appear to lead to an increase in services in the Amazon region, perhaps as a consequence of tourists visiting the region to purchase electronics, as well as some gains in municipal real GDP per capita relative to the counterfactual. But as Possebom recognizes, this cost-benefit analysis is for the local economy only, and the local analysis does not consider the fact that most of the ZFM's costs are borne by cities outside the Amazon region. Meanwhile, the ZFM has run large trade deficits since the 1990s, suggesting that it is little more than an assembly platform for components imported from elsewhere, with little in the way of spillover effects for higher value Brazilian industrial production (Egan, 2015). Further, these trade deficits have increased significantly since the turn of the century, with exports falling from 12 percent of total sales in 2003 to 2 percent in 2013. Imports per worker in 2012 were US$100,000; exports per worker were only US$8,000 (Bekerman and Dulcich, 2017). The cost of job creation in the ZFM is quite high, especially relative to the quality of the jobs that were created. And perhaps most importantly, there is little sign that firms in the ZFM have incorporated new technologies or increased productivity and competitiveness (Miranda, 2013). In sum, for more than half a century, the ZFM has been an expensive trade-off, with an annual cost of around 0.4 percent of GDP and 8.5 percent of national tax expenditures in 2018, with few spillovers and little national developmental impact.

Automotive Policy

Oftentimes, industrial programs are portrayed as relics of development-alism, occurring only under leftist presidents, like Dilma Rousseff, who are seen as sympathetic to state interventionist policies. The auto industry has long been the subject of developmental admiration, not least because it embodies one of the most relevant of developmental precepts, with its backward linkages to metalworking and mining, and its forward linkages to a host of mechanical industries and supplier chains. But even presidents of a "neoliberal" bent have adopted sectoral policies for the auto industry: President Collor undertook sectoral negotiations to help out the industry and President Cardoso adopted the special automotive regime in the late 1990s. The Workers' Party governments of the new century adopted the Inovar Auto regime. Regardless of the president, though, the historical record shows only inconstant attention to issues of reciprocity and effect-ive control in the implementation of these policies.

Under Collor, sectoral chambers were created to coordinate various aspects of industrial policy, in ways that would open the decision-making process in "a more democratic" fashion (Comin, 1998; cited in Schapiro, 2017). Central to these chambers was the notion of tripartite negotiation between government, employees and employers. In the automotive sector, the sectoral chamber between 1991 and 1992 adopted a number of measures to address declining production levels, which were almost 10 percent lower in 1992 than in 1980, as well as the 14 percent decline in industrial jobs in the ABC region of São Paulo, where the auto industry was then centered (Schapiro, 2017). These included a reduction in car prices and a commitment to lower profits by the car companies, a cut in taxes by the government, and worker acceptance of more stringent wage policies. Collor's measures were not developmentalist in conceit, but they did reflect a societal desire for a robust government response to crisis in the sector, and the Collor administration was willing to flex the state's muscle to make them happen.

Under Cardoso, the government initially adopted a wave of reforms intended to move away from an activist state to a more liberal, regulatory state. However, the post-stabilization period from 1995 to 1998 was marked by considerable concern with growing trade imbalances and rising import competition, with the adoption of "neo-activist" policies to succor import-competing sectors (Veiga, 2004, 178–9). The government adopted industrial and export promotion policies that privileged many of the same sectors and firms that had benefited from state intervention in the 1960s and 1970s (including the automotive industry, electronics and IT, textiles and shoe producers), under a policy set described as "discriminatory trade liberalization" (Veiga and Ventura-Dias, 2004, 102). The expedient neo-activist approach was nowhere more evident than in the 1995 creation of a "new automotive regime," which represented an "incompatible," "drastic departure" from "neoliberal" policies (Gómez Mera, 2007, 113–14). The automotive regime responded to complaints about the overvalued exchange rate[15] and foreign competition (especially from Argentina), with investment incentives, quantitative import restrictions and subsidized BNDES credit (Gómez Mera, 2007, 127; Almeida, 2009, 13; Montero, 2014b; Schapiro, 2017). Responding to pressures from within the presidential coalition, the regime also sought to build up industry in the northeast of the country through tax incentives to newly located firms (Suzigan and Furtado, 2006; Gómez Mera, 2007; Coronel et al., 2014; Schapiro, 2017). As Gómez Mera (2007, 114) demonstrated, the automotive regime was made possible by a combination of private sector pressures on the "more permeable elements" of the government, who were defenders of developmentalism, as well as the reluctant conversion of more neoliberal policymakers who sought to use the regime to neutralize opposition to macroeconomic policy and the overvalued exchange rate they believed was necessary to keeping prices in check.

Under Rousseff's PBM, the government adopted a policy set known as Inovar Auto. As the name indicates, this was conceived in a more self-consciously developmental fashion, with the goal of increasing innovation in the industry. Through a combination of local content requirements[16] and tax advantages, the government hoped to increase the proportion of global production that was produced in Brazil (Michaud, 2015). As the Development Ministry noted when it introduced the plan in 2012, the key goals were to improve spending on R&D, increase technological content of vehicles produced in country, increase energy efficiency, lower the cost of cars, and increase auto safety. Somewhat less prominently, the proposal also had more conjunctural policy concerns in mind, including the trade balance (Schapiro, 2017).

Over time, a number of criticisms have been leveled at the various governments' automotive incentive programs. One of the problems with these policies is that it can be hard to estimate the counterfactual: would jobs, production, or sales have increased more with or without the government-led policies, for example? Thus, criticism of the Collor plan or Rousseff plans for failing to generate auto industry jobs may be unfounded, or at least difficult to prove, as might be the criticism of the Cardoso and Rousseff plans for failing to significantly reverse trade deficits in the auto sector, since there is no way to demonstrate what would have transpired in their absence. A sturdier critique comes from analyzing the politics of these policies: a variety of authors trace how these programs emerge less from a self-conscious desire to address shortcomings in national industrial development than from political pressure to address the whining of ministers, legislators, the car manufacturers association, or other noisy players. A related critique is that too often these policies were simply a reaction to conjunctural problems (Coronel et al., 2014; Botelho, 2015). As a consequence, they were often expensive and had only temporary effect, serving primarily to buy off opposition to macroeconomic policy.[17]

A final series of critiques concerns the developmental impact of the policies. In terms of sins of omission, Cardoso's automotive regime was called out for failing to contain incentives for domestic innovation among multinational firms (Egan, 2015) and Rousseff's policies for failing to push for investment in newer technologies such as electric cars (Schapiro, 2017). As for sins of commission, Rousseff's policies actually did call for additional innovation, but failed to obtain it: in a post mortem in 2017, Finance Ministry staff noted that although it received R$6.6 billion in tax breaks between 2011 and 2014, the auto industry actually reduced R&D spending, both as a share of net revenue (from 1.39 percent to 1.11 percent) and as a share of total innovation spending (from 16 percent to 10 percent) (Carneiro, 2017).[18]

Meanwhile, there are concerns about the effectiveness of such policies in the broader economic context in which they were designed: Brazil's inward-looking economic policies mean that fewer than a fifth of cars are exported, most of which end up in Argentina; similarly, the high tax rate means that tax incentives may improve the domestic competitiveness of cars by comparison to other fully taxed consumer products produced in Brazil, but it does not do much to improve the competitiveness of Brazilian cars versus those produced elsewhere. Finally, the control imposed over these policies has been lackluster. One of the few examples of such control illustrates the point: the Cardoso Auto Regime was contested in the TCU, whose auditors calculated that the more than US$1.8 billion in taxes foregone between 1996 and 1998 had been ineffective, with employment falling by more than a fifth among auto companies (Gerchmann, 2000). Notably in this case, the TCU appears to have been activated by the governor of Rio Grande do Sul, who had lost out on some major carmakers' decisions to relocate to Bahia under tax incentives intended to spur the development of the north and northeastern regions. Further, even though the TCU recommended cessation of the tax benefits, ultimately the matter was considered a political decision, not subject to TCU oversight. As Schapiro notes, drawing on Evans' evocative imagery, in the case of the auto industry, the state has been less effective at midwifery than husbandry, failing to induce existing firms into new and more challenging kinds of production, and perhaps meeting only the complex, but less demanding task of facing some of the challenges of global competition (Evans, 1995, 13–14; Schapiro, 2017).

Ethanol

The ZFM and the automotive industry are, in some ways, fairly traditional economic policymaking: at their simplest, they aimed to build out regional industrial production and enhance innovation and competitiveness. The ethanol industry, by contrast, represents an even more ambitious effort to transition an entire sector from a long historical comparative advantage in sugar production toward a relatively new and dynamic new fuel source, ethanol, with the potential for developing new production technologies, forward linkages into eco-friendly renewable energy and engines, and corresponding movement up the production frontier, with all the associated gains for industrial and human capital that might come from such a move.

With these ideas in mind, the Brazilian government has long been active in the ethanol space, beginning with the Proálcool program established in 1975.[19] These programs have aimed to develop new markets beyond sugar alone, including various types of sugar and sugar substitutes, anhydrous and hydrous alcohol,[20] as well as bagasse for use in electric generation.

Three phases are evident in the contemporary state's role: 1) from the Proálcool program and into the late 1980s, with a heavy state effort that relied heavily on subsidies, production quotas, and government export controls (Ramos, 2016); 2) a regulatory approach in the 1990s and early 2000s, in which many aspects of state control began to be removed from the direct control of the executive branch; and 3) the neo-developmentalism of the Workers' Party years, which brought the private sector introduction of the flex car in 2003, as well as the public sector Incentive Program for Alternative Energy Sources (Proinfa) beginning in 2002. Particularly in the second and third periods, from the 1990s to the present, policy could be described as neither entirely hands-off, nor entirely hands-on: policymakers were not strategically active in the ethanol space, and many policies grew vegetatively, yet policymakers did not resist the temptation to play a role. Ultimately, though, all three periods are marked by serious government failures.

The federal government's overall policy ambivalence may have emerged because the regulatory issues associated with ethanol production are complex. Policymakers may be asked to smooth demand and supply in national markets, in a naturally cyclical industry that faces robust international competition from a variety of products (including substitutes), has enormous demands for credit, and must reconcile a wide variety of competitive, labor, and environmental demands. Ethanol production fits into a variety of policy buckets – including energy policy, agricultural policy, and labor policy – and ethanol producers come in a wide variety of shapes and sizes, ranging from small family operations to large multinational enterprises. As a consequence, regulation falls into a variety of organizational bailiwicks, including the ministries of agriculture, labor, finance, and environment; public banks; regulatory agencies such as the National Petroleum Agency (ANP) and the energy regulatory ANEEL; state governments; and a welter of coordinating and consultative bodies such as the Interministerial Council for Sugar and Alcohol (CIMA[21]), and the sectoral fund for sugar and alcohol (CSAA) in the Ministry of Science. So, by nature, there are a number of avenues by which the state might play a role, a variety of different policy arenas in which it could play a role, and a host of potential demandants for a state role. But coordinating those various possible policy interventions is a supremely complex task.

The first phase Proálcool program was an indubitable success in promoting ethanol production, which rose from nothing in 1975 to more than 11 billion liters in 1989 and then continued to grow more slowly, to 15 billion liters by the outset of the PT governments. The combination of public and private sector incentives for alcohol consumption drove another spurt of fast growth in the 2000s, with production doubling in the first decade of the century to nearly 30 billion liters. Together, by 2016, sugar-based products accounted for 16 percent of total energy supply in Brazil, upwards of R$40 billion of GDP, and more than one million jobs (Santos, 2016; Santos, Garcia, et al., 2016, 11, 17).

Proálcool created a dynamic new industry out of doughty old sugar plantations, partly through the application of subsidies that totaled US$7 billion between 1975 and 1989 (Stattman, 2013). This was no small achievement, requiring the reduction of production costs to a third of their previous levels, a productivity improvement which made ethanol competitive with gasoline without any subsidies by 2004 (Lucon and Goldemberg, 2009, 125; Ramos, 2016, 65). This is not to say there were no bumps in the road; two in particular were momentous. Proálcool's success helped encourage the adoption of a fleet of alcohol-driven cars by the 1980s, and fully three-quarters of cars in 1986 were ethanol-fueled (Stattman, 2013). But in light of repeated producer crises, by 1989 and 1990, ethanol supply was so spotty as to obliterate demand for alcohol-driven vehicles and, in consequence, for ethanol itself (Ramos, 2016, 61). The second failure was of political economy: the concentration of sugar producers and their relative importance to the smooth functioning of ethanol markets allowed them to hold policymakers at the state and federal levels hostage. As a consequence, one of the more ubiquitous stories about Proálcool and its aftermath relates to the relatively frequent bailouts of indebted sugar farmers, many of whom ran up enormous debts, in particular to the government and state-owned banks: *usineiro* debts in 2014 were on the order of R$63 billion, unpaid pension taxes in the sector totaled R$2.24 trillion, and a significant proportion of firms were routinely under bankruptcy protection (Ramos, 2011; Veiga Filho, 2012; Almeida and Kassai, 2013; McKay et al., 2016; Ramos, 2016).[22]

Policies toward ethanol remained largely state-oriented through the 1990s. Indeed, despite the fact that the Collor and Cardoso governments are widely referred to as "neoliberal," many of the structures of the Proálcool program remained intact throughout 1999, with the consequence that one representative of the UNICA sugar producer association referred to the period until 2004 as one of "government-driven" development. This was not a heavy-handed government intervention with the goal of restarting the ethanol program, but the government nonetheless continued to play a significant role in guiding the market. Although the state monopoly on the foreign sale of sugar came to an end in 1989 and the Institute for Sugar and Alcohol (IAA) was closed after nearly sixty years in 1990, prices for cane, sugar, and hydrated alcohol were only freed in 1999, with deregulation having been put off on multiple occasions due to political pressures (Moraes and Zilberman, 2014; Ramos, 2016, 63).[23] Furthermore, in the wake of the Real Plan, the government pushed the ethanol industry to further improve productivity (Rosillo-Calle and Cortez, 1998; Stattman, 2013).

The third phase, under the Workers' Party, did utilize government policy with considerable aplomb. But it was the private sector's development of the "flex car" and its emergence in local markets in 2004 that changed the dynamics of ethanol forever.[24] After the introduction of the flex car, consumers no longer faced the binary choice of the 1980s between a gasoline-driven car or an ethanol car, which locked in a consumer to one fuel market or another until they sold their car. The flex car enabled consumers to instead choose between ethanol and gasoline every time they went to the pump. The popular rule of thumb was that any time the price of ethanol was less than 70 percent that of gasoline, it made sense to buy ethanol; when the ratio rose above 70 percent, it was time to switch back to gasoline. By 2018, fully 80 percent of cars sold in Brazil were flex models, ensuring a steady demand, provided the cost of ethanol could be kept below the 70 percent threshold (Reuters, 2018).

The euphoria produced by the flex car was perhaps best epitomized by President Lula during a visit to the state of Goiás, where the president exclaimed, "the ethanol producers who ten years ago were the bandits of agrobusiness are becoming national and global heroes ..." (Agência Estado, 2007). There is no small irony to this statement, given that as a presidential candidate in the previous two decades, Lula had often criticized the *usineiros* (ethanol producers) as self-serving parasites, paralleled in their venality and abuse of the state only by bankers. But his change of heart reflected the dynamism of the times.

Sugar production doubled during the 2000s, with labor productivity in sugar fields improving at rates that were far faster than productivity growth in industry (although productivity still remains about 25 percent lower). The private sector invested more than R$30 billion in new projects and the expansion of existing capacity (Bertão and Costa, 2014). The government built out its regulatory structure around the sector, with a National Energy Policy law in 1997 followed by a national agricultural plan (PNA) and then a national energy plan (PNE 2030) in 2007. Despite the private sector turn of ethanol markets, furthermore, the government continued to play a significant role, with policies including subsidized loans from the BNDES to producers,[25] quality control measures, support for construction of infrastructure to stock alcohol, financial support to R&D programs through the Science Ministry, and sale of electricity from bagasse combustion. The government established the PAISS (*Plano de Apoio à Inovação Tecnológica no Setor Sucroquimico e Sucroenergético*) to assist firms with research and innovation, and through Embrapa, established an agro-energy research lab, while the corporate-owned Sugarcane Technology Center (CTC) received more than half its funding from BNDES and FINEP (a research funding agency within the Ministry of Science and Technology). From 2004 onward, the ethanol sector was incorporated into all the PT's development plans – PITCE in 2003, PDP in 2008, and as a strategic sector in the PBM in 2011, with more than R$4 billion in planned investments before 2014 (Corrêa et al., 2017). Most important, of course, were three public policies: 1) the tax breaks given for purchase of flex cars; 2) the tax breaks on ethanol sales, which are greater than would be needed to compensate for the fewer kilometers obtained relative to a liter of the gasoline-anhydrous fuel mixture (Gorter et al., 2013); and 3) the requirement that anhydrous ethanol be added to all gasoline sold nationwide, at levels that varied from 18 percent to 27 percent, guaranteeing a steady market for ethanol.

These were heady times to be an ethanol producer, and many firms overreached, seeking out new land, boosting capital expenditures on equipment, and borrowing to expand. By the end of the first decade of the new century, a crisis was brewing. Already, there was an important constraint on ethanol producers, originating from the fact that distribution of ethanol was highly concentrated in three groups: Petrobras, Cosan, and Ipiranga (itself partly owned by Petrobras). Government regulations prohibited direct sales to gas stations, so this oligopoly essentially determined the end price of ethanol to consumers, and meant that there was no way for ethanol producers to increase their margins on sales.[26] Rising agricultural production costs and the increasing cost of private credit began to take their toll by the second half of the decade.

In mid-2008, the government began to reduce the cost of gasoline, using its power as Petrobras' majority shareholder as well as its role as

Economic Rents and Controls in Brazil

a regulator. Gasoline prices had been rising more or less steadily from 2001 through 2006 but were then held steady for the next four years, as the governments of Lula and then Rousseff sought to keep inflation in check and stimulate growth. To achieve this, the first move was to reduce the obtusely-named CIDE tax (*Contribuição sobre Intervenção no Domínio Econômico*) on gasoline, which imposed billions in losses on ethanol producers by increasing the price of ethanol above its 70 percent threshold relative to gasoline. The CIDE began to be reduced in mid-2008, reached zero in mid-2012, and was reinstated again only in May 2015. Gasoline prices were held in check by Petrobras. Ethanol producers responded by holding their own prices in check, but the proportion of ethanol prices to gasoline prices remained above 60 percent nationally from 2009 onward, which in light of the significant variation in state-by-state prices, meant that prices remained above the 70 percent threshold in significant portions of the national territory during this period. As sugar producers moved away from ethanol and into sugar instead, the paradoxical effect was to drive up the price of ethanol, and the national average price surpassed 70 percent of gasoline during a majority of months in the 2010 decade (Almeida and Zanlorenssi, 2017).

The consequences of the gasoline price controls were significant. Of 402 ethanol producers in 2009, 60 shut down by 2013, and of the remaining producers, firms representing a third of total capacity were facing significant economic hardship. Possibly as many as 120 *usinas* were shut down as a consequence of the policy (Silva, 2019), with the obvious implication that the sector became increasingly concentrated. The ten largest firms were responsible for 30 percent of national production in 2005; this figure rose to 43 percent seven years later after the bankruptcies and more than fifty mergers (Santos, Garcia, et al., 2016, 25). The crisis attracted foreign capital, with the percentage of foreign ownership of mills rising from 3 percent in 2006 to 33 percent six years later (McKay et al., 2016).

Ultimately, the central problem was of broader strategic control: the consequences of the public sector decision to hold prices steady in one corner of the energy market had enormously deleterious consequences in the ethanol market, suggesting a total lack of synergy and coordination between policymakers in the two policy domains. As Roberto Rodrigues, Agriculture Minister under Lula, put it: "It is not appropriate to subsidize the price of gasoline while ethanol is submitted to market rules. The country has no strategy for the alcohol sector" (Veiga Filho, 2012, translation by author). Similarly, critics noted that there was no cross-sector coordination of strategy for the automotive industry: the government offered the auto industry a reduction in the IPI tax, but asked only for employment to be preserved in return, when it might well have been able to use the IPI tax to push automakers to improve ethanol efficiency to a level below the 70 percent threshold (Mello, 2014).

There were also concerns about policies that the government did not implement, or which seemed unproductive in the long term. Ethanol prices are remarkably volatile, subject as they are to seasonal factors, the global price of sugar, and labor costs (Almeida and Zanlorenssi, 2017) and critics point to the fact that the government had no program in place to stabilize them, which might help producers to weather the storm (Santos, Garcia, et al., 2016, 22). Some policies, such as the Rousseff administration's 2011 provisional measure reducing the required levels of anhydrous ethanol in gasoline, were sparked more by short-term concerns about inflation than with the longer-term viability of the sector (Flexor and Kato, 2011). Investments in new plant and equipment are not insignificant, and there are few public incentives that would make them safer long-term investments, especially given the absence of a clear and lasting sectoral policy that provides continuity and is not subject to current events and political pressures (Santos, Vian, et al., 2016, 283). Finally, tech investment is largely private sector, with the bulk coming from big firms like Monsanto, Bayer, Dupont, Syngenta, and Petrobras, raising questions about the need for Embrapa expenditures and BNDES lending.

Controlling Developmental Policies

In sum, across all three policy areas since the Collor administration, a variety of characteristics listed at the beginning of this section have been present: a poorly functioning strategic process, weak targeting, high costs, little strategic recalibration, and the absence of reciprocity. Policies intended to create new firms in areas in which Brazil has no comparative advantage have benefited established MNCs, as in the Manaus free zone and the automotive industry, with only minimal counterpart reciprocity. Policies intended to help generate new technologies in areas where Brazil does have a comparative advantage, such as sugar and ethanol, have been subverted by poor strategic coordination across policy domains.

Democratic Brazil has seen the pervasive use of rents intended to preserve and build local industry. Yet the overall strategy followed by

Economic Rents and Controls in Brazil

policymakers has often been ad hoc in nature, allowing developmental strategy to become intertwined with other policy objectives. Industrial policy has all too often been a response to crisis conditions.[27] Even on developmental grounds, Brazilian performance can be roundly criticized. Writing only a few years into the democratic regime, Jenkins (1991) noted that the key difference between Latin America and the newly industrializing East Asian economies was the effectiveness of state intervention. Even before the transition, it was clear that the government was vulnerable to pressures from firms and the middle class (Skidmore, 1973; Evans, 1979; Jenkins, 1991). There were concerns that tax incentives had "lost the selectivity required for effective inducements toward the state's developmental goals" (Varsano, 1982, in Weyland, 1998). Moreover, the use of incentives under crisis conditions may be preordained to failure: if firms are indebted, they may only use the incentives to cover their losses; if they are not indebted, they may invest the additional revenues in financial assets such as government debt (Carvalho, 2018, location 857–9).

In the intervening three decades, little has changed. Use of the tools of developmentalism has seldom demanded a counterpart commitment by firms to meet clear goals of productivity or competitiveness, nor to commit to improve the quality of their labor force (Fiori, 1992, 181). Even when such counterpart commitments are established, industry has not always met their obligations (e.g., Wiziack and Prado, 2017). Once created, rents rarely sunset on a preestablished timetable. Mechanisms of control have either been missing, are incomplete, or do not function; often controls are too under-strategized to effectively guide firm behavior in ways that drive the economy forward.[28] Across a variety of governments and development plans, there has been little effort to institute a formal process for periodic strategic reviews that might evaluate and recalibrate policy in light of performance, or to collect public feedback on the course of policy implementation (Schapiro, 2013b, 129).[29] The most important consequence is that government appears to be following, rather than leading, with all the best developmentalist motivations dissolving into a morass that imposes society-wide costs in exchange for firm or sector benefits, with little to show in return.

The use of rents as incentives has degraded over time, into uses that are far from their developmental roots, such as emergency palliative measures (e.g., tax exemptions for keeping employment levels unchanged), or even "directly unproductive rent-seeking," i.e. corruption (Bhagwati, 1982). Critics conclude that the system is so stacked that policymaking has been overwhelmingly dominated by unproductive rent-seeking, with the

180   *Rents, Control, and Reciprocity*

notable effect of pushing growth, employment, and better income distribution into secondary, or residual, status among policy priorities (Lisboa and Latif, 2013; Villela, 2015).

WHY DOES LACKLUSTER CONTROL PERSIST?

So, what is it that explains the poor performance of the developmental state, particularly its inability to drive firms and sectors in new directions that are net positives for the economy and society? Four factors help to answer this question: the resoluteness and short time horizons of policy-making in a coalitional system; the parochialism of politics and the corresponding difficulty of building an upgrading coalition; weak strategic coordination of developmental policies; and weak oversight over development policies, agencies, and beneficiaries.

Resoluteness and Short Time Horizons of the Fragmented Coalitional System

As Chapter 5 discussed, the electoral system and the fragmented Congress it produces means that – at least since 1990 – the president's party has never held more than a fifth of seats in the lower house and the president must therefore build a multiparty coalition. The president's strong powers ensure that she is *primus inter pares* in the negotiation of the coalition, but she has been constantly constrained by the need to provide her allies with a variety of rewards in the ongoing bargaining game of coalitional presidentialism (Abranches, 1988; Palermo, 2000, 2016; Mainwaring et al., 2017; Chaisty et al., 2018).

Although the institutions of the developmental state have been modified over the past generation, the overall framework may survive at least in part because it provides valuable resources for the tool kit of coalitional presidentialism, providing the president with governing strategies that would otherwise be untenable. Pension funds, SOEs, state banks, and minority shareholding provide the goods that bind together the coalition, while giving the president policy tools and maneuverability that are not available in the limited discretionary budget she controls. These bodies are also home to powerful constituencies that contribute to the resoluteness of policy and the continuity of the structure of the developmental state over time. Under governments of both the PSDB and PT, who governed from 1994 to 2016, this pattern was reflected in a division between kitchen cabinet ministries, controlled by the president's closest confidantes and

Why Does Lackluster Control Persist?

leading the overall direction of policy, and implementing ministries, which controlled many of the goodies that emerge from governing, such as public contracts and appointments. The governing party received a claim to the paternity of successful policies, while allied coalition parties obtained many benefits from oversight of key elements of the state.

There are several implications of the coalitional presidential bargaining game for policymakers' ability to control developmental strategies. As in democracies everywhere, policymaking is often associated with a particular political-electoral timetable, with politicians timing their demands to electoral calculations. This is not always conducive to developing the longer-term strategies that would be needed to develop newcomer firms or to encourage "Schumpeterian" innovators (Schapiro, 2013a, 126).[30]

In the Brazilian case, furthermore, the fragmentation of the state that results from the constant negotiation and renegotiation of coalitions further breaks up decision-making into various subdomains controlled by different parties and coalitions. This fragmentation is not conducive to consistent policymaking, which as a result tends to be both short-term and focused on meeting interest group demands (Schapiro, 2013a, 119; Botelho, 2015; Limoeiro and Schneider, 2017). As Suzigan and Furtado demonstrate in the case of Lula's PITCE development plan, fragmentation led to a highly diffuse policymaking process: politicized decision-making bodies, for example, such as CNDI and MDIC, coexisted with politically autonomous agencies like BNDES. There was little centralized decision-making power: the CNDI met sporadically, and the ABDI, which theoretically was responsible for overall coordination of the plan, was frequently overpowered by other agencies, while lacking the formal power to enforce policy choices (Suzigan and Furtado, 2006; Schapiro, 2013a; Arbix et al., 2017). In this context, it is perhaps unsurprising that the state demanded very little in return for the sectoral incentives it offered: political pressure against reciprocal counterpart commitments was strong, and there was little interagency coordination to present a unified government demand across all the competing agencies.

The fissiparous party system further contributes to the resoluteness of policy, meaning that it is hard to change policy direction decisively in ways that might break from past practice or hurt entrenched interests. As Chapter 5 noted, the large number of potential veto players and the coalitional system that emerges from elections have meant that even though the executive branch often gets its way, policy change is usually parametric rather than paradigmatic.

Parochialism and the Difficulty of Building an Upgrading Coalition

A number of factors complicate the construction of "upgrading coalitions," which might push for more effective developmental policies (Doner and Schneider, 2016). Any incipient upgrading coalition faces institutional barriers. Pressure from voters has only a weak direct effect on the political system, because of the weakness of parties in the electoral arena and the weakness of vertical accountability that would enable voters to drive elected representatives in a particular direction, evaluate their performance, and hold them responsible. The open-list proportional representation (OLPR) system used to elect members of the Chamber of Deputies makes it difficult for voters to punish or reward policy performance. Party fragmentation, intraparty vote transfers, and inorganic parties contribute to weak vertical links between elected representatives and their constituents. Voters have a hard time identifying who they have elected and because they cannot easily do so, deputies exert less effort than might be expected to claim authorship or responsibility for policy. Intraparty competition means that campaigns can be quite expensive; making legislators more receptive to campaign funders.[31]

Further, the party system engenders a certain pragmatism in government relations. Parties are ideologically indistinguishable at many moments of the political process. Although the PSDB and PT stood out for nearly two decades as poles on either side of the political spectrum, they were surrounded by an amorphous alphabet soup of parties, with little separating the middle parties from each other. In this context, firm pragmatism in political donations and in the cultivation of political relationships seems eminently rational: declared ideology may be a less important signal than simply knowing which party leaders are likely to control core ministries, preside over legislative committees, or act as "*padrinhos*" (godfathers) to particular appointees. Incumbent firms are thus less focused on developing alternative political platforms and movements than on ensuring the relative profitability or market share of their firm relative to its peers.

Because the electoral system generates competition within political parties, it generates incentives either to cultivate a personal vote, or given the incentives of being part of a larger grouping within Congress, to seek political advantage by joining on to sectoral legislative blocs that cut across party lines. They share a common pursuit of sectoral privileges, or rents, that might include looser environmental regulation (*bancada ruralista*), tax breaks for churches (*evangélicos*), or better pension benefits

Why Does Lackluster Control Persist?

for high-risk professions (police unions). Real opposition in Congress seldom is expressed in an effort to outright block legislation. Rather, legislators seek to disfigure projects and extract sectoral benefits through this threat. Congressmen apply pressure at critical moments, for example when rapporteurs are selected for particular legislation, when the congressional leadership is up for renewal, or when the executive branch is contemplating a cabinet overhaul aimed at buying support for its next big legislative push (Lamounier, 2005, 211).

The possibility that politicians will use such leverage to sectoral advantage diminishes the incentives to mobilize for public goods that would be sector- or economy-wide, since the very existence of gatekeepers and corporate relationships with those gatekeepers suggest that any reform push is likely to fall prey to multiple special interest demands. The very existence of sectoral benefits undermines collective action. As Gonçalves (2012, 116) notes with regard to tax reform, there is a huge path dependency problem: dissatisfaction with the tax system has not yielded successful tax reform, but the growing and persistent use of sectoral tax breaks has increased the political costs of reversing sectoral breaks, while also making broader tax reform an ever more distant possibility by undermining the collective will to push for reform. The most organized sectors are more efficient at getting the policies they desire, so even when collective organization is possible, the resulting reforms may redound to the benefit of narrow sectoral interests (Frassão, 2016, 23). As elsewhere, the ability of politically influential firms to use regulation and policy to obstruct market entry may suppress competition and have a cumulative effect upon the country's capacity for growth (Doner and Ramsay, 2000, 147).

As a consequence, incumbent domestic firms have few incentives to push for collective upgrades, such as educational or economic policy reforms that may have uncertain long-term effects and immediate consequences on their bottom lines. Due to the structure of the Brazilian labor market, most domestic firms have little need for highly skilled labor (Schneider, 2013, 150). As a consequence, there is little evidence of domestic firms pushing for broader public goods such as education reform or stricter labor regulation that might create incentives for the development of a pool of high-skilled labor. This is especially the case if they are already gaining from sectoral or firm-specific incentives. Foreign investors and MNCs benefit from similar incumbent privilege: the MNC-dominated auto industry, for example, which has been a beneficiary of industrial policy throughout the entire past generation, received tax benefits in PBM in exchange for abiding by loose local content requirements and undemanding R&D spending requirements (Wade, 2018, 204). Foreign firms that are less privileged by developmental policies may also be reticent players in pushing for reform, in part because they may not have the same political networks or may be eager to avoid government scrutiny in an inward-looking economy with the possibility of legal discrimination by nationality (Schneider, 2013).

The absence of an upgrading coalition reinforces the subpar equilibrium by giving firms further reason to engage in the pursuit of individual interests. At the broadest level, the relative weakness of large business federations, the possibility that the strong executive could rapidly adopt potentially significant policy change,[32] and the subsequent need to establish counter-balancing checks in the legislature, jointly create incentives for defensive legislative liaisons and defensive campaign contributions by firms (Scheffer and Bahia, 2011; Schneider, 2013; Boas et al., 2014). Leading firms work to ensure access to information about regulation, ensure more favorable terms or a veto over impending change, and perhaps to obtain particularistic rents, through public contracts, public regulation, tax breaks, or sectoral incentives. Although this is common to business-politics relations worldwide, the scale of the state in Brazil, and the relative lack of control, mean that this pursuit eliminates many of the incentives for firms to work together for upgrading policies.

Interfirm relations in Brazilian corporate life are governed by a combination of contracts and competition, on the one hand, and interwoven relationships that are not market-determined, on the other (Lazzarini, 2010). Because those interwoven relationships so often involve state actors – such as pension funds, SOEs, or state banks – there is a very strong incentive to seek narrow gains from building stronger political links between firms and politicians. Chapter 5 noted the importance of high-level brokers who can serve a fiduciary role, credibly committing the president to particular priorities. Legislative brokers also are a recurring storyline of Brazilian business life: one of the titans of Brazil's privatization process, banker Daniel Dantas, was very close to Senator Heráclito Fortes; the owners of the JBS meatpacking empire were well-connected to Senator Aécio Neves; mining and oil entrepreneur Eike Batista used his close ties to Rio governor Sérgio Cabral to build connections to federal politicians, including Presidents Lula and Rousseff; at various moments in time, corporations have seen PMDB heavyweights Michel Temer, Romero Jucá, and Eduardo Cunha as the go-to problem solvers in Brasília; and so forth, seemingly ad infinitum. Meanwhile, even bureaucrats in highly professionalized technocratic spheres of the state may seek out political connections: the testimony of long-time Petrobras executive Paulo Roberto Costa in the Lava Jato case demonstrated, for example, that even when they are not political appointees, senior executives within SOEs may need political sponsors (*padrinhos*) if their careers are to prosper.

The consequence of these political calculations is a steady flywheel of compensatory policymaking. Ineffective government policies lead to the high cost of doing business, widely referred to as the *custo Brasil*. Since firms' competitiveness is hurt by the *custo Brasil*, firms demand compensatory policies, which governments are willing to provide in part because many of the instruments they can employ to meet firm demands – e.g., tax breaks, tariffs, loans – are fiscally opaque, while firms pay handsomely for the privilege. Yet such policies may increase the *custo Brasil* by deepening the regulatory thicket and increasing the need for a state bureaucracy to oversee the new policies. The consequence is inertia that keeps the equilibrium in place, simultaneously increasing the *custo Brasil* through these policies, on the one hand, while seeking to compensate for it, on the other.

Weak Strategic Coordination

Fragmented authority means that the Brazilian state is not well-structured to coordinate and control the strategic implementation of complex developmental policies. In other middle-income countries, this lackluster control might be easily explained by a weak and underfunded state, but this explanation is less convincing in the case of Brazil's federal government, even by comparison to previous periods in Brazilian history.[33] As Chapter 7 will show, the federal bureaucracy has among the hemisphere's highest levels of *state capacity*, understood as a professional bureaucracy with the ability to implement policy free of undue external influence (e.g., Evans and Rauch, 1999, 2000).

Indeed, over the past three decades, as Chapter 7 demonstrates, some of the most impressive reforms to the developmental state apparatus have originated within the federal bureaucracy, operating below the radar screen of the political system to "smuggle" through reforms. The plurality of stakeholders and the complexity of policy issues has provided technocrats with breathing space, while the shared consensus among technocrats gave them considerable political power, as did the still-current notion that policymaking should somehow be "protected" from politics (Weyland, 2002; Abers and Keck, 2013, 43; Kaplan, 2013; Dargent, 2014, 2015).

Yet if individual bureaucracies have sometimes been effective change makers, with the capacity to drive forward reform in specific arenas, the state as a whole has failed to achieve collective coherence. The central problem, paraphrasing Boschi, has been weak *state capabilities*, including the ability to define priorities among the conflicting demands made upon the government; to target resources where they are most effective; to innovate when old policies show signs of failure; to coordinate among competing objectives; to impose losses on powerful groups; to ensure the effective implementation of policies after their definition; to represent diffuse and unorganized interests, in addition to powerful and more organized ones; to ensure political stability so that public policies will have time to mature; to ensure consistency between the different spheres of policy; and to ensure effective coordination between different actors in the same policy sphere (Boschi, 2018, 341–2, drawing on Weaver and Rockman, 1993; Stein et al., 2006).

Central to the issue of state capabilities is coordination: there are very few effective efforts to coordinate across the various government agencies.[34] Leadership on developmental policy typically comes from the presidency, but the short-term political demands on the president are not propitious to long-term strategizing. Further, the next step in the policymaking process is often the Finance Ministry, whose attention to the fiscal imperative often makes development policies subordinate to more immediate concerns, or privileges the use of fiscally opaque policy instruments such as tax breaks and credit incentives.[35] As policy implementation moves down the hierarchy of the bureaucracy, it is fragmented into a variety of distinct agencies, which are not always working in tandem or responding to the same incentives.

Absent is a pilot agency with the political strength, technical capacity, and embedded autonomy vis-à-vis firms to drive the economy in a strategic direction (De Toni, 2014; Stein and Herrlein Júnior, 2016). Upon the return to democracy, officials discovered that out of nearly 20,000 agencies in the federal government, nearly 900 had the purpose of coordinating agencies (Grindle, 2012, 210)! This situation has improved somewhat under democracy, but the coalitional system and the strength of extant developmental bureaucracies imposes strong counterpressures against coordination. Even under an elected government heavy with developmentalists who recognized the foundational importance of coordination, the ABDI was unable to fulfill this function in the PBM, serving more as a clearing house for demands than a muscular director of strategic coordination. Like many of its predecessors, from the outset ABDI was a weak peer to long-established bodies such as public banks, the BNDES, and the economic policy agencies of the federal bureaucracy. The agencies of the developmental state, in other words, were able to absorb and overpower the body that was designed to guide them. In the absence of a clear pilot agency, there are very few incentives for civil servants or ministries to worry about their role in a collective developmental strategy (Schapiro, 2013a, 35–9). Most rents are provided without specifying an agency that will monitor their effects (Folha, 2018a). The result is that there is a certain improvisational nature to developmental policymaking, with little strategic coordination, low reciprocity, and only glancing evaluation of long-term policy effects (Suzigan and Furtado, 2006, 167–8; De Toni, 2014).[36] The consequence of this weak coordination is, all too often, "erratic trajectories that often pull the country off the developmental path" (Arbix et al., 2017).

Weak Oversight of Developmental Policies, Agencies, and Beneficiaries

Oversight in a democracy involves a number of different actors and processes. At their broadest, these include vertical and horizontal accountability; more narrowly, these may include a variety of processes for ensuring that policy is coherent, cost-effective, and meets probity criteria.

The issues of vertical accountability in Brazil were addressed in Chapter 5. Suffice it to note here that while there is vigorous electoral competition, once elections take place, the coalitional system tends to coalesce in ways that conflate the interests of legislative majorities with those of the executive branch, blunting the incentives for oversight of the government. Under these conditions, electoral accountability by voters is like pushing on wet spaghetti: there are many ways in which even clear voter demands may be diluted and distorted by the political system.

Horizontal accountability has also been weak. Checks and balances are constantly diluted by coalitional politics. The intermingled logic of coalitional presidentialism, in which neither elected branch is completely autonomous of the other, means that effective congressional oversight of the executive branch is often undermined by intra-coalitional bargaining. Congress, which in theory should exercise a significant check on the executive, often fails to do so because representatives are so compromised by their participation in the governing coalition (Chaia and Teixeira, 2001; Figueiredo, 2001; Werneck Vianna, 2002, 15; Hiroi, 2013; Pavão, 2015).[37] Executive oversight of the legislative branch, meanwhile, is all too often considered a secondary preoccupation next to the need to preserve governability (Arantes et al., 2010; Schapiro, 2013b, 126).

From the perspective of direct administrative oversight of developmental policies and agencies, there are a wide number of organizations that can play a role, including congressional committees, regulatory agencies, and the TCU accounting court. All do play some role in oversight, but these efforts are frequently either undermined by the coalitional system or overpowered by the relative autonomy of executive agencies.

With regard to the coalitional system, both regulatory agencies and the accounting courts have been populated at their highest peaks by politicians from the presidential coalition (or their designated appointees), and in many cases, by appointees from the least programmatic and most transactional parties within the coalition.[38] Naturally, these appointments reflect the interests of key constituencies, and thereby undermine genuine and effective oversight. The TCU accounting court offers recurring and tragic evidence of this dynamic: all too often its well-funded and high capacity bureaucracy has alerted its ministers to misspending, inefficiency, and even questionable transactions, only to have those ministers ignore or even reject the staff's reports (Taylor, 2019). Regulatory agencies' independence, similarly, has been diluted over time, thereby allowing for considerable presidential or coalitional influence (Prado et al., 2016, 391).

With regard to the imbalance between overseers and overseen, oversight bodies are at a disadvantage with regard to major executive agencies or semi-autonomous agencies like the BNDES. The budgetary autonomy of the BNDES means that it owes little to the legislative branch or any other oversight body: for example, it was only after a truly deafening roar of criticism that the bank began to comply with requests for greater transparency about its lending practices during the early 2010s (Colby, 2013; Prado et al., 2016). The TCU has no authority to oversee some important actors, such as the pension funds of SOEs and public banks (Dieguez, 2014, 74). Meanwhile, the executive branch under numerous presidents has – often quite reasonably, in light of both political costs and concern for the efficiency of the policymaking process – feared the interference of the legislature in policymaking, preferring to preserve top policymaking bodies from legislative oversight. Given the absence of a strong pilot agency, mentioned in the previous section, or strong horizontal oversight, there is little pressure on agencies to demand the sacrifices that would be needed to make the developmental policies function

Why Does Lackluster Control Persist?

more equitably, with the consequence that narrow interests generally prevail over broader goals.

The role of law enforcement bodies is a final complicating factor. The independence of the judiciary and the *Ministério Público* prosecutorial body contributes to exacerbating uncertainty about policy, in a variety of ways. First, these bodies add more decisionmakers to the mix, oftentimes representing entirely new and distinct interests. The *Ministério Público*, for example, challenged many of the infrastructure projects undertaken in recent years, delaying or even halting their progress (Pires and Gomide, 2014; Prado et al., 2016). The courts, meanwhile, have long been recognized as an important site for policymaking, enabling a variety of interested parties to utilize the veto point offered by the judiciary to bend policy to their desired ends (Arantes, 1997, 2005; Werneck Vianna, 2002; Taylor, 2008). There are democratically legitimate reasons for courts to play a role in the policy process, of course, but it must also be acknowledged that this role often scrambles policymaking in significant ways and makes strategic implementation of development plans far more challenging. Further, the hydra-headed court system, with considerable latitude for highly individualized decision-making by judges, means that it can be extremely difficult to foresee the direction of policy questions that are judicialized (see, e.g., Arguelhes and Ribeiro, 2018).

The second effect is the failure of the courts to prevent the most egregious abuses of the coalitional presidential system, whose currencies of coalition-building often fade over into either ethically troubling forms of influence peddling, or directly into corruption. Corruption, of course, may lead to highly particularistic behaviors, such as legislation written at the behest of a particular firm or sector, or contracts written for particular companies, or simple bid-rigging. As a consequence of a long tradition of impunity, corruption has become an embedded institution: as some of the confessed criminals involved in Lava Jato noted, their illicit exchanges with politicians were simply "a rule of the game" in public sector contracts (Moro, 2018, 161).

A variety of destabilizing forces may change these patterns of behavior. State capacity among accountability agencies has been improving over the course of the past generation, in part due to the strong guarantees of civil service tenure and autonomy in the 1988 Constitution (Praça and Taylor, 2014; LaForge, 2017). The country has come a long way since 2003, when the landmark Banestado case investigating money laundering by leading political figures and firms was almost stymied by inability to buy paper, hire telephone lines, rent a copying machine, or reimburse federal police for their travel expenditures (Marques, 2003). Under a concerted effort begun during the Lula presidency, the numbers of civil servants in accountability agencies expanded rapidly: for instance, the Federal Police rose from 7,431 in 2004 to 14,160 in 2017, and the CGU from nothing to nearly 2,200 staff in the past fifteen years.[39] Partly in consequence of these budgetary and staffing gains, but also because of a strong tradition of merit-based hiring, the volume of anti-corruption actions has risen markedly: the number of arrests for corruption by federal police rose from 473 in 2013 to 4,122 in 2016 and the number of civil servants fired for malfeasance more than doubled, from 268 in 2003 to more than 500 a year between 2011 and 2016 (CGU, 2016; Godoy and Bramatti, 2017).[40] Legislative accountability bodies such as the TCU and congressional committees of inquiry (CPIs) have generated enormous amounts of data and copious reports, and executive bodies such as the Comptroller General (CGU) and the Finance Ministry police development agencies to ensure that procedural rules are being followed. The vibrant media is also an important multiplier of accountability efforts (McCann, 2008; Michener, 2010; Porto, 2011).

But largely because of the strength of political ties to the governing coalition, and the weakness of the judiciary as an accountability institution, these checks have generated only occasional corrective effects. As Bonvecchi (2015, 902) noted, "checks and balances at the federal level . . . seem to stop before looking into how the wheels of decision-making are greased." There are multiple issues that undermine control of corrupt rent-seeking. The first are lingering weaknesses of oversight agencies. The TCU is politicized, slow, and its decisions are subject to three levels of review (Figueiredo, 2001; Pessanha, 2009; Speck, 2011). The Federal Police and CGU have expanded in size and power but remain subordinate to the president: as the Temer administration demonstrated, they can be successfully sidelined through the skillful use of appointments, reassignments, and budgetary reallocations.

Second, there is virtually no judicial accountability, especially for political and economic elites. As the chief Lava Jato prosecutor concluded morosely: the judicial system is made not to function; impunity is *designed* into the system (Dallagnol, 2017, 13). Slow trial times, congested courts, and the original jurisdiction of the high court in cases involving sitting politicians ("*foro privilegiado*") all contribute to weak policing of the relations between economic and political actors. Even in the cases of civil servants charged with corruption, who are thought to be more subject to control than other elites because they can be punished administratively as

Why Does Lackluster Control Persist?

well as face civil liability and criminal prosecution, the rate of judicial conviction in corruption cases is only 3.2 percent, a rate that suggests that the efficacy of the judiciary in fighting civil service corruption is "negligible" (Alencar and Gico, 2011, 90).

Practical impunity for politicians has traditionally been almost absolute, a phenomenon best exemplified by the fact that even though leading businessmen have been jailed in the Lava Jato investigation, on current trends, no more than a handful of sitting federal politicians are likely to receive a final sentence from the high courts within a decade of the investigation's first arrests in 2014 (Taylor, 2017).[41] The number of prosecuted cases of corruption has been very low until recently, and although the number of corruption cases has begun to rise, especially in lower courts, convictions remain rare (Levcovitz, 2017). At the federal level, of more than 500 federal politicians on trial between 1988 and 2015, only 16 were convicted, and only 8 served time (Bretas, 2015). Between 2011 and 2016, fewer than 6 percent of STF cases were decided against defendants, and fewer than 1 percent led to conviction (Da Ros and Taylor, 2019). While it could be that all of those defendants faced spurious and politically motivated charges, this seems unlikely, in light of the massive evidence of corruption that has emerged in recent years and the enormous professional costs police and prosecutors pay for investigating and indicting powerful political actors.

The hurdles to effective judicial sanction (whose causes are described in greater detail in this note[42]) make it very difficult to dislodge corrupt elites from their positions of power within the system. My count in Chapter 5 showed that 28 percent of all federal politicians serving between 2000 and 2016 were under investigation or indictment for various crimes, but only a handful have actually been convicted. The saddest aspect of this, however, is that most of these cases will never go to a proper trial. Rates of conviction are very low, but equally troubling is that a large proportion of cases are simply never heard by the courts, meaning that there is no chance for politicians to either clear their names, or for citizens to see effective punishment of corrupt acts. Nullification of cases based on the statute of limitations is the most likely result, at least for politicians in the high courts,[43] with more than 177 investigations and 34 criminal cases reaching the statute of limitations in the high court since 1990 (Dallagnol, 2017, 36).

The likelihood of judicial sanction for wrongdoing by business elites is also very low. Wealthy defendants' efforts are facilitated by the slow pace of the court system and its tendency toward irresolution (Holston, 2008).

In a poll of business executives, although 38 percent of respondents think efforts by governments and enforcement authorities to combat fraud, bribery, and corruption have increased, 70 percent felt that authorities are not effective in securing convictions (Ernst and Young, 2016). Despite increasing enforcement by the CVM securities and exchange commission since passage of an insider trading law in 2001, only two cases had been effectively resolved in the courts by 2018 (Prado, 2019).

The difficulty of effectively imposing sanctions feeds back into the system, decreasing the relative costs of corruption, allowing criminals to intimidate witnesses and whistleblowers and discouraging accountability agents from doing their job. After years of frustrated attempts to investigate and prosecute high level crimes, even the most dedicated police and prosecutors may become disheartened witnesses to criminality, rather than undertaking Sisyphean efforts that they know are unlikely to yield tangible results. The consequence is that patrolling the boundaries between the political system, the developmental state, and business interests is an infrequent and unproductive endeavor.

CONCLUSION

The Brazilian developmental state under democracy has been ineffective at the essentially political act of controlling the distribution of rents in ways that channel business energies in strategically productive long-term directions. The causes of such weak control are multiple, including political factors associated with the functioning of the coalitional presidential system, bureaucratic factors such as the fragmentation of oversight, economic factors such as the strength and political influence of incumbent firms, and judicial factors such as the toothless policing of campaign finance and the illicit links between firms, the developmental state apparatus, and the political realm.

Institutional complementarities between the political system, the DHME and the developmental state drive toward the subpar equilibrium described in this chapter. The combination of coalitional presidentialism, party fragmentation, OLPR, expensive electoral campaigns, and weak enforcement of both campaign finance and anti-corruption provisions enable close links between the three spheres. The fragmentation of decision-making that results from the constant negotiation and renegotiation of coalitions breaks up decision-making into various subdomains controlled by different parties and coalitions. As the major political scandals of the past three decades have repeatedly illustrated, the process of coalition-building is plagued by ethical dangers that have only been partially addressed by the growing capacity of some accountability agencies. Even this partial improvement in probity is still embryonic, and constantly butting up against the fact that the ultimate arbiter of accountability, the judiciary, has been largely inoperative in breaking the illicit links between firms, state actors, and the political system.

These cross-domain complementarities undermine the possibility of control, and thereby permit sectoral and firm-level rent-seeking that is pernicious to longer-term developmental objectives. The most important consequence is that government appears to be following rather than leading firms, with all the best developmentalist motivations dissolving into a morass of unproductive rent-seeking that imposes society-wide costs in exchange for firm- or sector-specific benefits.

The Brazilian political system may "work" in the sense that it provides short-term governability and has not fallen into the fractured and unstable pattern of executive-legislative relations that Linz and others feared might result from the difficult combination of a powerful president and a fragmented legislature (Lamounier, 1992; Mainwaring, 1993; Linz, 1994). Yet it is ineffective in meeting longer-term strategic policy objectives. As a consequence, it is perhaps little surprise that the state has demanded very little in return for the sectoral incentives it has offered, that strategic review is weak, that developmental policies are driven more by short-term electoral considerations or crisis resolution than long-term strategy, and that in consequence, incumbent firms are the chief beneficiaries of policymaking, with little to show for it in terms of long-term growth performance.

7

The Autonomous Bureaucracy and Incremental Change

... it is in the hands of men of government to promote or delay the progress of a nation.

Monteiro Lobato, 1933[1]

The first six chapters of this book have emphasized the ways in which complementarities across the economic and political spheres reinforce each other, and thus often contribute to reinforcing the power of current elites and reproducing the institutional status quo. But it is also the case that the past three decades have brought important changes to Brazil, in a diverse set of policy areas and in ways that drew international attention, such as the implementation of fiscal reforms that are seen as a model for middle-income countries, the implementation of a well-regarded public human immunodeficiency viruses (HIV) program, and the successful prosecution of leading politicians in a hemisphere-wide bribery scheme. All of these successful cases of change share a central actor: the federal civil service.[2]

As these examples demonstrate, the bureaucracy has been a central player in many policy innovations under democracy, contributing and often driving some of the most significant episodes of institutional change, despite changes in political leadership and in the governing coalition. Bureaucracies worldwide have increasingly become active players in policy formulation in the twentieth century, of course. But the Brazil-specific argument of this chapter is that the very complementarities that constrain certain forms of change in the political system contribute to making change more likely via the civil service. This protagonism has both positive and negative effects.

The first section of the chapter addresses the increasing capacity and autonomy of the federal bureaucracy, in the context of the institutional complementarities laid out previously in the book. The second section illustrates how epistemic communities within the bureaucracy have guided a variety of innovations across a host of unconnected policy arenas. Although policy innovation by the bureaucracy is incremental, slow, and often restricted to particular "islands of excellence" within the archipelago of state agencies, it has nonetheless been central to some of the most important accomplishments of the past generation, helping to reform institutions from within. Change led by the bureaucracy has limits, though, not least of which is that incremental reform may make change away from the overarching systemic equilibrium less likely, by reinforcing commitment to beliefs and practices. The final section discusses these limits and how they fit into the broader institutional complementarities discussed in earlier chapters.

THE EMERGING POWER OF BUREAUCRACY

Against a long academic tradition that highlights the persistence of patrimonialism and patronage in the Brazilian state, it is in some ways surprising to discover that the Brazilian state is comparatively quite capable. In a comprehensive analysis of the eighteen largest Latin American countries, for example, the Brazilian federal bureaucracy placed highest with regard to hiring on merit criteria, far ahead of second place Chile, and more than twice as high as the regional average. Brazil also led the region with regard to functional capacity, with a score nearly twice the regional average (Zuvanic and Iacoviello, 2010).[3]

Brazilian history over the past century has been, in many ways, a story about the emergence of a motley bureaucracy, combining features that are often simultaneously Weberian and patrimonial.[4] But when we consider that the *tenentismo* of the 1920s emerged in part because of exasperation at the complete absence of a capable state, a century later, the scale and breadth of that state is impressive. Getúlio Vargas' pre-World War II efforts to reform the civil service by introducing merit in hiring and promotion were an important starting point, but they were of necessity partial and focused on building capacity only in a few highly strategic agencies (Pereira, 2016). The 1945–64 Republic brought a regression toward patronage, and while the subsequent military regime prided itself on the technocracy it established in the economic field – developmental practice requires a highly technocratic corps, after all – professionalism

196 The Autonomous Bureaucracy and Incremental Change

was underwhelming elsewhere in the state structure, in part because the military found patronage a "good way to pursue its goals" (Grindle, 2012, 208). For most of the second half of the twentieth century the patronage system "persisted and reasserted itself," even as the career civil service also expanded (Hagopian, 1996; Grindle, 2012, 201).

Even as late as the 1985 democratic transition, most public employees were not hired on the basis of public examinations or merit criteria (Schneider, 1991; Evans, 1995). Lobbying by civil servants and the progressivism of constitutional drafters combined to make the 1988 Constitution an instrument for Weberian reforms that greatly expanded merit-based hiring, tenure protections, and salary guarantees (Heredia and Schneider, 2003).[5] Civil service reforms in the mid-1990s further attempted to improve bureaucratic efficiency and responsiveness, while moving in a classically Weberian direction through a regular hiring schedule, better structured careers, and a more uniform set of pay and merit arrangements. The pace of merit hiring has shifted significantly over the past sixty years: fewer than one in five federal civil servants were hired on merit in 1962; this number fell to under one in ten in 1985, but then rose continuously to more than 85 percent in 2009 (Pereira, 2016, citing Graham, 1968). These gains have been matched by increasing educational levels, with university degree-holding individuals rising from 39.2 percent of newly hired civil servants in 1992 to 94.1 percent in 2001 (Grindle, 2012).

The emergence of a reasonably meritocratic and capable civil service with what the public administration literature refers to as "neutral competence" (Kaufman, 1956) was not unexpected. Yet this process did not stop at neutral competence, and indeed, the Brazilian federal bureaucracy has emerged as an autonomous actor in its own right, capable of acting of its own volition, loosened from the bidding of elected politicians, and sometimes even against politicians' self-interest. This is somewhat surprising, given that in much of the literature on public administration, the assumption is that the bureaucracy will be inert or passive except in response to external stimuli (Zuvanic and Iacoviello, 2010, 147–8).

Perhaps the most influential explanation of the rise of the bureaucracy as an autonomous actor with the capacity for proactive action is Geddes' top-down model of the "politician's dilemma," which suggests that, because Brazilian presidents have sought progress in some policy areas and therefore must build effective bureaucracies in what historically was a sea of patronage, they provided political insulation to some agencies while allowing others to be used as the playthings of patronage-oriented politicians. This model picks up on and extends a long tradition of thinking about Brazil's bureaucracy as marked by the coexistence of "islands of excellence" or "pockets of efficiency" alongside their almost polar opposite, agencies marked by both low capacity and low autonomy from politicians (Benevides, 1976; Souza, 1976; Evans, 1979, 1995, 257; D'Araújo, 1982; Martins, 1985; Willis, 1986; Schneider, 1991; Geddes, 1994; Loureiro, 1997, 2009; Nunes, 1997; Grindle, 2012; Pereira, 2016; Bersch et al., 2017a, 2017b). But the model seems to assume that the civil service is a passive actor, with one possible implication being that what the president giveth, she may also taketh away. If presidential insulation is the explanation for the rise of the bureaucracy, an autonomous bureaucracy acting against the president's interests might well find itself quickly shut down. And in a coalitional presidential system, any action that threatened the broader presidential coalition would also likely lead to pushback against the offending bureaucracy, contributing to bureaucratic inertia and passivity.

Another explanation emerges from the complexity of policymaking and the power this provides technocrats.[6] Especially in the larger nations of Latin America, the complex economic conditions of the post-Depression century have led politicians to give great pride of place to technocrats who promised industrial development or, later, provided a recipe for tackling hyperinflation. In the 1990s and 2000s, the expert preferences of these technocrats trumped others because of the imperative to maintain macroeconomic stability, but also because the plurality of stakeholders and the complexity of policy issues provided technocrats with breathing space, while the shared consensus among technocrats gave them considerable political power (Weyland, 2002; Kaplan, 2013; Dargent, 2014, 2015). The Brazilian bureaucracy was also well-positioned to take advantage of the uncertainty of the transitional period: strategic efforts to consciously alter institutions prospered under these conditions, with civil servants able to exploit the gaps between the behavior expected of the institution and the actual behavior that takes place within it (Deeg and Jackson, 2007). This institutional malleability has provided both motivation and space for determined bureaucratic entrepreneurs seeking to solve particular policy problems in the post-authoritarian era.

The bureaucracy has also been empowered by the developmental state, which requires a large and efficacious bureaucracy to administer the many state institutions charged with guiding economic performance[7]; state-centric norms, which as Chapters 3 and 5 noted, have long led

198 *The Autonomous Bureaucracy and Incremental Change*

Brazilians to look to the state to resolve problems of citizenship and serve as the protector of economic, civil, and political rights; and a coalitional system, which requires a standing bureaucracy that can function despite the constant rejiggering of coalition partners at the top of many ministries. The extraordinary number of veto players plays a role in empowering the bureaucracy, too: as the capacity of the political system to produce changes to the status quo declines, the likelihood that the bureaucracy may play a role increases (Tsebelis, 2000, 443). All of these factors are undergirded by the letter of the 1988 Constitution's strong guarantees of bureaucratic autonomy and capacity, such as merit hiring, high salaries and benefits, and tenure protections.

In the post-constitutional decades, practices and rules governing presidential appointments have steadily moved in the bureaucracy's favor, ensuring greater autonomy. In a state as extensive as the Brazilian, with 1.15 million federal employees (of whom nearly 70 percent are civil servants), the task of presidential oversight is especially complex, and there are therefore a high number of political appointees in the bureaucracy.[8] But the number of politically affiliated personnel in any federal agency never surpasses 25 percent, and in most cases is much lower, with an average of 11 percent in the most important ninety-five federal agencies in 2011 (Bersch et al., 2017b, 112). Many appointees, furthermore, are actually civil servants. For years, some agencies actually drew up informal limits of their own on how many external appointees they would tolerate, but in 2005, Lula's presidential Decree 5497 formalized this ceiling, guaranteeing 75 percent of political appointments in the lower ranks of political appointments to civil servants.[9]

As a consequence, by the early years of this century, leading scholars of the Brazilian bureaucracy concluded that the supposed clientelistic politicization of appointments within the federal government was nothing but a "myth of Brasília" (Loureiro et al., 2010; Souza, 2013). The policy expertise of civil servants helps to protect them from political appointees, either by lowering the likelihood that purely political appointments will be made in the first place, or by lowering the likelihood that such appointees will be able to influence the bureaucracy that serves under them (Praça et al., 2011). Many agencies are protected from political appointments by some combination of norms about technocracy (e.g., Central Bank and Finance Ministry), specialized skill sets (e.g., Federal Police and CGU), constitutional guarantees (e.g., the Ministério Público), or by the statutory protections introduced since the turn of the century. Where politicization persists, it is impermanent: turnover of appointees is highest among the most senior appointment positions which tend to be most politicized, and political appointees tend to turn over more quickly than civil servants appointed to high level jobs (Lopez et al., 2014). This combination of historically low proportions of external appointees and high turnover among external appointees has left the bureaucracy with considerable room to develop policies of its own, especially as top-down mandates to the bureaucracy are often either short-lived or themselves reflective of civil service preferences. Politicization's deleterious effects on bureaucratic autonomy are further tempered by the existence of multiple parties across the coalition, and the tendency to populate agencies with representatives from multiple parties. Few federal agencies are clearly dominated by a single political party (Bersch et al., 2017b, 112). This means that bureaucracies respond to multiple principals, which is in some ways akin to responding to none. As Tsebelis (2000, 466) summarized the theoretical point, "[m]any veto players create space for bureaucracies to play their principals against each other," providing them with more freedom of maneuver.

Even as autonomy increased, the advanced qualifications of the civil service helped to build *esprit de corps* that also empowered the bureaucracy relative to its principals. Evans and Rauch (1999, 752) argue that, "[b]ureaucrats who see themselves as having joined their confreres in office by virtue of sharing similar abilities are more likely to internalize shared norms and goals than are those who know they owe their office to the favor of a particular kinsman or patron." Careers within the federal civil service are prized in part because public sector wages are high by comparison to their private sector counterparts, leading to highly competitive public service exams, which usually attract multiple candidates for any opening. This pattern of qualified recruitment holds as one moves up the bureaucratic hierarchy, and in surveys and interviews with civil servants, Cavalcante and Lotta (2015) find that technical competence and professional experience are the primary drivers of mid-level appointments.[10] Although there may be significantly different points of view within a bureaucracy, the shared commitment of many civil servants to their work as a "vocation," in service to a particular cause; the shared patterns of thinking about particular problems; and the group cohesion these shared ideas and approaches produce can be powerful collective instruments as bureaucrats navigate the political space (Wilson, 1989; Zuvanic and Iacoviello, 2010, 169; Polga-Hecimovich and Trelles, 2016; Wolford, 2016).

The emergence of a capable and autonomous bureaucracy has two important limits. The first is the extent of its autonomy. Bureaucrats cannot be so autonomous that the government as a whole loses its ability to operate. Indeed, one of the common threads of the vignettes explored later in this chapter is the development of tools to constrain bureaucracies elsewhere in government: bringing spending at the state and federal level under control, ensuring that health priorities are implemented by subnational bureaucracies, and ensuring the accountability of political actors. The second limit is a consequence of the existence of multiple veto players in the political system. The large number of veto players and their diverse interests creates a narrow path for meaningful reform in most policy spheres. While the large number of veto players may empower the bureaucracy, as Tsebelis argued, the path toward effective reform is still restricted by the discrete preferences of a large number of veto players.

Multiple veto players and jurisdictional "entanglement" have contributed to a defining feature of Brazilian democracy: policy incrementalism. Unlike its neighbors elsewhere in the region, Brazil has not "powered through" important reforms, but instead engaged in incremental "problem-solving" (Bersch, 2016, 2019). Such incrementalism, usually spearheaded by a high-capacity bureaucratic agency, has been a defining feature of advances in a variety of different policy realms: fiscal matters, environmental policy, trade reform, transportation, health, sentencing reform, anti-corruption policies, judicial reform, and central bank autonomy, among others (Loureiro and Abrucio, 2004; Armijo and Kearney, 2008; Taylor, 2008, 29–34; Taylor, 2009; Montero, 2014a, 11–14; Praça and Taylor, 2014; Nunes, 2015; Bersch, 2016, 2019; Hochstetler, 2017).

With these possibilities in mind, the following vignettes seek to demonstrate how epistemic communities within the bureaucracy have developed shared interpretative frameworks that guide policy change, enabling incremental changes to move forward against various, often significant, forms of opposition.[11]

INCREMENTAL INSTITUTIONAL CHANGE THROUGH THE BUREAUCRACY

The importance of bureaucratic autonomy to policy change in Brazil is evident in three different policy areas that influence Brazilians' development outcomes, but developed independently of each other: fiscal policy, HIV treatment in a universal national healthcare system, and anti-corruption efforts. Despite covering quite different policy arenas, these

Institutional Change through the Bureaucracy 201

three areas share two features common to the bureaucracy-led reform process: the construction of a strong consensus among civil servants, and the use of various stratagems to curb or elide outright opposition from powerful veto players, including "smuggling" reform below the radar, wooing external constituencies to overcome opposition from the political system, and efforts to "lock in" reform by law and treaty.[12]

The Economic Policy Bureaucracy and Fiscal Reform, 1988–2000

A significant amount of policymakers' energy since the 1985 transition to democracy has been focused on the fiscal reorganization of the state. Between 1985 and 2000, a variety of major changes were implemented, bookended by the creation of a centralized system of budget control under the auspices of the Treasury Secretariat in the 1980s and the 2000 passage of the Fiscal Responsibility Law (FRL). These initiatives originated from within the bureaucracy, but they are also interesting because they demonstrate a shift away from the policymaking patterns of the authoritarian past, in which much macroeconomic policymaking was centralized within insulated, "restricted decision-making arenas," dominated by the so-called "economic team" (*equipe econômica*), with strong presidential protection, little public oversight, and very little coordination with political parties (Loureiro, 2009, 129).[13]

The strength of the bureaucracy proved to be the greatest in economic policy agencies that had a long tradition as "pockets of efficiency," isolated from politics (Sola 1994, 171). Yet in part because of its increasing willingness to engage external stakeholders in policy deliberations, this economic policy bureaucracy by the late 2010s had managed to overhaul the institutions of fiscal policy, establishing at least three central principles that broadly guide decision-making today: primary surplus targets, a spending ceiling, and the "golden rule" on lending.[14] All were buttressed by a changed "culture" regarding fiscal matters, as well as stronger enforcement mechanisms, which together help to explain some of the unnerved reaction to Dilma Rousseff's fiscally disastrous presidency and the increasing debt-to-GDP ratio it engendered (e.g., Cysne and Gomes, 2017). But at least initially, fiscal reform was not a societal demand but rather a requirement of the bureaucracy itself (Bresser-Pereira, 2017). Achieving this consensus was made possible by shared values among bureaucrats: as Gouvêa (1994) illustrated, the camaraderie between a group of young civil servants united by their careers, by their isolation in Brasília, and by their overall depoliticization at a time of considerable political upheaval helped to generate the necessary solidarity.

The first major changes emerged immediately following the transition, as civil servants worked to rationalize the chaotic allocation of public resources in a context of increasing inflation (Sola, 1994, 154; Giambiagi, 2008). Preliminary studies conducted within the Finance Ministry in 1983 suggested a massive overhaul of public finances was overdue. A working group of more than 150 leading economic technocrats met in August 1984 under the leadership of Mailson da Nóbrega, secretary-general in the Finance Ministry, to discuss how best to reform public finances before the new democratic government took office. Their eight major institutional reforms were approved by the National Monetary Council, the senior policymaking body, in December. Implementation was initially halted by a court injunction filed by a congressman with close ties to the Banco do Brasil, which stood to lose power in the reform (Nóbrega, 2005, 300–3). The injunction was eventually overturned, and most of the policy recommendations were implemented during 1985 and 1986. Much of this early effort focused on disentangling monetary and fiscal policy, in part by ending Central Bank lending to the Banco do Brasil (the so-called *conta movimento*), eliminating the Central Bank's developmental loan program, and generally working to provide the Central Bank greater autonomy from fiscal issues (Gouvêa, 1994; Loureiro and Abrucio, 2004; Nóbrega, 2005, 232). A key change in this process was the creation of a Treasury Secretariat within the Ministry of Finance, which assumed the management of the debt.

Given the absolute priority of economic stabilization on the political agenda during the first decade of democratic rule, the economic policy bureaucracy was well-placed to influence subsequent paths of institutional development. A large number of the remaining recommendations from Nóbrega's working group were slipped into the Cruzado and Bresser stabilization plans, including, most importantly, creation of the Integrated Financial Administration System (SIAFI), which centralized the management of the entire federal budget in a single system (Olivieri, 2010). By 1987, all expenditures were required to be registered on the system, permitting greater control over spending. This strategy of using stabilization plans to implement policy recommendations was widely enough employed that it became known among civil servants as "smuggling": proposals which had been drawn up by the bureaucracy as desiderata in the past were inserted into sometimes only tangentially-related legislation, whether it was economic stabilization plans or packages written to respond to financial crises (Nóbrega and Loyola, 2006, 83, fn. 12).[15] Even when they were not smuggling reforms into place, the civil service

Institutional Change through the Bureaucracy

took advantage of the leverage that politically salient policies provided to introduce institutional improvements: the end of the *conta movimento* took place during the preparation of the Cruzado stabilization plan, while the end of Central Bank development operations and the transfer of debt management to the Treasury were implemented on the eve of the Bresser stabilization plan (Nóbrega and Loyola, 2006, 72). Similarly, the renegotiation of the foreign debt, which would culminate in Brazil's 1993 acceptance of the Brady Plan, helped civil servants to push forward their effort to split the functions of the Treasury and Central Bank (Nóbrega and Loyola, 2006, 75). Market crises, which would be frequent over the subsequent decade, also provided opportunities for the government to push its desired reforms (Tavares, 2005, 95).

Thus, even before the 1988 Constitution was drafted, significant changes in the fiscal order had taken place. Partly as a consequence, the constituent assembly focused less on changing the institutional framework than on defending the new framework against challenges from the progressive faction that dominated the early stages of constitutional debate in the Constituent Assembly (Taylor, 2009, 503). Central to these efforts, both defensive and proactive, was the strong consensus within the economic civil service on which policies to follow, as well as the existence of a competent bureaucracy to implement those policies (Loureiro, 2001). As a consequence, as Nóbrega and Loyola (2006, 73) note: "The long held dream of absolute separation between the Central Bank and the Treasury was achieved paradoxically thanks to a Constitution that is not recognized by its prudence in fiscal and financial matters .... The chapter on public finances is one of the best in the Brazilian Constitution." The articles on public finance set clear ground rules on legislative oversight over federal taxation and budgeting and apply these principles to state and municipal governments as well.

This is not to suggest that the Constitution in any way facilitated fiscal management: indeed, the constitutionalization of fiscal federalism – the uneven transfer of revenues across the units of the federation – posed a central challenge, making the task of balancing the budget and fighting inflation all the more difficult. Further, the Constitution's drafters kicked many fiscal issues down the road, to be resolved by subsequent legislation. Indeed, much of the period between the Constitution and the 1994 Real Plan was spent renegotiating the constitution's implicit fiscal pact. The failure of the 1986 Cruzado Plan and the subsequent five stabilization efforts over the ensuing eight years can be chalked up to a large degree to the enormous political complexity of this renegotiation, which redounded

204 The Autonomous Bureaucracy and Incremental Change

in the absence of a credible fiscal adjustment. Failing to achieve this consensus, economic plans from the Cruzado through the second Collor plan instead relied heavily on gimmicks such as price freezes that provided temporary relief against inflation but fell apart when the deeper fiscal reforms needed to effectively signal government commitment failed to materialize (Baer and Coes, 2006).

If the 1980s were largely about the bureaucracy gaining access to fiscal instruments that it lacked under the military regime, the failure of the ambitious stabilization plans of the late 1980s meant that the early 1990s were centered around using those instruments to begin to effectively constrain spending by the federal government. The Collor and Franco administrations managed to cobble together a neutral fiscal policy, with the primary deficit running near zero. But this budgetary achievement was somewhat artificial, given that it was only made possible by hyperinflation, which allowed the government to gain revenues through seigniorage while using price increases to eat away at real benefits. The upshot was that the federal government was essentially running a "repressed deficit" that did not directly resolve deeper structural fiscal issues (Giambiagi, 2008).

Over the course of the early 1990s, though, the economic bureaucracy – assisted by a coterie of experts who came from outside government but worked closely with top civil servants – began to accumulate the experiences of past economic plans to develop ideas for achieving a temporary fiscal adjustment that could then be deepened so as to ensure lasting stabilization. This learning process by the bureaucracy was incremental, slow, and seldom smooth. By virtue of the existence of a permanent corps of civil servants, though, it was possible to draw lessons from past plans and the political challenges that fiscal containment efforts had confronted (Loureiro and Abrucio, 2004). Achieving a consensus about the fiscal roots of the hyperinflationary spiral was a significant milestone (Sodré, 2002; Tavares, 2005, 89). This process of policy learning had two important consequences. First, there was a belief that the gimmicky price freezes of the past could not function, and surprises or shocks would be of only limited value (Loureiro, 1997; Loureiro and Abrucio, 2004). Second, and partly as a consequence of this emphasis on transparency and credibility-building, there was a consensus throughout the economic policy bureaucracy that significant fiscal commitments would be needed to sustain any stabilization plan (Giambiagi, 2008). While some of the more brilliant technical aspects of the Real Plan (such as the gradual introduction of the "Real Unit of Value" [URV] to align relative prices before the implementation of the Real as the new currency) were largely drawn up by academic whiz kids such as Gustavo Franco brought in from outside the bureaucracy, the fiscal tools used to provide credibility to the plan were the result of years of careful construction by civil servants.

When Fernando Henrique Cardoso was inaugurated as president only six months after the introduction of the Real, he was able to draw on a deep bench of reform proposals and tools built up by this bureaucracy since the early 1980s. Cardoso's first term administration, for example, was able to draw on a newly effective Central Bank (Sola and Kugelmas, 2002), as well as the powerful Finance Ministry, whose power had grown with the expansion of the Federal Revenue Secretariat (SRF) and the National Treasury Secretariat (STN). In consequence of this reinforced SRF, tax collection rose in real terms over the course of the Cardoso administration from 22 percent to 34 percent of GDP (a gain achieved through effectiveness improvements as much as tax increases), while the STN achieved near complete control over the size and pace of spending by other federal government entities (Loureiro and Abrucio, 1999, 2004, 54).[16]

That being said, the job of fiscal construction remained incomplete. It quickly became clear that the fiscal foundations of the Real Plan were more temporary than might otherwise be desirable, in large part because of the federal government's inability to claw back enough constitutional transfers to states and municipalities, and in part because of electoral politics. The Real Plan was made possible in part by passage of the Emergency Social Fund (FSE), a 1993 constitutional amendment which temporarily allowed some constitutionally mandated transfers to remain in federal hands. The administration also managed to increase the revenues collected through "contributions" (such as the CPMF) whose revenues were not susceptible to the same revenue distribution to subnational governments as regular taxes. There had been a qualitative shift in public finance management (Tavares, 2005, 91). But partly as a consequence of greater transparency, it became evident that permanent fiscal adjustment was far from complete, as the full public sector's average annual primary surplus of 2.8 percent of GDP in 1990–4 declined to a deficit of 0.2 percent of GDP in the 1995–8 period, and the debt's share of the economy began to rise (Giambiagi, 2008). Meanwhile, the end of inflation suddenly pulled the sheets back on the dire situation of many states and municipalities, who clamored for succor. The strength of governors and mayors, and their influence on sitting legislators, meant that Cardoso faced the enormous challenge of trying to clamp down on subnational deficits, even as he

206   *The Autonomous Bureaucracy and Incremental Change*

was seeking to approve a constitutional amendment permitting reelection. By the mid-1990s, consensus within the government was "we have control over federal spending and no control over state spending," in the words of former BNDES president Luiz Carlos Mendonça de Barros (cited in Leite, 2005, 62, translation by author).

The Real Plan's temporary fiscal foundation was always contingent on the next set of reforms – which SOEs would be sold, what sort of pension reform would pass, which civil service amendments would withstand judicial scrutiny, and so forth. In this sequential process of policy learning, as the key bottlenecks to effective fiscal management at the federal level were addressed, it became increasingly clear that the necessary next step would be to address the subnational fiscal problem. Key to this effort would be eliminating the moral hazard problem associated with recurrent federal rescues of insolvent state banks and the extortive pattern by which new governors would visit Brasília to convince policymakers that the overstuffed public payrolls in their states were not their doing, but were a legacy of past administrations that required a "one-time" rescue plan (Tavares, 2005, 86).[17] The task gained greater urgency because the Real Plan greatly undermined subnational finances, given that many state governments were reliant on the inflationary tax to survive, while banks owned by the states were reliant on the inflationary float. Meanwhile, the exchange rate anchor for the Real, and the attendant necessity for high interest rates to defend the exchange rate, hurt heavily indebted state governments (Loureiro and Abrucio, 2004).

The constant renegotiation of state and municipal debts over the decade through 1995 were a "permanent" source of fiscal indiscipline and of tensions between state banks and the federal government (Nóbrega and Loyola, 2006, 74). Federal politicians, especially presidents, had a very hard time rejecting the demands of powerful state governors, who could mobilize state legislative delegations against administration policies or instead mobilize (or fail to mobilize) key sectors of the electorate. Partly as a consequence of this political reality, recurrent efforts to renegotiate state debts and state banks' balance sheets were an exercise in futility, as policy plans were overridden by political necessity. Seven different debt accords between the federal government and the states were negotiated in the decade from 1988 to 1997, and all seven fell apart (Loureiro, 2001; Loureiro and Abrucio, 2004).

The first step toward resolving this long-festering crisis was driven by Central Bank president Gustavo Loyola, a career civil servant, in a two-

Institutional Change through the Bureaucracy

pronged process aimed at addressing the structural vulnerabilities of both the private and public banking sectors. These plans, PROER for the private banks (*Programa de Estímulo à Reestruturação e ao Fortalecimento do Sistema Financeiro Nacional*, November 1995) and PROES (*Programa de Incentivo à Redução do Setor Público na Atividade Bancária*, February 1997) for the public banks, led to the restructuring of the banking sector, including the sale or closure of state-owned banks in all twenty-seven states.

The renegotiation of state debts was an integral part of this same process of cleansing the subnational fiscal mess. A scandal in late 1996 revealed that state and municipal governments were issuing bonds to pay off judicial debts, one of the few legal ways for states to issue debt.[18] The judicial debt bonds were fraudulently issued so as to obtain funds to pay off current expenditures. The ensuing renegotiation led to an overhaul of subnational debts on favorable repayment terms, in exchange for states' commitment to primary surplus targets, privatizations, and revenue targets, on penalty of federal withholding of revenue transfers.

The renegotiation included R$132 billion in refinancing, for twenty-five of the twenty-seven states, which was negotiated in each case by the STN bureaucracy (Sodré, 2002; Loureiro and Abrucio, 2004; Giambiagi, 2008). Provisional measures drafted by the bureaucracy placed limits on state debt issuance. More lastingly, the civil service drafted a statute which would be approved as Law 9.496 in 1997, setting out stringent conditions for renegotiation. Career civil servant and former Planning Minister Martus Tavares identified this law as the most relevant constraint on subnational debt up until that point (Tavares, 2005). It was backed by equally strict Senate resolutions on state debts that transferred further power for debt supervision to the STN (Loureiro, 2001). This was a delegation of substantial regulatory power by the legislature to the bureaucracy, perhaps because senators knew that they could not be trusted to credibly commit to overseeing their fellow state politicians: far better to bind themselves by moving such complex decisions to the bureaucracy (Loureiro, 2001; Loureiro and Abrucio, 2004). Under the immense pressure that was brought to bear by the combination of domestic support for stabilization and international market pressures to address Brazil's fiscal vulnerability, this calculus made reasonable sense to a majority.

In parallel to the renegotiation of state debts, the government had been working on a civil service reform that aimed to make the public service

208 *The Autonomous Bureaucracy and Incremental Change*

more efficient and fiscally sustainable. The June 1998 constitutional amendment for civil service reform imposed a requirement that the government draft a complementary law on fiscal principles within six months. This idea had been bandied about since at least the introduction of the proposed draft civil service amendment in 1996, giving the bureaucracy time to prepare its own version of the fiscal reform bill.

At heart, the economic bureaucracy wanted to undertake a reform that would lead to a "structural change" in the fiscal regime, so as to end – once and for all – the constant renegotiation that had become the bugbear of fiscal management (Afonso, 2010, 5). Top civil servants realized that the market was not going to be eternally satisfied by a series of fiscal band aids that dealt with crises in one-off fashion. In the memorable words of Martus Tavares, doing so was like serving a tiger small steaks; feeding it by dribs and drabs meant that the tiger's hunger would never be sated (Tavares, in Leite 2005, 85).[19] Legislators, meanwhile, were making it clear that the executive branch could not keep returning to Congress to ask for more sacrifice.

In mid-1997, a working group of civil servants had come together under the auspices of the BNDES to brainstorm how best to improve the management of public finances (Puttomatti, 2002, 5); the BNDES was involved by virtue of the bank's participation in debt negotiations associated with the privatization process. This process accelerated with the Russian crisis in August 1998. The Planning Ministry created two working groups. The first focused on emergency, short-term fiscal measures. The second aimed at coming up with a long-term plan. This second team was led by the executive secretary in the Planning Ministry, Martus Tavares, alongside BNDES manager José Roberto Afonso, a former legislative staffer who had advised congressman José Serra as the latter headed the fiscal committee during the Constituent Assembly. This working group drew on their expertise, past legislation, and a study of the experiences of New Zealand, the EU, and the US to develop the kernel of the 2000 FRL. The staff of the Planning Ministry then drew up an initial draft of the amendment (CPDOC, 2009).

In October, the Cardoso administration announced a letter of intentions with the IMF, in which it committed to a Fiscal Stability Program (PEF), which included as one of its key pillars the formal submission of the FRL to Congress by December (Tavares, 2005, 92). Ironically, the IMF did not impose the FRL on the federal government; instead, it was the Brazilian civil servants that pressured the IMF to include the proposal in the letter of intentions (against the opposition of some IMF staffers). In the final quarter of 1998, the working group pushed forward on the project, drawing heavily on staffers' past experience in a variety of agencies, including the Treasury, the Federal Control Secretary (a precursor to the CGU), the Central Bank, and BNDES, as well as consultations with staff from other agencies around the federal government (Leite, 2005, 88–90).

Rather than send the proposal directly to Congress, the executive branch sent a preliminary draft (*anteprojeto*) while opening up the same draft for public consultation. For the first time, a fiscal bill was being debated in public: a draft was opened up for review online, and senior civil servants held regular meetings with state and municipal finance secretaries, with business groups, and with civil society (Afonso, 2010, 6). This deliberative process contributed to a far more consensual amendment proposal. Even governors of the opposition Workers' Party voiced support for the proposal's provisions, including some of its most contentious restrictions on public payrolls (Leite, 2005, 98; Afonso, 2010). However, the proposal was insufficient to ensure the credibility of the Real Plan against the incessant tidal waves of balance of payments instability brought by the Mexican, Russian, and Asian crises (Baer and Coes, 2006). The federal government's mounting debt (ironically, in part a consequence of the process of clearing out subnational liabilities) and failure to tackle the fiscal adjustment as rapidly as markets sought proved unfortunate as international conditions began to shift.

One fateful consequence of the complex debt negotiations was former president, then-governor, Itamar Franco's decision to fight the privatization of his state's electric company by defaulting on his state's debt, a decision that led to a complete collapse in market faith, culminating in the catastrophic January 1999 devaluation. The devaluation, though, may have pushed Congress in the right direction, for the prudent macroeconomic response to the newly floating exchange rate required fiscal reform. In the absence of an exchange rate anchor, the government turned to the *tripé* of a floating exchange rate, fiscal surpluses, and inflation targeting. Fiscal responsibility would be central to keep foreign capital from fleeing while holding inflation in check. Most of government was on board, even the courts: in the wake of Franco's default, the Finance Ministry took the unprecedented decision to block constitutional transfers to Minas Gerais, a decision that was backed by the STF (Loureiro, 2001, 89).

At its core, the FRL sought to achieve three aims: planning, transparency, and control at all three levels of the federation (Cruz and Afonso, 2018). It sought to improve the efficacy of budgets as planning instruments, increase public access to fiscal information, and impose clear

The Autonomous Bureaucracy and Incremental Change

controls on public spending and public debt (Sodré, 2002). Personnel spending was limited as a share of revenue, debt ceilings were imposed, and certain outlays were prohibited in the runup to elections.

Several innovations are noteworthy. Article 35 of the FRL prohibits the renegotiation of debts with other levels of government, thus blocking new review of past debt agreements and eliminating a major source of moral hazard (Giambiagi, 2008). The FRL established spending limits not just vertically, up the three levels of the federation, but also horizontally, setting clear limits for the executive, legislative, and judicial branches. Failure to comply can be punished through legal and administrative action against individual policymakers, but also, and perhaps even more consequentially, subnational governments' failure to comply can be punished through retention of constitutional transfers and prohibition of future agreements with the federal government (Tavares et al., 1999). Congress passed the FRL rapidly, with 385 deputies in favor and only 86 against in the Chamber, and 60 senators in favor and 10 against in the Senate; it became law in May 2000.

In the course of the fifteen years following the transition to democracy, a strong consensus had developed within the economic policy bureaucracy on the need to achieve a series of improvements in fiscal governance. This drive culminated in 2000 with the passage and implementation of the FRL, but more importantly, it also led to a change in the "culture" of political actors in Brazil, some of whom voluntarily surrendered their regulatory power to the civil service and others of whom agreed to limit their potential freedom of action as governors or mayors (Loureiro and Abrucio, 2004; Tavares, 2005, 95). A "profound change" took place in the relationship between the federal government and subnational politicians, "turning the page" on the country's fiscal history and providing greater effectiveness and credibility to the government (Tavares, 2005, 88, 98). Populism is not dead, but neither is the irresponsible use of public monies tolerated as it was in the past. The political fiscal cycle around elections was largely tamed.

Clearly, this accomplishment is not irreversible, and the commitment to fiscal responsibility has sometimes wavered in the intervening years. Despite eleven major laws on the books to limit fiscal profligacy (O Globo, 2018a), a variety of actors have found ways to water down their efficacy, most notably by circumventing personnel spending limits through special housing allowances and other *jeitinhos*. Nor has the federal government always been the guardian of fiscal rectitude that the FRL envisions it to be, as the fiscal decline of the Rousseff years demonstrated. Most importantly,

Institutional Change through the Bureaucracy

the bureaucracy, which has in some regards been a force for change on the fiscal front, has also sometimes been an obstacle to that same change: the 1980s efforts to separate the Central Bank from the Banco do Brasil, for example, was fought by many civil servants (Nóbrega and Loyola, 2006), as were efforts to include limits on Central Bank debt issuance in the FRL (Leite, 2005, 99). The *jeitinhos* to boost salaries at the expense of fiscal responsibility are also often the result of creative ingenuity by civil servants acting self-interestedly.

Yet after looking more closely at the progress that has been made on fiscal issues, it is clear that the bureaucracy was the most relevant mobilizing force, even against the opposition of powerful political actors. Civil servants have generated new ideas, such as the brainstorm that led to the FRL or the working group that contributed to the creation of the STN. The economic policy bureaucracy has slowly closed fiscal spigots and increased the transparency of the fiscal accounts, improving the public disclosure of statistical data (Giambiagi, 2008, 579–80). The STN has achieved effective control over the disbursal of public funds and various institutional "locks" have been put in place to make a reversion to profligacy more difficult, including the constitutionalization of fiscal law, the sale of state banks, and the strengthening of legal controls over administrators. Civil servants have also encouraged policy in particular directions and not others, smuggling in their ideas, pushing pet projects, and taking advantage of crisis moments to reach commonly held goals.

Creation of the SUS and HIV/AIDS Policy

The construction of the democratic health care system was a two-step process. The late authoritarian years and the early years of democracy were marked by considerable policy dynamism by a group of actors outside the state, whose strategic pincer movement at both the grassroots and institutional levels contributed to a remarkable two-decade long process of institutional reform. The 1985 transition, 1988 Constitution, and 1990 Organic Law for Health were all a consequence of the remarkable energy devoted by these groups to institutional change during the regime transition.

In the realm of health provision, much of this energy came from outside government, through the well-documented efforts of the *"sanitarista"* movement of doctors, health professionals, and academics (Escorel, 2008; Falleti, 2010; McGuire, 2010; Sugiyama, 2012). Years of subtle efforts to "infiltrate the state" helped *sanitaristas* to gain a foothold in government and push through reforms that codified and institutionalized their core objectives of universal health care and decentralized health care provision (Falleti, 2010). But once the Organic Law governing the health care system was approved in 1990, institutions settled into more stable patterns, in which the large number of potential veto players limited many significant forms of change. Once the major institutional overhaul was completed, the second pattern of change began, with the bureaucracy playing a central role in adoption of most major policy initiatives – on such diverse topics as Farmacia Popular, HIV/AIDS, diabetes, and family health initiatives – within the constraints created by the *sanitaristas'* new institutions.

The story of healthcare in Brazil cannot be understood without reference to the social debt built up by the military regime's exclusionary social policies. At least half of the population in the economic "miracle" years remained outside the formal labor market, and they were therefore excluded from the formal structures of assistance provided via INAMPS (Instituto Nacional de Assistência Médica da Previdência Social) (Escorel et al., 2005, 61). Preventive public health was the "poor cousin of curative medical care," receiving only 15 percent of public health spending in the late 1970s (Dowbor, 2009, 192; Mayka, 2019a).

Beginning in the late 1960s, many universities began to create departments of preventive medicine, which would become havens for *sanitaristas*, who sought greater attention to primary care for a broader swathe of the population. *Sanitaristas* slowly moved into key bureaucracies, such as the INAMPS, the health ministry, IPEA, and FINEP in the federal government. Others, particularly those who had been repressed and exiled by the regime, found safety in the Pan-American Health Organization. From these institutional havens, *sanitaristas* were able to channel support back to their university departments, such as UERJ, Fiocruz, and the Centro Brasileiro de Estudos da Saúde (CEBES). CEBES, created at the University of São Paulo in 1976, soon began to publish a journal, *Saúde em Debate*, which became a central sounding board for the movement's ideas (Escorel et al., 2005; Mayka, 2019a, 2019b). CEBES remained an important clearinghouse decades later, carrying forward key ideals such as privileging preventive over curative care, health as a human right, improved care for the rural and urban poor, decentralized and universal health care provision (Weyland, 1995; Arretche, 2004; Sugiyama, 2008; Falleti, 2010; Bersch, 2019). Many changes took place "gradually and under the noses of ... the military regime" (Falleti, 2010) but began to crescendo by the late 1980s.

Sanitaristas helped to organize a wide variety of initiatives that tied together health policy across Brazil's federal system, among which the most important were the so-called *Ações Integradas de Saúde* (AIS), which sought to bring to bear all of the resources of the federal and state governments in an integrated fashion at the local level. The AIS were created by the *Ministério da Previdência e Assistência Social* in 1981 and had spread to all states by May 1984, under the leadership of one of the most prominent *sanitarista* doctors, Eleutério Rodriguez Neto, who encouraged bottom-up pressures by state secretaries of health to neutralize opposition at the federal level (Rodriguez Neto et al., 2003, 47; Falleti, 2010). The AIS program linked advocates across the federation, as well as setting the principles that would guide the 1987 proposal for a nationwide Unified and Decentralized Health System (*Sistema Unificado e Descentralizado de Saúde*, SUDS), an important precursor of the Integrated Health System (*Sistema Único de Saúde*, SUS) that would be implemented the following year.

The Eighth National Health Conference, held in 1986 and attended by more than 4,000 health care professionals and advocates, developed a final conference report that summarized the aims of the *sanitaristas*: universalism, equity, decentralization, regionalization, and community participation (Escorel et al., 2005, 79; Mayka, 2019a, 2019b). These principles were carried forward by the *Comissão Nacional de Reforma Sanitária* (CNRS), a body that drafted the principles for healthcare debated in the Constituent Assembly, as well as the new Lei do SUS, the law governing the Integrated Health System (SUS).[20] The organization of the *sanitaristas* helped them achieve their goal, and this remarkable period of institutional ferment reached a crescendo with the 1988 Constitution, whose Article 196 declared a universal right to health.[21]

The same reform coalition which had coalesced at the 1986 National Health Conference continued to play a central role in health policy following the Constitution: notably, it mobilized nationally to overcome President Collor's reluctance to approve participatory health provisions, forcing passage of the Organic Law of Health (LOS 8.080), in 1990.[22] The resulting changes were "a sweeping overhaul of the health sector" that created participatory health councils at the federal, state, and municipal levels,[23] "extended universal coverage to all Brazilians, eliminated existing state agencies, and decentralized financing and administration of health policy" (Mayka, 2019a).

This triumphant process put in place a new institutional structure, which gradually settled into place over the next decade, most notably through a series of six regulatory orders implemented between 1991 and 2002 that dismantled the INAMPS, began the decentralization process, set up funds transfers to state and municipal governments, and defined the roles and responsibilities of key agencies, including by giving health councils the responsibility to approve all federal funds transfers, a powerful lever over states and municipalities. It was not until 2000 that full adoption at the municipal level was completed (Mayka, 2019a, 2019b), and even after this moment, *sanitarista* control over leadership positions in the SUS national and subnational hierarchy were essential to ensuring effective implementation of SUS mandates (Gibson, 2017). But the institutional framework for a universal healthcare system, driven from the center but implemented at the local level, was in place.

The results of the *sanitarista* infiltration of the bureaucracy are perhaps nowhere better demonstrated than in the remarkable improvement in health care outcomes in the post-1980 period. While starting from a low base, life expectancy and infant mortality improved more than twice as fast in Brazil in the quarter century following 1985 as they did in the remainder of Latin America (Bersch, 2019; citing Gragnolati et al., 2013). Notably, reform successes "often cascaded from one area of health policy to another" (Bersch, 2019), enabling self-sustaining cycles of improvement across a variety of different fields of health care.

The HIV epidemic, however, posed an early challenge to the new health care system. One of the central problems in HIV policy has been to reassert federal power over the subnational level, so as to ensure that key policy initiatives are implemented by sometimes recalcitrant and frequently overburdened state and municipal governments, for whom HIV is only one of many competing priorities. But doing so posed a unique conundrum: how could the federal bureaucracy reassert control over subnational governments that had gained spending and policy autonomy in the Constitution? Decentralization through SUS also meant that the federal health care bureaucracy had few instruments to guide policy in the direction it desired. It could not make spending decisions for subnational governments, and it did not have good information about local implementation.

The federal response to HIV and AIDS included efforts to produce generic drugs at large scale, even if it meant threatening large multinational pharmaceutical companies with compulsory licensing of their antiretroviral drugs (ARVs). Initial efforts were led by Health Minister José Serra, who declared in 1996 that citizens would have guaranteed free access to ARVs. With the coordinated action of civil service officials and social mobilization, this promise was cemented into a 1996 law guaranteeing free and universal access to drugs for HIV/AIDS treatment (Law 9.313) (Nunn, 2009; Rich, 2013). By the late 1990s, seven non-patented ARVs were being produced at large scale in Brazil, and the remaining eleven ARVs in the national treatment guidelines were under patent, purchased from MNC pharmaceutical producers (Nunn, 2009, 3–4). By 1997, many of these drugs were available at clinics throughout the national health care system, with nearly 200,000 individuals under treatment by the end of the decade (this number would rise to over half a million by 2016) (Ministry of Health, 2017). The high cost of several of these ARVs led the Health Ministry to threaten to issue compulsory licenses for local production in 2001, enabling it to meet demand across all of the treatment guidelines.[24] These federal efforts to ensure supply at the national level required a parallel effort to ensure that demand was being met at the local level. Given that decentralization shifted most health care spending to the local level, the challenge became ensuring that the municipalities that were now the central providers of health (and education) actually followed through on national HIV policies (Montero, 2001; Arretche, 2002, 2004; Rich and Gómez, 2012).

Federal health officials pushed to build on preexisting relations with civil society to monitor subnational governments, while also developing strategies to mobilize local civil society groups where none existed previously. The central problem was one of ensuring that information about treatment provision was finding its way up the federal structure and that subnational governments were complying with federal policies. Rich's comprehensive analysis of this process notes that it led to the remarkable pattern by which federal bureaucrats built up local civil society groups which monitored local policy implementation and provided a mobilizable corps of allies who encouraged local policy implementation. Federal civil servants mobilized local grassroots as "watchdogs and policy advocates— monitoring subnational government behavior, sanctioning the politicians who fail to comply with national standards, and pursuing legislative and judicial policy protections" (Rich, 2013). Federal health officials sometimes used carrots, such as a discretionary fiscal transfer program, to provide funding to municipalities that complied with the national AIDS program's policy objectives (Gómez, 2014, 930). But they also encouraged punitive measures: most remarkably, federal officials actively pushed their allies in local civil society to confront local governments in court, if necessary, to meet needs in the HIV field (Rich, 2013).[25]

216 *The Autonomous Bureaucracy and Incremental Change*

To achieve their goals, during the 1990s, top officials in the AIDS program undertook a conscientious effort to bring civil society AIDS movement activists into government, in a process similar to the *sanitarista* colonization of the Health Ministry in the 1980s. In 1992, Lair Guerra, the program director for AIDS in the Health Ministry, worked hard to integrate civil society into the policy process, hiring leading figures as consultants and as civil servants, often relying on funds from the World Bank and administrative support from UNESCO (Rich, 2013, citing to Câmara and Lima, 2000; Galvão, 2000; Stern, 2003; World Bank, 2004). Federal officials developed strategic relationships with civil society, including through a unit, the Civil Society and Human Rights sector (CSHR) specifically designed to "monitor, mobilize, and strengthen local civil society groups that work with HIV/AIDS throughout the country" (Rich, 2013, 9–10). CSHR built and used participatory councils to engender political support, build networks of mutual support and trust, and ensure information flows from the subnational level to the federal civil service. Rich (2013, 9–10) notes that this strategy implied a "strikingly large amount" of transfers to civil society, on the order of 10 percent of the HIV prevention budget, to more than 4,000 projects in the decade after 1999. Again remarkably, much of this money centered on political advocacy projects. Federal officials used "legal aid" project funding to encourage civil society associations to undertake judicial action against the state. Although judicial inoperancy is also a factor in the health care arena,[26] at civil servants' prompting, civil society employed courts as an important venue to ensure that recalcitrant local governments were forced to respond to HIV patients' needs.

Improving Anti-Corruption Efforts

A third case of autonomous bureaucratic activism is the creation of the National Strategy for Combating Corruption and Money Laundering (ENCCLA), which is both a strategy and an interagency working group first inaugurated in 2003.[27] There are many examples of advances made by bureaucracies in the anti-corruption field over the past generation, such as the expanding power of prosecutors, the creation and increasing control over subnational governments exercised by the Comptroller General (CGU), and improvements in transparency and oversight by individual bureaucracies. Among all of these possibilities, the ENCCLA case is of interest because it is a bureaucratic initiative that sought to generate pressures for ongoing reform over time across a wide variety of agencies.

Although it began in the executive branch, furthermore, the initiative is significant in its reach, bringing together participants from all three branches of government, the Ministério Público, state governments, civil society, and both private sector and public banks. The annual meeting to develop the strategy expanded over time from thirty largely executive agencies in 2003 to more than ninety distinct entities in 2017.[28]

The ENCCLA exercise is unique because it was a conscientiously designed effort to create an epistemic community that could span the famously siloed and compartmentalized anti-corruption bodies present in the federal government. Over the years, these efforts would be expanded, furthermore, across all three levels of the federation. The impetus for ENCCLA arose in part because of Brazil's treaty obligations: in 1998, Brazil adopted new anti-money laundering (AML) legislation that brought it in line with international conventions (Law 9.613/1998). Studies by the Council of Federal Justice (CJF) of the law's implementation, however, found a variety of problems, including the fact that virtually no AML cases had been prosecuted since the law's implementation (Augustinis, 2011; Chagas, 2012, 44; Silva, 2012, 801).[29] Although the law had led to the creation of a financial intelligence office in the executive branch, known as COAF, its implementation left much to be desired, in part because even when the COAF flagged suspicious activity reports, these alerts triggered few concrete actions, since other agencies lacked the capacity and procedures to investigate money laundering (Aranovich, 2007; Araújo, 2012; Rodrigues, 2012). The 1998 law itself covered only a limited set of crimes and did not tackle predicate crimes such as corruption or fraud. Effective prosecution was hindered by the fact that few judges or prosecutors had the expertise to handle money laundering cases (LaForge, 2017). The cooperation that was needed between the various agencies involved in uncovering, investigating, and prosecuting financial crimes was hampered by formalism, overlapping responsibilities, bureaucratic rivalry, and the uncharted waters of the new law (Taylor and Buranelli, 2007).

Dissatisfaction with the judiciary's performance in money laundering cases led one entrepreneurial judge, STJ minister Gilson Dipp, to champion the creation of specialized AML courts, which – after a lengthy process of convincing his peers – were quickly established by judicial administrative fiat in May 2003. Dipp's efforts found an institutional home within a commission created by the Council of Federal Justice (CJF), with the participation of a variety of executive agencies involved in financial crimes, including the Central Bank and COAF. These efforts

The Autonomous Bureaucracy and Incremental Change

were closely watched by the Justice Ministry: government lawyers recognized the opportunity the new courts offered, shared the judges' dissatisfaction with the AML law's implementation, and saw value in the cross-agency dialogue that the CJF had sponsored.

Within months of the AML courts' creation, Justice Minister Márcio Thomaz Bastos moved to create a new Department of Asset Recovery and International Legal Cooperation (DRCI) within the ministry to oversee asset recovery. This top-down effort was met by a bottom-up effort by the new head of DRCI, government lawyer Antenor Madruga, who determined that greater cross-government cooperation was essential (Bastos, 2012; Abramovay, 2018). He faced a difficult challenge, in that the executive branch could not force the different branches of government to cooperate, and any effort that looked as though it was directed by the executive branch might raise the hackles of judges and prosecutors sensitive to any infringement of judicial independence. To overcome these institutional barriers, Madruga adopted a "soft law" approach that relied on a combination of peer pressure, carrots, and sticks to bring together the first attendees of the ENCCLA group. He obtained financing for a four-day retreat, enlisted Bastos – a respected criminal defense lawyer – to ensure that the right people were in the room and portrayed the interagency group as an "elite club" (Bastos, 2012; LaForge, 2017). Bastos' attendance at the first meeting sent a clear signal about the group's importance, and word of the conference spread widely across government, leading many agencies to seek out invitations in subsequent years.

ENCCLA developed a robust set of governance practices. Foremost among these were informality and rule by consensus. Hierarchy was eschewed, as were efforts to formalize the working group in the *Diário Oficial*, in the hopes of ensuring quicker action (Madruga, 2012, 34). While formally administered through DRCI,[30] the annual ENCCLA sessions were marked by significant brainstorming, debate, and even conflict among the wide variety of agencies present. Only the proposals that achieved consensus would move forward. At the end of the day, the group would come up with around a dozen suggested actions for the coming year, an agency would be asked to volunteer to oversee each action, and then the suggested actions would be released to the waiting press corps. In this way, peer pressure and the desire not to be seen falling down on the job led to forward movement on a variety of different fronts (Madruga, 2012, 34–5).

Just as important as the work product was the community-building exercise, which enabled civil servants from a broad range of agencies that had few links to each other to build networks. The informal tone of ENCCLA's meetings helped to overcome hierarchy and institutional deference, for example, between federal police and judges. As one prominent member, a federal police officer, noted, when one civil servant needs help from another agency, he now knows whom to call at that agency for help and he can count on that help to be forthcoming (Saadi, 2012, 16). The process allows individual bureaucrats to better understand the constraints their peers in other agencies face, as well as to understand why certain reform recommendations make sense (or do not) from the perspective of their colleagues elsewhere in government (Augustinis, 2011; Corrêa, 2011; Power and Taylor, 2011, 294; Praça and Taylor, 2014). Peer pressure can push some agencies into actions they might otherwise shirk: the Central Bank, for example, was finally convinced of the need for changes in its financial supervision practices after meetings with the group. This network has also frequently served a defensive purpose: when special AML courts were being heavily criticized in 2012, for example, the group included as one of its top recommendations a statement in their defense; when Congress pushed for an amnesty on the repatriation of funds from overseas accounts, ENCCLA released a strong letter of opposition; and when politicians mulled the possibility of a law preventing "abuse of authority" as a way to inhibit police and prosecutors' investigations, ENCCLA protested publicly (Macedo, 2011; O Estado de S. Paulo, 2016).

ENCCLA has not magically fixed all of the problems that have undermined anti-corruption efforts. But it has provided an overarching framework for continuously improving anti-corruption efforts, in ways that are decidedly gradual and incremental, but nonetheless routinized. Often the discussion of reform alternatives among potentially reluctant bureaucracies has enhanced the likelihood of reform, either by eliminating sticking points, or convincing reluctant agencies of the depth of the problem. Among ENCCLA's most important policy accomplishments have been:

- Training and community-building: A training program focused on corruption and financial crimes cases (known by its acronym PNLD[31]), which has trained more than 15,000 civil servants since its creation. In addition to its obvious capacity building objective, the PNLD training program had the ulterior goal of generating new networks of civil servants, by bringing together police, prosecutors and judges from the same jurisdictions, as well as by promoting new

220 The Autonomous Bureaucracy and Incremental Change

leaders in ENCCLA by recruiting them as instructors in the training program (LaForge, 2017).

- Legislation: Revisions to the 1998 AML law, including expanding it to ensure that any misdemeanor or felony can now be considered to be a predicate offense for pressing money laundering charges.[32] A broad set of legislative proposals were approved between 2012 and 2013, directly informed by ENCCLA, including the revised AML law (12.683/2012), a plea bargaining law (12.850/2013), and a corporate bribery law (12.846/2013). As a former top aide to Bastos noted, bills that had received the ENCCLA imprimatur had a stamp of government-wide support that absorbed potential veto players and nearly guaranteed legislative passage (LaForge, 2017; Abramovay, 2018; see also Cardozo, 2012). Furthermore, there was a constant risk that new criminal laws would be invalidated on constitutional grounds; the consensual drafting of such bills by experts in the field helped to ensure that they did not fall afoul of the courts (Araújo, 2012, 68). ENCCLA support did not guarantee quick passage – Law 12.683 took eight years to make it through Congress, for example – but it did ensure that reform ideas remained on the docket of legislative priorities.
- Information: over the years, ENCCLA proposed the creation of a variety of databases that permit agencies across government to share information on bribe paying companies, civil servants who faced civil penalties for administrative improbity, and an inventory of more than 2 million seized assets. It drove the creation of a national listing of bank clients, with a uniform reporting system (Saadi, 2012), as well as the creation of an internal wiki index on money laundering and corruption, known as WICCLA. ENCCLA pushed for oversight of politically exposed persons (PEP) by COAF, which put in place regulations governing those high-ranking politicians and required banks to accompany these persons' transactions. ENCCLA pushed for the streamlining of case reporting in the courts, so as to make all case types uniform across the entire state and federal judiciary. It also created a single model for all birth, marriage, and death certificates nationwide, and created a central database of these records.
- Structures: In the same way that the federal court system was able to create specialized AML courts, ENCCLA recommended that both the federal police and state prosecutors create specialized bodies: AML groups within the police and a National Group for Combating

Institutional Change through the Bureaucracy

Criminal Organizations, which brought together state prosecutors from across the country.

- Processes: Among the most important accomplishments was an effort to expedite the famously slow process of legally breaking bank secrecy protections and using the information thus collected. The System of Bank Transactions (*Sistema de Movimentações Bancárias*, SIMBA) was created at ENCCLA's urging to identify where a target's bank accounts are held, and to facilitate information requests directly to that specific bank, rather than the old practice of notifying all national banks of the investigation[33] and then painstakingly compiling their responses. A second procedural reform was the creation of a national network of anti-money laundering "labs," known as REDE-LAB, which sought to streamline the extremely laborious process of evaluating the data emerging from the lifting of tax, bank, and phone secrecy. Most states today have their own labs, whose staff can help investigators deal with the huge volumes of data collected on targets, providing the technological knowhow needed to parse it all.

The whole of government approach represented by ENCCLA has been extremely important to driving change, and many of the leaders in efforts to combat corruption in recent years are past participants: Judges Fausto De Sanctis and Sérgio Moro, prosecutor Deltan Dallagnol, and many federal police officers. Most important, the ENCCLA process has been "auto-catalytic" or self-starting: the process is driven from the bottom up, and while it is kept in annual motion by the Justice Ministry's DRCI, civil servants across a wide range of agencies have taken advantage of the venue provided by ENCCLA to push forward proposals about how best to tackle the bottlenecks to accountability they encounter in their daily work (Praça and Taylor, 2014).

ENCCLA by itself is no panacea, and it has been criticized on a number of fronts. As executive branch commitment to the program has flagged since the mid-2010s, the attendees have become less prominent leaders within their agencies, and the proposals that emerged out of ENCCLA became more anodyne than in the past. The capacity of ENCCLA is never greater than the capacity of its member agencies, and some agencies have been unable to achieve the targets in programs they sponsored (France, 2017). Some of the most needed reforms have either not emerged from ENCCLA (e.g., adequate definitions of beneficial ownership), have failed to produce the required change (e.g., a 2017 proposal to improve the selection process for ministers on state accounting tribunals), have taken years to approve (e.g., the reform to the 1998 AML law), or simply have not been approved (e.g., changes in the statutes of limitation, first proposed by ENCCLA in 2005) (Transparency International, 2015; OECD, 2017b). To some degree, ENCCLA was also a victim of its own success: by 2012, pictures of the annual meeting could no longer capture the scale of the plenary session in a single frame, given the large number of representatives in the room. With such scale, some of the benefits of a tight-knit community are lost. Nonetheless, for more than a decade, ENCCLA served as a powerful vehicle for bureaucracy-driven changes that responded pragmatically to practical concerns about the weakness of anti-corruption efforts.

CONCLUSION

The focus of political scientists on coalitional presidentialism and executive-legislative relations has largely overlooked one source of many policy improvements in the past generation: the bureaucracy.[34] This chapter has already pointed out many of the substantive improvements to the civil service that have emerged since the 1985 transition, including the profound change in patterns of recruitment, which has enabled it to overcome much of the "grammar" of clientelism that had marked the bureaucracy for decades (Nunes, 1997). The chapter has also shown the remarkable changes that the bureaucracy has designed, championed, and implemented in the fiscal, health, and anti-corruption fields. In most cases, bureaucratic-driven change has been incremental. Indeed, many efforts at wholesale change have been catastrophic, as for example in the cases of the Cruzado and Collor stabilization plans, which generated immediate economic pain, presaged significant political upheaval, and spawned a generation worth of court-clogging litigation. Wholesale change is the least savvy political strategy in a multiparty coalitional system with a multitude of potential veto players. Indeed, because other actors oftentimes have an active veto over institutional change, many of the most relevant changes in the institutional framework are only possible via small bureaucratic initiatives at the margin which, if continued over time, can add up to significant reform over the long haul, as in the three vignettes described here.

   As a consequence, many of the bureaucracy's initiatives have been designed to take place below the radar, purposefully hiding policy initiatives or their intention from the veto players who could stymie change.

Conclusion 223

Bureaucratic entrepreneurs in the economic policy arena "smuggled" legislation into unrelated proposals, took advantage of crises to effect their desired changes, enlisted external bodies like the IMF to push domestic policy objectives, and used public consultations to overcome congressional opposition. They then sought to lock in gains through statutory changes, constitutional amendments, and even international treaties. Bureaucrats in the health policy arena encouraged civil society actions against political opposition, even going so far as to encourage civil society to contest policy in the courts. In the ENCCLA case, politicians hurt by many changes simply "didn't realize what was going on," in the words of Justice Ministry official Pedro Abramovay, until the accumulation of various reforms was perhaps too weighty to reverse course (LaForge, 2017; Abramovay, 2018). This is not to say that legislators have always been oblivious; they have often caught on to important initiatives that run against their interests and smothered them. But in part because the multi-party system allows a wide variety of coalitions to coalesce behind bureaucratic initiatives, in part because of the executive's protagonism in driving forward legislation, and in part because legislative deliberation has been frenzied for much of the past thirty years, there has been ample room for bureaucratic innovations to find their way into policy. And there are of course also ample opportunities for bureaucrats to change the status quo without statutory reforms: some of the changes described here have been accomplished simply by budget allocation, administrative fiat, internal ministerial decree, and the reallocation of personnel.

The remaining pages of this chapter adopt a more critical lens, focusing on seven problematic aspects of the civil service's role, and the manner by which the bureaucracy's primacy as an agent of change contributes to reinforcing the institutional complementarities already highlighted in this book.

The need for bureaucratic insulation may generate a perverse cycle. Politicization of the federal bureaucracy is far less pervasive than it once was, and the worst forms of politicization have been largely overcome by distributing political appointments to a wide number of parties within the same agency, thus ensuring some intra-coalitional oversight (Bersch et al., 2017b). This makes it harder for parties to monopolize agency outcomes, while providing greater space for programmatic action by the bureaucracy. However, the trade-off is that the bureaucracy is strengthened to the detriment of parties. Empirical research shows that political appointments tend to lead to greater levels of corruption within agencies; and that agency capacity and agency autonomy provide a partial antidote (Bersch

224 *The Autonomous Bureaucracy and Incremental Change*

et al., 2017b). Knowing this, politicians on both the executive and legislative sides of the coalition face perverse incentives. A "vicious cycle" ensues, whereby some agencies are insulated from partisan demands; political appointees therefore cannot obtain programmatic experience that might provide them with electoral reputations; they therefore rely on more parochial, clientelist goods; and as a consequence, party politicians are only appointed to the least programmatic and most clientelist of agencies (Loureiro, 2010, 321). Over the long haul, this is likely to diminish bureaucratic capacity in many agencies that provide important potential payoffs to political appointees, such as agencies charged with infrastructure investment. Within those agencies, furthermore, research suggests that appointees may drive spending toward the projects most likely to provide them with electoral funds, thereby distorting public investment decisions toward quick or lucrative projects (Armijo and Rhodes, 2017).

Second, the bureaucracy is not always clearly responsive to a principal. This chapter provided three examples of bureaucracy-led policy change. Literally dozens, and possibly hundreds of other examples of such bureaucratic activism could be offered, ranging from the stimulus programs developed for many agricultural sectors to the Minha Casa, Minha Vida lower income housing program to the expansion of social services to prison populations. All of these examples involve bureaucratic actors across great portions of the developmental state, including the BNDES, agencies like the Embrapa agricultural research agency, ministries within each domain such as the Cities Ministry, and public banks, with their robust portfolios of subsidized loans. This is a powerful set of instruments that few presidents elsewhere in Latin America have at their disposal.[35] Given the broad expanse of governmental bodies and policy arenas, though, presidents seldom are aware of everything that is being done or contemplated in their names, allowing the bureaucracy to take policy matters into its own hands, rather than waiting for explicit directives from above. In "technocratic democracies," while elected representatives have nominal control over policy, the framing of policy alternatives is largely in the hands of experts (Centeno and Silva, 1998, 11; Vergara and Encinas, 2016). Slightly more unique to the Brazilian case, though, is that the civil service in most cases acts with little oversight from Congress. Rather than the "iron triangles" of the North American policy literature, which describe a relationship between an interest group, a congressional

Conclusion

committee and an executive agency, in Brazil the Congress is often excluded, sometimes intentionally.[36] Agents everywhere seek to shirk control by their principals. But when the civil service is a key source of change in a context of multiple principals, such shirking becomes much easier. As the stratagems of "smuggling," "locks," and enlistment of external actors have demonstrated, civil servants have become quite talented at finding ways "around" the political system. This may allow incremental change, but it also contributes to a cacophony of objectives that do not always respond to a central organizing principle.

A third issue is that the bureaucracy is an expensive change agent, which imposes an important drag on the fiscal accounts, deepens the fiscal imperative of policy, and contributes to the regressivity of public spending. The public sector accounts for only 11.4 percent of the labor force, versus an average of 19.3 percent in the OECD, and its scale is therefore not out of line in per capita terms. But spending has been rising at a steady pace since the turn of the century and spending on the civil service stands at 13 percent of GDP, making it considerably higher than other emerging markets (9 percent on average) or Latin American governments (8 percent on average). It also makes the wage bill the second largest primary spending item at the federal level, after pensions (an expense to which the public sector also contributes inordinately) (Karpowicz and Soto, 2018). The wage bill is six times greater than public investment and compresses the fiscal space that could otherwise be used on investment (Grindle, 2012, 145). Civil servants earn about 30 percent more than their private sector counterparts, holding other variables constant (Karpowicz and Soto, 2018, 229). The public sector wage bill is regressive: 80 percent of civil servants earn wages that put them in the top income quintile nationally, and public sector wages and benefits may be responsible for 24 percent of inequality (Medeiros and Souza, 2013).

Fourth, although the civil service has led important reforms, the bureaucracy is not always an efficient change agent. There is nothing about bureaucratic autonomy that guarantees effective change: political systems with many veto players provide the space for bureaucratic autonomy, but space is a necessary but not sufficient condition for civil servants to actually drive forward change (Tsebelis, 2000, 472, fn. 11). There are clearly large numbers of talented civil servants who are deeply committed to effecting positive change, whether it is by implementing more credible economic plans or mobilizing the public to petition Congress for anti-corruption reforms. But not all bureaucrats fit this ethos, and even those who are may be constrained by the regulations they labor under: the World Economic Forum (WEF) rated the quality of Brazilian government efficiency to be 124th out of 148 countries (Polga-Hecimovich, 2019). In the health care arena, for example, success on HIV was not paralleled in the field of tuberculosis control; the national TB program remained anemic for fifteen years even as the TB epidemic grew significantly (Rich and Gómez, 2012).[37] In other cases, bureaucratic rivalries got in the way of reform even among high-capacity bureaucrats: a study of national statistical systems across Latin America, for example, singles out Brazil, where the strength of the IBGE has blocked the development of other agencies in the broader national statistical system (Dargent et al., 2018, 34–5). Meanwhile, the jurisdictional "entanglement" (Abers and Keck, 2013) and multiple veto players in the federal system mean that even capable civil servants may find the narrow paths to reform blocked by a variety of forms of resistance. The possibility of resistance tends to privilege narrow efforts by small cohorts of trusted peers and undermine interagency coordination, feeding back into the central problem raised in the last chapter, Chapter 6, that is, the absence of effective strategic control.

Fifth, the civil service is not always public-regarding. Bureaucratic autonomy and activism may be a good thing if the reforms sought are considered positive and worthwhile but, as elsewhere, this is not always the case. One of the conundrums posed by the active role of the bureaucracy is that it has sometimes been engaged in self-serving behavior rather than selflessly contributing to broader societal improvements. Indeed, as Ames (2001) memorably phrased it, too often the Brazilian state "serves itself." As noted above, the federal bureaucracy is not especially large by international standards, but it is quite expensive. The 1988 Constitution was emblematic of "rent-seeking" by civil servants, who were able to cement in place tenure and pension provisions that are regressive and rigid (Bresser-Pereira, 2003, 95). The public sector unions which emerged to defend these privileges expanded at an astonishing clip, from 137 unions in 1989 to 1,882 by 2015 (Santos, 2007, 243; Campos, 2016, 11). Reversing the fiscal cost of the civil service has proven to be enormously challenging, as it engenders both political and judicial opposition. Indeed, the Brazilian state has long been marked by corporatism and the defense of the "corporate" rights of the public sector. But this corporatist

Conclusion

227

"grammar" no longer is rigidly determined by constitutional rules, as in the Vargas years, but instead by the enthusiastic defense of the rights of the "public servant" against "neoliberal" reformers who seek to take away the "rights" guaranteed by the Constitution (Nunes, 1997; Souza, 2013). Together, this means that even as pockets of the bureaucracy are active in bringing social improvements and policy innovations, the bureaucracy's great expense reinforces the essential social bargain of redistribution without growth.

Sixth, some policy changes may be less likely because there is considerable variation in the capacity and autonomy of bureaucracies. On the policy demand side, one consequence of agency variation is that an efficiency-seeking president may seek out the preexisting "islands of excellence" to implement policy, "even if it means making ideological sacrifices to do so" (Polga-Hecimovich, 2019). Consider the use of the BNDES to manage the national privatization plan during the reform years under Collor and Cardoso: while there is no way to establish the counterfactual, one wonders if the outcomes of privatization – inter alia, the emphasis on national buyers, cross-shareholding, and the government as minority investor model – might have been different under the charge of an equally high-capacity, but less developmentally-oriented agency. On the supply side, it may be that such high-capacity agencies are more likely to supply policies that stand a good chance of being effectively implemented, thus generating a feedback loop in favor of developmentalism.

Seventh, relying on the bureaucracy as an agent of change, especially incremental change, requires enormous technical competence, and reinforces the primacy of the developmental state. Technical competence is needed from policy designers, who must plan several steps ahead, negotiate with multiple political actors and members of society, and frame and reframe their ideas almost continuously (Loureiro and Abrucio, 2004). Furthermore, recourse to the civil service to resolve problems generates a self-fulfilling prophecy: as societal actors turn to the state to resolve problems, they reinforce a reliance on the state as the change agent, generating further pressure for state action, in a reinforcing cycle that crowds out problem-solving by other organizations within society. This instinct to turn to the state is longstanding, as exemplified by Monteiro Lobato's epigraph.

In sum, while the bureaucracy has often been an effective source of reforms and institutional change, its success has not been preordained. Further, the civil service's effectiveness in undertaking incremental reform may even perpetuate the institutional complementarities described earlier in this book. The bureaucracy increases the cost of the state apparatus, even as it permits reforms that tinker with the institutions of the developmental state, provide benefits to the political coalitions of coalitional presidentialism, and contribute to delivering somewhat better policy outcomes. In doing so, bureaucratic activism enables incremental changes that allow the overall institutional equilibrium of the developmental state to be preserved, rather than succumbing to more radical demands for wholesale change.

8

Conclusion

The resumption of development ... also requires creativity in the political realm. This only manifests when a high degree of collective will is summed to an acute perception of the historical moment.

Celso Furtado, 1984[1]

We are masters of our own destiny.

President Dilma Rousseff, citing economist Celso Furtado at the launch of Plano Brasil Maior, August 2011[2]

On November 25, 2011, the petroleum tanker *Celso Furtado* was launched in Rio de Janeiro. This immense 183-meter long ship, with capacity to carry fifty-six million liters of oil, was a triumph of Brazilian naval shipbuilding, winning an award from the British Royal Institute of Naval Architects as one of the most significant new ships launched worldwide that year (Transpetro, 2012). The *Celso Furtado* was also the encapsulation of the five institutional features that have guided Brazilian democracy since 1985: the economy, characterized by i) a developmental state and ii) a unique developmental hierarchical market economy (DHME); the political system, marked by iii) the interparty negotiations associated with coalitional presidentialism and iv) weak judicial and administrative control over policy initiatives; and v) a strong high-capacity bureaucracy capable of leading massive public-private projects. It also was a concrete example of the manner by which these various institutional features generated overlapping incentives that pushed actors to a joint equilibrium, physically manifested in this case in the throng of dignitaries milling about near the *Furtado*.

229

230 *Conclusion*

A Brazilian shipyard had designed and built the ship, with a consortium of Brazilian private sector companies taking the lead, incentivized by prodding from high-ranking officials and the carrot of generous financing. The *Celso Furtado* was built over the course of thirty months, drawing on R$180 million in resources from the naval shipbuilding fund known as PROMEF (*Programa de Modernização e Expansão da Frota*), as one of the flagship programs of the Growth Acceleration Program (PAC) of infrastructure investments championed by the Workers' Party governments (Rede Brasil Atual, 2011). At government urging, and despite shipbuilder complaints, the domestic content ratio on the *Furtado* was 74 percent. The PROMEF program was made administratively possible by a host of capable public agencies and state-owned enterprises (SOEs), including the national development bank, various ministries, and the crown jewel of SOEs, Petrobras, and its logistical subsidiary Transpetro. The *Furtado* was built under the oversight of Transpetro at the Mauá Shipbuilding Plant, a joint venture between the Brazilian plant and Singaporean shipbuilder Jurong. In the years from the beginning of PROMEF to the launch of the *Furtado*, government incentives helped to boost employment in the shipbuilding sector from two thousand to more than sixty thousand (Rede Brasil Atual, 2011).

The name of the ship paid homage to Brazil's most influential developmentalist economist, the longtime proponent of a state-led, internally oriented developmental strategy and Brazil's first Planning Minister. His ideas were top of mind at events surrounding the launch. As President Rousseff noted proudly,

> ... Brazilian workers know how to build ships ... As Celso Furtado said, growth is one thing; development is another ... This ship is a very important step in the resurgence of our naval industry. We are now building ships, making investments and creating jobs here in Brazil, rather than exporting them to other countries .... (Presidência da República, 2011)

Politically, the launch allowed representatives of several different political parties in the coalition, as well as some members of the opposition, to share in the glory of the new ship. A veritable *Who's Who* of the governing coalition was assembled. In addition to Rousseff, the dignitaries included Rio governor Sérgio Cabral (PMDB) and vice governor Luiz Pezão (PMDB), Mining and Energy Minister Edison Lobão (PMDB), Communications Minister Helena Chagas, Senators Lindberg Faria (PT) and Benedito de Lira (PP), and deputies Chico D'Angelo (PT) and Filipe Pereira (PSC). Members of the ostensible opposition were also present,

Conclusion

notably Alagoas governor Teotônio Vilela (PSDB). The stellar audience was rounded out by top executives in the Petrobras directorate, including president Maria das Graças Foster and directors Paulo Roberto Costa and Guilherme Estrella; representatives of petroleum and naval industry unions; and a number of business executives, including Transpetro president Sérgio Machado, Correios president Wagner Pinheiro, and Manuel Ribeiro, head of the Mauá facility.

The institutional complementarities within and across the five arenas of the political economy had been placed under considerable strain by the end of the 2010 decade. Stresses included weak growth and recession, fiscal crisis, the Lava Jato investigations, and the political upheaval between the massive street protests of 2013 and the shocking election of Jair Bolsonaro five years later. As the sad aftermath of the *Celso Furtado* launch illustrates, the cumulative effect of these stressors was concrete. As would become evident a few years after the launch, much of Petrobras' effort to reap the discovery of pre-salt oil by developing homegrown infrastructure capacity was deeply corrupt, motivated in large part because corruption offered an immediate solution to the demands of the expensive electoral and coalitional systems. By 2018, eight dignitaries who had participated in the *Furtado*'s launch had been indicted, jailed, or had admitted guilt through plea bargains. One of PROMEF and Rousseff's biggest champions, former president Lula, was jailed in 2018. The Mauá shipyard temporarily shut its doors in 2015 in the face of financial troubles and labor litigation, laying off several hundred workers (G1, 2015). The PROMEF fund lost funding under emergency fiscal cuts implemented during the Temer administration, and contracts for a third of the forty-six ships planned in 2011 were cancelled in 2016. There was growing unease about the continued viability of past policy choices and the sustainability of the developmentalist policy tool kit.

The *Celso Furtado* story was emblematic of the broader patterns of institutional performance over much of the generation that began in 1985. Institutional complementarities across various dimensions of the political economy provided incentives that drove actors toward a self-sustaining but ultimately unproductive equilibrium. The developmental state apparatus was employed to drive new industry, in joint efforts between foreign companies, SOEs, and private Brazilian firms; the project was made possible by state funding and guided toward particular policy goals by qualified bureaucrats; together with other Transpetro projects, there were opportunities for both licit and illicit transfers to coalition members; and with the important exception of the unprecedented Lava

Jato investigation, such transfers and the inefficiencies they generated remained largely hidden from public eye because of lackluster oversight and control. The existence of these complementarities factored into actors' decision-making processes and raised the cost of moving to alternate ways of organizing the economy: firms expected guidance and support; policymakers and bureaucrats saw incentivizing the development of local industry as their role; policymakers and politicians saw side payments as the way business was done; and many Brazilians applauded the development of homegrown industrial capacity for contributing to job creation and economic growth. The complementarities between these institutional arenas – in shipbuilding, as in so many other fields – contributed to the permanence of a particular Brazilian "variety of capitalism," to Brazil's failure to converge to the neoliberal norm adopted in much of Latin America over the course of the past generation, as well as to the preservation of a particular way of politics.

An open question for Brazil in the 2020s was whether the multiple and overlapping crises of the 2010s would destabilize the equilibrium that had remained in place for the previous generation. The tanker *Furtado* remained impervious, steadily plying the Brazilian coast as it transported oil to and from Brazil's various refineries. But the political economy equilibrium may have been shaken.

To evaluate the extent to which the events of the 2010s changed the stability of the overall political economy equilibrium, this concluding chapter first summarizes the contributions of this book to our understanding of Brazil's political economy under democracy. The second section describes how past reform efforts failed to move the political economy away from the status quo equilibrium. The third evaluates the complementarities across institutions and the ways in which complementarities may shape the pace and scope of change. The final section concludes with an evaluation of the "stress test" posed by the Bolsonaro administration, to evaluate the extent to which the changes that his administration has put in motion might permanently destabilize the political economy equilibrium that has governed Brazil since the return to democracy a generation ago.

INSTITUTIONAL COMPLEMENTARITIES WITHIN AND ACROSS THE POLITICAL ECONOMY

This book has highlighted the degree to which the political economy of Brazilian democracy is held in equilibrium by the macroeconomics of the developmental state, a DHME, coalitional presidentialism, weak

Complementarities in Brazil's Political Economy 233

controls, and an autonomous bureaucracy which generate mutually reinforcing incentives that drive diverse actors, such as politicians, bureaucrats, and executives, toward common preferences and behaviors.

For most of the generation between 1985 and 2018, the most significant constraints on policymaking within this system were fiscal, resulting from the need to simultaneously fulfill promises made in the central institutional guidepost of the democratic period, the 1988 Constitution; and to address the high inequality pervasive in Brazilian society, all without rekindling the legacy of hyperinflation, with its devastating effects on transparency and social order. The Constitution was written with an eye to protecting and enhancing many privileges, especially for the upper middle-class employed by the state, through salary, tenure, and pension guarantees. In part because the median voter's income was below mean income, however, there were also strong redistributive pressures (Armijo, 2005; Melo et al., 2014). Jointly, these pressures for middle-class benefits and redistribution increased expenditures steadily, with only the fear of a return to hyperinflation curbing politicians' most prolific inclinations.

Together, these pressures also drove the dirty secret of Brazil's otherwise strong presidency: there was only ever marginal room in the budget for new discretionary spending, and much of this discretion was frequently eroded by the need for fiscal containment, as well as by the need to finance programs that were politically untouchable, such as the *Bolsa Família* conditional cash transfer program. The pincer of personnel spending and limited discretionary funding also had the important effect of lowering the government's capacity to invest, thereby relegating economic growth to residual priority (Pessôa, 2011). Incumbents faced continued pressure to increase tax revenue, found little opportunity to increase public investment (particularly in infrastructure), and fell back on the use of opaque policy tools that had less visible, indirect impacts on the fiscal bottom line.

Many of these opaque tools were made possible by the infrastructure of the developmental state inherited from the authoritarian regime. Policy instruments built up over the course of much of the twentieth century – such as subsidized lending by the National Bank for Economic and Social Development (BNDES), tax incentives, domestic content requirements, regulatory licensing, state control over public prices, credit provision, cross-shareholding, and investment by state-controlled pension funds – could be used with very little direct or immediately observable impact on the fiscal results, since they were not immediately accounted for in the budget and, in some cases, were not even directly disclosed by government agencies. Since the immediate fiscal impact of using entities such as the BNDES or Petrobras was only indirectly observable, and their potential political utility was significant, there was little incentive to divest the state of these powerful tools, even under reformist presidents. The capacity of civil servants in these organizations protected them and made them valuable instruments for presidents across the ideological spectrum. Meanwhile, new taxes were implemented in complex, indirect, and nontransparent ways that raised few hackles because their nontransparency generated a "fiscal illusion" that made it difficult for voters to correctly perceive their cost or become aware of their distortionary and regressive effects (Nogueira et al., 2015). The opaqueness of these tax and spending decisions helped to make them politically viable, but also meant that the state was not forced into a broad bargain with society about the boundaries and limits of revenue and spending. Once fixed in place, furthermore, such decisions tended to be very difficult to reverse, because the beneficiaries were concentrated, the costs were diffuse, the policies' opacity made it hard to debate their costs and benefits, and they were often embedded in rigid legal frameworks (Lisboa and Latif, 2013, 10, 40; Mancuso and Moreira, 2013).

In the context of spending constraints and the low public investment that resulted from the squeezed fiscal situation, foreign investment gained importance. Policymakers of every stripe worried about investor confidence and did what they could to encourage foreign firms to move into Brazil's protected economy. This effort enhanced the fiscal imperative, as governments sought to convince investors that their investments would be safe from inflationary tax. But the importance of foreign investment in an investment-hungry economy also gave the government incentives to provide investors with guarantees of equality behind protective barriers, allowing foreign multinational corporations (MNCs) into the country, and providing them with treatment similar to that provided to domestic firms. One consequence was an HME marked by the presence of multinationals in high value-added manufacturing, alongside large domestically-owned firms dominating commodities and typically oligopolistic sectors, similar to that described by Schneider (2013). Yet the resulting HME was significantly different from the one that Schneider described for Latin America as a whole. Enforcement of domestic laws could be quite different for foreign and domestic firms, there was a strong state-oriented sector uncommon to other Latin American HMEs, and credit was available from state banks, meaning that private businesses, by and large, tended not to engage in the diversification across sectors that was common

Complementarities in Brazil's Political Economy   235

to other HMEs in the region. Further, the state was able to exert considerable power over many businesses, especially in the highly concentrated sectors dominated by national firms, through cross-shareholding and the strategic deployment of its developmental policy tool kit.

The deployment of these state policy tools reinforced incentives toward defensive political action by firms seeking to maintain the status quo and to protect their individual firm's interests. They were helped in this regard by the large number of veto players that emerged from Brazil's complex combination of a fissiparous party system, fragmented legislature, and multiparty presidential cabinets. Facing a panoply of government pressures, firms of various sorts – family-owned firms, market-traded national firms, and MNCs – responded defensively, seeking to reciprocate government influence over business. On the licit side of the ledger, firms used a variety of tools in tandem, including various forms of associational pressure and campaign donations. More adventurous business executives conscientiously cultivated relationships with key politicians: Eike Batista's rise, for example, was in many ways propelled by his good fortune to have been born of a father who had run the Vale mining company (at the time, owned by the state) and had close ties to government officials associated with the regulation of mining; his early business ties with leading politicians such as Tasso Jereissati, José Sarney, and Delcídio Amaral; and his insistent efforts to court the Lula and Rousseff administrations (Gaspar, 2014, 67–92). Nor was Batista unusual: as Chapter 5 demonstrated, many large firms cultivated long-term reciprocal relationships with key politicians.

An important consequence of this pattern of particularistic relationships is that business lobbying was not focused on collective action for the purpose of reducing economy-wide inefficiencies. Private returns to political mobilization for the purposes of providing collective goods were low, whether it was reducing regulation or taxes, or improving education and public security. Instead, much of the effort by politically active firms was designed to ensure access to information about regulation, ensure more favorable terms or at least a veto over impending change, and perhaps to obtain firm-level rents, through public contracts, public regulation, tax breaks, or sectoral incentives. As a result, redistributive policies designed to benefit the poor ended up instead benefiting wealthier groups, while generating inefficiencies that reduced overall economic productivity to the detriment of all (Mendes, 2014, 64; Carvalho, 2016). Furthermore, the flexibility of policymaking was deeply limited by the practice of earmarking fiscal revenues to specific expenditure items, a practice established in

236   *Conclusion*

the 1988 Constitution and extended in subsequent years, which ensured that any debate over tax and revenue quickly became a zero-sum spat between competing interest groups (Carvalho, 2016, 113). As an example, private returns to investment in human capital were low, undermining incentives for businesses to lobby for sorely needed education reform; as a consequence, while education budgets expanded nearly 50 percent in the quarter century after 1990, largely because of constitutionally mandated transfers, there were few quality gains because businesses and even the middle class had little individual incentive to hound politicians to provide the broader collective good of a high-quality education. The consequences were brutal: calculations suggest that about two-thirds of the difference in income per capita between Brazil and South Korea, for example, was explained by the education gap (Bezerra and Cavalcanti, 2009; Lisboa and Latif, 2013, 21).

The incentives for political actors, meanwhile, reinforced this equilibrium. The tendency of the party system toward fragmentation was exacerbated by the fact that many party leaders were less ideological leaders than entrepreneurs. The incentives to form new parties were significant, given the powers of party leaders in Congress, the public campaign funds that flowed to parties, and the national status accrued by party leaders. Candidate-centered electoral laws provided further incentives to eschew ideology and program, and especially in the lower house, open list proportional representation weakened vertical accountability to voters and increased the gains from being responsible instead to campaign funders. As a consequence, it was not just that parties were *unable* to organize around national issues, it may be that they did not *wish* to do so, since their bread was, in fact, buttered by defending particular interests over collective or programmatic goals.

The potential governability nightmare that might result from this fragmented system, and which was feared by many analysts in the late 1980s and early 1990s, was avoided in part because instruments of coalition management permitted some governability. But governability was often obtained through the nontransparent exchange of the political currencies made possible by the developmental institutions of the state. The relations between politicians and their funders mixed elements that spanned a range of behaviors from legal to blatantly illegal. The scale of the state in Brazil provided ample opportunities for avarice to prosper, across a wide range of different fields, ranging from health care and dam construction to oil refining and meatpacking. Avarice, meanwhile, found few barriers aside from personal ethics. Horizontal accountability was far more tenuous

Complementarities in Brazil's Political Economy   237

than would be needed to challenge, punish, or eradicate the worst abuses within government. Weak judicial accountability, in particular, meant that few elites inside or outside government were punished for corrupting the political system. Although this pattern may have changed for business leaders – witness the jailing of top executives during the late 2010s for wrongdoing at firms as diverse as the multinational Philips and SBM, the family-owned Odebrecht, the market-listed OGX, and state-owned Transpetro – it is not clear that the calculus changed significantly for politicians. This is especially the case for federal political elites, who are protected by formal institutional rules, such as politicians' right to trial under the original jurisdiction of the high court (the so-called *foro privilegiado*), as well as informal norms about the gentle treatment that should be dispensed to white collar criminals.

Coalitional presidentialism also meant that it was extremely difficult for development policies to be effectively controlled. The manner by which crosscutting coalitions undermined typical conceptions of checks and balances, legislative oversight, and bureaucratic process complicated efforts by the state to effectively implement policies that fulfilled broader strategies, that led rather than followed firms, and that were capable of ensuring reciprocity, whereby firms were pushed up the innovation and productivity frontiers in response to government incentives.

If these institutional complementarities give the impression of stasis and immobility, one complementarity in particular contributed to permitting incremental changes over time. The large number of veto players in the political system, combined with the relatively capable civil service required by the developmental state, provided the autonomous bureaucracy space to carry forward long-term policy initiatives of its own. As Chapter 7 illustrated, civil servants drove major reforms across a variety of unrelated areas, such as fiscal reform in the 1980s, the effort to respond to HIV in the 1990s, and the anti-corruption reforms of the 2000s. The federal bureaucracy on many occasions was able to overcome opposition from political actors because of its autonomy within the executive branch, the strength of the executive relative to Congress, the multiple principals generated by the fissiparous party system, and by adapting a number of stratagems such as operating below the radar of potential political opponents, appealing to civil society for support, and trying to lock in policy choices. The incrementalism of the resulting policy reforms was often spectacularly slow, but significant changes accumulated over time, and bricolage drawing on extant institutional components may, other things equal, have been able to achieve more lasting change than more radical reform efforts that generated pushback.

Simultaneously, however, the significant role of the bureaucracy reinforced the prevailing equilibrium in the other domains of the political economy. The autonomy of the bureaucracy permitted particularistic solutions to sector or firm-specific problems to be hardened into law with little political oversight. The bureaucracy and the burden it imposed on new market entrants protected incumbent firms, reducing the overall competitiveness of firm life. The scale of the state bureaucracy and the privileges it was accorded over time contributed to the fiscal constraint and limited opportunities to expand investment. The existence of high-capacity bureaucracies, meanwhile, provided a ready tool to politicians in times of crisis, in a self-sustaining cycle: the shifting roles of the BNDES over time, under politicians as diverse as Collor, Cardoso, Lula, Rousseff, and Temer were an illustration that, once in place, such agencies reinforced the institutional foundations of the developmental state, even as they were put to new uses.

In sum, it is difficult to understand the policy evolution of the past generation without reference to the complementarities between these institutional arenas, and the way in which they generated incentives that tended to reinforce the political economy equilibrium, neutering, sidelining, or absorbing major reform. These complementarities helped to explain the continuities of various aspects of economic policymaking, including the resilience of state institutions and developmentalist ideas, even under supposedly "neoliberal" reformers. The reinforcing incentives they generated drove Brazilian society toward several implicit bargains: the implicit preference for redistribution over growth, for a strong state role in the economy, for a system of control marked by conciliation rather than effective strategic guidance, and for a powerful government bureaucracy that simultaneously served as the most effective engine of change, but also undercut other spending possibilities that might be more beneficial for economic growth.

REFORM AND REGRESSION

As the 2010s drew to a close, Brazil faced a difficult choice between two ideal paths: developmentalist and neoliberal. The first path Brazil could follow would be to make the developmental state *truly* developmental: enabling the state to implement strong controls over developmental policies; to strategize more clearly about the objectives of developmentalism in a competitive global economy; to adopt meaningful policies to move the economy up the value-added production frontier; and to put in place the strong controls needed to achieve all of the above. The odds of achieving this outcome were slim: only a few developmental states – such as Taiwan, Japan, and South Korea – can claim truly enduring developmental success, and they began the process as far more equitable and less heterogeneous societies than Brazil, in which such coordination was politically easier (though never easy) to achieve.

The second, equally challenging path would be to move toward a smaller, neoliberal state, providing a modicum of social welfare, but greatly diminishing the state's ambition to harness the economy or drive firms into new spaces. The challenge of this second path would also be political: reshaping a state that has played an enormous economic role for seven decades, and that still served as a leading employer for about eleven million workers nationwide, accounting for fully 10 percent of the economically active population and much of the middle and upper middle class. Further, contrary to the most simplistic libertarianism, movement toward a market-economy would not mean abdicating control: it would require instituting a regulatory apparatus that was far less prone to sectoral and political pressures than the regulatory agency framework designed in the 1990s had become, and making certain that controls imposed on elites were effective so as to avoid a deepening of oligopolistic practices. Nor is success guaranteed: not only would a move to a less inward-looking and state-centric economy make Brazil more vulnerable to the boom and bust commodities cycles that have plagued it for centuries, but it would also run up against the social and political challenges of altering state protections in a society that is permeated by remarkable inequality.

What might cause an equilibrium shift that moved Brazil out of its current institutional equilibrium and into a new one, either of more effective developmentalism or a more liberal, social democratic market model? There is a tendency to think about Brazil's evolution in terms of two steps forward, one step back. But this metaphor assumes that all that is required is continued progress and renewed effort. The metaphor of an equilibrium, especially one that is held in place by overlapping incentives across more than one institutional domain, instead suggests a certain stasis, unless actors' incentives in multiple domains are simultaneously pushed away from equilibrium.

Indeed, one of the most remarkable things about Brazil in the post-transition moment was its imperviousness to reform. Even in the cases of

240   Conclusion

leading reformers such as Cardoso and Lula, whose presidencies were marked by significant reform (albeit in different domains), there was a certain inertia to the system – a difficulty in moving off one equilibrium point and moving on to another – that meant that, despite "hyperactive" reform, the overall political economy equilibrium did not shift significantly. The equilibrium established by complementary underlying institutions tended to exert a gravitational force, pulling policymakers and economic actors back into recurring patterns of behavior that date back decades: a developmental policy set that dates to the immediate postwar period; a system of industrial supports and business-state relations that reached maturity under the military regime; a coalitional system that has its roots in the Second Republic (1946–64); tenuous controls whose frailty was exacerbated by the return to democracy; and a bureaucracy whose capacity and autonomy can be traced to the *varguista* reforms of the 1930s.

The most proactive reformer of the past generation, Fernando Henrique Cardoso, restructured the developmental state apparatus away from state ownership of enterprise, but replaced this state ownership with a fiscally-preferable alternative that removed the state as majority shareholder but nonetheless maintained state influence in formerly public firms through minority shares and cross-shareholding (Lazzarini, 2010; Musacchio and Lazzarini, 2014). The Cardoso administration maintained a preference for domestic ownership of privatized firms and preserved a central role for the five major SOEs: Petrobras, Eletrobras, the Correios and two of Brazil's largest banks, Banco do Brasil and Caixa Econômica Federal (CEF). The BNDES was rethought and put to new ends but remained a powerful potential tool for policymakers of any ideological stripe, alongside other fiscally opaque tools, such as state-guided pension funds, and fiscally illusionary taxes, such as the CPMF. The state bureaucracy was reformed and trimmed of dead wood, strengthening it as a tool for future presidents. Despite its reformist efforts, the ideational commitment of Cardoso's party to the institutions of the developmental state was strong, a commitment perhaps best exemplified by the fact that Cardoso's heir as PSDB standard bearer, José Serra, spent much of Cardoso's second term leading a feud between the "developmentalists" he commanded and the "neoliberals" in the Finance Ministry. Upon running for president in 2002, the most marked characteristic of Serra's campaign was a determined effort to run away from Cardoso's reformist record. Four years later, the PSDB presidential candidate, Geraldo Alckmin, underlined this trend by not-so-subtly donning a jacket emblazoned with the logos of

Reform and Regression

major SOEs, alongside a biker's cap covered in Banco do Brasil insignia. If politicians have the pulse of the voter, the behavior of these politicians suggest that the incidence of "neoliberalism" had reverted to match broader societal preferences for developmentalism.

Cardoso pushed through thirty-five constitutional amendments, more than any other president, accounting for a third of all amendments passed between the 1988 Constitution and 2018. But in undertaking these reforms, he deepened patterns of coalitional presidentialism, pulling together seven different legislative coalitions over his presidency, which were held together by budgetary amendments, ministerial appointments, and a variety of other incentives that have since been referred to as the "toolbox" of coalitional presidential systems (Chaisty et al., 2018). Although Cardoso began accountability reforms, including an effort to make courts more efficient and create comptroller functions within the federal government, these reforms improved fiscal control but did not significantly remake control mechanisms for either political actors or developmental policies. Furthermore, even a highly capable politician like Cardoso was frequently thwarted in his reforms of state control mechanisms by the need to preserve a governing coalition that would permit him to confront the various economic and political crises that beleaguered his administration.

A similar reversion to equilibrium occurred under Lula, who spent three electoral cycles (1989, 1994, and 1998) campaigning against the politics of the coalitional presidential system. Lula was famous for expressing, as a catchy 1995 song by the band *Paralamas do Sucesso* put it, his belief that Brasília was run by "three hundred swindlers with law degrees" who ran the country on the basis of "lobby, conspiracy, bribes, and side payments."[3] But by 2002, after his three previous losses, Lula threatened not to run again unless his Workers' Party agreed to play coalition politics. Lula went so far as to join forces with the ideologically distant Liberal Party of his vice-presidential running mate, businessman José Alencar. Five months into his first year in office, Lula had pulled together a legislative coalition that surpassed 70 percent of the Chamber of Deputies, with the broadest ideological diversity of parties seen until that point.[4] Arguably, it was the combination of broad coalition-making, horse-trading of appointments in the bureaucracy and SOEs, the illicit transfers that were the motivation for these appointments, and weak control mechanisms that made possible the first scandal of the Lula presidency, the *mensalão* scheme. Partly in consequence of this scandal, the Workers' Party governments of Lula and then Rousseff deepened their

242   Conclusion

commitment to strengthening accountability institutions that would eliminate some of the worst incentives generated by the combination of a developmental state with coalition politics and weak control. Although they significantly remade the Comptroller General's Office, the Federal Police, and a variety of other agencies, this was insufficient to temper the patterns of political economy that were revealed in the Lava Jato case, and in the shipbuilding experience detailed at the outset of this chapter. Similarly, efforts to encourage strategic administrative control of development programs like *Plano Brasil Maior* by empowering a pilot agency, the ABDI, came to naught in part because the government agencies and private sector firms that ABDI would theoretically oversee could not be reined in, and had the political muscle to bypass the pilot agency.

COMPLEMENTARITIES, EQUILIBRIA, CHANGE

Table 8.1 summarizes some of the most important complementarities between the five domains described in this book, which generated incentives that pushed actors toward a common equilibrium. These complementarities presumably do not require further elaboration at this point. Suffice it to note one space where complementarities are not present: the cell marked by an asterisk, representing the alignment of incentives between weak control mechanisms and an active bureaucracy. Mechanisms of control are actually relatively robust with regard to the bureaucracy, presumably because in order for the bureaucracy to serve any purpose for the executive, it must itself be relatively constrained, fiscally, ethically, and strategically. Indeed, one of the key complaints in Brasília in recent years has been the immobilization of the bureaucracy by "excessive" controls that make the bureaucracy rigid and incapable of creative innovations. In the opposite direction, the autonomous bureaucracy has in many cases worked to improve weak controls, as Chapter 7 illustrated, contributing to temporarily destabilizing the institutional equilibrium in other domains during the *mensalão* and Lava Jato investigations.

The notion of institutional complementarities provides at least three insights into institutional change. The first is that in a system marked by considerable complementarities, ease of change in a *given* institution does not necessarily imply depth of change away from a status quo equilibrium that is jointly determined by complementarities across *multiple* institutions. In other words, in a system of institutional complementarities, incremental changes may sometimes "snap back" to the status quo

TABLE 8.1 *Incentive alignment across complementary institutions*

	Developmental state	DHME	Coalitional politics	Weak control mechanisms	Autonomous bureaucracy
Developmental state		• Fiscal constraint and fiscally opaque policies overlap with incentives to utilize the policy tool kit of DHME • Patterns of developmentalism share incentives with DHME: concentrated state funding; privileging incumbent firms; lingering preference for national firms, especially in financial sector; segmentation	• Fiscally opaque policies coincide with incentives for bargaining in coalitional politics • Scale of developmental state provides incentives for horse-trading of appointments and ministerial influence	• Reliance on fiscally opaque policies overlaps with incentives for weakened controls	• Developmental state drives incentives to develop strong high capacity bureaucracy
DHME	• the complex demands of DHME share incentives (and objectives) with developmental state apparatus		• DHME increases incentives for firms to engage in politics, particularly defensive parochialism	• DHME and sectoral concentration creates incentives for firms and politicians to resist control	• the complicated policy framework of DHME overlaps with incentives for developing bureaucratic autonomy

(continued)

TABLE 8.1 *(continued)*

	Developmental state	DHME	Coalitional politics	Weak control mechanisms	Autonomous bureaucracy
Coalitional politics	• the veto players of the political system undergird incentives for defense of developmental institutions	• Parochialism reinforces incentives in favor of oligopolistic national firms • incentives of politicians as entrepreneurs align with particularism of DHME		• Coalitional politics facilitates parochialism which reinforces incentives toward weak control	• In a system with multiple veto players, need for performance creates incentives to preserve an autonomous bureaucracy • defensive parochialism generates incentives to preserve state bureaucracies across a variety of sectors
Weak control mechanisms	• weak control mechanisms reinforce incentives to maintain generous fiscally opaque developmental state organizations	• weak control mechanisms reinforce incentives for policies that benefit incumbent firms	• weak control mechanisms overlap with incentives to facilitate coalitional bargaining	✳	

| Autonomous bureaucracy | • an autonomous bureaucracy reinforces incentives for reliance on state to resolve issues;
• an autonomous bureaucracy reinforces incentives for maintaining developmental state apparatus | • the need for the bureaucracy to prove its worth aligns with the incentives of firms seeking support and nurturing | • an autonomous bureaucracy undergirds incentives that reinforce hierarchy of firms by privileging incumbent firms | • principals in the executive and legislative branch tolerate an autonomous bureaucracy as a means of achieving policy change, but the same impetus also drives toward weak controls over the relations between state and market |

ante.[5] This happens because the systemic equilibrium is set by incentives aligning across multiple institutions. By way of example, even though the Temer administration approved a constitutional amendment imposing a fiscal ceiling on primary expenditure, the actual imposition of the fiscal ceiling over the long haul is still very much an open question, given the depth of the fiscal crisis, the cost of the developmental state and the autonomous bureaucracy, as well as resort to opaque economic instruments to sidestep fiscal constraints. On the face of it, the amendment suggests a move away from equilibrium, but there is a strong possibility that as the fiscal ceiling is phased in, the incentives derived from these other institutions could lead to a reversion to the status quo ante, of continued fiscal permissiveness.

A second, somewhat counterintuitive, insight is that the more rigidly preferences are structured against a move away from equilibrium, the more likely that – other things being equal – an incremental change will result in an abrupt equilibrium shift. The more rigid preferences and behaviors are, the more rapidly structural change may take place once the equilibrium is tipped (this point is illustrated graphically in this note[6]). Third, partly in consequence of the first and second points, some institutions are likely to be more influential in establishing the status quo equilibrium than others.[7] This suggests a hierarchy of institutions, with the implication that changing some institutions may have broader effects across the entire ecosystem of institutions than changes to other institutions.

In the Brazilian case, the institutions referred to here as the developmental state and coalitional presidentialism are the hierarchically superior institutions of the five institutions described. Within their individual spheres, the DHME, weak control mechanisms, and the autonomous bureaucracy are each important and have achieved a certain equilibrium. But scholars have neglected that the broader systemic equilibrium is given not just by the individual institutional equilibrium, but by the joint equilibrium established with the developmental state and coalitional presidentialism.[8] This may help to explain why it is that, although incrementalism has been the guiding pattern of reform since almost the moment the military went back to its barracks in 1985, the overall political economy equilibrium looks relatively stable, with SOEs, public banks, private firms, politicians, and bureaucrats reverting to longstanding political and economic practices.

Two conditioning factors are worth keeping in mind. The first is that this entire discussion presupposes that there is more than one political economy equilibrium. That is not always the case (Stephenson, 2020),

The Bolsonaro "Stress Test"

although the existence of multiple equilibria seems likely. In the case of the political economy, the examples of South Korea and Chile suggest that there are at least two alternative potential equilibria that Brazil could aim for: a more effective developmental state or a more market-oriented "neoliberal" state. And in the political realm, the diverse mixtures of consociational and majoritarian dimensions of democracy suggest more than one equilibrium is also available (Lijphart, 1999). The second factor is that I have said nothing about the conditions under which a move away from equilibrium is more or less likely to take place. Shifts away from equilibrium seem more likely to succeed under conditions that alter the stability of preferences, such as moments of crisis. Crises, as Gourevitch (1986, 34) noted, are "open moments when system-creating choices are made" and as such, they may enable more change than might otherwise be possible. As Brazil enters the third decade of the twenty-first century, conditions would seemingly be propitious for change: the country has been through the worst economic recession in a century and one of the most foundation-shattering political scandals of all time. But as this book goes to press, despite more than a half-decade of crisis, and even though preferences seem to be in flux, the political economy does not appear to have yet moved toward a new equilibrium. How might this status quo change?

THE BOLSONARO "STRESS TEST": SHIFTING THE EQUILIBRIUM?

This book was concluded at the end of the first eighteen months of Jair Bolsonaro's presidency. The election of Bolsonaro, a conservative former military officer who pulled together an unlikely coalition of evangelical moral conservatives, "neoliberal" economic reformers, and law and order types, all fed up with the malaise of the 2010s, suggested that change was in the air. The election suggested that public preferences were shifting, with the dramatic expansion of the president's party, an historic turnover in incumbent legislators, and the weakening of the parties that had largely dominated politics since the return to democracy. Bolsonaro took on the mantle of reform during his inaugural speech to Congress, inviting legislators to help him pass reforms to "free Brazil, definitively, of the yoke of corruption, of crime, of economic irresponsibility, and of ideological submission. We have before us a unique opportunity to rebuild our country ..." (Folha, 2019a). Speaking before the public at the presidential palace later in the day, Bolsonaro proclaimed, "[w]e will propose and

248 *Conclusion*

implement needed reforms. We will increase infrastructure, de-bureaucratize, simplify, and eliminate the mistrust and weight of government on those who work and produce" (G1, 2019a).

This emphasis on reform and change means that the Bolsonaro administration served as a "stress test" for the stability of the political economy equilibrium that prevailed during the 1985–2018 generation.[9] But, of course, Bolsonaro was not the first politician to come into office promising change. Was there something about his reforms that was more likely to change the underlying patterns of political economic organization? Let us consider his administration's actions and plans across all five institutional arenas, keeping in mind that, as the introduction emphasized, there is no reason that institutional complementarities must be stasis-inducing. The literature on institutional complementarity recognizes that complementarity can be a source of change as much as stability: changes in one arena may drive adjustment in others, destabilizing the incentives that drive toward a common equilibrium, and potentially even leading to the collapse of the overall system (Amable, 2016).[10] Is there anything about Bolsonaro's reforms that suggests that his presidency could lead to a momentous reconfiguration of the institutional equilibrium that has persisted since the 1985 transition?

Bolsonaro's most influential cabinet member during his first year in office was Economics Minister Paulo Guedes, an unabashed "neoliberal" with a Ph.D. from the University of Chicago who had railed against the policy errors of the Rousseff administration, the timidity of Cardoso's reforms, and the overextended and self-serving state. Bolsonaro gave Guedes extraordinary power, including by unifying under his control most of the ministries that used to dispute control of economic policy, including the Finance, Planning, and Industry portfolios. Guedes was a minister with a clear desire to shift the institutional path of Brazilian democracy in a more neoliberal direction, and unprecedented power to achieve that goal.

In his first months in office, Guedes pushed forward a significant social security reform, which stood to realize savings of R\$800 million (US\$ 193 million). He installed reformers in the trade secretariat, Central Bank, BNDES, and public banks; argued for "de-indexing" and "un-linking" the mandatory transfers in the federal budget, so as to increase discretionary spending as a share of the budget; and promised infrastructure reform, tax reform, and regulatory reforms. He vowed to reduce service on the debt by applying privatization revenues to the principal balance. Through Mercosur, Brazil reached a trade agreement

The Bolsonaro "Stress Test"

with the European Union that – if ratified – promised to significantly increase inter-bloc trade, procurement, and services. The Central Bank launched a new Agenda BC+ to increase the supply of private sector credit and reduce its cost, alongside a credit registry initiative known as the *cadastro positivo*. The government sent a bill to Congress that would establish Central Bank autonomy. Lending by public banks was trimmed, and the BNDES lending rate was raised to reduce the implicit credit subsidies to large firms.

On the public side of business, the new privatizations secretary, Salim Mattar, said the government hoped to sell off two of the five big SOEs, keeping only Petrobras, Banco do Brasil, and CEF in government hands, and began shrinking their size by selling off subsidiaries. The government was helped along by a high court decision arguing that the sale of subsidiaries did not require previous legislative approval. Mattar also suggested selling off all of BNDESPar's holdings in private firms, estimated at R$110 billion. The government sold twelve airport concessions for more than R$2.3 billion and announced plans for the sale of another R$1.6 trillion in concessions for airports, highways, ports, and electric transmission capacity (Sant'Ana, 2019). Petrobras sold off 30 percent of its distributor, BR Distribuidora, for R$9.6 billion, relinquishing majority control. The state oil company also began to auction off oilfields estimated to be worth R$107 billion.

Meanwhile, the fabric of firm life was rent by a combination of global pressures and the Lava Jato investigations. Contextually, the rise of China and its simultaneous effects on global commodity prices and industrial prices had contributed to deindustrialization over the course of the 2010s. Manufacturing suffered a secular decline as a share of the economy from its peak in 1985, when it reached 21.8 percent of GDP, to 11.7 percent in 2016 (FIESP, 2017, 6). Agricultural states within Brazil grew at "Chinese" rates, and agricultural production became more efficient and more competitive, growing to account for as much as a quarter of the economy (Klein and Luna, 2019). From 2013, China became Brazil's largest export market, accounting for 28 percent of exports in 2018, including four-fifths of its soy, half its petroleum and iron ore, and two-fifths of its paper and pulp (Freire, 2018). This had enormous effects on Brazilian firms; but unlike his predecessors, Guedes seemed averse to providing supports to industrial firms hit by competition from Chinese manufactured goods.

In part because of the accumulated evidence of the first two decades of the century that "state champions" are not always effective flagbearers for the developmental state, there was declining support, within government or outside it, for propping up industry. Under the Workers' Party, market leaders such as meatpacker JBS chose, with government backing, to ravenously acquire competitors at home and abroad so as to achieve global scale. But as soon as it reached global scale, JBS also adopted global pretensions: it reportedly considered shifting its corporate residence to a lower tax domicile, such as Ireland, Holland, or Luxembourg. Successful champions that did not expand as forcefully, such as Embraer, found themselves in the crosshairs of larger international rivals, such as Boeing, which signed a deal to acquire 80 percent of Embraer's passenger jet business (Landim and Fernandes, 2018; Rochabrun, 2019).[11] In this context of increasingly global capitalism, dominated by transnational firms, the very concept of "Brazilian-ness" lost some of its meaning, changing the incentives for government intervention. Certainly, the Guedes economic team showed considerably less interest in nurturing state champions than its predecessors.

During the second half of the 2010s, the Lava Jato investigations upended an oligopolistic business segment with enormous political influence, the construction sector, and complicated some of the least transparent pressures brought to bear by other business actors. This perhaps made it easier for the Bolsonaro government to stave off political pressures for policies that would support business during a sputtering recovery. Whatever the cause, the Guedes ministry focused on helping out smaller firms via deregulation rather than industrial policy: one good example of this approach was the government's provisional measure on "economic liberty," reducing regulation on smaller firms and watering down labor protections.[12] Meanwhile, Minister Guedes struggled for control of the "Sistema S," trying to pry its R$18 billion budget out of the hands of big industrial and commercial federations and imposing stricter public transparency regulations (Carneiro and Wiziack, 2019; Michener and Mohallem, 2020). Guedes hoped to use "Sistema S" funds to carry out employment training and other programs that the government could not otherwise afford. Labor reforms undertaken by Temer began to bite, cutting union income by more than 85 percent and dramatically reducing the number of labor lawsuits (Istoé, 2018).

In the political realm, the 2018 election was a sea change, with the rate of incumbent reelection falling to 48.9 percent of the Chamber of Deputies, its lowest level since 1994. A record 243 deputies were complete newcomers to the Chamber (Folha, 2018c). Bolsonaro's party, the PSL, rose from eight to fifty-two deputies, coming in a close second behind the largest party, the PT (fifty-four), and surpassing both the MDB (thirty-four) and the PSDB (twenty-nine), the three parties which together had dominated politics since at least 1994. Bolsonaro made it quite clear that he had little interest in playing the traditional presidential role of coalition broker, arguing that if Congress wanted reform, it must step up and fill a leadership role. He reduced the number of ministries and filled many of the existing ministries with army officers and others from outside the party system. At various stages in the pension reform, Bolsonaro seemed willing to allow the amendment to be guided by Chamber president Rodrigo Maia, even if this led to a significant dilution of his administration's objectives, and even though there was a significant risk that pension reform might fail completely. A number of reforms with deferred implementation also stood to shape the political system. In October 2017, Congress ended the possibility of *"coligações,"* or interparty alliances, and put in place a performance threshold that should gradually come into effect in coming electoral cycles. This could reduce the degree of party fragmentation, and perhaps ameliorate the intra-coalitional bargaining that has been common to all presidencies.

The first year and a half of the Bolsonaro administration reshaped the political controls over the developmental state in a number of ways. The first was simply a reticence to engage in any kind of industrial policy at all. For example, at one of the first meetings of the SUFRAMA (Superintendency of the Free Trade Zone of Manaus) that Guedes presided over, he created a small firestorm with the provocative question: "You mean that I have to leave Brazil all screwed up, all messed up because, otherwise, there are no benefits for Manaus?" (Maisonnave, 2019). As this illustrated, under a government with less overt industrial policy, fewer controls over industrial policy would presumably be needed. Yet even neoliberal policies require some sort of control, most notably through independent regulatory oversight of different industries and financial markets to prevent market-damaging anticompetitive practices. In July 2019, Bolsonaro signed into law a new bill aligning the rules and procedures for all eleven regulatory agencies, increasing their budgetary and administrative autonomy from sectoral ministries, and requiring them to conduct annual strategic reports. Second, the Bolsonaro administration followed in the footsteps of Temer in attempting to realign public prices at market levels so as to diminish the need for continuous control and management of public prices and their ripple effects throughout the economy. Third, Bolsonaro nominated as Justice Minister Sérgio Moro, the judge who headed the Lava Jato investigations, who put forth a reform that would tighten laws on corruption and money laundering. Moro attempted to reverse the dismantling of control bodies like the Federal Police which occurred under the Temer presidency. Meanwhile, external pressures in the Lava Jato investigations, such as the involvement of the US Department of Justice and the US Securities and Exchange Commission, increased pressure on Brazilian firms and MNCs active in Brazil to improve compliance mechanisms that would mitigate the likelihood of bribery and other improper influence peddling as tools of business. The number of companies with such compliance programs has risen from virtually nothing to an overwhelming majority of large firms over the past decade.

Finally, the autonomous bureaucracy. As noted earlier, the number of ministers peaked at a remarkable thirty-nine under Rousseff in 2015 but was cut to fewer than two dozen under Temer and Bolsonaro. Most notably, after eight decades and immense influence on politics, the Labor Ministry was shuttered. Economics Minister Guedes announced that he would suspend public examinations for hiring new civil servants which in light of the wave of retirements expected in coming years, will shrink the number of civil servants, if not their per capita cost.

In sum, as Brazil entered the third decade of the twenty-first century, the Bolsonaro administration appeared poised to bring a significant amount of change across all five institutional domains. But would it be sufficient to push the overall equilibrium of Brazil's political economy toward a new mix of preferences and behaviors? Here we are constrained theoretically as well as empirically. Theoretically, it is impossible to know exactly where the country is at present: Is it closer to a stable equilibrium, or on the verge of a major tipping point? Is it dealing with institutions that are more susceptible to difficult but potentially rapid change, or that permit easier but incremental change?[13] Empirically, too, it is hard to foresee which forces are likely to prevail: reformers such as Guedes, or counterreformers in some firms, members of Congress or, for that matter, the president himself, whose commitment to reform often appears wavering.

INSTITUTIONS SNAPPING BACK TO EQUILIBRIUM

President Bolsonaro repeatedly showed a certain lack of alignment with his advisors on economic matters. During the presidential campaign, he sought to evade criticism of his contradictory postures by admitting his ignorance of economics and making a show of deferring to Minister Guedes on all things related to economic policy. But as candidate and

Institutions Snapping Back to Equilibrium

president, Bolsonaro showed that old habits die hard, and that the temptation to use the tools of the developmental state was a natural one for politicians accustomed to them. As a candidate, Bolsonaro publicly repudiated Guedes' plan to raise taxes, saying "nobody can stand more taxes" (Cruz, 2018). When word leaked of an idea to recreate the CPMF tax on financial transactions, Bolsonaro quashed the idea publicly. After the election, Bolsonaro criticized Guedes' social security reform, promising to protect certain professions, such as police and military officers, from the proposed changes. Bolsonaro publicly demanded in early 2019 that the Banco do Brasil lower its interest rates for the agriculture sector, raising "alarm bells among investors wary of government meddling" (Lima, 2019). When a major tailings dam collapsed in Minas Gerais, leading to the tragic loss of hundreds of lives, both Bolsonaro's vice president and his presidential chief of staff Onyx Lorenzoni suggested that government should use its golden shares and influence with state-guided pension funds to replace senior executives at Vale (Kastner, 2019).

With regard to the organization of firms, pervasive ideas about the role of the state in the economy were deeply embedded and intertwined with special interests, making them politically difficult to confront. Even mild reforms faced pushback. After announcing cuts in local content requirements for oil exploration and a reduction in tariff protections in 2017, for example, the Temer administration was forced to backtrack in the face of strong opposition from a local suppliers group, Abimaq (Reuters, 2017). The Petrobras president, Pedro Parente, resigned a year into his new job in the face of the government's inability to undertake needed price readjustments, which had triggered a massively disruptive nationwide truckers' strike. The BNDES' move to end subsidized lending provoked backlash from industrial associations such as FIESP, which complained about the uncompetitive lending rates prevalent in the rest of society. Although the Bolsonaro administration continued to work for readjustments in public prices, it was hemmed in by similar pressure from politically powerful businesses and professions. In April 2019, Bolsonaro prohibited Petrobras from raising prices by more than 5 percent after facing considerable pressures from truckers; in July, the ANTT transport regulator responded to ministerial pressure and withdrew its rules regarding minimum freight rates in response to new threats from truckers.

On privatization, when more radical reformers suggested that his administration would privatize all SOEs, Bolsonaro pushed back. Even though plans had been underway under Temer in preparation for Eletrobras' privatization, during the election Bolsonaro publicly rejected calls for the company's sale, arguing that it would put Brazil "in the hands of China" (Surran, 2018). Bolsonaro ultimately reversed course, and Eletrobras may hit the auction block in the early 2020s. Reflecting the opposition from many senators, though, in September 2019, Senate president David Alcolumbre was quoted saying, "Why are we going to start with this if there's resistance?" (Reuters, 2019). With regard to the private sector, Bolsonaro's instincts also seemed reflexively inward-looking. In January 2019, when asked about the purchase of Embraer's civil aviation division by Boeing, Bolsonaro fretted about the loss of "our patrimony." His predecessor's comments on the sale had been no more encouraging: Temer argued that while foreign capital in Embraer was welcome, shifting shareholder control to Boeing was "out of the question" (Fernandes and Ventura, 2017). Meanwhile, even seemingly market-oriented moves are often not quite so purely market-based as they appear: past concession purchases have been financed by as much as 70 percent public capital, such as BNDES funds (Lazzarini et al., 2017).

During the debate over reforms to regulatory agencies, one proposal was for Congress to control nominations so as to make the agencies more autonomous from the executive branch, where sectoral ministries have often overridden and weakened agencies through appointments and tight budgetary controls. Informed of this possibility, Bolsonaro asked, to the eternal delight of internet trolls, "What, do they want me to be the Queen of England?," presumably referring to the merely ceremonial functions of the crown sovereign. When the reform was passed in July 2019, Bolsonaro vetoed several clauses that had been designed to augment agency autonomy, most notably one that would have forced the president to choose the regulatory agency heads from a list of three nominees chosen by the legislative branch. These vetoes meant that all directors would continue to be picked freely by the President, and that there would be no restrictions on revolving door hiring practices.

Meanwhile, there were few plans for action in a number of microeconomic areas, such as the oligopolies in the banking sector, the high levels of informality, or the inequality of social policy. Tax reform was bandied about as a possibility but raised a bewildering number of issues that ensure it will be a multiyear, incremental proposition. Even newly dynamic areas of the economy appeared to be falling into existing patterns of political and economic organization: agricultural producers, for example, played by the prevailing rules of the political system, organizing an influential "ruralist" caucus in Congress dedicated to forwarding their interests, seeking out special credit programs and state loans, and otherwise pushing

Institutions Snapping Back to Equilibrium

for parochial gains. Bolsonaro courted the sector with a variety of plum appointments in the Agriculture Ministry, including naming a former president of the ruralist caucus as minister, and radically weakening the environment portfolio. Oligopolies in other sectors continued to pull the equilibrium back to its original starting point. For example, the dynamic expansion of financial technology firms (*fin-tech*) and start-ups was once thought likely to revolutionize the oligopolistic banking sector. But one iconic start-up, the brokerage XP Investimentos – once referred to as "Brazil's Charles Schwab" for the likelihood that it would upend the financial market – has sold 49.9 percent of its shares to banking giant Itaú. While the Central Bank put some restrictions on the sale, for example barring Itaú from purchasing any more shares of XP for eight years, it was hard to avoid the conclusion that one of the few financial market disruptors to emerge in recent years had been neutered (Napolitano, 2018). Similarly, in the auto industry, the end of the five-year R$7.5 billion Inovar Auto incentive program in 2017 was met by a new program known as Rota 2030, which offered tax incentives of up to R$1.5 billion a year in exchange for increased spending on research and development.

Nor was it clear that the broader population's perspective on the economy had changed significantly. It is worth recalling that past changes to developmental models in postwar Latin America occurred only when there was a combination of political will, ideological change, and social change (Kaufman, 1990). While there was immense dissatisfaction in Brazil at the end of the 2010s, preferences continued to lean in a largely developmental direction. This may be an outcome of many factors, as Chapter 3 illustrated: the perceived success of developmentalist practice; inequality's effects on citizens' attitudes toward the state; the undisputed costs of reform; and the strong constituencies arrayed in defense of portions of the status quo. Whatever the reason, polls during the first year of Bolsonaro's presidency showed support for privatization nationwide at only about 40 percent; likewise, on labor reform, only about two-fifths of the population declared themselves in favor, with 57 percent against (Gielow, 2019).

In the political realm, Congress was renewed by the 2018 elections, but this did nothing to change the underlying trend toward fragmentation: from 1999 to 2019, the effective number of parties (as calculated by the Laakso-Taagapera formula) rose more or less steadily from 6.7 to 16.5. The largest party in 1999 held 21 percent of the lower house seats, but only 11 percent in 2019.[14] With the average number of legislators per party falling, the Bolsonaro government's initial reticence to play the coalitional game had a high cost in terms of the discombobulation of the legislative agenda. The party that Bolsonaro had joined for the 2018 election, the PSL, seemed as lost as anyone, with multiple voices speaking on behalf of the party. Ultimately the conflict was solved in time-honored fashion, as Bolsonaro left the PSL to found a new party. The most notable effect was to dilute the pension reform from the most ambitious draft put forward by Guedes, which would have treated all professions equally and instituted a market capitalization scheme that was designed to increase equity investment. Whatever its merits, this diluted pension reform thus served as only one more incremental step toward solving the fiscal quandary. As an influential economist concluded, the tepid results of reform meant that either a tendentious tax reform would be needed, spending would have to be further cut, or the government would be forced to inflate its way out of the political problem (Pessôa, 2019).

The Bolsonaro administration also backed away from its principled early stance against horse-trading. By the president's fourth month in office, the government was openly negotiating appointments and budget amendments to obtain support for legislative proposals, and in early June, the administration held direct meetings with the leadership of both houses of Congress and party leaders to negotiate the pace and contents of reform. The power of party leaders appeared to have reasserted itself in ways that reverted to traditional patterns of executive-legislative relations. Congress also took advantage of Bolsonaro's absence to approve a constitutional amendment making collective budget amendments by state caucuses binding on the executive branch, directly contradicting Guedes' goal of removing all earmarked and discretion-reducing instruments of budget management. To push the pension reform through the lower house, the administration agreed to a deal increasing permissible budget amendments for each legislator by R$10 million, on top of the original R$15 million, at a total cost of more than R$3 billion (Bragon, 2019). By the end of his first year, Bolsonaro's "new politics" appeared to be nothing more than a "chaotic" version of the old coalitional politics (Limongi, 2019, 43). Early in his second year, Bolsonaro threw in the towel, exchanging subministerial appointments responsible for nearly R$75 billion in federal funds for legislative support from the highly pliable "Centrão" parties (Benites, 2020).

The imposition of controls on the developmental state has proven difficult, and a rather low priority. Reciprocity remains an issue, because even though BNDES lending and industrial incentives have diminished,

Institutions Snapping Back to Equilibrium 257

they have not gone away. Perhaps most emblematically, after coming out strongly against the special interests of the Zona Franca de Manaus trade zone, within a few weeks, Minister Guedes had tempered his public statements, arguing that "the government was not going to target the essence and the economic heart of Brazilian regions . . ." Guedes presided over a July meeting of SUFRAMA that approved the addition of twenty-six new projects in the ZFM, while expanding sixty-one existing projects, at a cost of US$650 million (Maisonnave, 2019). Governmental strategic initiatives seemed focused on reducing fiscal costs rather than improving supervision by a market-oriented state. Regulatory reform was focused more on changing regulatory policy direction than on freeing regulatory agencies from political interference and ensuring that they were genuinely market-regulating, as the "Queen of England" episode illustrated.

In the realm of legal control, a wave of bad news swamped the Bolsonaro administration. The president's son was accused of illegitimate campaign transactions, and the PSL was accused of using fake candidates to fraudulently obtain public campaign funds. Despite the turnover in Congress, about one-fifth of the members of the new Chamber and one-third of the Senate had cases pending in the high court, complicating passage of Justice Minister Moro's anticrime and anti-corruption measures, which were heavily watered down. Anti-corruption gains over the past decade seemed more tenuous than the bombastic headlines of Lava Jato suggested: few other high-level investigations prospered, and the Lava Jato prosecutions of political elites seemed caught in a morass of high court irresolution and self-inflicted wounds. There were honest disagreements about the correct application of legal doctrine on issues that remained contentious under Brazilian law, such as racketeering, preventive detention, plea bargaining, jail upon unsuccessful appeal, and the extent of original jurisdiction. But there were also less well-intentioned legislative forays that suggested the political system would not give up easily in a tug of war with rising accountability institutions. Indeed, President Temer appears to have been backed by a slim plurality in Congress *precisely* because he was perceived to have done so much on behalf of legislators fearing prosecution (Londoño, 2017).[15] These counterpressures lingered under Bolsonaro. Notably, Moro resigned his ministry in April 2020, alleging pressure from Bolsonaro to interfere in the Federal Police. The high court also made a number of decisions that complicated effective legal punishment for those involved in corruption. One of the most consequential was a decision to move all corruption cases involving campaign finance out of the regular judiciary and into the even less effective electoral court system. In sum, while the public's frustration with judicial irresoluteness has grown, there were clear impediments – both well-intentioned and salutary brakes on the punitive impetus, as well as poorly intentioned efforts to undermine accountability – that will slow and dilute any changes.

Finally, with regard to the bureaucracy, meetings with civil servants during visits to Brasília in 2019 produced reiterated expressions of two sorts: we are keeping our heads down to avoid drawing unwelcome attention from this administration; and we have been immobilized by all the attention to probity, which falls inordinately on the civil service and makes it hard to do our jobs. Ironically, these comments hinted at the possibility that the cumulative effect of Bolsonaro's reformism, and the tightening of anti-corruption efforts over the longer haul, might be a diminution of the bureaucracy's ability to autonomously foment incremental change. Further, the high cost of the bureaucracy remains an important constraint: to comply with the new constitutional amendment establishing a fiscal ceiling, federal personnel expenditures must fall by fully one percentage point of GDP by 2023 (Karpowicz and Soto, 2018).

This book has focused on the forces that hold Brazil's political economy in an equilibrium that the title labels "decadent developmentalism." Any change in the fabric of Brazil's political economy must take into account institutional complementarities that are specific to Brazil and that generate country specific, mutually reinforcing incentives to actors in both the economic and political spheres. The five institutional domains described here, though, have not been equal in their impact on the stability of the overall political economy equilibrium.

Reforms to three of the institutional domains – while possibly impactful in their own right – seemed unlikely to shift the overall political economy equilibrium. The weakness of control mechanisms resulted in large part from the context of weak checks and balances engendered by coalitional presidentialism, defensive parochialism by business interests in the political sphere, and the absence of clear disciplining of incumbent politicians by voters. This helped to explain why, despite a variety of efforts to improve both administrative and judicial controls, the institutional equilibrium of weak control persisted into the 2020s. The institution kept snapping back, in other words, to an equilibrium of weak control, guided in part by the incentives generated by other, complementary institutions. Bureaucratic autonomy in some ways co-evolved with the developmental state. Under democracy, with its vastly larger number of veto players, bureaucratic autonomy provided a modicum of

Institutions Snapping Back to Equilibrium 259

incremental reforms necessary to deliver basic public goods. Yet reforming the civil service was unlikely to significantly alter the incentives in other institutional domains; the autonomous bureaucracy is a hierarchically subordinate institution to coalitional presidentialism. In the same manner, the DHME is the hierarchically subordinate institution to the developmental state.

Two central institutions thus seemed likely to be the most relevant for reformers seeking to move Brazil's economic policy set in either a truly developmentalist or a neoliberal direction: the developmental state and coalitional presidentialism. These institutions are intertwined because steering capital in any economy – neoliberal, developmentalist, or otherwise – is an inherently political act. Yet although the developmental state has been the target of reform for almost the entirety of the past generation, the overall political economy equilibrium seems not to have shifted significantly toward a more effective economic model capable of producing equitable growth. Further, as the push and pull of Bolsonaro's early reforms demonstrates, even under radical reformers, there has been a tendency for old behaviors and preferences to persist and reestablish themselves. Given the multiple complementarities across the political and economic domains, changes to political institutions are thus as important to changing the underlying incentives of the developmental state economy as changes in the economic institutions themselves.

If policymakers truly wish to move away from the decadent developmental equilibrium, they may benefit from the insight in Celso Furtado's admonition in the epigraph to this chapter: it is vital to consider how the political system drives incentives toward parochialism, toward oligopoly, and toward the use of the developmental tool kit, even when the massive weight of the evidence suggests this tool kit is incapable of delivering equitable growth. To master its destiny, Brazil must not focus solely on economic reforms, but instead needs to consider ways of making the political system more strategically coherent, answerable to the electorate, and capable of controlling and effectively guiding elites.

Notes

1 INTRODUCTION

1. World Bank World Development Indicators.
2. Brazil has grown slightly faster than Argentina, Mexico, and Venezuela since 1988, although over the past fifteen years, Argentina has outgrown Brazil.
3. Nor is Brazil's relative stagnation the result of the recent growth shocks generated by the country's triple crises post-2013. Although the scale of Brazil's relative losses, especially against the wealthy nations, would be slightly smaller if the graph were to compare 1985 with 2013 or 2009, in the depths of the global financial crisis, the overall pattern remains the same.
4. The "demographic dividend" refers to a period in which the working age population is growing more quickly than the total population, thus permitting an accrual of savings that help growth. The working age population accounted for more than 50 percent of the total population by the mid-1990s. Recent Brazilian government studies suggest the dividend came to an end in 2018 (Bôas, 2018).
5. World Bank World Development Indicators.
6. https://fred.stlouisfed.org/series/RTFPNABRA632NRUG, July 3, 2018.
7. Another approach is to measure inequality by using data on income declared to the Revenue Service; a 2019 study by Tendências Consultoria found that both measures had been rising since 2014, but also that inequality measured by income declarations was nearly twice the level of inequality measured by household census data (G1, 2019a).
8. Indeed, because of the state's role in guiding firms and markets, some authors prefer to use the term "state capitalism" rather than "developmental state." There is considerable overlap between the two concepts as applied to Brazil. Trubek (2013, 4), for example, argues that in Brazil's "new developmental" state, "government plays an active role in mobilizing resources, stimulating investment, and promoting innovation ... employ[ing] industrial policy ... [and using] an active social policy to eliminate poverty, reduce inequality, and

Notes to pages 11–13 261

stimulate domestic demand." This broad conceptualization covers motivations that go beyond firm-government relations alone, ranging across macroeconomic, regulatory, and social policies as well. Musacchio and Lazzarini (2014, 2), define state capitalism narrowly as "the widespread influence of the government in the economy, either by owning majority or minority equity positions in companies or by providing subsidized credit and/or other privileges to private companies."

I use the term "developmentalism" because it encapsulates several broad aspects of state behavior, including ideas, institutions, and policies. Analytically, the notion of state developmentalism ascribes intentionality to state action: rather than simply affirming a role for the state in the economy, which is common to all capitalist systems, developmentalism points to the fact that the state's role has a concrete objective, and the theoretical core of developmentalism suggests a set of assumptions that ground these actions. Another reason to use the "developmental state" moniker is that the comparative use of the concept of "state capitalism" outside Brazil is ambiguous. Even authors who argue for a globally applicable notion of state capitalism make the point that it is "hardly monolithic; instead, it is better understood as a continuum, just as free-market capitalism runs along a continuum from extreme laissez-faire economics to a French or Scandinavian model of a highly regulated market economy" (Kurlantzick, 2016, 7). Brazil combines government-controlled firms with a predominantly market economy and emerging capital markets, yet because of developmentalist influence, the government encourages national control of strategic sectors, engages in industrial policy, and holds dominant positions in banking. Politically, too, Brazil is an outlier among so-called "state capitalist" nations: Brazil is not authoritarian, nor does it rely on a single-party state, as do so many state capitalist nations (Bremmer, 2010, 4–5; Tsai and Naughton, 2015).

9. Institutional complementarities are not the only causes: veto players and veto points, sunk costs, and coordination problems may also be sources of a bias toward stability (Pierson, 2004; Deeg and Jackson, 2007). But institutional complementarities contribute to all of the other forms of resistance to change.

10. I do not claim that institutional complementarities explain any and all interactions involving these institutions, or that all complementarities are equally strong. Indeed, as past authors have noted, some complementarities between institutions are stronger than others, depending on the "coupling" between institutions (Campbell, 2010). This book evaluates both within-domain complementarities (e.g., the relationship between state-owned enterprises and fiscal policy in the developmental state), as well as cross-domain complementarities (e.g., between the developmental state and coalitional presidentialism). Understandably, within-domain complementarities are likely to be much stronger than cross-domain complementarities, and some within-domain complementarities will be stronger than others.

11. I am informed by Hutchcroft and Kuhonta (2018), who explore the Northian and Huntingtonian conceptions of institutions.

262 *Notes to pages 14–19*

12. This is not to say that institutions can never have an organizational face, however. As Streeck and Thelen (2005, 12) point out, "organizations come to be regarded as institutions to the extent that their existence and operation become in a specific way publicly guaranteed and privileged, by becoming backed up by societal norms and the enforcement capacities related to them ...."

13. Institutional change is necessarily incremental in this model: because institutions are determined by the collective preferences and actions of individuals, any change is the result of changes in the proportions of individuals behaving in a particular way. A similar point is made by Amable and Palombarini (2009). Of course, over time incremental changes at the margin may add up to a significant transformation (Streeck and Thelen, 2005; Deeg, 2007; Taylor, 2009; Bersch, 2019).

14. A point that is well established by threshold models (e.g., Granovetter, 1978; Kuran, 1991).

15. Institutions may be considered "compatible" if their coexistence does not undermine each other but also does not enhance it (Deeg, 2007).

16. It is worth noting here what my conceptualization does not claim. Institutional change (or stasis) is not brought about because of emotions like fear of change (or of continuity; contra Campbell, 2010), but instead by the fact that the institutions are held in place by overlapping incentive structures that guide the choice of individual strategies. Similarly, complementarity is not about the benefits one institution provides to another (contra Campbell, 2010). It is about how the incentives an institution generates help to reinforce similar incentives generated by another institution. Finally, complementarity is relational and depends on the actor (Campbell, 2010): while firms might react in one way to a shift in incentives provided by the developmental state, business associations or labor might react in quite another way.

17. For critiques of the extension of the concept of an Asian developmentalist state, see Hundt and Uttam (2017) and Carney et al. (2009).

18. Institutions cannot be "functional" because although they may arise to address a particular problem, they quickly become autonomous "with respect to the precise conditions of the emergence of the institution" (Amable and Palombarini, 2009, 133). Institutional complementarity is not planned, and in fact, key Brazilian institutions evolved at different points in time: the developmental state and DHME in the postwar period; the logic of coalitional presidentialism in the second republic, with reinforcement in the third (Abranches, 2018); the lack of control in part as an outcome of the 1988 Constitution; and the strong and autonomous bureaucracy in the 1930s, strengthened in the 1988 Constitution and subsequent reforms.

19. As a consequence of their strategic nature, institutions cannot be judged on whether they are good, viable, efficient, or functional. Because institutions are the consequence of multiple actors' strategic decisions, they are haphazard and in no way "rational." While we may judge the *effects* of the institutions and the likelihood that they will deliver outcomes we prefer, we should not ascribe motives to those institutions, or otherwise anthropomorphize them. There are a variety of criteria we might choose from to judge an institution's effects, such as the institution's effects on equity and justice, its profit

Notes to page 19 263

outcomes, or its health implications. But while each of us might have normative preferences about the various ways institutions might be structured, the simple fact of the matter is that the "institution" – that is, the established rules of the game – is a passive, unresponsive, blameless thing. Not only can we not judge it, it doesn't care what we think. It has neither normative feelings, nor normative value in and of itself.

20. Aoki (2013, 235) makes a similar point, noting that institutions are "endorsed and reconfirmed" by the recursive state of play among agents.

21. Throughout this book, I assume that there are multiple equilibria.

22. This model for thinking about institutions is inspired by Stephenson's (2020) discussion of incremental change in the anti-corruption field. To conceptualize matters in the context of a single institution, it may be useful to imagine an "S-curve" representing preferences and incidence of behaviors (the preference-incidence, or P-I line), as in Figure A. There will be stable equilibria, E^l and E^r, at the bottom and top of the "S" and an unstable equilibrium, E^m, in the middle. The vertical axis represents the proportion of the population with a preference for boarding the subway on their right, and the horizontal axis represents the proportion of the population following the rule of entering subway cars on their right. The $45°$ line represents where these proportions are equivalent, and the three equilibria therefore are attained where the s-curve meets that $45°$ line. The E^m equilibrium is "unstable" because any small shift away from E^m would cause the system to quickly shift to a different equilibrium by virtue of the steep vertical slope around E^m. By contrast, small local perturbations at E^l or E^r – the late subway rider racing onto the train, or the rider who stumbled on her way out of the train – would get wiped out quickly, and the tendency would be for preferences and incidence to return to the same equilibrium.

Institutional complementarity could be modeled as a separate P-I line for each institution, but it could also be assumed – as I do here – that the P-I-line curve for any given institution reflects preferences derived from other institutions. By way of example, a P-I curve for driving would be much "boxier" than the P-I curve for subway boarding shown in Figure A, given that any deviation from E^l and E^r would be extremely dangerous. As a consequence, the P-I curve would look like a fairly flat horizontal line at E^l and E^r, and a steep vertical line around E^m. If highway driving and subway boarding are complementary, though, we need not show both P-I lines; it is sufficient to assume that the P-I line for subway boarding is slightly more rounded – the line from E^l to E^r is more parallel to the horizontal axis and the slope around E^m is steeper – than it would otherwise be in the absence of the complementary institution.

The three paths for change described in the main text of this section can be depicted graphically. In the first case of no change, exemplified by the failure of the Cardoso administration to approve Central Bank independence, no movement took place and the equilibrium persisted at an equilibrium like E^r. The second path, of change that is subsequently swamped, could take place either as movement along the P-I curve or as movement to a new P-I curve that then reverts to the original status quo (Figure B, arrows 1a and 1b). In the case

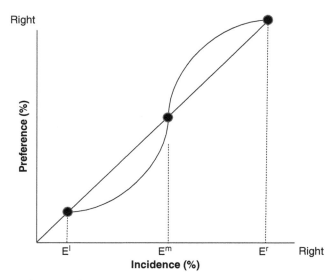

FIGURE A Subway loading at three equilibria.
Source: Author, drawing on Stephenson (2020).

of arrows 1a, a determined group tries to change the status quo, perhaps through collective effort to change behaviors, but is overwhelmed by broader society, and the push reverts to previous practice. In the case of arrow 1b, reformers actually shift the P-I curve upward, perhaps through a concerted policy push, but after the policy push, groups with contrary preferences push the equilibrium back to the original P-I curve and the original E^r.

Figure C shows the third path, of successful change, either through a big push (arrow 2), or through an accumulation of small changes (arrows 3 and 4). If sufficiently strong, as in arrow 2, this push could shift the P-I curve to the right, such that the equilibrium moves in one fell swoop from E^1 to E^6. The other possibility is incremental change. Note that one of the most significant implications of this model is that even small, incremental changes may be capable of triggering abrupt equilibria shifts. Initially, the shift in the P-I curve demonstrated by arrow 3 would lead to a shift from E^1 to E^2. But the next small incremental change, shown by arrow 4, would lead to a much more momentous change in equilibrium from E^2 to E^6.

23. Arida presentation at Primeiro Fórum de Regulação, "Banco Central do Brasil: para além da independência," Escola de Direito Fundação Getulio Vargas, São Paulo, June 12, 2019.
24. As Deeg (2007) notes, the "historical-political approach eschews equilibrium analysis and conceives of institutions (and 'equilibriums') as continuously evolving in nontrivial ways. This approach sees institutions as more or less

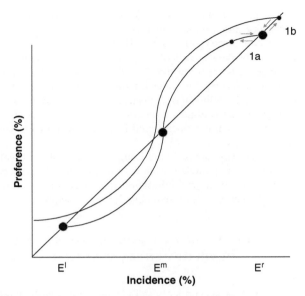

FIGURE B Reversion to equilibrium.
Source: Author.

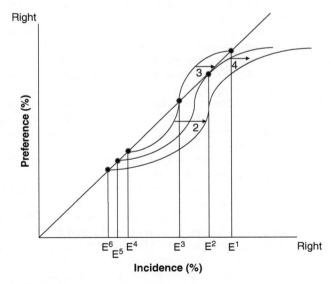

FIGURE C Shifting preference-incidence curves.
Source: Author.

266 *Notes to pages 24–40*

constantly changing; in many instances smaller or gradual changes add up over time to major institutional transformation (e.g., Pierson, 2004; Crouch, 2005; Morgan et al., 2005; Streeck and Thelen, 2005)."

25. Taylor (2020) maps the key axes of the political economy of democracy, and draws out the pervasive tensions that have driven the slow but steady changes that have been underway for much of the past generation, including the emergence of fiscal discipline, more effective instruments of monetary authority, stable patterns of coalition formation and electoral competition, the deepening of bureaucratic capacity, and incremental reforms across a wide range of policy arenas.

26. Armijo (2017, 231, 245) notes that although it is not a sharp break from the developmentalism of the authoritarian regime, the "new" developmentalism does bring a significant new emphasis on macroeconomic stability, global integration, and an emphasis on reducing domestic inequality.

2 THE MACROECONOMIC FOUNDATIONS OF THE DEVELOPMENTAL STATE

1. Leahy (2011).
2. As with the inflation targets under both Lula and Dilma, with increasing dirty floating of the exchange rate under Finance Minister Mantega, and at the outset of President Rousseff's second term, when the fiscal situation deteriorated and manipulation of the fiscal results became especially pronounced.
3. As Melo et al. (2014) note, "[t]he fallout of the trauma of hyperinflation was that beliefs about the value of social inclusion gave away to beliefs in social inclusion *cum* fiscal stability."
4. Amable (2016, 82), citing Boyer (2007), notes that "More generally, the viability of an accumulation regime depends on the compatibility between five institutional forms: competition, the wage-labour nexus, the monetary and financial regimes, the state and the type of integration of the national economy into the world system."
5. It is common to assume that foreign investment is incompatible with inward-looking developmentalism. Yet the developmental state often combines inward-looking development with the search for external sources of finance. See, for example, Sikkink (1991, 30–1).
6. Data on the tax burden and government spending as a share of GDP are from www.heritage.org, September 18, 2018.
7. This expansion in tax collections occurred in two spurts: the first in the early years of the military regime, and the second in the wake of the Real Plan. The military regime's new tax code included introduction of a value-added tax (VAT), the world's first; as well as creating the Federal Revenue Secretariat (SRF) (Melo et al., 2014). The Real Plan spurred revenue increases from improved administration and greater transparency. Melo et al. (2014, note 29) note that revenue from seigniorage reached a maximum of 8 percent of GDP in the 1983–7 period, but this was moderate compared with rates of 12 to 25 percent in Argentina.

Notes to pages 41–5 267

8. The anti-reform momentum has several root causes: 1) much reform can only take place via constitutional amendment, which requires significant political mobilization; 2) among those who pay the individual income tax, those most likely to face a higher tax rate from reform include influential civil servants, judges, and politicians; 3) in the private sector, many high-income workers have established their own firms to reduce their tax liability, thus weakening their support for reform; 4) the middle class has been resistant to property tax increases that might offset reductions in more regressive taxes; 5) the corporate beneficiaries of fiscal incentives (such as reductions in the tax on industrial production [*Imposto sobre Produtos Industrializados*, IPI] or in the tax on the movement of goods and services [*Imposto sobre Circulação de Mercadorias e Serviços*, ICMS]) are more concerned about preserving their sectoral gains than about the inefficiencies created by taxing consumption; and 6) governments have been reluctant to push forward tax reform, for fear that after negotiation with Congress, the post-reform system might be either worse than the status quo, or damaging to the fiscal accounts (Afonso, 2013; Melo et al., 2014). The result is that most change has been incremental.

9. Nogueira et al. (2015) analyze the following benefits: family wage (*salário família*), the unemployment benefit, the wage bonus paid to employees who lose their job (known as PIS/PASEP after the private sector contribution, *Programa de Integração Social*, PIS, and the public sector contribution, *Programa de Formação do Patrimônio do Servidor Público*, PASEP), the *Bolsa Família*, and the old age assistance benefit (*benefício de prestação continuada*).

10. According to the World Bank's Doing Business Project (2014), tax paperwork to file corporate income taxes, sales taxes, and labor taxes eats up 2,600 hours a year, the highest in the world. This compares with 334 hours in Mexico, 291 in Chile, and 405 in Argentina. Brazil was 167th in the world in ease of opening a business, 177th in tax efficiency, and 123rd in trade bureaucracy.

11. Net public sector debt stood at a moderate 36.8 percent of GDP in 2014, in steady decline from 60 percent in 2002. Brazil has been a net foreign creditor for most of the years since the turn of the century (and ran mild net foreign debt of less than 0.1 percent of GDP in the remaining years).

12. Data on subsidies is from author calculations for 1997–2014; percentages for *Bolsa Família* and PAC are for period from 2003 to 2011, calculated by Giambiagi and Castelar Pinheiro (2012).

13. Total public investment by all levels of government has been around 4.5 percent of GDP.

14. As Mansueto Almeida (2013b) notes, between social security, social transfers, labor payments, education, and health care, 13.6 percent of GDP is spent, or nearly 80 percent of federal spending (17.34 percent of GDP).

15. Other effects include the regressivity of debt payments: as Mattei and Pereira (2015, 3, 13) note, around 5 percent of GDP went to paying interest on the public debt, earnings which were largely directed to Brazil's richest families. Federal interest payments in 2011 were about R$170 billion, by contrast to the R$11 billion spent on the *Bolsa Família* program.

268 *Notes to pages 46–8*

16. Nogueira et al. (2015) discuss a similar, but distinct concept, of the "fiscal illusion," whereby the cost of public services appears lower than it actually is. Among the causes of the fiscal illusion is the use of indirect taxes (which account for fully 49.7 percent of taxes); the complexity of the tax system's 18,000 regulations; the use of cascading taxation, where taxes fall on previously taxed goods; the numerous small changes in the basic tax system, which was altered almost 250 thousand times between 1988 and 2010; and the use of income from state enterprises to finance public expenditures. As Silva and Siqueira (2012) demonstrate, higher levels of indirect taxes also make it harder for taxpayers to realize how much they are paying in taxes.
17. Regulations push private banks to channel credit to agriculture, small loans, and mortgages.
18. As Fraga et al. (2003, 382–3) note, "fiscal and financial dominance leads to fear that the monetary policy regime will break down, leading inflationary expectations to rise." Briefly put, financial dominance is when the conduct of monetary policy is compromised by a weak or overleveraged financial system, or by the presence of government-owned banks. Fiscal dominance is when the conduct of monetary policy is compromised by weak fiscal policy that necessitates tighter monetary policy. There is a vibrant debate on whether Brazil suffers from fiscal dominance; the relevant point here, though, is simply that the fiscal accounts exert considerable pressure on monetary policymakers.
19. The exceptions were in 2002–03, as uncertainty about the possibility of a Lula presidency roiled expectations, and in late 2015 and early 2016, as the Rousseff administration's fiscal profligacy and political troubles raised uncertainty.
20. Although mechanisms of indexation have been reduced, key prices such as rents, electricity, telephony, and the minimum wage remain linked to specific inflation indices (Afonso et al., 2016).
21. The Central Bank contributed significantly to the effectiveness of indexation through its use of debt instruments such as the *Obrigações Reajustáveis do Tesouro Nacional* (ORTNs) and *Letras do Tesouro Nacional* (LTN), which offered fixed monetary correction and had daily liquidity. Further, banks were permitted to carry out operations valued at up to thirty times their equity (Luna and Klein, 2006, 82, 88).
22. That said, the debt burden is among the largest of the emerging market economies, and the fiscal crisis of the late 2010s means that the debt is likely to continue to grow into the mid-2020s.
23. Government debt is only slightly higher than in the rest of Latin America, but borrowing costs are significantly higher. Brazil's interest expenditures were nearly 8 percent of GDP in 2014, by contrast to under 3 percent in Colombia, under 1 percent in Peru, and around 0.5 percent in Chile (World Bank, 2017b, 35).
24. I am indebted to Mario Schapiro for helping me disentangle these issues. See Schapiro and Taylor (2020) for an explanation of the Central Bank's relationship with the financial sector.
25. Not only did inflation discourage long-term lending, but it also discouraged private banks from providing credit, given that credit intermediation was less

Notes to pages 49–51 269

lucrative than the inflation float or reinvestment of depositors' funds (Andrezo and Lima, 1999, 202; cited in McQuerry, 2001, 33).

26. Crisostomo et al. (2014) note that despite recent advances, external funding to firms is limited because capital markets are less developed than those in more advanced economies, minority shareholder and creditor protections are weak, there is high ownership concentration, and interest rates remain high.

27. Of all of these contributions, fulfilling social objectives is perhaps the least self-evident. Noting that access to finance is particularly important to fighting inequality in a country that is marked by high financial returns, Mettenheim and Lima (2014) argue that financial inclusion policies are an extremely important aspect of state banks' work. Access to banking has been deepened since 2000 by the adoption of conditional cash transfer programs, which consolidated transfers into the single *Cartão do Cidadão*, distributed by the CEF to over 130 million users. Public banks have benefited disproportionately from the creation of "simplified accounts" by the Central Bank, which have boosted account holders from 20 percent of the population in 2000 to 45 percent in 2010 (Mettenheim and Lima, 2014, 1455). These accounts, which can be opened without proof of income, have been complemented by federal banks' automatic extension of overdraft privileges to simplified account holders maintaining a minimum balance, generating what is in essence a small payroll loan. Both Banco do Brasil and the CEF have captive control over large sources of capital, such as the *Fundo de Amparo ao Trabalhador* (FAT), a fund financed through PIS/PASEP payroll deductions. Equally important, their implicit government backing contributes to greater client confidence, and more stable savings deposits (Mettenheim and Lima, 2014).

28. President Lula fired the head of the Banco do Brasil when he refused to lower lending rates (Mettenheim, 2010, 90).

29. The World Bank (2018a) draws on Central Bank data to report that the funds dedicated to earmarked lending are Treasury (7 percent of GDP); the payroll savings contributions in the *Fundo de Garantia por Tempo de Serviço* (FGTS; 5 percent); FAT (4 percent); and other constitutional funds (0.2 percent).

30. The Long-Term Interest Rate (*Taxa de Juros de Longo Prazo*, TJLP) was used through 2018 for the BNDES' lending; the Referential Rate (*Taxa Referencial*, TR) in the housing finance market dominated by the CEF; and specific rates for different segments of the agricultural credit market dominated by the Banco do Brasil.

31. Overperformance on the Basel requirements may also be driven by the fact that Brazilian banks carry large volumes of public debt, due to its high guaranteed returns (Schapiro and Taylor, 2020).

32. Foreign banks ramped up sharply from 7 percent of total banking assets in 1990 to a peak of 30 percent in 2001, before retreating to 16 percent in 2018 (Banco Central do Brasil, 2018, 142).

33. For a chronological list of development plans, see Cypher (2015).

34. The establishment of regulatory bodies for industry was a strategy to ensure that the privatization process did not redound in monopolies that would exploit gains to scale or monopoly control of key markets (Trubek, Coutinho, et al., 2013, 32). Constitutional amendments approved in 1995

270   *Notes to pages 52–5*

began the process of establishing regulatory bodies for the telecommunications industry and the oil sector. Between 1996 and 2005, eight more federal regulatory agencies were created, for the electric sector, health inspection, private health care services, water, water transportation, ground transportation, cinema, and aviation (National Electrical Energy Agency, ANEEL – 1996; the National Telecommunications Agency, ANATEL – 1997; the National Petroleum, Natural Gas, and Biofuels Agency, ANP – 1997; the National Health Surveillance Agency, ANVISA – 1999; the National Supplemental Health Agency, ANS – 2000; the National Water Agency, ANA – 2000; the National Waterway Transportation Agency, ANTAQ – 2001; the National Land Transportation Agency, ANTT – 2001; the National Cinema Agency, ANCINE – 2001; and the National Civil Aviation Agency, ANAC – 2005) (Freitas, 2014).The regulators were provided institutional independence through a variety of mechanisms, including fixed and staggered terms of office for commissioners, congressional approval of presidential nominations, and alternative sources of funding. The goal was to signal to investors Brazil's "regulatory commitment" to a stable set of rules and avoid the opportunism and pressures inherent in the electoral cycle (Abranches, 1999; Prado, 2008) as well as arbitrary intervention that might hurt investors' returns once investments had been made (Correa et al., 2008).

35. These terms refer to exploration and production (upstream); refining and transportation (midstream); and distribution and sales (downstream).

36. The ANP has not been entirely toothless with regard to Petrobras, but it is interesting to note that some of its fines against the company in the 2010s have concerned noncompliance with local content requirements, a decidedly developmentalist policy objective (USTR, 2013).

37. Respectively, the Federal Trade Commission (FTC) and the Office of Fair Trade (OFT).

38. Regulatory agencies have been brought under presidential control through reduced budgets and failure to fill vacancies (Prado et al., 2016), although there are efforts to push back, such as attempts by corporate lawyers to impose legal constraints on regulatory discretion (Sá e Silva and Trubek, 2018, 920).

39. Changes to the trappings of trade protection include elimination of the Law of Similars (which banned imports of locally-produced products) and the CACEX foreign trade department, which maintained an intricate system of controls over thousands of imports (Villela, 2015, 168). Important constraints have been placed on trade policy by international agreements, such as the WTO and Mercosur; by markets, via ratings agencies and the floating exchange rate; and by domestic business groups. There has been less space for the deep protectionism of the 1940–80s: under WTO strictures, it was no longer possible to impose an effective tariff on automobiles of 308 percent, as in 1987 (Cardoso, 2009, 10).

40. Oliveira et al. (2019, 12–15) make the important point that average MFN tariff rates on agricultural goods are actually lower in Brazil than in peers such as China, India, and Mexico (and have been for the entire period from 1989 to 2016), while for manufactured goods, tariff rates have always been among the

Notes to pages 55–65 271

highest in this grouping of countries. They further make the point that Brazil's services trade restrictiveness is higher than the average calculated by the OECD in almost all service sectors.

41. "Brazil's tariff regime is more protectionist than an average Latin America and the Caribbean (LAC) or upper-middle-income country (which have TTRIs of 7.8 and 6.9 percent, respectively). Based on its TTRI, Brazil is ranked 93rd out of 125 countries, where 1st is least restrictive" (World Bank, 2010). Although import tariffs under Mercosur and WTO were capped at 35 percent, and Brazil's applied tariff averaged 11.64 percent in 2011, the average bound tariff was 31.4 percent.

42. It is also worth noting that trade policy may be further constrained by foreign policy. Foreign policy objectives have included fostering greater South-South dialogue, organizing counter-hegemonic coalitions that permit Brazil to maintain and extend its dominant position in South America, and expanding Brazil's influence in the WTO and among the BRIC nations (Hornbeck, 2006, 6; Baumann, 2009, 11; Onuki, 2010). They have been guided by adherence to a somewhat defensive nationalism, distilled from various currents of Brazilian thought, including a nationalistic critique of the role of the United States, strains of dependency and center-periphery thought, and a tradition of foreign policy realism aimed at preserving an autonomous national industrial strategy (Soares de Lima, 1990, 1994, 2005; Veiga, 2004, 2007; Maia and Taylor, 2015; Burges, 2017). Brazil has perceived the largest external threats to its sovereignty as being economic, rather than security-oriented, which has contributed to the strong developmentalist tint of foreign policy (Soares de Lima, 2005, 5; Mares and Trinkunas, 2016). The foreign ministry, Itamaraty, fought developed countries' efforts to expand the Uruguay Round agenda to include issues of intellectual property, services, and investment, and has been a major proponent of creating clear rules on antidumping and controversy resolution, in part because of economic interests, but also because of a longer commitment to the notion of reciprocal and equal trading relations. Moreover, business leaders frequently toe the government line rather than pushing the government for opening (Oliveira, 2011, 186–9).

43. That said, the small scope of Brazilian trade suggests that exchange rate appreciation is not the likely or primary cause of Brazil's ongoing deindustrialization, underway since the 1980s and often associated with "Dutch disease" (Cypher, 2015).

3 CONTINUITY THROUGH CHANGE: IDEAS AS BALLAST FOR THE DEVELOPMENTAL STATE

1. Schwartsman (2018), translation by author.
2. Smith and Bernardes (2013), translation by author.
3. Ideas interact with interests and preferences. The rules and roles inherent in ideas act as scripts for appropriate behavior and provide guidance that either enables or constrains action. The actions of state actors may be guided less by self-interest than by a "logic of appropriateness" (Finnemore, 1996)

272

Notes to pages 65–8

regarding the obligations and duties most important in that particular context. In some cases, ideas may actually push against self-interest, as in the case of the bureaucrat who stays late to help a distraught citizen, guided by a self-conception of the appropriate role of a public-spirited civil servant. In other cases, ideas may reinforce self-interest, as with the bureaucrat who refuses to help a friend extra-officially, fearing punishment and drawing on the idea of bureaucratic neutrality for justification.

4. The literature on the effect of ideas on economic policy has a long and distinguished lineage, including Bielschowsky (1988), Sikkink (1991), and Sola (1998) on Brazil, as well as the broader perspectives offered by Polanyi (1957), Weir and Skocpol (1985), Hall (1989), Hirschman (1989), Goldstein and Keohane (1993), Love (1996, 2005), and Ruggie (2008).

5. For example, Love (1996, 220) notes that "... in 1933 Argentina had to sell 73 percent more than before the Depression to obtain the same quantity of (manufactured) imports."

6. Cardoso and Helwege (2000[1992],158) note that, "In practice, ISI differed from protectionism in industrialized countries. Whereas protectionism in developed countries has typically been aimed at helping specific industries, ISI was adopted as an economy-wide strategy." The primary advocate of structuralism, Raúl Prebisch, was well-acquainted with Keynesian thought, having published a textbook on the subject in 1947.

7. As Toye and Toye (2003) note, Prebisch and Singer published similar papers at nearly the same time, and although Prebisch won much of the credit, he relied heavily on Singer's previous work. They point out, however, that Prebisch did make "a contribution distinct from that made by Singer. This was to advance a cyclical-cum structural mechanism to explain the decline, one more complicated than the purely structural interpretation of Singer" (459). A rich discussion of the eclectic influences on Prebisch can be found in Love (1996), who mentions a diverse set of intellectuals and policymakers, including Alejandro Bunge, Victor Emilio Estrada, Werner Sombart, Mihail Manoilescu, François Perroux, and Charles Kindleberger.

8. One reason this was possible, Prebisch and Singer argued, was due to the "power of organized labor and oligopolistic industries in the developed world. The former were able to maintain high wages, and the latter to control production rates instead of reducing prices, when demand fell. Neither of these conditions held for primary commodities, or for the countries producing them" (Ficker, 2005, 147).

9. With the benefit of hindsight, it does not take much imagination to see how such beliefs could be harnessed in favor of a broader argument relating to the dependence of periphery countries. Where Cardoso and Faletto (1973[1967]) innovated in the depiction of this "dependency theory" was in illustrating how dependency affects the class structure and politics *within* those peripheral nations. Indeed, while their argument builds on and reinforces the structuralist approach, it goes beyond by illustrating how political alliances associated with dependent "underdevelopment" in the *international* arena function to sustain dominant political elites in the *domestic* arena.

Notes to pages 68–71

10. Of course, not all of the structuralist prescriptions were followed. Prebisch's views were more far-ranging than the Prebisch-Singer thesis alone would indicate, and many of his other prescriptions were ignored by policymakers of the era. Noting that development does not take place spontaneously, Prebisch argued that states needed to engage in a rational effort at reforming social structures to permit better social mobility and distribution of wealth, all in the service of deeper net capital formation (Prebisch, 1963, 13). Without greater capital investment, industrialization would be continuously undermined by the "extravagant consumption" of the upper classes, who would not allocate capital toward industry without government guidance. Prebisch further suggested addressing problems of agricultural production, such as land tenure and unsatisfactory investment, education, and the geographical imbalance in income between urban and rural centers.

11. I use the term "liberal" in the classical sense, rather than by reference to its secondary (largely American) usage as a synonym for progressive. In the pantheon of ideas, liberalism is often considered close to, but not coterminous with, laissez-faire free market fundamentalism, privileging private actors over the state. Other terms often used in Latin America when discussing economic liberalism include neoliberal, orthodox, outward-oriented, reformist, non-contextual, and noninterventionist. My general reference here is to a "mean and lean" Anglo-Saxon variety of capitalism, akin to that described as a liberal market economy (LME) by Hall and Soskice (2001). This is by contrast to the developmentalist school, which overlaps with but is never perfectly coincident with terms such as structuralism, heterodox economics, inward-looking, dirigiste, contextual, and interventionist. Equating either liberalism or developmentalism with all of this associated terminological baggage can lead to a loss of nuance. But the heuristic shorthand of "liberal" and "developmentalist" will facilitate communication of the central argument about the embeddedness of developmental ideas in Brazil.

12. As Carvalho (2002) explored in depth, this historical process reverses the Marshallian sequence of rights-granting specific to England, where expanding civil rights in the eighteenth century contributed to the expansion of political rights in the nineteenth, and then the expansion of social rights in the twentieth.

13. The shadow of the Washington Consensus has grown over time, with some critics retroactively using the term to encompass any "neoliberal," radical free-market reforms and other observers using it retroactively to depict the reforms of the 1990s in aggregate fashion, with little attention to the disparities across the countries that implemented them. In light of this somewhat lazy approach to the term, it is worth remembering that the "Washington Consensus" sought only to summarize a general consensus forming at the international financial institutions (IFIs) headquartered in Washington, DC, regarding the likeliest forms of achieving stable growth in Latin American nations (Williamson, 1990). This new consensus represented a significant break: through the 1970s, most international financial institutions had taken an "implicitly pro-ISI stance" (Love, 2005, 106). The summary list of Washington Consensus policy recommendations does not truly deserve the

274 *Notes to pages 73–9*

moniker of "neoliberalism," especially if this is interpreted as free-market fundamentalism, with little space for the state to play a role. Briefly, the Consensus summarized by Williamson (1990) included the need for fiscal discipline, reordering public expenditures, tax reform, liberalizing interest rates, a competitive exchange rate, trade liberalization, liberalization of inward foreign direct investment (FDI), privatization, deregulation, and property rights. Indeed, the question here was not so much whether the government should intervene in the economy, but rather, in what way (Evans, 1995, 10; Kingstone, 2011).

Williamson (2002) highlighted some of the ambiguities and oversights of his initial formulation, which led to some of its more radical adherents pushing for rapid trade opening, immediate financial liberalization, radical privatization, or a minimal state. As he noted, many of the countries who critics claim were undone by the Washington Consensus – most notably Argentina and Brazil in the late 1990s – had in fact ignored its suggestions, both by fixing their exchange rates in ways that became "grossly uncompetitive" and by failing to get their fiscal houses in order (Williamson, 2002; Fraga, 2004, 98).

14. Others have referred to this as getting "prices wrong" (Amsden, 1989; Haggard, 2018); purposely setting prices wrong in the hopes of spurring investment in new directions.

15. Relative to the past, developmentalism as practiced in its "new" variant may be more focused on avoiding debt and fiscal crises, and escaping balance of payments disequilibria, while also addressing inequality and avoiding repressive politics. Bresser-Pereira (2011, 2016) argues that it should go further, recognizing that in an increasingly competitive global economy, the state must be fiscally strengthened and state capacity increased; exchange rate management will be required to avoid over-appreciation; trade must be liberalized, but without unilateral, nonreciprocal opening; and labor markets must be flexibilized, but without eliminating protections.

16. Cox and McCubbins (2001) argue that there is a trade-off between a political system's decisiveness (is its ability to make policy decisions) and its resoluteness (its ability to commit to policy decisions) (Shugart and Haggard, 2001, 6). Using different language, Stark and Bruszt (1998a, 1998b), and Crisp et al. (2011), among others, argue that political and institutional conditions that constrain executive autonomy tend to produce more coherent and stable policy.

17. The concept of "natural openness" suggests that scale and geographic location are important to trade, and that the bigger a country is, the less it will trade as a share of the economy. But even by these standards, Brazil is a trade laggard.

18. Chile is an outlier by contrast to the rest of Latin America, where the "neoliberal" reforms of the Washington Consensus years also did little to change hearts and minds, in part because they were less successful than previous policies: Latin America's reformist era coincided with the worst twenty-five years of growth in a century (Easterly, 2001; Coatsworth, 2005, 137; Love, 2005).

Notes to pages 79–87 275

19. If anything, the years suggested here as liberal may be overstated. For example, with regard to 1994–2002, as one economist noted in conversation with me, "although the opposition was able to stamp [President Cardoso] as a 'neoliberal,' he was a long way from being one. He only changed the dosage a little bit ..."

20. A survey experiment by Lazzarini (2018) showed that support for privatization declined when the respondents were informed that it would be used to pay off the public debt. Polling improves when respondents are told privatization revenues will fund social programs, that the public will be permitted to purchase shares in the privatized firms, or that privatization will be accompanied by regulatory efforts to guarantee service quality. Lazzarini also finds considerable differences across socioeconomic groups, with wealthier and more educated respondents supporting privatization more.

21. There is some ambiguity in survey responses when we compare Brazil with its regional peers. Latinobarometro polls since 2010 find, for example, that Brazilians are more conservative, more desirous of free markets, and more approving of privatization than their Chilean peers. However, any such cross-national comparison may fall prey to relative contextual factors that affect response rates, since there is no absolute measure of state intervention in the economy that all publics are being asked to respond to. If asked whether they are conservative, for example, Brazilians may not interpret the question in the same way as Chileans or Argentines on its economic, social, and political dimensions. Further, there is ample survey evidence for Brazilian statist beliefs: for example, a 2018 poll showed that 76 percent believe the government is the party most responsible for investing in the country and making the economy grow (Freire, 2018).

22. The inclusion of accountants is only a factor in Argentina, where in the 1950–70s, many economists earned an accounting degree.

23. Other Argentine institutions that have harbored economists outside government or academia include *Fundación de Investigaciones Económicas Latinoamericanas* (FIEL), *Centro de Implementación de Políticas Públicas para la Equidad y el Crecimiento* (CIPPEC), and *Fundación de Investigaciones para el Desarrollo* (FIDE) (Bouzas, 2012).

24. Codato and Cavalieri (2015) tentatively place the University of São Paulo in the orthodox column but note the diverse educational backgrounds of its faculty.

25. Another home for liberals has been the economics department at the Fundação Getulio Vargas in Rio (FGV-EPGE), but PUC-Rio has produced more policymakers over the years (Prado, 2005, 65).

26. It is worth noting, furthermore, that Bulhões and Gudin were considered "liberals" largely in contrast to their developmentalist colleagues. But their pragmatic liberalism would have placed them to the left of many of the Argentine or Chilean liberals of the 1960s and 1970s. As a result, they were able to stomach ISI policies, and in fact contributed greatly to industrialization policies under Kubitschek, prior to their work for the military regime.

27. This is not to imply, however, that there were not debates within the ranks of the *técnicos*. Sola (1998) and Bielschowsky (1988) document the important

276   *Notes to pages 87–92*

debate between "nationalist" and "cosmopolitan" *técnicos* beginning in the immediate postwar period. As a prominent representative of the former group, Mario Henrique Simonsen soon gained the upper hand over the more liberal, cosmopolitan vision of his primary opponent, Eugenio Gudin. But it is worth noting that both men agreed that the state had an important role to play in development. A purely anecdotal example of their conflictual but cordial relationship is the fact that they edited a book together in 1978, on the "Controversy of Planning in the Brazilian Economy."

28. The Central Bank has been a haven for liberals, harboring Eugenio Gudin in the 1950s, Gustavo Franco in the 1990s, and Henrique Meirelles in the 2000s. Codato and Cavalieri (2015) find that foreign degrees predominated among Central Bank directors from 1995 to 2014.

29. Indeed, a number of authors have noted that policy has been far from consensual, and important pockets of dissension have always been a feature of bureaucratic politics in the developmental state. See particularly Sola (1988), Bielschowsky (1988), and Guimarães (2005). Meanwhile, the Finance Ministry has never been a monopoly of neoliberals; e.g., Guido Mantega's eight-year term as minister (2006–15).

30. For example, since the 1990s, Trubek (2013) notes that certain neoliberal tenets have been dominant, including central bank independence, inflation control, resistance to deficit finance, and low tariffs. In all of these cases, however, it is possible to make the case that Brazil is far less neoliberal than most of its regional peers both in terms of policy and practice. Other authors have similarly pointed to hybridity in the Brazilian case (e.g., Boschi, 2011, 11; Morais and Saad-Filho, 2012; Hochstetler and Montero, 2013).

31. Ministers in the PSDB and PT administrations show no significant differences in prior professional experience or expertise for their respective portfolios (Codato and Franz, 2018, 795).

4 THE DEVELOPMENTAL HIERARCHICAL MARKET ECONOMY

1. Dieguez (2014, 276), translation by author.
2. Paduan (2016, 198), translation by author.
3. The government share of real GDP per capita is significantly higher than in other large Latin American economies.
4. As Laurence Whitehead notes, the relationship between state and market tends more to the state in "state capitalism," but it does not fully neglect the market: "... state capitalism also requires a major autonomous role for private markets. Corporations and productive enterprises need legal security to produce many goods and ... on the basis of business competition within a fairly predictable and reliable framework of rules and regulations upheld by the public authorities. This is the 'capitalist' dimension of state capitalism. Thus, centrally planned economies with SOE monopolies are excluded." However, he continues, "... in the last analysis state authority over allocative decisions can over-ride market outcomes (or if not, then at least restructure

Notes to pages 92–4   277

and 'distort' them). Admittedly this is a universal feature of all really existing market economies (contrary to free market ideological theory). But under state capitalism it is not just a phenomenon at the margins. It is the political economy heart of the system." (Personal correspondence among members of the International Political Science Association's Research Committee 51, cited with permission.)

5. Throughout this chapter and the next, I draw on data I have compiled about the 504 largest firms (by adjusted net worth) operating in Brazil, as well as the fifteen largest banks, drawing on databases created by *Revista Exame* and *Valor Econômico*. References to "largest firms" and "leading firms," are to this list of 519 enterprises. Although this listing might be criticized for failing to analyze mid-sized companies, it goes relatively deep into the structure of firm life, given that these top firms jointly account for more than half of GDP.

6. The number of family-owned firms is much smaller among the leading 500-plus firms, than it is in the broader population of firms: according to the IBGE, 90 percent of firms in the overall economy are family-owned (Rizzo and Velasco, 2018, 199).

7. One notable exception to this general rule is the Votorantim group, a family-owned company which for many years had a remarkably diversified set of interests, including cement, construction, banking, metallurgy, energy, and paper and pulp production.

8. Abreu (2019) notes that the market capitalization of the BM&F Bovespa is only 17th in the world, even though Brazil's economy is the eighth largest in the world.

9. Equity sales do not necessarily imply, however, that firms are *not* organized in a way that parallels HMEs: stock markets in Brazil, for example, have permitted firms to issue as much as two-thirds of their shares as nonvoting, allowing shareholders to continue to maintain dominance even after they open their firms to external investors.

10. The sum of listed public firms and unlisted public firms; listed private firms and unlisted private firms in Table 4.1.

11. The data on firm net worth (*patrimônio líquido ajustado*) is drawn from the 2015 report, which includes data for the years 2011–14, corrected for inflation. Net worth data has been averaged over the full period. Because approximately 15 percent of firms did not provide any data on net worth, but did provide sales figures, missing net worth values were estimated on the basis of the average sales/equity ratio for other companies in that firm's sector.

12. There are two caveats worth keeping in mind here. The first is that the measure of nationality used here is a blunt one: firms are considered either Brazilian or foreign, based on *Valor* and *Exame*'s analysis of share ownership. In real life, of course, minority shareholders may be Brazilian, even in the sectors on the left-hand side of the figure. Second, of course, there is no sector in which Brazilian firms are completely absent. So, while Schneider's insight about the likely sectoral specialization of firms in HMEs appears to hold in the Brazilian case, there is intra-sectoral variation, and there are firms that escape the overall pattern. But overall, the HME model appears to hold with regard to firm specialization.

278 *Notes to pages 95–100*

13. The Pearson correlation between concentration and foreign ownership is 0.365, but it is not statistically significant.
14. Other state banks also lend, as noted in Chapter 2. Further, they also have investment funds. The Caixa Econômica Federal (CEF), for example, manages the FI-FGTS, a R$32 billion investment fund backed by employment taxes. The Banco do Brasil is a significant asset investor, too, with equity holdings of the ten largest Brazilian firms (Kasznar and Oliveira, 2019).
15. Musacchio and Lazzarini (2014, 251) note that since the 1980s, retained earnings have been more important to BNDES than payroll taxes. Long-term, low-interest loans became especially significant after 2009. Yet as much as 40 percent of FAT payroll funds are directed to BNDES operations (Kröger, 2012).
16. These rates may have been less concessional in the 2010s than in the past, however: it has been estimated that during the 1980s, a combination of inflation and generosity meant that borrowing companies effectively repaid only about 26 percent of their loans in real terms (Najberg, 1989; in Musacchio and Lazzarini, 2014, 245).
17. Armijo notes that of the BNDES' total loan portfolio in mid-2012, 39 percent went to the top five borrowers, and a further 28 percent to the next fifty (Armijo, 2017, 236).
18. There are sixteen companies of diverse sizes in the financial services sector, twenty-one associated with Eletrobras, thirty-eight with Petrobras, and another thirty-one associated with various logistical tasks, from mail delivery (Correios) to docks and warehousing.
19. Privatization had begun under military rule and continued through the Sarney and Collor administrations, before picking up pace under Cardoso. Total privatizations in the 1990s reached more than US$105bn.
20. Technically, SOEs can be either mixed enterprises (*sociedades de economia mista*), when the state holds the majority of the voting stock, or public enterprises (*empresas públicas*), when the state is the sole shareholder (Parglender, 2016).
21. The largest federal public sector pension funds are Previ, Funcef, Petros, and Postalis, belonging, respectively, to workers at Banco do Brasil, CEF, Petrobras, and Correios. Together, the first three funds in 2010 accounted for 46.8 percent of the total investment value of Brazil's 275 pension funds (Casanova and Kassum, 2014, 38, citing data from ABRAPP; Datz, 2013). Rising wages and pension reforms increased the scale of state-controlled pension funds from R$75 billion in 1994 to R$670 billion in 2015 (Abu-El-Haj, 2016); Brazil's pension assets are the highest of all the developing countries, accounting for about 18 percent of GDP (Kröger, 2012; Datz, 2013).
22. That pension funds would be used as a tool of state leverage is not coincidental: there are eighty-nine public foundations in Brazil, which in 2015 controlled more than R$450 billion in assets, two-thirds of which are in four funds (Petros, Previ, Funcef, and Postalis). The funds themselves are not public resources, as they originate from the private savings of workers at public companies (Datz, 2013). However, as Parglender (2016) notes, the

Notes to pages 100–5 279

governance structure of these funds is "particularly conducive to political interference," since the SOEs themselves appoint half of the board members and the director of the fund. Under the Lula administration, former union leaders ran the three biggest funds (Sérgio Rosa, Previ; Wagner Pinheiro, Petros; and Guilherme Lacerda, Funcef), while the PT's largest coalition ally, the PMDB, controlled Postalis (Casado et al., 2016). One outcome of political control is that the allocation of the public pension funds' assets is quite different from that of private funds, with a much higher allocation to equity investments than to fixed income (Parglender, 2016).

23. These figures are estimates by the author, based on data from BNDESPar, Petros, and Previ. The Funcef pension fund did not publish data in 2010 on its specific share holdings, so I estimated the likely holdings of Funcef using baseline averages from Petros and Previ to estimate the proportions of Funcef's R$15bn in portfolio investment that were likely to have gone to the top private companies, as a share of total portfolio investments.

24. To make the Oi merger a possibility, for example, the government was forced to change the telecom law; to permit the purchase of Gol by foreign shareholders, changes were made to the aviation law.

25. Musacchio and Lazzarini (2014, 109) point to important reforms intended to improve minority rights, although they also note the irony that these may have increased the government's leverage as a minority shareholder. The Joint Stock Company Law of 2001 (10.303) instituted legal protections for minority shareholders; including the right to elect members of the board; as well as two-thirds qualified majority rule.

26. The project description can be found here: https://reporterbrasil.org.br/2014/06/relacoes-entre-empresas-brasileiras-estao-na-plataforma-eles-mandam/. The analysis of Vale has been deactivated, however.

27. Vale had been privatized in 1997, but the state retained a stake in the company. Vale estimated that it provided $2.7bn in revenue to the government in 2009, including $1.3bn in taxes and the remainder in royalties on mineral extraction (Musacchio and Lazzarini, 2014, 224).

28. Although it is hard to compare total domestic content requirements across countries, an Organization for Economic Cooperation and Development (OECD) study shows that although Brazilian trade and investment restrictions are lower than those found in other large emerging economies, such as China and India, they remain far above the OECD average. As of 2013, Brazilian product market regulation was more than 70 percent above the OECD average. Tariff barriers were thirty-two times greater; other barriers to trade and investment were nearly 1.8 times greater; and barriers to trade facilitation were 2.6 times greater (Koske et al., 2015).

29. The BNDES runs a specific program for medical equipment, PROFARMA, to finance equipment imports, but various laws allow the government to make preferential purchases of local equipment, and imports face stiff regulatory controls through ANVISA.

30. This leads to sometimes ironic situations: for example, the owner of JetBlue, David Neeleman, was born of US parents in Brazil and left the country as a young boy. He has long been a resident of Connecticut. Local birth, however,

280 *Notes to pages 106–7*

permitted him to open a local carrier, Azul, despite laws that forbid foreign ownership of airlines. This national preference in the airline industry was altered by law in 2017.

31. In this, I follow Trubek, Coutinho, et al. (2013, 42), who claim with regard to the "new state activism" of the 2000s that, "[t]he Brazilian government has been feeling the stones as it crosses the river – to quote Deng Xiaoping – not following some worked out blueprint."

32. Schneider (2004, 118) refers to counterpart commitments as reciprocity, and notes that effective reciprocity requires that policymakers have adequate information, sufficient authority, and political protection.

33. Labor reforms under Cardoso altered work timetables, pensions, and judicial processes. They also introduced flexible temporary contracts and eliminated automatic wage readjustments for inflation. Rousseff introduced a law that substantially weakened the right to strike. Overall, however, few of the guarantees for formal sector workers were substantially altered and the overall system – marked by government control over labor activities – was very resilient through 2018, when research for this book concluded (Moraes, 2014; Coslovksy et al., 2017).

34. Vargas' *Estado Novo* has cast a long shadow over the evolution of both labor policy and social policy. Vargas' primary goal was to organize urban, industrial workers into a corporatist structure, whereby a single union represented all workers in each category, and where government recognition was essential to obtaining all of the benefits of union membership. Rural workers and informal urban workers were not offered the same protections. Meanwhile, labor protections offered to the formal sector form a set of tightly interlocking political and economic mechanisms. Obligatory contributions until 2017 funded both worker unions and trade associations. These compulsory "contributions" funded both unions and the so-called "S system" (composed of the Agency for Micro and Small Enterprise, SEBRAE, and the commercial and industrial training services SESI, SESC, SENAI, and SENAC), which provided association leaders with lush revenues – estimated to have been on the order of R\$2.75 billion in union taxes and R\$16 billion in association revenues in 2016 (Folha, 2017b). Unions, funded by the automatic union tax, proved easy to create under democracy, especially because the 1988 Constitution eliminated the need for new unions to receive prior Labor Ministry recognition (Hall, 2009, 154). Partly as a consequence, Brazil has more than 17,000 unions. The government's fiscal accounts benefit from taxes on labor that are central to financing social security (Pochmann and Santos, 1998; Scherer, 2015), while severance provision through the FGTS (*Fundo de Garantia de Tempo de Serviço*) functions as a forced employment insurance plan whose funds provide low-cost funding to the CEF, the federal government savings bank. Together, labor-related contributions that flow to the government coffers sum to a 27.8 percent tax on the payroll bill (Scherer, 2015), which has a dissuasive impact on formal hiring. Despite the costs imposed by the system, workers in the formal sector are reluctant to see reforms that might undermine cherished gains, such as the year-end 13th salary, paid annual vacations, and unemployment benefits. As Hall (2009, 151) notes, although

Notes to pages 110–22 281

the system has "practically no open defenders," a number of beneficiaries see some positive aspects of the system. Given the interlocking nature of these benefits, and the wide range of potential beneficiaries – ranging from associations to the government itself – it has been difficult to dismantle any of them, except for minor changes at the margins, such as Temer's flexibilization reforms in 2017. Even these have been contested in the courts, with more than 120 decisions upholding the union contribution by employees.

35. State policies have increasingly emphasized innovation, including a new Innovation Law in 2004 and a *Lei do Bem* of 2005, both of which aimed to improve interactions between government and academia, as well as provide incentives for research and development (R&D) spending. The FINEP manages much of this innovation system, including financing to firms and grants to universities, with some modest support from BNDES lending (Hochstetler and Montero, 2013, 1492–5; Schapiro, 2013a). Innovation is also a frequently espoused objective of the broader industrial programs implemented by diverse presidents, such as the Lula's *Política Industrial, Tecnológica e de Comércio Exterior* (PITCE, 2004) and Rousseff's *Brasil Maior* (2011), which may have made these industrial plans more palatable to some of their critics.

36. Drawing on IPEA data, Almeida (2009, 21) noted that Brazilian exports were 60 percent low technology and commodities, while world exports were 60 percent medium and high technology.

37. Brazilian figures from Instituto Paulo Montenegro (2018); global figures from Vágvölgyi et al. (2016).

38. The Brazilian National Plan for Education established in 2014 sought to triple the number of students enrolled in upper secondary vocational programs by 2024.

39. Members of the poorest quintile of the population represent 41.7 percent of primary school students and only 3.8 percent of students in higher education; members of the richest quintile represent 7.9 percent of primary school students and 39.9 percent of higher education. Ministério da Fazenda (2017), using data from the 2015 household survey (PNAD).

40. One exception was the PRONATEC program, aimed at expanding vocational education, with a budget of R$4.7 billion in 2015 and R$1.6 billion in 2016.

41. It is impossible to measure the effect of debt service on family incomes, but it is a source of inequality: public bond holders received nearly ten times the transfers that were made via *Bolsa Família* in 2014 (Medeiros and Souza, 2013, 28; Mendonça, 2015).

5 COALITIONAL PRESIDENTIALISM AND DEFENSIVE PAROCHIALISM

1. Guandalini (2006), translation by author.
2. O Globo (2017), Folha (2018b), translation by author.
3. Constitutional amendments require two votes in each house of Congress, with three-fifths support in each vote (308 deputies and 49 senators). Complementary laws require an absolute majority. Ordinary laws are

282   *Notes to pages 123–3*

approved by simple majority. The count above runs from law 7.672 on September 23, 1988 to Law 13.413 on December 29, 2016.

4. Brazil is an exception to the rule that most PR systems are run on the basis of closed lists (Ames, 1995, 406–33; Samuels, 1999, 487–9; Power, 2010, 26).

5. There are thirty-five parties registered officially at the *Tribunal Superior Eleitoral* (TSE).

6. Electoral turnover and party fragmentation in the Senate are less pronounced but malapportionment of seats has meant that there is enormous disparity of representation: states that represent only 13 percent of the population can block legislation supported by senators representing 87 percent of the population (Souza, 1999). Disproportionality is a problem of territorially representative bodies the world over, but in the Brazilian case, overrepresentation tends to benefit precisely those states with "particularly unequal income distribution and strong traditions of local oligarchic control," and is associated with higher budgetary transfers (Stepan, 2000, 165; Hiroi, 2016).

7. Indeed, a central fear of early analysts of Brazilian democracy was the "contradictory combination of highly plebiscitarian and extremely consociational procedures, practices, and symbols," with a president elected as the "direct incarnation of the people" facing a multiplicity of vetoes and counterweights from a fragmented party system, Congress, and federalism.

The focus of this book is on the federal government, so I will not digress into the complexities of Brazilian federalism, which are the subject of a large and vibrant literature. Suffice it to note that the central government has grown much stronger than initially feared after the 1988 Constitution, when the astounding imbalance between revenues collected by the federal government and mandatory transfers to states and municipalities helped to fuel the fiscal spiral that fed hyperinflation, and fears arose about the "demos-constraining" nature of federalism, which would enable regional minorities to block provision of public goods, including economic stabilization (Montero, 2000; Stepan, 2000; Ames, 2001; Samuels and Mainwaring, 2004).

Imbalances between fiscal revenues and fiscal transfers among the levels of the federation were adjusted in the federal government's favor. The monetary authority of states – particularly their ability to borrow from state banks – was strictly curtailed by the PROES program for overhauling state banks in the late 1990s. Much social provision has been centralized within the federal sphere, and the central government has managed to bypass state and local governments in getting funds to citizens on the ground (Fenwick, 2009, 2010). Where the federal government seeks policy influence it has found it: Arretche (2002), for example, finds that in four arenas of social policy – elementary education, health, housing, and sanitation – federal dominance of policymaking is nearly total, with the only major pushback coming against efforts to privatize the states' sanitation companies. The federal government dominates legislation on the taxation, spending, and policymaking authority of subnational units: most legislation on federal issues does not require supermajorities, and the ease with which the presidential coalition has passed legislation has meant that the only recourse for state and local governments has been appeals to the Supreme Federal Tribunal (*Supremo*

Tribunal Federal, STF) (Arretche, 2013, 135). But although the ability of states to challenge the constitutionality of laws in the STF is very broad, and hundreds of cases have been brought to adjudicate issues between the states and the central government, the STF has overwhelmingly decided cases in the federal government's favor; the STF has been a "judge from the center and for the center" (Oliveira, 2009; Canello, 2016, 230, translation by author).

8. Rules on provisional measures have been amended to limit presidential prerogatives, but they still permit the executive to alter the status quo before seeking congressional support.

9. For many years, it was common practice for the president's party to gain substantial membership – as high as 30 to 40 percent growth – after an election. The STF in 2007 ruled against unrestricted party switching. As Freitas (2012, 952) notes, even after the court decisions, a significant (if smaller) proportion of deputies continued to switch parties, especially to join new parties.

10. Party leaders control key aspects of election campaigns, such as who is included in the party lists, the distribution of party campaign funds, and the distribution of exposure during the party's free campaign airtime (Schmitt et al., 1999; Figueiredo and Limongi, 2002).

11. Most successful budget amendments have been proposed by state-wide legislative blocs and powerful party figures chosen as committee rapporteurs, demonstrating the importance of working together or with the leadership.

12. Uncertainty gives legislators leverage over presidents. Presidents at the very minimum require a defensive coalition to protect themselves against impeachment: for this, a mere 172 votes in the Chamber and 28 in the Senate suffice. To get anything done, they need a full majority (257 seats in the Chamber; 41 in the Senate) and to get the full power of constitutional amendment that has been essential to governance since 1988, they need a three-fifths majority (308 in the Chamber; 49 in the Senate) or perhaps even more (to lower the leverage of the last holdouts) (Melo, 2018, 165).

13. Chaisty et al. (2018, 209) warn that the survey was conducted contemporaneously with the Lava Jato investigation, which may have altered Brazilian legislators' perspectives.

14. Melo and Câmara (2012) note that the three poles of Brazilian politics are: on the left, the PT, PSB, PDT, and PCdoB; on the right, PSDB, DEM, and PPS; and in the center, PMDB, PP, PTB, and PR.

15. One senior prosecutor in São Paulo estimated that 70 percent of malfeasance is discovered because of politicians ratting out their peers (Bechara, 2019).

16. Presentation by Justice Barroso at *Centro de Estudos em Política e Economia do Setor Público* (CEPESP), *Fundação Getulio Vargas* (FGV-Rio), July 30, 2019.

17. The word "lobby" has a bad connotation in Brazil, perhaps because of its association with backroom dealings under authoritarian rule, or influence-peddling scandals since the return to democracy (Jobim and Souza, 2018, 62–6; Melo, 2018, 150; Seligman and Bandeira, 2018, 227). Many firms thus prefer the term "government relations," arguing that that it is natural to have interest groups in a plural society, and that policymakers may gain valuable

284   *Notes to pages 131–2*

information that enhances government effectiveness by dialoguing with interested parties before undertaking policy reform. But Brazilian firms are also skittish about lobbying because despite repeated legislative proposals since the 1970s, Congress still has not passed regulations governing the practice. That said, the right to lobby is broadly protected by the rights enumerated in the Constitution, and there is even an association of professionals in government affairs, the *Associação Brasileira de Relações Institucionais e Governamentais* (ABRIG) (Santos, 2007, 410; Jobim and Souza, 2018, 59–62).

18. Authors associated with this school include Schneider, Weyland, Kingstone, and Power and Doctor (Mancuso, 2004, 511). Corporatism is both a structure of interest representation and a system of policymaking (Schmitter, 1982; Molina and Rhodes, 2002). At its core, the term corporatism refers to a particular way of incorporating interest groups into the state, which contrasts with pluralism in that the key corporations are given monopoly or near monopoly representation in negotiations with the state (Schmitter, 1971; Winkler, 1976; Schmitter and Lehmbruch, 1979; Wiarda, 1981; Lehmbruch and Schmitter, 1982). In the Brazilian case, corporatism is generally associated with the monopoly on labor representation designed during the Getúlio Vargas presidency, and more recently, the mandatory representation of civil society and business interests in deliberative bodies. A central theme is the power of the state, and its ability to rely "on corporatist forms of organization to ensure the dominant position of the state over society," in a hierarchical system that permits opposition but coopts it to operate within established rules (Roett, 1978, 43–4; Faoro, 2001[1975]). Corporatism in Brazil has been understood more broadly to refer to the manner of interest representation in all types of policymaking. These might include business and labor representation on economic advisory boards like the Council of Economic and Social Development (CDES), or even more broadly, the representation of key interest groups in the institutions established by the 1988 Constitution. There is considerable path dependence – the state has created powerful groups that have compulsory membership, monopoly over their professional sphere, a role recognized by the state, and legal instruments and access to venues which enable them to continue to press for favorable policies or block policies that endanger their interests (Schmitter, 1971; Wiarda, 1973, 1981, 2004; Malloy, 1977; Power and Doctor, 2004; Taylor, 2008, 111; Schneider, 2013, 192). One consequence is that corporatist structures have been resilient to pressures to change, helped along by the benefits they provide, which may contribute to widespread interest in their continuity; the weakness of non-corporatist organizations, particularly in business; and the institutionalization of corporatism within the legal framework (Power and Doctor, 2004, 18).

19. Reforms to union tax contributions by workers during the Temer administration, were not matched by a reduction in compulsory contributions to business associations.

20. There is considerable distance between these two schools of thought. The first school, with its emphasis on the fragmented, anemic, corporatist, and low capacity of business pressure groups, has perhaps been slow to recognize the

Notes to pages 133–5 285

shifts that have taken place in the past two decades in Brazil. The second school, with its emphasis on the new effectiveness of business pressures, has perhaps underappreciated the comparative perspective: Brazilian business may be better organized today than it was two or three decades ago, but its associations are still relatively weak by comparison to peak associations in Mexico or Chile. This is not to say that business is incapable of collective action, only that it has less of a permanent influence on policymakers and must mobilize to make itself heard. Further, the various authors have slightly different research interests – ranging from the broad (the threat that collective action poses to the democratic regime) (Kingstone, 2000) to the narrow (the influence of the construction industry) (Mancuso, 2003). Shifting economic conditions have also kept the contextual environment in constant flux: important changes in the international and domestic firmament such as trade liberalization and foreign direct investment have altered the competitive environment for industry since the 1980s (Kingstone, 2000, 202; Mancuso, 2004), and thus made the accumulation of knowledge particularly challenging.

21. Even as industrial associations expanded, corporatist bodies were preserved in the structure of the post-transition legal system (Power and Doctor, 2004, 18; Mancuso, 2007). Simultaneously, however, new forms of organization and influence emerged. Old representative monopolies, such as the General Confederation of Labor (CGT) and National Confederation of Agriculture (CAN), have even been supplanted by upstarts that are unrecognized by the state, such as the CUT labor union and the UDR ruralist union. Democracy permitted considerable organizational hybridity, as in the case of the *Movimento Brasil Competitivo* (MBC), whose membership includes many domestic firms, alongside major MNCs. MBC emerged in the early 1990s out of a government-sponsored program to increase productivity; partly in consequence, MBC retains strong connections to government, with a variety of ministers serving on its board (Movimento Brasil Competitivo, 2018). Yet its focus is largely on reforms to improve the efficiency of the bureaucracy, without any strong emphasis on international competitiveness or economic opening.

22. There are also a variety of other voluntary associations for banks that widen this menu. Small and medium banks may use the *Associação Brasileira de Bancos* (ABBC); foreign banks may use the *Associação de Bancos Brasileiros Internacionais* (ABBI), trading firms may use *Associação Nacional das Instituições do Mercado Aberto* (ANDIMA), and investment banks have *Associação Nacional dos Bancos de Investimento* (ANBID) (Minella, 2007).

23. Formally, this is known as the *Frente Parlamentar Mista da Agropecuária*, and included 228 deputies and 27 senators as members in the 2015 legislature.

24. Other *"bancadas"* include evangelicals, law and order types, labor unions, supplementary health insurance companies, and financial institutions (DIAP, 2011; Scheffer and Bahia, 2011).

25. Members of the *Colégio de Líderes* received an average of R$2.2 million in donations. By contrast, the average for all 5,500 candidates was only R$213 thousand in personal donations.

286 · *Notes to pages 135–43*

26. There are at least two reasons for this common structure: first, it seeks to remove some of the pressures for bottom-line performance that might otherwise be brought to bear in the realm of government affairs (including corruption); and second, to ensure that government affairs has a coherent global strategy that is not specific to the Brazilian market alone.

27. Interview with an executive at a Fortune 500 MNC with extensive operations in Brazil, May 2018.

28. In January 2014, Brazil passed Law 12.846, which imposes penalties on firms found to be involved in corrupt acts. Enforcement remains a work in progress. But as the 2016 Odebrecht-Braskem settlement with the US Department of Justice and the US Securities and Exchange Commission (SEC) illustrated, Brazilian firms also face an increased risk of foreign enforcement actions.

29. This decision pushed donations into other channels, especially to individual donations, which are still permitted up to the high limit of 10 percent of income. Given the fungibility of resources and the extent to which corporate donations were dominated by Brazilian firms, this migration is significant, suggesting that corporate money will find other paths into politics. Evaluating corporate donations in 2014 will thus help us to better understand the past and speculate productively about the future. It should be noted that the ban on corporate contributions is only one of a slew of ever-evolving norms on political campaigns; this legislation has been under continuous flux for much of the past thirty years, with variation in the rules for threshold barriers for small parties, party loyalty, and cross-party alliances (*coligações eleitorais*), among other significant changes (Marchetti, 2008; Marchetti and Cortez, 2009). For a discussion of the 2015 STF decision and its likely impacts, see Speck (2016b).

30. Speck and Campos (2014, 21), covering the 2010–13 electoral cycle.

31. This data was compiled by Anna Petherick, to whom I am grateful, and is drawn from the US Federal Electoral Commission. It should be noted that the method of calculating advertising expenditures by the two electoral bodies may not be entirely comparable. Data from www.fec.gov, accessed August 13, 2016.

32. Campaign expenditures were estimated at the midpoint.

33. The Law of Political Parties in 1995 and the Electoral Law of 1997 shifted the terrain significantly (Speck, 2010).

34. BNDES' officials argue that these findings are overwrought, and that the BNDES governance structure requires so many reviews, and so many decisions by collective bodies, that it would be very hard to make a rational choice to favor a particular firm or donor. As one former BNDES official said to me, citing Raymundo Faoro, "not everything that is rational is true" (*"nem tudo que é racional é verdadeiro"*).

35. In large majoritarian elections, including the presidential race, if no candidate receives a simple majority in the first round, a second round is held between the two leading candidates.

36. Although the rules theoretically prohibit donations by foreign companies, companies listed in the *Exame* magazine's list of 504 largest firms or *Valor Econômico*'s list of top banks as foreign-controlled firms accounted for about

Notes to pages 145–5 287

11 percent of donations in 2014. This is unlikely to be a sign that laws were broken and may have more to do with the fact that the measure of control may vary from the business world (where minority shareholding and cross-shareholding may give foreigners actual control) to the legal world (where legal residence is what matters). Although Santander is a Spanish banking company, for example, its subsidiary is a Brazilian company that can legally donate to campaigns.

37. Table 5.3 reports on a Tobit regression for total campaign contributions by firms that were among the top 519 nationwide. The data is compiled from several sources:

-the *Revista Exame*'s firm-level data for the four years from 2011–14, which provides information on joint net equity (*patrimônio liquido ajustado*) as well as sector;

-the TSE campaign finance data for the 2014 federal election;

-databases compiled by the author on membership in the CDES, BNDES loans, and investments by SOEs' pension funds (sourced from annual reports for Funcef, Previ, Petros; shareholdings belonging to BNDESPar; online membership rosters for the CDES; and annual management reports by BNDES).

Model selection was determined by the fact that campaign donors face two decisions: one discrete choice (whether or not to donate), and one continuous choice (how much to donate). I initially used a Heckman selection model but decided that there is no good reason to believe that one independent variable was driving selection directly, so instead moved to a Tobit model.

In both the Heckman and the Tobit models, ten firms were dropped: media firms (which are not permitted to donate because they receive public subsidies), the regional Unimed operators (since contributions are largely made by the central Unimed structure), and JBS, the meatpacking firm, which was a clear outlier in terms of the scale of its contributions during this electoral cycle, declaring more than R$300 million in donations.

The independent variables are as follows:

CDES membership: a dummy based on membership between 2010 and 2014 on the CDES, an advisory business council;

BNDES loan value: a continuous variable of loans from the BNDES from 2012 to 2015;

Presence of BNDES loan: a dummy variable marking the presence of a loan;

SOE pension fund: a dummy variable to indicate share ownership by one of the three big pension funds (Petros, Previ, and Funcef). A continuous variable of share value was not possible, due to data limitations;

Firm size: as measured by joint net equity from *Revista Exame*;

Brazilianness of sector: a measure of how much of a sector's joint net equity belonged to Brazilian firms.

Sector concentration is a Herfindahl-Hirschman index of concentration, calculated as the sum of squares of firms' shares of joint net equity within its sector.

Sectoral dummies: whether a company is from a particular sector (e.g., construction).

288 *Notes to pages 147–51*

38. Readers may reasonably complain that Lava Jato is largely a scandal about the PT's years in power, that it only allows us to see corruption that has actually been uncovered, and that there are many accusations that have never led to conviction. All of these critiques have merit. With regard to analyzing cases only during the PT years, in some ways, this is a backhanded compliment to the strengthening of oversight bodies that took place under the PT's watch. There were not many credible police investigations before the turn of the century, for a variety of reasons having to do with the politicization and low capacity of oversight bodies. The number of operations undertaken by the federal police under the PT rose steadily from 18 in 2003 to 550 in 2016 (Polícia Federal, 2017), as the police budget and workforce expanded (Arantes, 2011). Even when police investigations moved forward, however, the likelihood of judicial conviction was remote: "[e]ven in the intensely investigated Collor case in Brazil, only two of his men were convicted, and one, his private pilot, for tax evasion" (Fleischer, 2002, 7).

39. This is not to say that other forms of corruption are not present, such as petty corruption by police and the motor vehicles department. But in terms of scale and potential damage to the democratic political regime, grand corruption is the most pernicious. A second caveat is that by claiming that there is a link between coalitional presidentialism and the developmental state, I am not suggesting that corruption is driven only by political objectives; personal enrichment is also a factor.

40. Costa said that he paid bribes to PSDB heavyweight Sérgio Guerra to prevent the creation of a congressional investigation (CPI) into Petrobras in 2010.

41. Later leniency agreements, such as in the SBM case, suggest that wrongdoing at Petrobras dated back at least to the 1990s. Federal agents were uninterested in pursuing wrongdoing during the Cardoso years, though, presumably because of short statutes of limitation.

42. The parties whose politicians were charged include: PT, PMDB, PSDB, PTC, PSB, SD, PR, PPS, PP, DEM, PCdoB, PRB, PTB, and PSD.

43. 13a Vara Federal Criminal de Curitiba, Ação Penal No 5046512–94.2016.4.04.7000/PR, July 12, 2017, at 535, 649, 773, 843, 860, and 868.

44. Because the Senate is elected in a one-third then two-third rotation, the database of officeholders also includes senators elected in 1998 who were serving the second half of their eight-year terms. Although they are not, strictly speaking, federal officeholders, governors frequently cycle in and out of federal office and the presidential cabinet, so I have included them here. I have not included *suplentes*. There is considerable movement in and out of the cabinet, which can expand and contract at the president's whim, but I have included all ministers who served more than a provisional role.

45. The database was created by combing through media reports on indictments and allegations, as well as the high court website.

46. Although they are not formally a part of the federal court system, the STJ and the STF are included here, since they serve as appeals courts for the federal trial and appeals courts.

47. Banestado, Mensalão, Satiagraha, Castelo de Areia, and Lava Jato.

Notes to pages 152–63 289

48. Foreign firms are present in Lava Jato, including major international players Rolls Royce, SBM, Maersk, Kawasaki, and Mitsubishi (Arruda and Zagaris, 2015, 94). But to a large degree, foreign companies' ties to corrupt SOE executives appear to have run directly through Petrobras functionaries, without intermediation by the political sphere (United States District Court, 2017). That is, they are not grand corruption, with intermediation by politicians, but rather direct bribes between foreign executives and SOE executives. The SBM deferred prosecution agreement, for example, mentions the payment of bribes to Petrobras officials between 1996 and 2012, but unlike the Odebrecht agreement, does not mention any Brazilian government officials.

49. Data from TSE, compiled by the "tribuna" project at https://github.com/raf apolo/tribuna. See also Belisário (2017).

50. The shift from particularism to ethical universalism is at its heart a collective action problem (Rothstein, 2011; Mungiu-Pippidi, 2015, 15; Rotberg, 2017, 11).

51. Electoral turnover in Brazil has been quite high, but politicians often move from one post to another, rather than exiting the political system as a whole.

52. Describing Brazil, Palermo (2016, 10) notes, "… the system does not work without an ingredient of corruption, as it is often a requirement for building alliances. But if so, the corruption is by itself a source of ungovernability …. In sum, corruption, which is necessary for good governance (at least under the coalitional presidentialism), is at the same time a disruptive factor of ungovernability."

53. Notably, Eike came from public sector wealth: his father had served as Minister of Mines and Energy under João Goulart, then as the influential CEO of Companhia Vale do Rio Doce, which at the time was an SOE.

6 RENTS, CONTROL, AND RECIPROCITY

1. Melo (2019), translation by author.

2. Amsden (2001, 9) notes that a "control mechanism involves a *sensor,* to detect the 'givens' in the process to be controlled; an *assessor,* to compare what is happening with what should happen; an *effector,* to change behavior; and a *communications network,* to transmit information between all functions."

3. A prior question is whether developmental states can be democratic. Historically, many successful developmental states have been authoritarian, which permitted rigid controls over the state's strategic direction, even as it had lamentable effects on economic and political rights. Although it may be more difficult, there is no a priori reason to believe that democracies cannot be successfully developmental. For a more comprehensive discussion see Prado et al. (2016).

4. Suzigan and Furtado (2006, 179), Arbix et al. (2017), and Schapiro (2013b, 129) attribute the weakness of ABDI to the fact that it is an autonomous parastatal agency, incorporated in the "S-system" rather than acting as a full-fledged federal agency.

290   *Notes to pages 163–5*

5. The so-called "contributions" are taxes that finance government labor and pension funds: PIS (Program of Social Integration) contributions fund private sector employees' labor benefits; PASEP (*Programa de Formação do Patrimônio do Servidor Público*) does the same for civil servants; and the Cofins (Contribution for the Financing of Social Security) funds the pension and healthcare system.

6. The APT was gradually withdrawn in the face of the fiscal crisis, although seventeen sectors remained protected as of September 2018. Many of the sectors that continued to benefit from relief were the usual suspects: shoe makers, leather producers, textile manufacturers, and construction firms.

7. Exposition of motives for Provisional Measure 540, at https://goo.gl/uHi3hM.

8. I am grateful to Chris DeSá for this quotation, and more generally, for his many contributions to my understanding of the *Plano Brasil Maior*.

9. The National Treasury only partially compensated the pension system for the shortfall generated by payroll tax relief.

10. Tax breaks have been widely used since the 1980s, at a scale that is monumental: about 20 percent of total federal revenue, or 4.1 percent of GDP in 2017, which was also the average share of tax breaks to GDP over the 2011–17 period (Pellegrini, 2018).

   Three things are striking about this. First, there is some variability in activism over time, but many of these breaks are recurrent across the entire democratic period. Second, only about one-fifth (21.4 percent) of tax breaks are truly developmental in nature. The remainder are guided either by concern about competitiveness (e.g., simplified taxes for small firms, to boost their efficiency), by social criteria (e.g., tax breaks for disabled elderly), or by emergency economic measures (e.g., tax breaks on pension contributions, aimed at preserving employment). Third, there is virtually no oversight: few tax breaks stipulate a particular agency to ensure that goals are met; there is little coordination between fiscal authorities and sectoral agencies; clear objectives are missing; no sunset date is written into most legislation, ensuring that benefits linger over time; and tax breaks tend to be regressive and inefficient (Pellegrini, 2018, 9–10). Between 1994 and 2009, more than fifty laws were written providing tax breaks on social contributions (taxes which are controlled exclusively by the federal government). These laws, which cumulatively cost more than twice the federal pension deficit, were largely focused on developmental objectives, such as export benefits, R&D investments, and generating incentives for firms to work with SOEs (Mancuso et al., 2010; Mancuso and Moreira, 2013). More than three-fifths of the laws were sectoral in nature. The process was executive-centric: nine in ten laws came out of the executive branch, the majority (79 percent) implemented by provisional measure, and more than half subsequently unaltered by Congress. Only one of the proposals included measurable objectives, and although the FRL requires an estimation of the budgetary effect of any exemption, only one-third included such an estimate. Nearly four-fifths (77 percent) were open-ended, with no cut-off date, and the same proportion had no counterpart commitment (Mancuso and Moreira, 2013). Even advocates of

Notes to pages 165–73 291

muscular industrial policy note that tax breaks may introduce irrationality into firm behavior. They may also generate "structural dependence" on the continuation of tax breaks to ensure firm competitiveness (Suzigan and Furtado, 2006, 180). Many proposals were virtually uncontested in Congress. Partly by virtue of implementation via provisional measure, tax incentives made it through Congress 3.5 times more quickly than other laws (Gonçalves, 2012, 41). Sectoral associations were often actively part of the process, cited in congressional speeches, and present at deliberations. Control over the tax breaks once they were implemented, furthermore, was punitive and procedural (i.e., were rules followed properly?) rather than oriented toward learning and correction. Said another way, the central preoccupation was with process, rather than ensuring that broader developmental objectives were achieved (Gonçalves, 2012, 108–9).

11. The effect of BNDES credits and tax breaks was often canceled out by a strengthening exchange rate (De Toni, 2014; Bresser-Pereira, 2017, 2019). Suzigan and Furtado note that high interest rates, a strong exchange rate, and an irrational tax system diminished the impact of industrial policy (2006, 179).

12. In some cases, such as the goal of increasing access to broadband, the government simply changed the benchmark, for example shifting its emphasis from broadband access to also include mobile access in determining whether it had met its goal (Baldocchi, 2014). Coronel et al. (2011) find that the PDP helped increase production and exports in the low and medium technology automotive and capital goods sectors but did not help high tech sectors.

13. https://fred.stlouisfed.org/series/NAEXKP01BRQ661S

14. These tax breaks are quite complex, but include exemption from import tariffs, export taxes, and the industrialized products tax (IPI); a 75 percent reduction in corporate taxes; exemption from PIS/PASEP, Cofins, and local property taxes, as well subsidies on freight to and from Manaus (Bekerman and Dulcich, 2017).

15. As one interviewee jokingly noted, in the 1980s and 1990s, it was said that there were two exchange rates. The official rate and the Anfavea [National Association of Automotive Manufacturers] rate, which was always 40 percent higher. *[Imitating two interlocutors:]* "Which exchange rate do you need?" "Aaaahh, it's too low, about 40 percent below where it needs to be ..." (Baumann, 2012).

16. Foreign firms could benefit from these incentives if sited in Brazil.

17. An additional concern may be simply that the international liberal order does not permit policymakers to go far enough: the Inovar Auto policies, for example, were ruled against by the WTO as discriminatory. Such constraints suggest that perhaps the government cannot productively engage against its own multilateral commitments.

18. Brazil's auto industry spends around 10 percent on R&D, by contrast to a global average of 13.7 percent (Carneiro, 2017).

19. State action in the sugar markets precedes Proálcool, with active regulation of sugar markets dating to the 1930s.

292   *Notes to pages 173–9*

20. Anhydrous alcohol is mixed with gasoline; hydrous alcohol is what is usually referred to as ethanol and used in ethanol-only or flex cars as a substitute for gasoline (Gorter et al., 2013).
21. CIMA was composed of representatives from the Agriculture, Finance, Development, and Mines and Energy ministries.
22. Lawsuits filed in the early 1990s alleged that the regulator at the time, the IAA, had fixed prices below production costs in a bid to control inflationary pressures. Estimates of the potential value of these lawsuits range from R$50 to R$174 billion.
23. Moraes and Zilberman (2014) make the point that the sugar industry was not a monolithic bloc: there were more efficient producers, who sought rapid deregulation, as well as less efficient producers, who were in favor of maintaining government support.
24. The flex car was not the sole example of private sector driven change: in 1998, sugar producers in São Paulo banded together to create Consecana (*Conselho dos Produtores de Cana-de-Açúcar, Açúcar e Álcool do Estado de São Paulo*), a private-sector governance body that determined that cane prices would henceforth be determined by sucrose content. There is some irony to the fact that the flex car was a private sector investment; as Stattman (2013) notes, the automobile industry had opposed Proálcool precisely because they did not desire a specific car engine adaptation for ethanol.
25. By 2010, subsidized credit for the sugar industry was on the order of US$3.1 billion a year (McKay et al., 2016).
26. The Bolsonaro government permitted direct sales to gas stations, however, this change will have minimal effect, given that Ipiranga and Petrobras branded stations may not purchase directly from competing firms, and Cosan has purchased the Esso brand stations and is unlikely to buy competitors' ethanol. Dieguez (2013, 23) reports that when Exxon Mobil was looking to sell the Esso gas station chain in Brazil, the owner of Cosan, Rubens Ometto, went to Brasília and told Lula and Rousseff that if Petrobras bought Esso, as was largely expected, he would sell Cosan to a multinational the next day. They withdrew Petrobras' plan, and Ometto bought Esso. Within three years, he sold half of Cosan to Shell.
27. Democratic governments have used instruments common to developmental states elsewhere: directed bank credit; public private partnerships in high-risk investments; antitrust policies more focused on international competitiveness than on domestic competition; government licensing and entry requirements for particular sectors; research and development funded or directed by the state; tariff protections for infant industry; and rents and price distortions as a way of guiding investment (Stein and Herrlein Júnior, 2016; drawing on Johnson, 1982; Woo-Cumings, 1999; Chang 1999, 2002 and Amsden, 2001). Less used in Brazil have been performance requirements for firms accessing state funds; recession cartels, to limit production in times of low demand; and negotiated exit or capacity scrapping, to lower supply in areas with excess production. There have of course been notable differences in direction under governments of different stripes. There are at least three "ideal" types of industrial policy: developmentalist; neoclassical; and neo-

Notes to page 179   293

Schumpeterian or "new developmental" (Schapiro, 2013a; Stein and Herrlein Júnior, 2016; Boschi, 2018). Pre-1985 development plans, under Kubitschek and then Geisel's Second National Development Plan (PND II), were old developmental, focused largely on shifting the economy away from commodity production and into heavy industry, especially metalworking and chemical goods (Suzigan and Furtado, 2006, 170). With the return to democracy, Sarney's Novo Política Industrial (NPI, 1988–9) was similarly old-developmental in conception, although it was stillborn in the context of the hyperinflation and debt crises of the 1980s. Under Collor, Franco, and Cardoso, industrial policy shifted more toward the neoclassical ideal, focused less on "vertical" sectoral supports and more toward "horizontal," economy wide efforts, with the creation of autonomous regulatory agencies, a reduction in industry-specific benefits, and an effort to improve industrial competitiveness through macroeconomic stabilization, with the hope that competition and economic opening would drive innovation (Coronel et al., 2014; Arbix et al., 2017).

But even more neoclassically oriented presidencies during the 1990s nonetheless also implemented sectoral policies. President Collor operated so-called "sectoral chambers" (*câmaras setoriais*) to negotiate specific policies, including automotive policy. His *Política Industrial e de Comércio Exterior* (PICE) included components of industrial policy, although many were subsequently abandoned, with the notable exception of trade opening (Suzigan and Furtado 2006, 172). Under Itamar Franco, sectoral pressures continued, resulting in the popular car regime, among other policies. Under the reformist Cardoso administration, automotive policy also took top booking as an industrial policy. Resende (2000) points out that explicit industrial policy was also carried out in the capital goods, aerospace, and toy manufacturing sectors, using a mix of import tariffs, import tax breaks, industrial production tax (IPI) breaks, domestic content requirements, regional incentives, export financing through the Finamex and Proex programs housed in the BNDES and Banco do Brasil, "Competitiveness forums" in the MDIC maintained dialogue with industrial leaders, albeit in the face of open hostility from the Finance Ministry (De Toni, 2014). Late in the Cardoso administration, the government created sectoral funds and proposed an innovation law, which would become the embryo of Lula's later innovation law (Suzigan and Furtado, 2006, 177; Almeida, 2009; Schapiro, 2013a; Egan, 2015). The simultaneous coexistence of "developmentalism" with "neoliberalism" reflected an "intrastate bargain," used to neutralize opposition to macroeconomic policy (Gómez-Mera, 2007, 114). Finally, the Workers' Party governments of 2003–16 sought to undertake new developmental, neo-Schumpeterian industrial policies, which included efforts to increase innovation and R&D. The central shift in the Workers' Party's "new" developmentalism, though, was that the state sought more to nudge the market than to dominate it, while also taking into account distributive issues and seeking more democratic input (Arbix and Martin, 2010; Schapiro, 2013a; Trubek, Coutinho, et al., 2013).

294   *Notes to pages 179–84*

The centrality of innovation to many development plans contributes to the fact that Brazil spends more than double the Latin American regional average on R&D, even though its levels of R&D are about half OECD levels (Limoeiro and Schneider, 2017, 4). But as Limoeiro and Schneider (2017) also note, innovation policies present a complex pattern that is simultaneously state-driven, in which innovation policy is implemented in a relatively closed economy, but in which MNCs account for about half of private R&D, the largest domestic firms do virtually no R&D, and there is only a small venture capital sector investing in start-ups.

28. By contrast, in other countries in which the state plays a central role in guiding economic behavior, such as South Korea, the state has done a great deal to discipline firms: beneficiaries often had to meet basic requirements, such as export targets or greater investments in research and development (Amsden, 1989; Almeida, 2009; Doner and Schneider, 2016).

29. Such strategic review is not entirely absent in Brazil: it has taken place in policy arenas that were marked by greater insulation from sectoral pressures, such as monetary policy and anticorruption, where strategic planning and review has been more commonplace (Schapiro, 2013b; LaForge, 2017). Despite improvements in recent years, good data can still be hard to find, in part because little firm-level performance data is demanded by government, while government agencies also lack incentives for, and the custom of, collecting and evaluating their strategic performance. The opaqueness of many policies that are subsumed under the rubric of developmental plans also complicates effective evaluation.

30. Almost by definition, bodies that permit public-private sector deliberation are more likely to benefit incumbent firms than future innovators: appointees to deliberative councils are nominated precisely because of their firms' current power and reputation, rather than their future promise. For similar reasons, it is perhaps unsurprising that BNDES loans have benefitted incumbent firms far more than new "Schumpeterian" competitors, even in loans dedicated to innovation policy (Almeida, 2009; Schapiro, 2013a; Lazzarini et al., 2015).

31. The Senate's majoritarian elections suggests there should be more direct responsibility-holding, but the incumbent advantage is so significant – name recognition, access to campaign finance, and the perks of proximity to the executive branch – that it complicates vertical electoral accountability (Lemos et al., 2010). Several factors contribute to senatorial longevity. The *suplente* system, whereby senators run for office alongside a second candidate who can fill in for them in case they step down temporarily, permits leading figures to resign to take up executive appointments. In their absence from the Senate, they will usually have a trusted loyalist as *suplente*, allowing them to simultaneously exert influence in the executive and legislative branches, and they can return to the Senate when they wish. Further, senatorial campaigns are expensive: elected senators typically spend five times what their competitors spend, and incumbents in the Senate spent two to four times more than their competitors (Lemos et al., 2010, 388–9).

32. For example, via changes in regulatory matters or via provisional measure.

33. In the 1970s, the developmental state was responsible for a number of feats, including the creation of SOEs that dramatically changed their sectors of the economy, such as Embraer (1969), Telebras (1972), Siderbras (1973), and the COBRA computing company (1974). Between the authoritarian regime and 2018, there was a change in focus, with developmental policies paying less interest to the creation of new SOEs (although some SOEs were created, such as the EPE energy research company, the Pre-Salt Petroleum company, and the Empresa Brasileira de Planejamento e Logística) (Coutinho et al., 2019). One possible explanation that has been offered for the relative inefficacy of the developmental state under democracy is the size of the state, but here the evidence is unconvincing. The developmental state under military rule consumed between 10 percent and 15 percent of GDP. Since 1985, government expenditure has been nearly three times as large, remaining between 35 and 40 percent (IMF, 2019). Of course, the fiscal demands on government have been significant under democracy, including higher debt payments and social policy expenses (Weyland, 1998), meaning that there is little discretionary funding available to invest in developmental enterprises. But there are a number of factors that suggest that the state should function better with regard to the implementation of developmental policies under democracy, including past developmental successes that can serve as a roadmap for effective planning, existing agencies and organizations of the developmental state, the much improved bureaucratic apparatus, and the improved controls that are expected of a democratic regime, with its institutionalization of oversight and accountability.

34. Cross-governmental capabilities have historically been hurt by the insulation needed to build up agency capacity. Over the past seventy years, the creation of "insulated" "pockets of efficiency" (*bolsões de eficiência*) – such as Petrobrás, the BNDE, the SUMOC, the DASP, Itamaraty, offices within the Banco do Brasil, the CACEX trade body – often aimed to bypass the state apparatus rather than transforming it (Martins, 1985; Geddes, 1990, 1994; Loureiro, 1997, 2009 a point also made more recently by Prado and Trebilcock, 2018). The problem with that strategy, as Evans (1995, 61–5) illustrates, is that it makes it hard to effectively coordinate policy. Further, the atomization of the bureaucracy that results is susceptible to particularistic interests that join forces informally with the bureaucracy, creating what Cardoso (1975) would term "*anéis burocráticos.*"

35. Ironically, even in the fiscal and monetary policy domains, renowned experts note that many improvements "did not result from prior appropriate strategic planning," but instead in response to crises. They conclude, "it is strange that there is no official body tasked with bringing together, integrating, and coordinating the authorities and the policies involved in Brazilian macroeconomic policymaking" (Afonso et al., 2016).

36. Suzigan and Furtado (2006, 173ff) argue that such coordination existed under the military but was lost because of the economic crises of the 1980s and 1990s, as well as intellectual hostility that made them ineffective by the 1990s.

296 *Notes to pages 187–91*

37. For a slightly more optimistic view, see Lemos and Power (2013), who note Congress' use of four oversight tools: *Propostas de Fiscalização e Controle*, information requests, ministerial audiences, and public audiences.
38. I am grateful to Luciano Da Ros for this observation.
39. 2017 data from Portal da Transparência; 2004 data from O Estado de S. Paulo (2014).
40. These levels of civil service dismissals by internal oversight agencies are similar to the proportions in the Canadian government (Figueiredo, 2019, 15).
41. The politicians jailed in Lava Jato were those who were not sitting politicians at the time of their conviction: e.g., Senator Delcidio Amaral of the PT and Eduardo Cunha of the PMDB, both expelled from Congress by their peers, and President Lula, who was no longer serving in office at the time of his conviction.
42. The sources of impunity are multiple, including ineffective courts, Brasília's distance – both geographic and relational – from the rest of the country, and the legal protections elites provide themselves.

    There is a strong consensus among academics that Brazilian courts are independent, powerful, well-staffed, and endowed with generous resources (Castro, 1997a, 1997b; Prillaman, 2000; Taylor, 2005; Zimmerman, 2008; Da Ros, 2010; Almeida, 2014; Engelmann and Bandeira, 2017). But simultaneously, the courts are inefficient in curbing wrongdoing, especially in cases of malfeasance by economic and political elites. Judicial inefficiency and capriciousness combine with judges' naked self-interest to generate impunity. High court congestion, high numbers of appeals, and the use of "monocratic" decisions by single judges on the high court, contribute to uncertainty, slow resolution of court cases, and a lack of accountability (Arguelhes and Hartmann, 2017; Da Ros and Taylor, 2019). In the words of one renowned scholar of the courts, "the legal system is not rationally functioning" (Rosenn, 2014, 313). The scarier possibility, which looks more plausible after the repeated failure of anti-corruption reforms, is that the system may in fact be functioning completely rationally, as political elites eschew reform and rely on the courts' inefficiency as a shield.

    Related to this is Brasília's distance from the remainder of the country, which contributes to the relatively small and intertwined elite community in the capital. Campante and Do (2014) demonstrate that in the US states, distance of the capital from major population centers influences the level of corruption. In the Brazilian case, the close-knit and relatively small size of the federal political elite engenders a certain tractability in intra-elite disputes. No one wishes to upset the apple cart in a set of interlocking relationships that may cross family relations, social organizations, and professional affiliations, and leads to what Palermo (2016, 20) has called a "culture of composition," which "appreciates pragmatism and negotiation, while being akin to cooptation and elitist conciliation." As Matias Spektor has written, "the relation between the STF and other branches is set by the exchange of favors and mutual protection. When things are going well, elected politicians generate opportunities for justices to consolidate their patronage networks in the bureaucratic structure of the judiciary. When things go badly,

Notes to pages 191–8 297

the bleeding is stanched through the STF's consent, support, and active intervention" (Spektor, 2018, translation by author).

Finally, politicians enjoy extraordinary protections from prosecution. Sitting federal politicians can only be tried under the original jurisdiction of the STF, a phenomenon widely known as the *"foro privilegiado,"* which has served as an effective "shield against accountability" (Moro, 2018, 159), in part because the STF is overly congested, but also because the court has traditionally been deferential to politicians.

43. NUPPS-ABJ (2019, 97) shows that the statute of limitations affects a relatively low volume of cases in the lower courts: just over 1 percent of cases of corruption, for example.

7 THE AUTONOMOUS BUREAUCRACY AND INCREMENTAL CHANGE

1. Monteiro Lobato 1933[2003], translation by author.
2. Throughout this chapter, "bureaucracy" and "civil service" are used interchangeably; except as noted, they refer here solely to the federal civil service.
3. In a comprehensive analysis of the eighteen largest Latin American countries, the Brazilian federal government bureaucracy placed highest with regard to hiring on merit criteria, far ahead of second place Chile, and more than twice as high as the regional average. The civil service's functional capacity score was nearly twice the regional average (Zuvanic and Iacoviello, 2010).
4. Abers and Keck (2013, 33) summarize this neatly: "The coexistence of dispersed and concentrated powers, of strong and weak parts of the state, and of different patterns of state-society interaction has been produced through a long series of unfinished, contradictory state reform processes. Another result of this history is a great deal of redundancy, overlap, and jurisdictional confusion among Brazilian institutions, a situation we call entanglement."
5. The Constitution required that all civil servants be hired through entrance exams (*concursos públicos*) that tested performance and academic qualifications. Tenure protections under the *Regime Jurídico Único* include rules protecting civil servants from dismissal, as well as pay equality (*isonomia*) among civil servants in the same job or same stage of a career (De Bonis, 2015).
6. Bureaucracies, after all, are not separate from other political bodies, and can only be understood in their broader political context (Polga-Hecimovich and Trelles, 2016).
7. Weber was clear "that a rational bureaucracy is a precondition for a fully developed capitalist system" (Grindle, 2012, 30). A developmental state places even greater demands on the bureaucracy needed to plan, guide, and implement activities, as Chapter 6 suggested.
8. There are 10.5 million government employees nationwide: roughly 10 percent in federal government, 30 percent in state governments, and 60 percent in municipal governments. Of the 1.15 million federal civil servants, 716

298 *Notes to pages 198–205*

thousand are civilians working in the executive branch or as government employees in SOEs (Boletim Estatístico de Pessoal, 2017).

9. The constitution established that appointment positions should preferably be filled by civil servants (Art. 37, V). Until the civil service reform in 1998, however, there were few real limits on the appointment powers of presidents. Decree 5.497 established tighter rules on more than 21,000 lower level appointment positions (DAS 1–4), obligating presidents to nominate active or retired civil servants to at least 75 percent of DAS 1–3 slots, and 50 percent of DAS 4 slots (Santos, 2009). A subsequent decree by President Michel Temer reduced this figure to 50 percent for DAS 1–3, maintained it for DAS 4, and instituted a new limit for the highest-ranking appointees, with a 60 percent quotient for DAS 5 and DAS 6. Rules for DAS slots favor civil servants: an outsider with a DAS position is paid the reference salary for that posting, while a career civil servant will receive his/her usual salary plus 60 percent of the DAS wage (De Bonis and Pacheco, 2010, 360).

10. Mid-level political appointees have levels of education that far surpass those of the overall population (63 percent hold higher degrees, against 11 percent of the adult population) (Cavalcante and Lotta, 2015).

11. Epistemic communities are broad groups with shared ideas that support particular reforms, even if they have never met in person or have never jointly developed strategic plans for achieving their goals. They are akin to "advocacy coalitions" (Sabatier, 1988) or "shared-action groups" (Heclo, 1978; McFarland, 2004; Da Ros, 2014, 52).

12. Vergara and Encinas (2016) coin the term "locks" or "*candados*" to describe the strategies used by civil servants in Peru to preserve the new post-reform status quo. I borrow their concept here but refer to it as "lock-in."

13. Loureiro (2009, 129) notes, "this technocratic decision-making pattern has been historically justified in several ways, whether by the need to develop the country (1950s and 1960s), to control the 'inflation monster' (1980s and 1990s), or more recently, to deal with external vulnerability. Arguing that development, monetary stability, and other issues are technically complex (that is, demand the exclusive competence of specialists and, therefore, cannot be open to competition among political forces), economists, regardless of their theoretical or ideological orientation, have thereby reinforced nondemocratic patterns of political action."

14. The golden rule stipulates that current expenditure must not be met by borrowing. Although it is laid out in the Constitution, the FRL reiterates that borrowing cannot exceed capital expenditure in ways that might finance current expenditure.

15. Bersch (2019) describes a similar phenomenon in the passage of bidding reforms, where reforms were kept below the radar of potential opposition forces, and the provisional measure imposing the change was submitted simultaneously with the much higher profile FRL, thereby providing it political cover. Abers and Keck (2013, 24, 201) also describe reformers working under the radar in Brazilian water politics.

16. The budgetary powers of the presidency are important to explaining the STN's increasing control over spending. Of particular importance is the fact

Notes to pages 206–17 299

that until 2019, the budget approved by Congress merely authorized expenditure, rather than requiring it. This meant that the STN had great control over the flow of expenditures over the course of the fiscal year and could also curtail budget outlays when needed (Loureiro and Abrucio, 2004).

17. Tavares notes, however, that the constitutional amendment permitting reelection was also important, because it forced new governors and mayors to lengthen their spending horizons.

18. Constitutional Amendment 3 limited debt issuance, except in cases of judicial debts pre-dating the 1988 Constitution.

19. The fixed exchange rate policy in place at the time generated a pernicious cycle, with the overvalued exchange rate and high interest rates increasing the cost of servicing the debt (Tavares, 2005, 91). The need to ensure capital inflows meant that policymakers were constantly working to retain market confidence, and newly established fiscal transparency ensured that markets would focus on the fiscal bottom line.

20. A central figure in these efforts was Dr. Sergio Arouca (Gibson, 2017, 758).

21. But as Nunn (2009) notes, the Constitution's establishment of a right to health somewhat ambiguously assigned this responsibility as a shared task of local, state, and federal governments, and it did not clarify what a right to health meant. Health institutions thus remained in an institutional limbo that only slowly began to be addressed with laws written in 1990, 1993, and 1996, and a 2000 constitutional amendment, which guaranteed set proportions of federal tax revenues to health care.

22. As Mayka (2019b) notes, Collor vetoed eleven key articles in the bill, which the coalition then recouped in a separate bill proposed and approved in late 1990, which Collor reluctantly signed into law.

23. The councils have a broad mandate to set policy, allocate funds, and oversee implementation; furthermore, their decisions have formal legal weight (Tatagiba, 2002; Mayka, 2019b, 275).

24. Under WTO rules, compulsory licenses allow governments to produce a drug (or allow a firm to produce it) without consent of the patent holder in cases of national public health emergency (Nunn, 2009, 4).

25. There are at least two paths to judicial intervention: litigants may seek to secure individual judgements providing them with AIDS treatments (Nunn, 2009) or alternately, they may encourage public prosecutors to file an *ação civil pública*, the rough equivalent of a class action lawsuit, on behalf of a broader constituency (Hoffman and Bentes, 2008, 117; Rich, 2019).

26. In health care as elsewhere, courts are slow-functioning, unable to implement binding policy decisions, and often privilege individual care without regard to its social cost (Oliveira and Noronha, 2011; Wang et al., 2014; Wang, 2015).

27. Initially, this grouping was known as ENCLA and focused only on money laundering. An additional "C" was added to the acronym in 2006, when the grouping was expanded to address corruption (Araújo, 2012, 71).

28. These include government agencies (such as the ABIN, AGU, BCB, BNDES, CADE, Casa Civil, Comissão de Ética, COAF, Gabinete de Segurança Institucional, INSS, Defense, MDIC, Justiça, CGU, Planejamento, Itamaraty, Federal police, Receita Federal), federal prosecutors, civil service

300 *Notes to pages 217–24*

professional associations (such as the ADPF, AJUFE, AMB, ATRICON, AMPCON, ANAPE, ANPR, CONACI, CONCPC, and CNPG), state police forces, representatives from both houses of Congress, state banks (Caixa and Banco do Brasil), state prosecutors, state and municipal agencies, regulatory bodies (CVM, PREVIC, SUSEP), judicial oversight bodies (CJF, CNJ, CNMP, CSJT), private sector associations (e.g., Febraban), and representatives from the legislative accounting tribunal (TCU), labor court (TST), and electoral court (TSE).

29. International pressure was essential to getting Brazil to sign on to the law, which may also explain why the law was slow to find traction among domestic law enforcement institutions. The law was implemented against a backdrop of significant international norms-making, including the United Nations Convention against Transnational Organized Crime (UNTOC), the OECD antibribery convention, the Financial Action Task Force (FATF), the Organization of American States (OAS) Inter-American Convention Against Corruption, and the United Nations Convention against Corruption (UNCAC) (Vaz Ferreira and Morosini, 2013; France, 2017).

30. ENCCLA has several overlapping structures. There is the annual plenary meeting, where the final recommendations are approved. A steering committee known as the *Gabinete de Gestão Integrada* meets quarterly to evaluate the current year's progress. Working groups hold regular meetings to move forward each of the current year's recommendations as well as to brainstorm for the next year. All are coordinated and overseen by the DRCI.

31. *Programa Nacional de Capacitação e Treinamento para o Combate à Corrupção e à Lavagem de Dinheiro.*

32. As Araújo (2012) notes, the first generation of AML laws focused on proceeds of drug trafficking, the second focused on proceeds of major crimes such as corruption, and the third, which included Law 12.683, were broader still, allowing charges to be brought for a wide variety of predicate crimes.

33. A practice which had the frequent consequence of alerting the target to an investigation.

34. This is not to suggest that bureaucracies are the only source of change, of course. Especially early in the democratic era, sweeping institutional change was commonplace through mobilization by social movements, interest groups, and professional associations. The 1987–88 Constituent Assembly proved a focal point for mobilization across a variety of causes and policy arenas, as well as an institutional space to effect change. Even after the Constitution was written, change has at times been driven by grassroots activists working through participatory institutions in, for example, river basin committees (Abers and Keck, 2013), education, housing (Wampler, 2009, 2015; Donaghy, 2011), social assistance, and health (Mayka, 2019a).

35. Mainwaring and Shugart (1997) distinguish between the legislative and partisan powers of the president. The importance of the bureaucracy to presidential success, however, suggests that perhaps we might wish to also consider the bureaucratic powers of the president, which are arguably quite broad in Brazil by contrast to other Latin American countries, and thereby contribute to the

Notes to pages 225–46

president's primacy in policymaking. I am grateful to Luciano Da Ros for highlighting this point.
36. Luciano Da Ros is also the instigator of this argument, and I am once again much obliged.
37. Meanwhile, it should be noted that HIV numbers have been creeping back up, suggesting that despite early successes, continued progress is not guaranteed.

8 CONCLUSION

1. Furtado (1984, 28), translation by author.
2. Baldocchi (2014), translation by author.
3. "É lobby, é conchavo, é propina e jeton … " (Vianna, 1995).
4. Dilma Rousseff would later pull together an even broader coalition.
5. A return to equilibrium is shown in Chapter 1, Figure B, arrows 1a and 1b (supra note 22).
6. Consider two institutions with preference-incidence lines 2a and 2b in Figure D. Preference-incidence line 2a shows a particularly malleable institution, such as subway boarding. Line 2b shows a much more rigid institution, such as road driving. Between points 4 and 5, the slope for road driving is much steeper than subway boarding, since the costs of being caught off equilibrium are consequential, especially by contrast to the relatively innocuous grumbles that would meet a subway rider boarding on the wrong side of the door. For any given shift in incidence between points 4 and 5, the likelihood of a substantial change in equilibrium is much greater for institution 2b than for institution 2a.

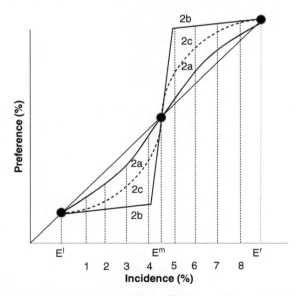

FIGURE D Incremental change under different preference-incidence curves.
Source: Author.

302   *Notes to pages 246–8*

The challenge is to move from E^l to point 4, or from E^r to point 5, without regressing back to the status quo equilibrium at E^l or E^r. The traffic engineer seeking to move society from driving on the right (E^r) to driving on the left (E^l) must first think of ways to get to point 5 without reverting (or "snapping back") to E^r, and then give an extra push to get over the cliff to E^m, then to points 4, 3, etc., at which point the "gravitational" pull of E^l is likely to dominate. Such a policy intervention might include a public awareness campaign in the months ahead of the move, a beefing up of traffic police in the weeks preceding the move, a lot of traffic cones and signage on the day of the change, and then constant vigilance in the ensuing months to ensure that the new equilibrium is maintained. Recent Brazilian history offers another example in this line: the Real Plan, and particularly its use of the Unit of Real Value (URV) to bring preferences in line, before pushing for a major shift in citizen behaviors regarding the indexation of prices. Another way of expressing the different types of change at work in P-I curves 2a and 2b is that the less steep the line, the easier change will be, but the less likely that each incremental change will add up to an equilibrium shift; the steeper the line, the harder change will be, but the more likely that each incremental change will lead to an equilibrium shift.

7. The point about hierarchically subordinate institutions may be illustrated by the subway example described in the Introduction. If passengers boarding the subway arrive at equilibrium E^r (board on one's right and disembark on one's right) partly because of the complementary institution of driving one's car on the right, it seems likely that until there is a change in the institution of driving on the right, occasional expressions of a preference for boarding the subway on the left are likely to be swamped by the actual behaviors of subway riders following the preference for adopting the same behavior on the subway as they do on the road. Furthermore, consider that the costs of driving on the left when the equilibrium behavior is to drive on the right are, to put it mildly, consequential: fender benders, potential injury, lawsuits, and death. The costs of boarding on the left, by contrast, are low, even when most people stick to boarding on the right.

8. So if the preference-incidence line for the developmental state looks a bit like line 2b, and the preference-incidence line for the autonomous bureaucracy looks like 2a, the joint set of complementary institutions may be more akin to line 2c.

9. I am grateful to Mario Schapiro and an anonymous reviewer for suggesting that Bolsonaro represented a "stress test" for my arguments.

10. The literature suggests that institutional complementarities need not lead to complete collapse resulting from the "unwinding of the previously 'positive' complementarities" but instead may lead to incremental, stepwise adjustments as changes in one arena lead to adjustment in other arenas (Streeck, 2005; Amable, 2016). Thus, change might take place via large "punctuated equilibria" or "critical junctures," or instead through the accretion of small and gradual changes that over time add up into major transformations. Change that drives the system to a tipping point in which it moves to a new equilibrium could come either through "direct" changes from within, such as

changes within a particular institutional domain, or through "contextual" changes in the overall institutional setting (Lamberson and Page, 2012). These contextual changes could be either due to the global context outside of Brazil, or instead due to the reverberating effect of institutional complementarities, as change in one domain sparks change in another.

11. This deal was called off in early 2020 in the context of the aviation industry's pandemic-related crisis (Rochabrun, 2020).

12. Provisional Measure 881 issued April 30, 2019.

13. Theoretically, it is impossible to know exactly where the country is at present: Is it closer to a stable equilibrium (e.g., E^1 in Figure D), or on the verge of a major tipping point (e.g., point 4)? Is it on a preference-incidence line that promises more difficult but potentially rapid change (e.g., line 2a), or one that promises easier but incremental change (e.g., line 2b)?

14. Data kindness of Felix Lopez, who calculated the index from datasets provided by Acir Almeida and the Brazilian Chamber of Deputies.

15. Within its first year in office, for example, the Temer administration had reduced the federal police budget and dismantled the police's specialized task force team. The former head of the *Ministério Público*, Rodrigo Janot, complained the Justice Ministry was slowing down joint cooperation with other countries. From January 2015 through 2018, the Comptroller General's Office (CGU) churned through seven different ministers.

References

Abers, Rebecca and Margaret Keck. 2013. *Practical Authority: Agency and Institutional Change in Brazilian Water Politics*. New York: Oxford University Press.

Abramovay, Pedro. 2018. Author interview with Abramovay, former National Secretary of Justice, Ministry of Justice, July 13.

Abranches, Sérgio. 1988. "Presidencialismo de coalizão: o dilema institucional brasileiro." *Dados, 31*: 5–38.

Abranches, Sérgio. 1999. "Reforma regulatória: conceitos, experiências e recomendações." *Revista do Serviço Público, April–June*, 19–51.

Abranches, Sérgio. 2016. "Clientelismo, petróleo e corrupção no presidencialismo de coalizão." *Ecopolítica*. March 17. sergioabranches.com.br

Abranches, Sérgio. 2018. *Presidencialismo de coalizão: raízes e evolução do modelo político brasileiro*. São Paulo: Editora Companhia das Letras.

Abreu, Marcelo de Paiva. 2007. "A quem beneficiam as políticas públicas no Brasil? Uma visão de longo prazo." Working Paper Departamento de Economia, PUC-Rio 554.

Abreu, Marcelo de Paiva. 2015. "Autarkic Obsession: A Long-term View of Brazil in the World Economy." Paper presented at Princeton-USP conference on the International Politics of Economic Globalization and Emerging Market Economies, March 19–20.

Abreu, Mariana Piaia. 2019. "Structure of Control in Financial Networks: An Application to the Brazilian Stock Market." *Physica A, 522*: 302–14.

Abrucio, Fernando Luiz. 2018. "Uma breve história da educação como política pública no Brasil." In Danilo Leite Dalmon, Caetano Siqueira, and Felipe Michel Braga (eds.), *Políticas educacionais no Brasil: o que podemos aprender com casos reais de implementação?*, 37–58. São Paulo: Edições SM.

Abu-El-Haj, Jawdat. 2016. "Brazilian Left Bonapartism and the Rise of Finance Capital: A critique of the Internal-Bourgeoisie Thesis." *Latin American Perspectives, 43*: 207–16.

References

Afonso, José Roberto R. 2010. Responsabilidade fiscal no Brasil: uma memória da lei. FGV Projetos. June 24, 2015. http://fgvprojetos.fgv.br/publicacao/respons abilidade-fiscal-uma-memoria-da-lei

Afonso, José Roberto R. 2013. "A economia política da reforma tributária: o caso brasileiro." September. Washington, DC: Woodrow Wilson Center for Scholars.

Afonso, José Roberto R., Eliana Cristina Araújo, and Bernardo Guelber Fajardo. 2016. "The Role of Fiscal and Monetary Policies in the Brazilian Economy: Understanding Recent Institutional Reforms and Economic Changes." *Quarterly Review of Economics and Finance*, 62: 41–55.

Afonso, José Roberto R., Julia Moraes Soares, and Kleber Pacheco de Castro. 2013. "Avaliação da estrutura e do desempenho do sistema tributário brasileiro: livro branco da tributação brasileira." Banco Interamericano de Desenvolvimento, Documento para discussão #IDB-DP-265.

Agência Estado. 2007. "Para Lula, usineiros são heróis mundiais." March 20.

Aggarwal, Vinod K. and Ralph Espach. 2004. "Diverging Trade Strategies in Latin America: A Framework for Analysis." In Vinod K. Aggarwal, Ralph Espach, and Joseph S. Tulchin (eds.), *The Strategic Dynamics of Latin American Trade*, 3–36. Stanford, CA: Stanford University Press.

Agosín, Manuel. 2012. Author interview with Agosín, Dean of the School of Economics and Business, Universidad de Chile, June 7.

Alencar, Carlos Higino Ribeiro de and Ivo Gico Jr. 2011. "Corrupção e Judiciário: a (in)eficácia do sistema judicial no combate à corrupção." *Revista Direito GV*, 7, 75–98.

Almeida, Acir dos Santos. 2018. "Governo presidencial condicionado: delegação e participação legislativa na Câmara dos Deputados." Unpublished Ph.D. Dissertation, Universidade Estadual do Rio de Janeiro, Instituto de Estudos Sociais e Políticos.

Almeida, Frederico de. 2014. "As elites da Justiça: instituições, profissões e poder na política da justiça brasileira." *Revista de Sociologia e Política*, 22: 77–95.

Almeida, Daniel B. de Castro and Frederico G. Jayme Jr. 2008. "Bank Consolidation and Credit Concentration in Brazil (1995–2004)." *CEPAL Review*, 95: 155–71.

Almeida, Isis and Lucia Kassai. 2013. "Brazil crushing sugar to ethanol with caps on fuel prices." *Bloomberg News*, December 19.

Almeida, Mansueto. 2009. "Desafios da real política industrial brasileira no século XXI." *IPEA Texto para Discussão* 1452.

Almeida, Mansueto. 2013a. "Padrões de política industrial: a velha, a nova e a brasileira." In Edmar Bacha and Monica de Bolle (eds.), *O futuro da industria no Brasil*, 273–94. Rio de Janeiro: Civilização Brasileira.

Almeida, Mansueto. 2013b. "O problema da carga tributária no Brasil." Blogpost of November 20. mansueto.wordpress.com, February 12, 2015.

Almeida, Maria Hermínia Tavares de. 1996. "Pragmatismo por necessidade: os rumos da reforma econômica no Brasil." *Dados*, 39: 213–34.

Almeida, Maria Hermínia Tavares de. 2005. "Recentralizando a federação?" *Revista de Sociologia e Política*, 24: 29–40.

References

Almeida, Rodolfo and Gabriel Zanlorenssi. 2017. "A trajetória do preço de combustível no Brasil nos últimos 17 anos." *Nexo*, October 16.

Almeida, Mansueto, Renato Lima-Oliveira, and Ben Ross Schneider. 2012. "Industrial Policy and State Owned Enterprises in Brazil: BNDES and Petrobras." Brasília: IPEA.

Alston, Lee J., Marcus André Melo, Bernardo Mueller, and Carlos Pereira. 2016. *Brazil in Transition: Beliefs, Leadership, and Institutional Change*. Princeton, NJ: Princeton University Press.

Amable, Bruno. 2003. *The Diversity of Modern Capitalism*. Oxford: Oxford University Press.

Amable, Bruno. 2016. "Institutional Complementarities in the Dynamic Comparative Analysis of Capitalism." *Journal of Institutional Economics*, 12: 79–103.

Amable, Bruno and Stefano Palombarini. 2009. "A Neorealist Approach to Institutional Change and the Diversity of Capitalism." *Socio-Economic Review*, 7: 123–43.

Amann, Edmund and Werner Baer. 2009. "The Macroeconomic Record of the Lula Administration, the Roots of Brazil's Inequality, and Attempts to Overcome Them." In Joseph L. Love and Werner Baer (eds.), *Brazil under Lula: Economy, Politics, and Society under the Worker-President*, 27–46. Basingstoke: Palgrave Macmillan.

Amann, Edmund and Armando Barrientos. 2016. "Introduction: Is There a Brazilian 'Development' Model?" *Quarterly Review of Economics and Finance*, 62: 7–11.

Amann, Edmund, Werner Baer, Thomas Trebat, and Juan Villa Lora. 2016. "Infrastructure and its Role in Brazil's Development Process." *Quarterly Review of Economics and Finance*, 62: 66–73.

Ames, Barry. 1995. "Electoral Strategy under Open-List Proportional Representation." *American Journal of Political Science*, 39: 406–33.

Ames, Barry. 2001. *The Deadlock of Democracy in Brazil*. Ann Arbor: University of Michigan Press.

Amsden, Alice H. 1989. *Asia's Next Giant: South Korea and Late Industrialization*. Oxford University Press: New York.

Amsden, Alice H. 1991. "Diffusion of Development: The Late-Industrializing Model and Greater East Asia." *American Economic Review*, 81: 282–6.

Amsden, Alice H. 2001. *The Rise of "the Rest": Challenges to the West from Late-Industrializing Economies*. Oxford: Oxford University Press.

Andrezo, Andrea Fernandes and Iran Siqueira Lima. 1999. *Mercado financeiro: aspectos históricos e conceituais*. São Paulo: Pioneira.

Aninat, Augusto. 2012. Author interview with Augusto Aninat, retired ambassador, former director of international economic relations, Universidad de Chile, June 5.

Aoki, Masahiko. 1994. "The Contingent Governance of Teams: Analysis of Institutional Complementarity." *International Economic Review*, 34: 657–76.

Aoki, Masahiko. 2001. *Toward a Comparative Institutional Analysis*. Cambridge, MA: MIT Press.

References

Aoki, Masahiko. 2013. "Historical Sources of Institutional Trajectories in Economic Development: China, Japan and Korea Compared." *Socio-Economic Review*, 11: 233–63.

Aranovich, Tatiana de Campos. 2007. "Estratégia Nacional de Combate à Corrupção e à Lavagem de Dinheiro: o Estado organizado contra o crime organizado." *Revista de Política Públicas e Gestão Governamental*, 6: 117–45.

Arantes, Rogério Bastos. 1997. *Judiciário e política no Brasil*. São Paulo: IDESP.

Arantes, Rogério Bastos. 2005. "Constitutionalism, the Expansion of Justice and the Judicialization of Politics in Brazil." In Rachel Sieder, Line Schjolden, and Alan Angell (eds.), *The Judicialization of Politics in Latin America*, 231–62. New York: Palgrave Macmillan.

Arantes, Rogério Bastos. 2011. "The Federal Police and the Ministério Público." In Timothy J. Power and Matthew M. Taylor (eds.), *Corruption and Democracy in Brazil: The Struggle for Accountability*, 184–217. Notre Dame, IN: University of Notre Dame Press.

Arantes, Rogério Bastos, Maria Rita Loureiro, Cláudio Couto, and Marco Antonio Carvalho Teixeira. 2010. "Controles democráticos sobre a administração pública no Brasil: Legislativo, Tribunais de Contas, Judiciário e Ministério Público." In Maria Rita Loureiro, Fernando Luiz Abrucio, and Regina Silvia Pacheco (eds.), *Burocracia e política no Brasil: desafios para o Estado democrático no século XXI*, 109–47. Rio de Janeiro: Editora FGV.

Araújo, Felipe Dantas de. 2012. "Uma análise da Estratégia Nacional Contra a Corrupção e a Lavagem de Dinheiro (ENCCLA) por suas diretrizes." *Revista Brasileira de Políticas Públicas*, Brasília, 2: 53–82.

Araújo, Victor, Graziele Silotto, and Lucas Rodrigues Cunha. 2015. "Capital politico e financiamento eleitoral no Brasil: uma análise empírica da estratégia das empresas na alocação de recursos de campanha." *Teoria & Sociedade*, 23: 126–58.

Arbix, Glauco and Scott B. Martin. 2010. "Beyond Developmentalism and Market Fundamentalism in Brazil: Inclusionary State Activism without Statism." Global Legal Studies Center and the Center for World Affairs and the Global Economy, University of Wisconsin-Madison.

Arbix, Glauco, Mario Sérgio Salerno, Guilherme Amaral, and Leonardo Melo Lins. 2017. "Avanços, equívocos e instabilidade das políticas de inovação no Brasil." *Novos Estudos CEBRAP*, 109 (November): 9–27.

Arguelhes, Diego Werneck and Ivar A. Hartmann. 2017. "Timing Control without Docket Control: How Individual Justices Shape the Brazilian Supreme Court's Agenda." *Journal of Law and Courts*, 5: 105–40.

Arguelhes, Diego Werneck and Leandro Molhano Ribeiro. 2018. "Ministrocracia: o Supremo Tribunal individual e o processo democrático brasileiro." *Novos Estudos CEBRAP*, 37: 13–32.

Armijo, Leslie Elliott. 2005. "Mass Democracy: The real reason that Brazil ended inflation?" *World Development*, 3: 2013–27.

Armijo, Leslie Elliott. 2017. "The Public Bank Trilemma: Brazil's New Developmentalism and the BNDES." In Peter R. Kingstone and Timothy J. Power (eds.), *Democratic Brazil Divided*, 230–47. Pittsburgh, PA: University of Pittsburgh Press.

References

Armijo, Leslie Elliott and Christine A. Kearney. 2008. "Does Democratization Alter the Policy Process? Trade Policymaking in Brazil." *Democratization, 15*: 991–1017.

Armijo, Leslie Elliott and Sybil D. Rhodes. 2017. "Explaining Infrastructure Underperformance in Brazil: Cash, Political Institutions, Corruption, and Policy Gestalts." *Policy Studies, 38*: 231–47.

Arretche, Marta. 2002. "Federalismo e relações intergovernamentais no Brasil: a reforma de programas sociais." *Dados, 45*: 431–58.

Arretche, Marta. 2004. "Toward a Unified and More Equitable System: Health Reform in Brazil." In Robert Kaufman and Joan Nelson (eds.), *Crucial Needs, Weak Incentives*, 155–88. Baltimore, MD: John Hopkins University Press.

Arretche, Marta. 2009. "Continuidades e descontinuidades da Federação Brasileira: de como 1988 facilitou 1995." *Dados, 52*: 377–423.

Arretche, Marta. 2013. "Demos-Constraining or Demos-Enabling Federalism? Political Institutions and Policy Change in Brazil." *Journal of Politics in Latin America, 5*: 133–50.

Arruda de Almeida, Mônica and Bruce Zagaris. 2015. "Political Capture in the Petrobras Scandal: The Sad Tale of an Oil Giant." *The Fletcher Forum of World Affairs, 39*: 87–99.

Augustinis, Viviane Franco de. 2011. "Gestão em redes para a construção de políticas públicas: um estudo sobre as atividades de prevenção e repressão à lavagem de dinheiro no Brasil." Unpublished Ph.D. Dissertation, Fundação Getulio Vargas-RJ.

Avelino, George, Ciro Biederman, and Arthur Fisch. 2017. "A corrida armamentista nas eleições brasileiras." CEPESP-FGV, June 13. https://cepesp.wordpress.com/2017/06/13/a-corrida-armamentista-nas-eleicoes-brasileiras/

Bacha, Edmar Lisboa. 2016. "Abre-te, Brasil." *Valor Econômico*, September 9.

Baer, Werner and Coes, Donald V. 2006. "The Impact of Politics on Fiscal Behavior: The Case of Brazil." *Economia Aplicada, 10*: 25–40.

Baerresen, Donald W., Martin Carnoy, and Joseph Grunwald. 1965. *Latin American Trade Patterns*. Washington, DC: The Brookings Institution.

Baird, Marcelo Fragano. 2012. "O lobby na regulação da propaganda de alimentos da Agência Nacional de Vigilância Sanitária – Anvisa." Unpublished M.A. Thesis, Department of Political Science, Universidade de São Paulo.

Baird, Marcelo Fragano and Ivan Filipe de Almeida Lopes Fernandes. 2014. "Flying in Clear Skies: Technical Arguments Influencing Anac Regulations." *Brazilian Political Science Review, 8*: 70–92.

Bairoch, Paul. 1972. "Free trade and European Economic Development in the 19th Century." *European Economic Review, 3*: 211–45.

Baker, Andy. 2003. "Why Is Trade Reform So Popular in Latin America? A Consumption-Based Theory of Trade Policy Preferences." *World Politics, 55*: 423–55.

Baker, Andy. 2009. *The Market and the Masses in Latin America: Policy Reform and Consumption in Liberalizing Economies*. New York: Cambridge University Press.

References 309

Balán, Manuel. 2011. "Competition by Denunciation: The Political Dynamics of Corruption Scandals in Argentina and Chile." *Comparative Politics*, 43: 459–78.

Balbachevsky, Elizabeth and Helena Sampaio. 2017. "Brazilian Postsecondary Education in the 21st Century: A Conservative Modernization." In Philip G. Altbach, Liz Reisberg, and Hans de Wit (eds.), *Responding to Massification: Differentiation in Postsecondary Education Worldwide*, 155–65. Rotterdam, The Netherlands: Sense Publishers.

Baldocchi, Gabriel. 2014. "O Plano Brasil Maior ficou bem menor." *Istoé Dinheiro*, October 17.

Ban, Cornel. 2013. "Brazil's Liberal Neo-Developmentalism: New Paradigm or Edited Orthodoxy." *Review of International Political Economy*, 20: 298–331.

Banco Central do Brasil. 2018. "Relatório de economia bancária." www .bcb.gov.br/publicacoes/relatorioeconomiabancaria

Bandeira-de-Mello, Rodrigo. 2015. "Financiamento de campanha não esgota a relação entre empresas e governo." *O Estado de S. Paulo*, April 8.

Bandeira-de-Mello, Rodrigo, Rosilene Marcon, and Anete Alberton. 2008. "Drivers of Discretionary Firm Donations in Brazil." *Brazilian Administration Review*, 5: 275–88.

Barbosa, Fernando de Holanda. 2006. "The Contagion Effect of Public Debt on Monetary Policy: The Brazilian Experience." *Brazilian Journal of Political Economy*, 26: 231–8.

Barbosa Filho, Fernando de Holanda. 2012. "An Estimation of the Underground Economy in Brazil." FGV working paper.

Bastos, Márcio Thomaz. 2012. "Uma estratégia de longo prazo para o Estado brasileiro." In Ricardo Andrade Saadi, Roberto Biasoli, and Ana Paula da Cunha (eds.), *ENCCLA: Estratégia Nacional de Combate à Corrupção e à Lavagem de Dinheiro: 10 anos de organização do Estado brasileiro contra o crime organizado*, 32–3. Brasília: Ministério da Justiça.

Batista, Henrique Gomes and Ruben Berta. 2015. "Governo revela que há 480 entidades sindicais milionárias." *O Globo*, August 25.

Batista, Mariana. 2012. "Mecanismos de participação e atuação de grupos de interesse no processo regulatório brasileiro: o caso da Agência Nacional de Energia Elétrica (Aneel)." *Revista de Administração Pública*, 46: 969–92.

Baumann, Renato. 2009. "The Geography of Brazilian External Trade: Right Option for a BRIC?" Paper presented at Conference on *The Political Economy of Trade Policy in the BRICS*. New Orleans, LA, March 27–28.

Baumann, Renato. 2012. Author interview with Baumann, trade specialist and researcher at IPEA, Brasília, May 22.

Bechara, Fábio Ramazzini. 2019. Author Interview with Bechara, senior prosecutor at the São Paulo Ministério Público and law professor at Mackenzie University, São Paulo, April 23.

Bekerman, Marta and Federico Dulcich. 2017. "Análisis comparativo de la Zona Franca de Manaos y el área aduanera especial de Tierra del Fuego." *Economia e Sociedade*, 26: 751–91.

Belisário, Adriano. 2017. "Mapeamento inédito mostra que doações legais da Odebrecht beneficiaram 1.087 candidatos desde 2002." *The Intercept Brasil*,

September 26. https://theintercept.com/2017/09/26/mapeamento-inedito-mostra-que-doacoes-legais-da-odebrecht-beneficiaram-1-087-candidatos-desde-2002

Benevides, Maria Vitória. 1976. *Governo Kubitschek: desenvolvimento econômico e estabilidade política*. São Paulo: Brasiliense.

Benites, Afonso. 2020. "Centrão já administra 73 bilhões de reais no Governo Bolsonaro." *El País*, May 22.

Bersch, Katherine S. 2016. "The Merits of Problem-Solving over Powering: Governance Reform in Brazil and Argentina." *Comparative Politics*, 48: 205–25.

Bersch, Katherine S. 2019. *When Democracies Deliver: Governance Reform in Latin America*. New York: Cambridge University Press.

Bersch, Katherine, Sérgio Praça, and Matthew M. Taylor. 2017a. "State Capacity and Bureaucratic Autonomy Within National States: Mapping the Archipelago of Excellence in Brazil." In Miguel Angel Centeno, Atul Kohli, and Deborah Yashar (eds.), *State Building in the Developing World*, 157–83. Cambridge: Cambridge University Press.

Bersch, Katherine, Sérgio Praça, and Matthew M. Taylor. 2017b. "State Capacity, Bureaucratic Politicization, and Corruption in the Brazilian State." *Governance*, 30: 105–24.

Bertão, Naiara Infante and Ana Clara Costa. 2014. "O problema do etanol não é só a Petrobras – mas a produtividade." *Veja*, August 23.

Bezerra, Jocildo and Tiago V. de V. Cavalcanti. 2009. "Brazil's Lack of Growth." In Joseph L. Love and Werner Baer (eds.), *Brazil under Lula: Economy, Politics, and Society under the Worker-President*, 67–89: Palgrave Macmillan.

Bhagwati, Jagdish N. 1982. "Directly Unproductive, Profit-Seeking (DUP) Activities." *Journal of Political Economy*, 90: 988–1002.

Bielschowsky, Ricardo. 1988. *Pensamento econômico brasileiro: o ciclo ideológico do desenvolvimentismo*. 5th ed. Rio de Janeiro: Contraponto.

Biglaiser, Glen. 2009. "The Internationalization of Ideas in Argentina 's Economics Profession." In Verónica Montecinos and John Markoff (eds.), *Economists in the Americas*, 63–99. Cheltenham, UK: Edward Elgar.

Biglaiser, Glen and Karl DeRouen. 2006. "Economic Reforms and Inflows of Foreign Direct Investment in Latin America." *Latin American Research Review*, 41: 51–75.

Blyth, Mark. 2003. "Structures Do Not Come with An Instruction Sheet: Interests, Ideas, and Progress in Political Science." *Perspectives on Politics*, 1: 695–706.

Blyth, Mark and Hendrik Spruyt. 2003. "Our Past as Prologue: Introduction to the Tenth Anniversary Issue of the Review of International Political Economy." *Review of International Political Economy*, 10: 607–20.

Bôas, Bruno Villas. 2018. "Brazil's Demographic Dividend Ends Earlier than Expected." *Valor International*, July 26.

Boas, Taylor C., F. Daniel Hidalgo, and Neal P. Richardson. 2014. "The Spoils of Victory: Campaign Donations and Government Contracts in Brazil." *The Journal of Politics*, 76: 415–29.

Boletim Estatístico de Pessoal, 2017. www.planejamento.gov.br/secretarias/up load/Arquivos/servidor/publicacoes/boletim_estatistico_pessoal/2017/bep-dezembro–2017

References

Bolle, Monica Baumgarten de. 2015. "Do Public Development Banks Hurt Growth? Evidence from Brazil." *Peterson Institute for International Economics Policy Brief*, Number PB15-16, September.

Bolle, Monica Baumgarten de. 2016. *Como matar a borboleta-azul: uma crônica da era Dilma*. Rio de Janeiro: Intrínseca.

Bonomo, Diego. 2012. Author interview with Diego Bonomo, US-Brazil Chamber of Commerce, January 26.

Bonvecchi, Alejandro. 2015. "Review: 'Melo and Pereira, Making Brazil Work'." *Perspectives on Politics*, *13*: 901–2.

Bonvecchi, Alejandro and Carlos Scartascini. 2014. "The Organization of the Executive Branch in Latin America: What We Know and What We Need to Know." *Latin American Politics & Society*, *56*: 144–65.

Boschi, Renato, (ed.). 2011. *Variedades de capitalismo, política e desenvolvimento na América Latina*. Belo Horizonte: Editora UFMG.

Boschi, Renato. 2018. "State Capabilities as a Challenge to Public Policy." In Ana Célia Castro and Fernando Filgueiras (eds.), *The State in the 21st Century*, 337–67. Brasília: ENAP.

Botelho, Svetlana Haspar Vasco. 2015. "Análise da política industrial recente: sugestões de uma agenda para o Brasil." Unpublished B.A. Thesis, Department of Economics, Universidade de Brasília.

Bourdoukan, Adla Youssef. 2009. "O bolso e a urna: financiamento político em perspectiva comparada." Unpublished Ph.D. dissertation, Department of Political Science, Universidade de São Paulo.

Bouzas, Roberto. 2012. Interview. Author interview with Roberto Bouzas, Professor, Universidad de San Andrés, Buenos Aires, June 19.

Boyer, Robert. 2007. "Capitalism Strikes Back: Why and What Consequences for Social Sciences?" *Revue de la Régulation*, *1*. journals.openedition.org/regulation/2142

Braga, Maria do Socorro and Jairo Pimentel Jr. 2011. "Os partidos políticos brasileiros realmente não importam?" *Opinião Pública*, *17*: 271–303.

Bragon, Ranier. 2019. "Contra mote de campanha, Bolsonaro mantém troca de favores com Congresso." *Folha de S. Paulo*, July 1.

Brandão, Gildo Marçal. 2001. "Idéias e intelectuais: modos de usar." *Lua Nova*, *54*: 25–34.

Bremmer, Ian. 2010. *The End of the Free Market*. New York: Portfolio.

Bresser-Pereira, Luiz Carlos. 2003. "The 1995 Public Management Reform in Brazil: Reflections of a Reformer." In Ben Ross Schneider and Blanca Heredia (eds.), *Reinventing Leviathan: The Politics of Administrative Reform in Developing Countries*, 89–112. University of Miami: North-South Center Press.

Bresser-Pereira, Luiz Carlos. 2011. "From Old to New Developmentalism in Latin America." In José Antonio Ocampo and Jaime Ros (eds.), *Handbook of Latin American Economics*, 108–29. Oxford: Oxford University Press.

Bresser-Pereira, Luiz Carlos. 2016. "Reflecting on New Developmentalism and Classical Developmentalism." *Review of Keynesian Economics*, *4*: 331–52.

Bresser-Pereira, Luiz Carlos. 2017. *The Political Construction of Brazil: Society, Economy, and State Since Independence*. Boulder, CO: Lynne Rienner Publishers.

Bresser-Pereira, Luiz Carlos. 2019. "40 anos de desindustrialização." *Jornal do Economista*, May.

Bretas, Valéria. "Em 3 décadas, STF só condenou 16 políticos por corrupção." *Revista Exame*. September 22, 2015.

Brey, Nathanael Kusch, Silvio Parodi Oliveira Camilo, Rosilene Marcon, and Rodrigo Bandeira-de-Mello. 2014. "Conexões políticas em estruturas de propriedade: o governo como acionista em uma análise descritiva." *Revista de Administração Mackenzie*, *15*: 98–124.

Buchanan, James and Gordon Tullock. 1962. *The Calculus of Consent*. Ann Arbor: University of Michigan Press.

Bulmer-Thomas, Victor. 1994. *The Economic History of Latin America since Independence*. Cambridge: Cambridge University Press.

Burges, Sean W. 2017. *Brazil in the World: The International Relations of a South American Giant*. Manchester: Manchester University Press.

Butler, Ines. 2012. Author interview with Ines Butler, Chief Researcher, Instituto de Estudios sobre la Realidad Argentina y Latinoamericana (IERAL), Fundación Mediterránea, Buenos Aires, June 12.

Câmara dos Deputados. 2011. *Diário da Câmara dos Deputados*, October. https://goo.gl/LcWkmP

Câmara, Cristina and Ronaldo Lima. 2000. "Histórica das ONGs/AIDS e sua contribuição no campo das lutas sociais." *Cadernos Abong*, *28*: 29–74.

Campante, Filipe R. and Quoc-Anh Do. 2014. "Isolated Capital Cities, Accountability and Corruption: Evidence from US States." *American Economic Review*, *104*: 2456–81.

Campbell, John L. 2010. "Institutional Reproduction and Change." In Glenn Morgan, John L. Campbell, Colin Crouch, Ove Kaj Pedersen, and Richard Whitley (eds.), *The Oxford Handbook of Comparative Institutional Analysis*, 87–117. Oxford: Oxford University Press.

Campello, Daniela. 2015. *The Politics of Market Discipline in Latin America: Globalization and Democracy*. New York: Cambridge University Press.

Campos, André Gambier. 2016. "Sindicatos no Brasil: o que esperar no futuro próximo?" *IPEA Texto para Discussão* 2262.

Campos, Mauro Macedo. 2009. "Democracia, partidos e eleições: os custos do sistema partidário-eleitoral no Brasil." Unpublished Ph.D. Dissertation, Universidade Federal de Minas Gerais.

Canêdo-Pinheiro, Mauricio. 2013. "Experiencias comparadas de politica industrial no pos-guerra: lições para o Brasil." In Fernando Veloso, Pedro Cavalcanti Ferreira, Fábio Giambiagi, and Samuel de Abreu Pessôa (eds.), *Desenvolvimento econômico: uma perspectiva brasileira*, 381–404. Rio de Janeiro: Editora Campus Elsevier.

Canello, Júlio. 2016. "Judicializando a Federação? O Supremo Tribunal Federal e os atos normativos estaduais." Unpublished Ph.D. dissertation, Instituto de Estudos Sociais e Políticos, Universidade do Estado do Rio de Janeiro (UERJ).

Canuto, Otaviano. 2018. "Benefits and Costs of Opening Brazil's Foreign Trade," Center for Macroeconomics and Development, August 8.

References 313

Canuto, Otaviano, Matheus Cavallari, and José Guilherme Reis. 2013. "The Brazilian Competitiveness Cliff." *Economic Premise (The World Bank Poverty Reduction and Economic Management Network)*, *105*: 1–8.

Canuto, Otaviano, Cornelius Fleischhaker, and Philip Schellekens. 2015. "The Curious Case of Brazil's Closedness to Trade." *VOX: CEPR's Policy Portal*, January 11. www.voxeu.org/article/brazil-s-closedness-trade

Cardoso, Adalberto. 2016. "Informality and Public Policies to Overcome It. The Case of Brazil." *Sociologia & Antropologia*, 6: 321–49.

Cardoso, Eliana. 2009. "A Brief History of Trade Policies in Brazil: From ISI, Export Promotion and Import Liberalization to Multilateral and Regional Agreements." Paper prepared for the conference on "The Political Economy of Trade Policy in the BRICS," New Orleans, LA, March.

Cardoso, Eliana and Ann Helwege. 2000 [1992]. "Import Substitution Industrialization." In Jeffry A. Frieden, Manuel Pastor Jr., and Michael Tomz (eds.), *Modern Political Economy and Latin America: Theory and Policy*, 155–64. Boulder, CO: Westview Press.

Cardoso, Fernando Henrique. 1975. *Autoritarismo e democratização*. Rio de Janeiro: Paz e Terra.

Cardoso, Fernando Henrique and Enzo Faletto. 1973 [1967]. *Dependência e desenvolvimento na América Latina: ensaio de interpretação sociológica*. 8th ed. Rio de Janeiro: Civilização Brasileira.

Cardozo, José Eduardo. 2012. "ENCCLA 10 anos: o mapa e a bússola." In Ricardo Andrade Saadi, Roberto Biasoli, Ana Paula da Cunha (eds.), *ENCCLA: Estratégia Nacional de Combate à Corrupção e à Lavagem de Dinheiro: 10 anos de organização do Estado brasileiro contra o crime organizado*, 9–10. Brasília: Ministério da Justiça.

Carey, John M. 2000. "Parchment, Equilibria, and Institutions." *Comparative Political Studies*, 33: 735–61.

Carneiro, Mariana. 2017. "Gasto com pesquisa na indústria automotiva caiu no Inovar-Auto." *Folha de S. Paulo*, December 21.

Carneiro, Mariana and Julio Wiziack. 2019. "Guedes trava batalha com Sistema S para assumir entidades e seu Caixa." *Folha de S. Paulo*, March 31.

Carney, Michael, Eric Gedajlovic, and Xiaohua Yang. 2009. "Varieties of Asian Capitalism: Toward an Institutional Theory of Asian Enterprise." *Asia Pacific Journal of Management*, 25: 361–80.

Carney, Richard W. 2016. "Varieties of Hierarchical Capitalism: Family and State Market Economies in Asia." *The Pacific Review*, 29: 137–63.

Carrasco, Vinicius and João Manoel Pinho de Mello. 2015. "Leis da oferta, a conta do subsídio à exportação de serviços de construção." *Revista Exame*, June 18.

Carson, Lindsey D. and Mariana Mota Prado. 2016. "Using Institutional Multiplicity to Address Corruption as a Collective Action Problem: Lessons from the Brazilian Case. " *The Quarterly Review of Economics and Finance*, 62: 56–65.

Cartier-Bresson, Jean. 1997. "Corruption Networks, Transaction Security and Illegal Social Exchange." In Paul Heywood (ed.), *Political Corruption*, 47–60. Oxford: Blackwell Publishers.

Carvalho, Fernando J. Cardim de. 2016. "Looking into the Abyss? Brazil at the Mid-2010s." *Journal of Post Keynesian Economics*, 39: 93–114.

Carvalho, José Murilo de. 2002. 3rd ed. *Cidadania no Brasil: o longo caminho.* Rio de Janeiro: Civilização Brasileira.

Carvalho, Laura. 2018. *Valsa brasileira: do boom ao caos econômico.* São Paulo: Todavia, Kindle edition.

Casado, José, Danielle Nogueira, Ramona Ordoñez, and Bruno Rosa. 2016. "Aparelhamento de fundos de pensão afeta 500 mil aposentados." *G1*, February 21.

Casanova, Lourdes and Julian Kassum. 2014. *The Political Economy of an Emerging Global Power: In Search of the Brazil Dream.* New York: Palgrave MacMillan.

Cassin, Richard L. 2018. "Petrobras Smashes the Top Ten List (and We Explain Why)." *The FCPA Blog*, September 28. https://fcpablog.com

Castro, Marcus Faro de. 1997a. "The Courts, Law, and Democracy in Brazil." *International Social Science Journal*, 49: 241–52.

Castro, Marcus Faro de. 1997b. "O Supremo Tribunal Federal e a judicialização da política." *Revista Brasileira de Ciências Sociais*, 12: 147–56.

Cavalcante, Pedro and Gabriela Lotta. (eds.). 2015. *Burocracia de médio escalão: perfil, trajetória e atuação.* Brasília: ENAP.

Centeno, Miguel A. and Patricio Silva. 1998. "The Politics of Expertise in Latin America: Introduction." In Miguel A. Centeno and Patricio Silva (eds.), *The Politics of Expertise in Latin America*, 1–12. Basingstoke: Macmillan Press.

CEPESP (Centro de Estudos em Política e Economia do Setor Público, FGV). 2019. "Os custos da campanha eleitoral no Brasil." Fundação Getulio Vargas, May 14.

CGU (Controladoría Geral da União). 2016. "Relatório de acompanhamento das punições expulsivas aplicadas a estatutários no âmbito da administração pública federal." www.cgu.gov.br/assuntos/atividade-disciplinar/relatorios-de-punicoes-expulsivas/arquivos/consolidado-por-ano-2003-a-2016.pdf

Chagas, Cláudia. 2012. "ENCCLA – A integração necessária." In Ricardo Andrade Saadi, Roberto Biasoli, and Ana Paula da Cunha (eds.), *ENCCLA: Estratégia Nacional de Combate à Corrupção e à Lavagem de Dinheiro: 10 anos de organização do Estado brasileiro contra o crime organizado*, 44–5. Brasília: Ministério da Justiça.

Chaia, Vera and Marco Antonio Teixeira. 2001. "Democracia e escândalos políticos." *São Paulo em Perspectiva*, 15: 62–75.

Chaisty, Paul, Nic Cheeseman, and Timothy J. Power. 2018. *Coalitional Presidentialism in Comparative Perspective: Minority Presidents in Multiparty Systems.* Oxford: Oxford University Press.

Chang, Ha-Joon. 1994. *The Political Economy of Industrial Policy.* London: Macmillan.

Chang, Ha-Joon. 1999. "The Economic Theory of the Developmental State." In Meredith Woo-Cumings (ed.), *The Developmental State*, 182–99. Ithaca, NY: Cornell University Press.

Chang, Ha-Joon. 2002. *Kicking Away the Ladder: Development Strategy in Historical Perspective.* London: Anthem Press.

References 315

Cheibub, José A., Adam Przeworski, and Sebastian M. Saiegh. 2004. "Government Coalitions and Legislative Success under Presidentialism and Parliamentarism." *British Journal of Political Science*, 34: 565–87.

Claessens, Stijn, Erik Feijen, and Luc Laeven. 2008. "Political Connections and Access to Finance: The Role of Campaign Contributions." *Journal of Financial Economics*, 88: 554–80.

Coatsworth, John H. 2005. "Structures, Endowments, and Institutions in the Economic History of Latin America." *Latin American Research Review*, 40: 126–44.

Codato, Adriano and Marco Cavalieri. 2015. "Diretores do Banco Central do Brasil nos governos Cardoso, Lula e Dilma: uma radiografia dos seus backgrounds educacionais." *Newsletter: The Observatory of Social and Political Elites of Brazil*, 2: 5.

Codato, Adriano and Paulo Franz. 2018. "Ministros-técnicos e ministros-políticos nos governos do PSDB e do PT." *Revista de Administração Pública*, 52: 776–96.

Cohen, Michael D., James March, and Johan P. Olsen. 1972. "A Garbage Can Model of Organizational Choice." *Administrative Science Quarterly*, 17: 1–25.

Colby, Seth Stevens. 2013. "Searching for Institutional Solutions to Industrial Policy Challenges: A Case Study of the Brazilian Development Bank." Unpublished Ph.D. dissertation, Johns Hopkins University.

Comin, Alexandre. 1998. *De volta para o futuro: política e reestruturação industrial no setor automobilístico nos anos 1990*. São Paulo: Anablume.

Coronel, Daniel Arruda, Antônio Carvalho Campos, André Filipe Zago de Azevedo, and Fátima Marília Andrade de Carvalho. 2011. "Impactos da política de desenvolvimento produtivo na economia brasileira: uma análise de equilíbrio geral computável." *Pesquisa e Planejamento Econômico*, 41: 337–65.

Coronel, Daniel Arruda, André Filipe Zago de Azevedo, and Antônio Carvalho Campos. 2014. "Política industrial e desenvolvimento econômico: a reatualização de um debate histórico." *Revista de Economia Política*, 34: 103–18.

Corrêa, Izabela Moreira. 2011. "Sistema de integridade: avanços e agenda de ação para a administração pública federal." In Leonardo Avritzer and Fernando Filgueiras, (eds.), *Corrupção e sistema político no Brasil*, 163–90. Rio de Janeiro: Editora Civilização Brasileira.

Correa, Paulo, Marcus Melo, Bernardo Mueller, and Carlos Pereira. 2008. "Regulatory Governance in Brazilian Infrastructure Industries." *The Quarterly Review of Economics and Finance*, 48: 202–16.

Corrêa, Victor, José Marcelo de Castro, and Cláudia Souza Passador. 2017. "Policy of Ethanol in Brazil: Current Scenario and Research Agenda." *Revista Capital Científico*, 15. revistas.unicentro.br/index.php/capitalcientifico/article/viewFile/4775/3441

Coslovsky, Salo, Roberto Pires, and Renato Bignami. 2017. "Resilience and Renewal: The Enforcement of Labor Laws in Brazil." *Latin American Politics and Society*, 59: 77–102.

Costa, Sérgio, Barbara Fritz, and Martina Sproll. 2015. "Dilma 2.0: From Economic Growth with Distribution to Stagnation and Increasing Inequalities?" *LASA Forum*, Summer 2015: Vol XLVI, Issue 3.

Coutinho, Diogo R., Clarissa Ferreira de Melo Mesquita, and Maria Virginia Nabuco do Amaral Mesquita Nasser. 2019. "Empresas estatais entre serviços públicos e atividades econômicas." *Revista Direito GV*, 15: 1–23.

Coutinho, Luciano. 2010. "A construção dos fundamentos para o crescimento sustentável da economia brasileira." In Ana Cláudia Além and Fabio Giambiagi (eds.), *O BNDES em um Brasil em transição*, 17–38. Rio de Janeiro: BNDES.

Cox, Gary W. and Mathew D. McCubbins. 2001. "The Institutional Determinants of Economic Policy Outcomes." In Stephan Haggard and Mathew D. McCubbins (eds.), *Presidents, Parliaments, and Policy*, 21–63. Cambridge: Cambridge University Press.

CPDOC. 2009. "Lei de Responsabilidade Fiscal." Verbete Temático. Faculdade Getúlio Vargas. www.fgv.br/cpdoc/acervo/dicionarios/verbete-tematico/lei-de-responsabilidade-fiscal

Crisostomo, Vicente Lima, Felix Javier Lopez Iturriaga, and Eleuterio Vallelado Gonzalez. 2014. "Financial Constraints for Investment in Brazil." *International Journal of Managerial Finance*, 10: 73–92.

Crisp, Brian F., Scott W. Desposato, and Kristin Kanthak. 2011. "Legislative Pivots, Presidential Powers, and Policy Stability." *Journal of Law, Economics, and Organization*, 27: 426–52.

Crouch, Colin. 2005. "Three meanings of complementarity," in edited "Dialogue on 'Institutional complementarity and political economy,'" between Colin Crouch, Wolfgang Streeck, Robert Boyer, Bruno Amable, Peter A. Hall, and Gregory Jackson. *Socio-Economic Review*, 3: 359–82.

Crouch, Colin. 2010. "Complementarity." In John L. Campbell Glenn Morgan, Colin Crouch, Ove Kaj Pedersen, and Richard Whitley (eds.), *The Oxford Handbook of Comparative Institutional Analysis*, 117–37. Oxford: Oxford University Press.

Cruz, Cláudia Ferreira and Luís Eduardo Afonso. 2018. "Fiscal Management and Pillars of the Fiscal Responsibility Law in Brazil: Evidence in Large Municipalities." *Brazilian Journal of Public Administration*, 52: 126–48.

Cruz, Valdo. 2018. "Bolsonaro enquadra Paulo Guedes e gera apreensão no mercado." *G1*, September 20.

Cunha, Paulo Roberto and Neli Aparecida de Mello-Théry. 2017. "Financiamento privado de campanha eleitoral: o agronegócio bancando a queda do Código Florestal brasileiro de 1965." *Guaju: Revista Brasileira de Desenvolvimento Territorial Sustentável*, 3: 3–31.

Cypher, James M. 2015. "Emerging Contradictions of Brazil's Neo-Developmentalism: Precarious Growth, Redistribution, and Deindustrialization." *Journal of Economic Issues*, 49: 617–48.

Cysne, Rubens Penha and Carlos Thadeu de F. Gomes. 2017. "Brasil: o custo do atraso no equacionamento da questão fiscal." *Revista de Economia Política*, 37: 704–18.

D'Araújo, Maria Celina. 1982. *O segundo governo Vargas (1951–54)*. Rio de Janeiro: Zahar Editores.

Da Ros, Luciano. 2010. "Judges in the Formation of the Nation State: Professional Experiences, Academic Background, and Geographic Circulation of Members

References

of the Supreme Courts of Brazil and the United States." *Brazilian Political Science Review*, 4: 102–30.

Da Ros, Luciano. 2014. "Mayors in the Dock: Judicial Responses to Local Corruption." Unpublished PhD dissertation, University of Illinois at Chicago.

Da Ros, Luciano and Matthew M. Taylor. 2019a. "Kickbacks, Crackdown, and Backlash: Legal Accountability in the Lava Jato Investigation." Paper presented at seminar on *"Política y derecho en América Latina: Nuevas preguntas, viejos desafíos,"* Universidad del Rosario, Bogotá, Colombia, October 25–26.

Da Ros, Luciano and Matthew M. Taylor. 2019b. "Juízes eficientes, Judiciário ineficiente no Brasil pós-1988." *Revista BIB*, 89: 1–31.

Dallagnol, Deltan. 2017. *A luta contra a corrupção: a Lava Jato e o futuro de um país marcado pela impunidade*. São Paulo: Primeira Pessoa.

Dargent, Eduardo. 2014. "Determinantes internacionales de la capacidad de las agencias estatales." *Apuntes*, 41: 9–40.

Dargent, Eduardo. 2015. *Technocracy and Democracy in Latin America: The Experts Running Government*. New York: Cambridge University Press.

Dargent, Eduardo, Gabriela Lotta, José Antonio Mejía, and Gilberto Moncada. 2018. *Who Wants to Know?: The Political Economy of Statistical Capacity in Latin America*. Washington, DC: Inter-American Development Bank.

Datz, Giselle. 2013. "Brazil's Pension Fund Developmentalism." *Competition and Change*, 17: 111–28.

De Bonis, Daniel. 2015. "Politicisation of the Federal Civil Service in Brazil: An Empirical Assessment." *The Public Sphere*, 3: 4–15.

De Bonis, Daniel. 2016. "Lógicas de recrutamento de elites dirigentes: padrões de mudança e continuidade no governo federal brasileiro." Unpublished Ph.D. dissertation, Fundação Getulio Vargas.

De Bonis, Daniel and Pacheco, Regina S. 2010. "Nem político nem burocrata: o debate sobre o dirigente público." In Fernando Luiz Abrucio, Maria Rita Loureiro, and Regina S. Pacheco (eds.), *Burocracia e política no Brasil: desafios para o Estado democrático no século XXI*, 273–295. São Paulo: FGV.

De Gregorio, José. 2009. "Implementation of Inflation Targets in Emerging Markets." In Gill Hammond, Ravi Kanbur, and Eswar Prasad (eds.), *Monetary Policy Frameworks for Emerging Markets*, 40–59. Cheltenham, UK: Edward Elgar.

De Toni, Jackson. 2014. "Dez anos da política industrial: conquistas e desafios a superar." *Carta Capital*, April 2, 2014.

Deeg, Richard. 2007. "Complementarity and institutional change in capitalist systems." *Journal of European Public Policy*, 14: 611–30.

Deeg, Richard and Gregory Jackson. 2007. "The State of the Art: Towards a More Dynamic Theory of Capitalist Variety." *Socio-Economic Review*, 5: 149–79.

Dezalay, Yves and Bryant G. Garth. 2002. *Internationalization of Palace Wars: Lawyers, Economists, and the Contest to Transform Latin American States*. Chicago: University of Chicago Press.

DIAP. 2011. "Bancadas informais no Congresso Nacional em 2011." *Radiografia do Novo Congresso 2011/2015*, Brasília: DIAP 2011.

318

References

Diaz-Alejandro, Carlos F. 1984. "Latin America in the 1930s." In Rosemary Thorp (ed.), *Latin America in the 1930s: The Role of the Periphery in World Crisis*, 17–49. New York: St. Martin's Press.

Dieguez, Consuelo. 2013. "Colheita amarga." *Revista piauí*, 78: 18–24.

Dieguez, Consuelo. 2014. *Bilhões e lágrimas: a economia brasileira e seus atores*. São Paulo: Portfolio-Penguin.

Diniz, Eli. 2010. "Estado, variedades de capitalismo e desenvolvimento em países emergentes." *Desenvolvimento em Debate*, 1: 7–27.

Diniz, Eli. 2011. "Depois do neoliberalismo: rediscutindo a articulação Estado e desenvolvimento no novo milênio." In Renato Boschi (ed.), *Variedades de capitalismo, política e desenvolvimento na América Latina*, 31–55. Belo Horizonte: Editora UFMG.

Diniz, Eli and Renato Boschi. 2000. "Globalização, herança corporativa e a representação dos interesses empresariais: novas configurações no cenário pós-reformas." In Renato Boschi, Eli Diniz, and Fabiano Santos (eds.), *Elites políticas e econômicas no Brasil contemporâneo: a desconstrução da ordem corporativa e o papel do Legislativo no cenário pós-reformas*, 15–90. Rio de Janeiro: Fundação Konrad Adenauer.

Donaghy, Maureen. 2011. "Do Participatory Governance Institutions Matter? Municipal Councils and Social Housing Programs in Brazil." *Comparative Politics*, 44: 83–102.

Doner, Richard F. and Ansil Ramsay. 2000. "Rent-seeking and Economic Development in Thailand." In Mushtaq H. Khan and Kwame Sundaram Jomo (eds.), *Rents, Rent-seeking and Economic Development: Theory and Evidence in Asia*, 145–81. Cambridge: Cambridge University Press.

Doner, Richard F. and Ben Ross Schneider. 2016. "The Middle-Income Trap: More Politics than Economics." *World Politics*, 68: 608–44.

Dowbor, Mónika. 2009. "Da inflexão pré-constitucional ao SUS municipalizado." *Lua Nova* 78: 185–222.

Doyle, David. 2014. "The Political Economy of Policy Volatility in Latin America." *Latin American Politics and Society*, 56: 1–21.

Easterly, William. 2001. "The Lost Decades: Developing Countries' Stagnation in Spite of Policy Reform 1980–1998." *Journal of Economic Growth*, 6: 135–57.

Economist. 1995. "A Survey of Brazil: Half-empty or Half-full?" April 29.

Egan, Patrick J. W. 2015. "Crawling Up the Value Chain: Domestic Institutions and Non-Traditional Foreign Direct Investment in Brazil, 1990–2010." *Brazilian Journal of Political Economy*, 35: 156–74.

Engelmann, Fabiano and Júlia Veiga Vieira Mâncio Bandeira. 2017. "A construção da autonomia política do Judiciário na América Latina: Um estudo comparativo entre Argentina, Brasil, Chile, Colômbia e Venezuela." *Dados*, 60: 903–36.

Ernst & Young Global Fraud Survey. 2016. www.ey.com/gl/en/services/assur ance/fraud-investigation–dispute-services/ey-global-fraud-survey-2016

Escorel, Sarah. 2008. "História das políticas de saúde no Brasil de 1964 a 1990: do golpe militar à reforma sanitária." In Lígia Gianovella Sarah Escorel, Lenaura de Vasconcelos Costa Lobato, José Carvalho de Noronha, and Antonio Ivo de

References   319

Carvalho (eds.), *Políticas e sistema de saúde no Brasil*, 385–434. Rio de Janeiro: Fiocruz.

Escorel, Sarah, Dilene Raimundo do Nascimento, and Flavio Coelho Edler. 2005. "As origens da reforma sanitária e do SUS." In Nísia Trindade Lima, Silvia Gerschman, Flavio Coelho Edler, and Julio Manuel Suárez (eds.), *Saúde e democracia: história e perspectivas do SUS*, 59–81. Rio de Janeiro: Fiocruz.

Evans, Peter B. 1979. *Dependent Development: The Alliance of Multinational, State, and Local Capital in Brazil*. Princeton, NJ: Princeton University Press.

Evans, Peter B. 1992. "The State as Problem and Solution: Predation, Embedded Autonomy, and Adjustment." In Stephan Haggard and Robert R. Kaufman (eds.), *The Politics of Economic Adjustment*, 139–91. Princeton, NJ: Princeton University Press.

Evans, Peter B. 1995. *Embedded Autonomy: States and Industrial Transformation*. Princeton, NJ: Princeton University Press.

Evans, Peter B. and James E. Rauch. 1999. "Bureaucracy and Growth: A Cross-National Analysis of the Effects of 'Weberian' State Structures on Economic Growth." *American Sociological Review*, 64: 748–65.

Evans, Peter B. and James E. Rauch. 2000. "Bureaucratic Structure and Bureaucratic Performance in Less Developed Countries." *Journal of Public Economics*, 75: 49–71.

Fagnani, Eduardo. 2018. "Introdução: A reforma tributária necessária." In Eduardo Fagnani (ed.), *A reforma tributária necessária*, 13–42. São Paulo: ANFIP/FENAFISCO/Plataforma Política Social.

Falleti, Tulia G. 2010. "Infiltrating the State: The Evolution of Health Care Reforms in Brazil, 1964–1988." In James Mahoney and Kathleen Thelen (eds.), *Explaining Institutional Change: Ambiguity, Agency, and Power*, 38–62. New York: Cambridge University Press.

Faoro, Raymundo. 2001 [1975]. *Os donos do poder: formação do patronato político brasileiro*. 3rd ed. Porto Alegre: Editora Globo.

Feenstra, Robert C., Robert Inklaar, and Marcel P. Timmer (2015), "The Next Generation of the Penn World Table." *American Economic Review*, 105: 3150–82. www.ggdc.net/pwt

Fenwick, Tracy B. 2009. "Avoiding Governors: The Success of *Bolsa Família*." *Latin American Research Review*, 44: 102–31.

Fenwick, Tracy B. 2010. "The Institutional Feasibility of National-Local Policy Collaboration: Insights from Brazil and Argentina." *Journal of Politics in Latin America*, 2: 155–83.

Fernandes, Leticia and Manoel Ventura. 2017. "Capital estrangeiro na Embraer é muito 'bem-vindo,' disse Temer." *O Globo*, December 22.

Ficker, Sandra Kuntz. 2005. "From Structuralism to the New Institutional Economics: The Impact of Theory on the Study of Foreign Trade in Latin America." *Latin American Research Review*, 40: 145–62.

FIESP. 2017. "Panorama da indústria de transformação brasileira." 14th ed., June 30. https://goo.gl/aUNqnW

Figueiredo, Argelina Cheibub. 2001. "Instituições e política no controle do Executivo." *Dados*, 44: 689–727.

References

Figueiredo, Argelina Cheibub and Fernando Limongi. 1999. *Executivo e legislativo na nova ordem constitucional*. Rio de Janeiro: Editora FGV.

Figueiredo, Argelina Cheibub and Fernando Limongi. 2002. "Incentivos eleitorais, partidos e política orçamentária." *Dados*, 45: 303–44.

Figueiredo, Fernanda Odilla Vasconcellos de. 2019. "Oversee and Punish: Understanding the Fight Against Corruption Involving Government Workers in the Federal Executive Branch in Brazil." Unpublished Ph.D. dissertation, Faculty of Social Science and Public Policy, King's College London.

Finnemore, Martha. 1996. *National Interests in International Society*. Ithaca, NY: Cornell University Press.

Fiori, José Luis. 1992. "The Political Economy of the Developmentalist State in Brazil." *CEPAL Review*, 47: 173–86.

Fishlow, Albert. 2011. *Starting Over: Brazil since 1985*. Washington, DC: The Brookings Institution Press.

Fleischer, David. 2002. "Corruption in Brazil: Defining, Measuring, and Reducing." Washington, DC: Center for Strategic and International Studies.

Fleischer, David. 2017. *Brazil Focus*, July 1.

Flexor, Georges and Karina Kato. 2011. "As difíceis relações entre o governo e os usineiros." *Carta Maior*, June 13.

Folha de S. Paulo. 1996. "Ex-deputado liberou Centrão." January 29.

Folha de S. Paulo. 2016. "Obsoleta e excludente." August 7.

Folha de S. Paulo. 2017a. "Ideologia nacional." April 7.

Folha de S. Paulo. 2017b. "A sombra do Leviatã." May 8.

Folha de S. Paulo. 2017c. "Tabu estatal." December 29.

Folha de S. Paulo. 2018a. "Sem fim, sem fins." January 9.

Folha de S. Paulo. 2018b. "Aécio na Justiça," April 17.

Folha de S. Paulo. 2018c. "Com reeleição abaixo de 50%, Câmara terá renovação recorde." October 9.

Folha de S. Paulo. 2019a. "Leía a íntegra do discurso de Bolsonaro na cerimônia de posse no Congresso." January 1.

Folha de S. Paulo. 2019b. "Datafolha aponta que apoio à privatização cresce com Bolsonaro, mas ainda é minoritário." September 9.

Fraga, Arminio. 2004. "Latin America since the 1990s: Rising from the Sickbed?" *Journal of Economic Perspectives*, 18: 89–106.

Fraga, Arminio, Ilan Goldfajn, and André Minella. 2003. "Inflation Targeting in Emerging Market Economies." *NBER Macroeconomics Annual*, 18: 365–400.

France, Guilherme de Jesus. 2017. "A evolução da legislação brasileira contra a corrupção." In Michael Freitas Mohallem and Carlos Emmanuel Joppert Ragazzo (eds.), *Diagnóstico institucional: primeiros passos para um Plano Nacional Anticorrupção*, 39–70. Rio de Janeiro: Escola de Direito do Rio de Janeiro da Fundação Getulio Vargas.

Frassão, Caroline de Souza. 2016. "Lobby e proteção da indústria: uma análise do Plano Brasil Maior." Paper presented at the 40th Annual Meeting of the ANPOCS.

Freire, Vinicius Torres. 2018. "Amanhã é dia de cair na real." *Folha de S. Paulo*, October 28.

References 321

Freitas, Andréa. 2012. "Migração partidária na Câmara dos Deputados de 1987 a 2009." *Dados*, 55: 951–86.

Freitas, Vladimir de. 2014. "The Role of Regulatory Agencies." *Environmental Policy and Law*, 44: 552–61.

Frieden, Jeffrey. 1991. *Debt, Development, and Democracy: Modern Political Economy and Latin America*. Princeton, NJ: Princeton University Press.

Friedman, Thomas L. 1999. *The Lexus and the Olive Tree: Understanding Globalization*. New York: Farrar, Straus Giroux.

Furtado, Celso. 1978 (2nd ed.). *Economic Development of Latin America: Historical Background and Contemporary Problems*. Suzette Macedo (trans.). Cambridge: Cambridge University Press.

Furtado, Celso. 1984. *Cultura e desenvolvimento em época de crise*. Rio de Janeiro: Paz e Terra.

G1. 2015. "Estaleiro Mauá, RJ, fechas as portas por causa de questões financeiras." July 3.

G1. 2019a. "Discursos de Bolsonaro." January 1.

G1. 2019b. "BNDES divulga lista como os 50 maiores clientes do banco." January 18.

Galvão, Jane. 2000. "AIDS no Brasil: a agenda de construção de uma epidemia." Rio de Janeiro: Associação Brasileira Interdisciplinar de AIDS.

Galvin, Daniel J. 2012. "The Transformation of Political Institutions: Investments in Institutional Resources and Gradual Change in National Party Committees." *Studies in American Political Development*, 26: 50–70.

Garcia, Felipe, Adolfo Sachsida e Alexandre Xavier Ywata de Carvalho. 2018. "Impacto da desoneração da folha de pagamento sobre o emprego: novas evidências." *IPEA Texto para Discussão* 2357.

Garcia, Mauricio and Helio Gastaldi Filho. April 2007. "A participação do Estado brasileiro na sociedade: percepções da população em relação ao processo de privatização." Paper presented at the First Latin American Congress on Public Opinion, Uruguay.

Garcia-Escribano, Mercedes, Carlos Goes, and Izabela Karpowicz. 2015. "Filling the Gap: Infrastructure Investment in Brazil." IMF Working Paper.

Gaspar, Malu. 2014. *Tudo ou nada: Eike Batista e a verdadeira história do Grupo X*, 4th ed. Rio de Janeiro: Editora Record.

Geddes, Barbara. 1990. "Building State Autonomy in Brazil, 1930–1964." *Comparative Politics*, 22: 217–35.

Geddes, Barbara. 1994. *Politician's Dilemma: Building State Capacity in Latin America*. Berkeley, CA: University of California Press.

George, Alexander L. and Andrew Bennett. 2005. *Case Studies and Theory Development in the Social Sciences*. Boston, MA: MIT Press.

Gerchmann, Léo. 2000. "TCU contesta Regime Automotivo do NE." *Folha de S. Paulo*, September 3.

Gerschenkron, Alexander. 1962. *Economic Backwardness in Historical Perspective: A Book of Essays*. Cambridge: Harvard University Press.

Giambiagi, Fabio. 2008. "18 anos de política fiscal no Brasil: 1991/2008." *Economia Aplicada*, 12: 535–80.

Giambiagi, Fabio and Armando Castelar Pinheiro. 2012. *Além da euforia: riscos e lacunas do modelo brasileiro de desenvolvimento*. Rio de Janeiro: Elsevier.

Gibson, Christopher L. 2017. "The Consequences of Movement Office-Holding for Health Policy Implementation and Social Development in Urban Brazil." *Social Forces*, 96: 751–78.

Gielow, Igor. 2019. "Brasileiro rejeita privatização, diz Datafolha." *Folha de S. Paulo*, January 5.

Gill, Indermit and Homi Kharas, together with Deepak Bhattasali, Milan Brahmbhatt, Gaurav Datt, Mona Haddad, Edward Mountfield, Radu Tatucu, and Ekaterina Vostroknutova. 2007. *An East Asian Renaissance: Ideas for Economic Growth*. Washington, DC: The World Bank.

Godoy, Marcelo and Daniel Bramatti. 2017. "Desde 2013, prisões por corrupção cresceram 288%." *O Estado de S. Paulo*, June 25.

Goldstein, Judith. 1993. *Ideas, Interests, and American Trade Policy*. Ithaca, NY: Cornell University Press.

Goldstein, Judith and Robert O. Keohane. 1993. "Ideas and Foreign Policy: An Analytical Framework." In Judith Goldstein and Robert O. Keohane (eds.), *Ideas and Foreign Policy: Beliefs, Institutions, and Political Change*, 3–30. Ithaca, NY: Cornell University Press.

Gómez, Eduardo J. 2014. "What Reverses Decentralization? Failed Policy Implementation, Civic Supporters, or Central Bureaucrats' expertise? The Case of Brazil's AIDs Program." *Administration & Society*, 46: 929–59.

Gómez-Mera, Laura. 2007. "Macroeconomic Concerns and Intrastate Bargains: Explaining Illiberal Policies in Brazil's Automobile Sector." *Latin American Politics & Society*, 49: 113–40.

Gonçalves, Maetê Pedroso. 2012. "O ciclo da política nacional de concessão de benefícios tributários (2003–2010)." Unpublished M.A. thesis, Departamento de Ciência Política, Universidade de São Paulo.

Gootenberg, Paul. 2004. "Between a Rock and a Softer Place: Reflections on some Recent Economic History of Latin America." *Latin American Research Review*, 39: 239–52.

Gorter, Harry de, Dusan Drabik, Erika M. Kliauga, and Govinda R. Timilsina. 2013. "An Economic Model of Brazil's Ethanol-Sugar Markets and Impacts of Fuel Policies." The World Bank, Policy Research Working Paper 6524.

Gourevitch, Peter. 1986. *Politics in Hard Times: Comparative Responses to International Economic Crises*. Ithaca, NY: Cornell University Press.

Gouvêa, Gilda Figueiredo Portugal. 1994. *Burocracia e elites burocráticas no Brasil*. São Paulo: Paulicéia.

Gozetto, Andréa Cristina Oliveira and Clive S. Thomas. 2014. "Interest Groups in Brazil: A New Era and Its Challenges." *Journal of Public Affairs*, 14: 212–39.

Gragnolati, Michele, Magnus Lindelow, and Bernard Couttolenc. 2013. *Twenty Years of Health System Reform in Brazil: An Assessment of the Sistema Único de Saúde*. Washington, DC: World Bank.

Graham, Lawrence. 1968. *Civil Service Reform in Brazil: Principles versus Practice*. Austin, TX: University of Texas Press.

Granovetter, Mark. 1978. "Threshold Models of Collective Behavior." *American Journal of Sociology*, 83: 1420–43.

References

Grindle, Merilee S. 2012. *Jobs for the Boys: Patronage and the State in Comparative Perspective.* Cambridge, MA: Harvard University Press.

Guandalini, Giuliano. 2006. "Por que o Brasil não cresce como a China e a Índia?" *Veja,* August 16: 86–94.

Guerriero, Ian Ramalho. 2012. "Formulação e avaliação de política industrial e o caso da PDP." 2012. Unpublished Ph.D. dissertation, Universidade Federal do Rio de Janeiro.

Guimarães, Alexandre Queiroz. 2005. "Historical Institutionalism and Economic Policymaking – Determinants of the Pattern of Economic Policy in Brazil, 1930–1960." *Bulletin of Latin American Research,* 24: 527–42.

Haas, Peter M. 1992. "Introduction: Epistemic Communities and International Policy Coordination." *International Organization,* 46: 1–35.

Haggard, Stephan. 2018. *Developmental States.* New York: Cambridge University Press.

Haggard, Stephan and Robert R. Kaufman. 1992. "Institutions and Economic Adjustment." In Stephan Haggard and Robert R. Kaufman (eds.), *The Politics of Economic Adjustment,* 3–40. Princeton, NJ: Princeton University Press.

Haggard, Stephan and Robert R. Kaufman. 2008. *Development, Democracy, and Welfare States: Latin America, East Asia and Eastern Europe.* Princeton, NJ: Princeton University Press.

Hagopian, Frances. 1996. *Traditional Politics and Regime Change in Brazil.* New York: Cambridge University Press.

Hagopian, Frances. 2016. "Brazil's Accountability Paradox." *Journal of Democracy,* 27: 119–28.

Hagopian, Frances, Carlos Gervasoni, and Juan Andrés Moraes. 2009. "From Patronage to Program: The Emergence of Party-Oriented Legislators in Brazil." *Comparative Political Studies,* 42: 360–91.

Hall, Michael M. 2009. "The Labor Policies of the Lula Government." In Joseph L. Love and Werner Baer (eds.), *Brazil under Lula: Economy, Politics, and Society under the Worker-President,* 151–65. New York: Palgrave Macmillan.

Hall, Peter A. 1989. "Conclusion: The Politics of Economic Ideas." In Peter A. Hall (ed.), *The Political Power of Economic Ideas: Keynesianism across Nations,* 361–91. Princeton, NJ: Princeton University Press.

Hall, Peter A. and Daniel W. Gingerich. 2009. "Varieties of Capitalism and Institutional Complementarities in the Political Economy." *British Journal of Political Science,* 39: 449–82.

Hall, Peter A. and Kathleen Thelen. 2009. "Institutional Change in Varieties of Capitalism." *Socio-Economic Review,* 7: 7–34.

Hall, Peter E. and David Soskice. 2001. *Varieties of Capitalism: The Institutional Foundations of Comparative Advantage.* Oxford: Oxford University Press.

Hartmann, Dominik, Cristian Jara-Figueroa, Miguel Guevara, Alex Simoes, and César A. Hidalgo. 2016. "The Structural Constraints of Income Inequality in Latin America." *Integration & Trade Journal,* 40: 70–85.

Haydu, Jeffrey. 1998. "Making Use of the Past: Time Periods as Cases to Compare and as Sequences of Problem Solving." *American Journal of Sociology,* 104: 339–71.

Heclo, Hugh. 1978. "Issue Networks and the Executive Establishment." In Anthony King (ed.), *The New American Political System*. Washington, DC: American Enterprise Institute.

Heredia, Blanca and Ben Ross Schneider. 2003. "The Political Economy of Administrative Reform in Developing Countries." In Ben Ross Schneider and Blanca Heredia (eds.), *Reinventing Leviathan: The Politics of Administrative Reform in Developing Countries*, 1–29. University of Miami: North-South Center Press.

Hermann, Jennifer. 2010. "Development Banks in the Financial-Liberalization Era: The Case of BNDES in Brazil." *CEPAL Review, 100*: 189–203.

Higgins, Sean and Claudiney Pereira. 2014. "The Effects of Brazil's Taxation and Social Spending on the Distribution of Household Income." In Nora Lustig, Carola Pessino, and John Scott (eds.), "The Redistributive Impact of Taxes and Social Spending in Latin America." Special Issue, *Public Finance Review, 42*: 346–67.

Hiroi, Taeko. 2013. "Governability and Accountability in Brazil: Dilemma of Coalitional Presidentialism." *The Journal of Social Science, 75*: 39–59.

Hiroi, Taeko. 2016. "Malapportionment and Redistribution in the Brazilian Congress." Paper presented at the 2016 Meeting of the Brazilian Studies Association. Providence, Rhode Island.

Hiroi, Taeko and Lucio Rennó. 2016. "Agenda Setting and Gridlock in a Multi-Party Coalitional Presidential System: The Case of Brazil." In Eduardo Alemán and George Tsebelis (eds.), *Legislative Institutions and Lawmaking in Latin America*, 62–89. Oxford: Oxford University Press.

Hirschman, Albert O. 1968. "The Political Economy of Import Substituting Industrialization in Latin America." *Quarterly Journal of Economics, 82*: 1–32.

Hirschman, Albert O. 1987. "On the Political Economy of Latin American Development." *Latin American Research Review, 22*: 7–36.

Hirschman, Albert O. 1981. *Essays in Trespassing: Economics to Politics and Beyond*. New York: Cambridge University Press.

Hirschman, Albert O. 1989. "How the Keynesian Revolution was Exported from the United States and Other Comments." In Peter A. Hall (ed.), *The Political Power of Economic Ideas: Keynesianism across Nations*, 347–59. Princeton, NJ: Princeton University Press.

Hochstetler, Kathryn. 2011. "The Politics of Comparatively Good Times: Brazil in the Global Financial Crisis." Paper presented at the *International Studies Association Annual Meeting*, Montreal, Canada.

Hochstetler, Kathryn. 2017. "Environmental Politics in Brazil the Cross-Pressures of Democracy, Development, and Global Projection." In Peter R. Kingstone and Timothy J. Power (eds.), *Democratic Brazil Divided*, 97–112. Pittsburgh, PA: University of Pittsburgh Press.

Hochstetler, Kathryn and Alfred P. Montero. 2013. "The Renewed Developmental State: The National Development Bank and the Brazil Model." *The Journal of Development Studies, 49*: 1484–99.

Hoffmann, Florian and Bentes, Fernando R. N. M. 2008. "Accountability for Social and Economic Rights in Brazil." In Varun Gauri and Daniel M. Brinks (eds.),

References

Courting Social Justice: Judicial Enforcement of Social and Economic Rights in the Developing World, 100–45. New York: Cambridge University Press.

Holland, Márcio, Angelo Gurgel, Claudia Cerqueira, et al. 2019. "Zona Franca de Manaus: impactos, efetividade e oportunidades." São Paulo: FGV-EESP (Fundação Getulio Vargas - Escola de Economia de São Paulo). https://eesp.fgv.br/sites/eesp.fgv.br/files/estudos_fgv_zonafranca_manaus_abril_2019v2.pdf

Holston, James. 2008. *Insurgent Citizenship: Disjunctions of Democracy and Modernity in Brazil*. Princeton, NJ: Princeton University Press.

Horch, Dan. 2015. "In Good Times or Bad, Brazilian Banks Profit." *The New York Times*, August 13.

Hornbeck, J. F. 2006. "Brazilian Trade Policy and the United States." Washington, DC: Congressional Research Service Report for Congress.

Hundt, David and Jitendra Uttam. 2017. *Varieties of Capitalism in Asia: Beyond the Developmental State*. London: Palgrave Macmillan.

Huntington, Samuel. 1968. *Political Order in Changing Societies*. New Haven, CT: Yale University Press.

Hutchcroft, Paul and Erik Martinez Kuhonta. 2018. "Upending the 'Rules of the Game': Toward Greater Clarity in the Conceptualization of Institutions." Paper presented at the Annual Meeting of the American Political Science Association, Boston, MA, 29 August–1 September.

IMF Data Mapper. 2019. "Government expenditure, percent of GDP." www.imf.org/external/datamapper/datasets

Instituto Paulo Montenegro. 2018. "INAF Brasil 2018: resultados preliminares." https://goo.gl/NhpKkv

IPSOS Public Affairs. 2007. "Pulso Brasil: Estadão."

IPSOS Public Affairs. 2015. "Estudio sobre la coyuntura política y la complejidad cultural Argentina 2015."

Istoé. 2018. "Seis meses após reforma trabalhista, arrecadação de sindicatos desaba 88%." June 4.

Iversen, Torben. 2005. *Capitalism, Democracy, and Welfare*. Cambridge: Cambridge University Press.

Jacobsen, John Kurt. 1995. "Much Ado about Ideas: The Cognitive Factor in Economic Policy." *World Politics*, 47: 283–310.

Jenkins, Rhys. 1991. "The Political Economy of Industrialization: A Comparison of Latin American and East Asian Newly Industrializing Countries." *Development and Change*, 22: 197–231.

Jobim, Nelson A. and Luciano Inácio de Souza. 2018. "A regulamentácão do lobby: análise comparada entre América Latina, Brasil e Estados Unidos." In Milton Seligman and Fernando Mello (eds.), *Lobby desvendado: democracia, políticas públicas e corrupção no Brasil contemporâneo*, 45–66. Rio de Janeiro: Record.

Johnson, Chalmers. 1982. *MITI and the Japanese Miracle: The Growth of Industrial Policy, 1925–1975*. Stanford, CA: Stanford University Press.

Jota. 2019. "Pesquisa de opinião nacional, 300 Dias de Bolsonaro." October 29–November 2.

Judd, Elizabeth. 2011. "*O Momento Mágico:* Managing Public Affairs in Brazil." Washington, DC: Foundation for Public Affairs.

Kahler, Miles. 1992. "External Influence, Conditionality, and the Politics of Adjustment." In Stephan Haggard and Robert R. Kaufman (eds.), *The Politics of Economic Adjustment*, 89–138. Princeton, NJ: Princeton University Press.

Kaplan, Stephen B. 2013. *Globalization and Austerity Politics in Latin America*. Cambridge, MA: Cambridge University Press.

Karpowicz, Izabela and Mauricio Soto. 2018. "Rightsizing the Public Sector Wage Bill." In Antonio Spilimbergo and Krishna Srinivasan (eds.), *Brazil: Boom, Bust, and the Road to Recovery*, 223–40. Washington, DC: International Monetary Fund.

Kasahara, Yuri. 2011. "A regulação do setor financeiro brasileiro: uma análise exploratória das relações entre Estado e setor privado." In Renato Boschi (ed.), *Variedades de capitalismo, política e desenvolvimento na América Latina*, 194–227. Belo Horizonte: Editora UFMG.

Kastner, Tássia. 2019. "Para XP, eventual mudança na diretoria, promovida pelo governo, seria prejudicial à companhia." *Folha de S. Paulo*, January 29.

Kasznar, Istvan Karoly and Ivandro de Almeida Oliveira. 2019. "The Effect of the Participation of Financial Companies in Non-Financial Companies in Brazil." *Cadernos Ebape.br*, 17: 212–28.

Kaufman, Herbert. 1956. "Emerging Conflicts in the Doctrines of Public Administration." *American Political Science Review*, 50: 1057–73.

Kaufman, Robert R. 1990. "How Societies Change Developmental Models or Keep Them: Reflections on the Latin American Experience in the 1930s and the Postwar World." In Gary Gereffi and Donald L. Wyman (eds.), *Manufacturing Miracles: Paths of Industrialization in Latin America and East Asia*, 110–38. Princeton, NJ: Princeton University Press.

Khan, Mushtaq H. 2000a. "Rents, Efficiency and Growth." In Mushtaq H. Khan and Kwame Sundaram Jomo (eds.), *Rents, Rent-seeking and Economic Development: Theory and Evidence in Asia*, 21–69. Cambridge: Cambridge University Press.

Khan, Mushtaq H. 2000b. "Rent-seeking as Process." In Mushtaq H. Khan and Kwame Sundaram Jomo (eds.), *Rents, Rent-seeking and Economic Development: Theory and Evidence in Asia*, 70–144. Cambridge: Cambridge University Press.

Khan, Mushtaq H. and Kwame Sundaram Jomo. 2000. "Introduction." In Mushtaq H. Khan and Kwame Sundaram Jomo (eds.), *Rents, Rent-seeking and Economic Development: Theory and Evidence in Asia*, 1–20. Cambridge: Cambridge University Press.

Khanna, Tarun and Yishay Yafeh. 2007. "Business Groups in Emerging Markets: Paragons or Parasites?" *Journal of Economic Literature*, 45: 331–72.

Kharas, Homi and Harinder Kohli. 2011. "What is the Middle Income Trap, Why Do Countries Fall into It, and How Can It Be Avoided?" *Global Journal of Emerging Market Economies*, 3: 281–9.

Kingstone, Peter R. 1999. *Crafting Coalitions for Reform: Business Preferences, Political Institutions, and Neoliberal Reform in Brazil*. University Park, PA: Pennsylvania State University Press.

Kingstone, Peter R. 2000. "Muddling Through Gridlock: Economic Policy Performance, Business Responses, and Democratic Sustainability." In Peter

References

R. Kingstone and Timothy J. Power (eds.), *Democratic Brazil: Actors, Institutions and Processes*, 185–203. Pittsburgh, PA: University of Pittsburgh Press.

Kingstone, Peter R. 2001. "Why Free Trade 'Losers' Support Free Trade: Industrialists and the Surprising Politics of Trade Reform in Brazil." *Comparative Political Studies*, 34: 986–1010.

Kingstone, Peter R. 2011. *The Political Economy of Latin America: Reflections on Neoliberalism and Development*. New York: Routledge.

Kingstone, Peter R. and Timothy J. Power (eds.). 2017. *Democratic Brazil Divided*. Pittsburgh, PA: University of Pittsburgh Press.

Klein, Herbert S. and Francisco Vidal Luna. 2019. *Feeding the World: Brazil's Transformation into a Modern Agricultural Economy*. Cambridge: Cambridge University Press.

Klüger, Elisa. 2018. "Mapping the Inflections in the Policies of the Brazilian National Economic and Social Development Bank During the Nineties and Two Thousands within Social Spaces and Networks." *Historical Social Research-Historische Sozialforschung*, 43: 274–302.

Kohli, Atul. 2004. *State-Directed Development: Political Power and Industrialization in the Global Periphery*. New York: Cambridge University Press.

Koske, Isabell, Isabelle Wanner, Rosamaria Bitetti, and Omar Barbiero. 2015. "The 2013 update of the OECD's database on product market regulation: Policy insights for OECD and non-OECD countries." *OECD Economics Department Working Papers*, No. 1200.

Kröger, Markus. 2012. "Neo-Mercantilist Capitalism and Post-2008 Cleavages in Economic Decision-making Power in Brazil." *Third World Quarterly*, 33: 887–901.

Krueger, Anne O. 1974. "The Political Economy of the Rent-Seeking Society." *The American Economic Review*, 64: 291–303.

Krueger, Anne O. 1990. "Government Failures in Development." *Journal of Economic Perspectives*, 4: 9–23.

Kuran, Timur. 1991. "Now Out of Never: The Element of Surprise in the East European Revolutions of 1989." *World Politics*, 44: 7–48.

Kurlantzick, Joshua. 2016. *State Capitalism: How the Return of Statism is Transforming the World*. Oxford: Oxford University Press.

Kurtz, Marcus J. 2013. *Latin American State Building in Comparative Perspective: Social Foundations of Institutional Order*. Cambridge: Cambridge University Press.

LaForge, Gordon. 2017. "The Sum of Its Parts: Coordinating Brazil's Fight Against Corruption, 2003–2016." *Innovations for Successful Societies*, Princeton University. http://successfulsocieties.princeton.edu

Lamberson, P. J. and Scott E. Page. 2012. "Tipping Points." SFI Working Paper 2012-02-002. Santa Fé Institute.

Lamounier, Bolivar. 1992. "Estrutura institucional e governabilidade na década de 1990." In João Paulo dos Reis Velloso (ed.), *O Brasil e as reformas políticas*, 24–47. Rio de Janeiro: Editora José Olympia.

Lamounier, Bolivar. 1994. "Brazil at an Impasse." *Journal of Democracy*, 5: 72–87.

References

Lamounier, Bolívar. 1996. "Brazil: The Hyperactive Paralysis Syndrome." In Jorge I. Domínguez and Abraham F. Lowenthal (eds.), *Constructing Democratic Governance: South America in the 1990s*, 166–87. Baltimore, MD: The Johns Hopkins University Press.

Lamounier, Bolivar. 2005. *Da Independência a Lula: dois séculos de política brasileira*. São Paulo: Augurium Editora.

Landim, Raquel and Anaïs Fernandes. 2018. "Boeing fica com 80% da divisão de jatos comerciais da Embraer por US $ 3,8 bi." *Folha de S. Paulo*, July 5.

Latin News. 2018. "Brazil: Petrobras wins out over politics." *Weekly Report*, 17 May.

Lazzarini, Sérgio G. 2010. *Capitalismo de laços: os donos do Brasil e suas conexões*. Rio de Janeiro: Elsevier–Campus.

Lazzarini, Sérgio G. 2018. "Percepções sobre propostas de privatização: análise preliminar com dados brasileiros." Mimeo, São Paulo: INSPER, August.

Lazzarini, Sérgio G., Thiago Lima, and Pedro Makhoul. 2017. "Como aumentar a atração do capital privado para projetos de infraestrutura no Brasil?" In Affonso Celso Pastore (ed.), *Infraestrutura: eficiência e ética*, 235–61. Rio de Janeiro: Elsevier.

Lazzarini, Sérgio G., Aldo Musacchio, Rodrigo Bandeira-de- Mello, and Rosilene Marcon. 2015. "What Do Development Banks Do? Evidence from Brazil, 2002–2009." *World Development*, 66: 237–53.

Leahy, Joe. 2011. "Brazil: Credit to Redeem." *Financial Times*, July 12.

Leahy, Joe. 2015. "BNDES: Lender of First Resort for Brazil's Tycoons." *Financial Times*, January 11.

Leal, Leila. 2015. "As desonerações tributárias concedidas ao setor privado e seus impactos sobre os trabalhadores." *Brasil de Fato*, January 15. https://goo.gl/hxLVfy

Leff, Nathaniel. 1968. *Economic Policy-Making and Development in Brazil 1947–1964*. New York: John Wiley & Sons.

Lehmbruch, Gerhard and Philippe C. Schmitter (eds.). 1982. *Patterns of Corporatist Policy-Making*. London: Sage.

Leite, Cristiane Kerches da Silva. 2005. "O processo de ordenamento fiscal no Brasil na década de 1990 e a Lei de Responsabilidade Fiscal." Unpublished Ph.D. dissertation, Department of Political Science, University of São Paulo.

Lemos, Leany B. and Timothy J. Power. 2013. "Determinantes do controle horizontal em parlamentos reativos: o caso do Brasil (1988–2005)." *Dados*, 56: 383–412.

Lemos, Leany Barreiro, João Henrique Pederiva, and Daniel Marcelino. 2010. "Porque dinheiro importa: dinâmica das contribuições eleitorais para o Congresso Nacional em 2002 e 2006." *Opinião Pública*, 16: 366–93.

Lengyel, Miguel. 2012. Interview. Author interview with Lengyel, Director, FLACSO Argentina, June 21.

Levcovitz, Silvio. 2017. "A corrupção e a atuação da Justiça Federal brasileira: 1991–2014." Unpublished M.A. Thesis, Unicamp.

Lijphart, Arend. *Patterns of Democracy: Government Forms and Performance in Thirty-Six Countries*. New Haven, CT: Yale University Press, 1999.

References

Lima Jr., Olavo Brasil de. 2000. "Presidential Elections: Centrality, Context and Implications." *Revista Brasileira de Ciências Sociais*, Special Issue 1: 53–72.

Lima, Mario Sergio. 2019. "An Economy on the Rocks? No Sweat for Brazil's Bust-Proof Banks." *Bloomberg*, May 26.

Limoeiro, Danilo and Ben Ross Schneider. 2017. "State-Led Innovation: SOEs, Institutional Fragmentation and Policy Making in Brazil." MIT-IPC Working Paper 17–004, September.

Limongi, Fernando. 2019. "Presidencialismo do desleixo: o modo Bolsonaro de governar." *Revista piauí, 158*: 40–3.

Limongi, Fernando and Rafael Cortez. 2010. "As eleições de 2010 e o quadro partidário." *Novos Estudos, 88*: 21–37.

Linz, Juan J. 1994. "Presidential or Parliamentary Democracy: Does It Make a Difference?" In Juan J. Linz and Arturo Valenzuela (eds.), *The Failure of Presidential Democracy*, 3–90. Baltimore, MD: Johns Hopkins University Press.

Lisboa, Marcos de Barros and Zeina Abdel Latif. 2013. "Democracy and Growth in Brazil." Insper Working Paper WPE 311.

Londoño, Ernesto. 2017. "Brazilian Lawmakers Reject Bribery Prosecution of President Michel Temer." *New York Times*, August 2.

Lopez, Felix Garcia, Maurício Bugarin, and Karina Bugarin. 2014. "Rotatividade nos cargos de confiança da Administração Federal brasileira (1999–2013)." *Revista do Serviço Público, 65*: 439–61.

Loureiro, Maria Rita. 1997. *Os economistas no governo: gestão econômica e democracia*. Rio de Janeiro: Editora FGV.

Loureiro, Maria Rita. 2001. "Instituições, política e ajuste fiscal." *Revista Brasileira de Ciências Sociais, 16*: 75–96.

Loureiro, Maria Rita. 2009. "Economists in the Brazilian Government: From Developmentalist State to Neoliberal Policies." In Verónica Montecinos and John Markoff (eds.), *Economists in the Americas*, 100–41. Cheltenham: Edward Elgar.

Loureiro, Maria Rita. 2010. "Democracia e políticas públicas: o papel da burocracia e dos partidos politicos." In Fabio de Sá e Silva, Felix Garcia Lopez, and Roberto Rocha C. Pires (eds.), *Estado, instituições e democracia: democracia*, 305–36. Brasília: IPEA.

Loureiro, Maria Rita and Fernando Abrucio. 1999. "Política e burocracia no presidencialismo brasileiro: o papel do Ministério da Fazenda no primeiro governo Fernando Henrique Cardoso." *Revista Brasileira de Ciências Sociais, 14*, 69–89.

Loureiro, Maria Rita and Fernando Abrucio. 2004. "Política e reformas fiscais no Brasil recente." *Revista de Economia Política*, 24: 50–72.

Loureiro, Maria Rita, Fernando Luiz Abrucio, and Regina Silvia Pacheco (eds.). 2010. *Burocracia e política no Brasil: desafios para o Estado democrático no século XXI*. Rio de Janeiro: Editora FGV.

Love, Joseph L. 1996. "Economic Ideas and Ideologies in Latin America since 1930." In Leslie Bethell (ed.), *Ideas and Ideologies in Twentieth Century Latin America*, 207–74. Cambridge: Cambridge University Press.

Love, Joseph L. 2005. "The Rise and Decline of Economic Structuralism in Latin America: New Dimensions." *Latin American Research Review*, 40: 100–25.

Love, Joseph L. 2009. "The Lula Government in Historical Perspective." In Joseph L. Love and Werner Baer (eds.), *Brazil under Lula: Economy, Politics, and Society under the Worker-President*, 305–15. New York: Palgrave Macmillan.

Lucon, Oswaldo and José Goldemberg. 2009. "Crise financeira, energia e sustentabilidade no Brasil." *Estudos Avancados*, 23: 121–30.

Luna, Francisco Vidal and Herbert S. Klein. 2006. *Brazil since 1980*. Cambridge: Cambridge University Press.

Lustig, Nora. 2016. "Domestic Resource Mobilization and the Poor." Background paper for Expert Group Meeting: "Strategies for eradicating poverty to achieve sustainable development for all." June 1–3. http://www.un.org/esa/socdev/egms/docs/2016/Poverty-SDGs/NoraLustig-paper.pdf

Lyne, Mona M. 2005. "Parties as Programmatic Agents: A Test of Institutional Theory in Brazil." *Party Politics*, 11: 193–216.

Lyne, Mona M. 2015. "Rethinking the Political Economy of Import Substitution Industrialization in Brazil: A Clientelist Model of Development Policymaking." *Latin American Politics and Society*, 57: 75–98.

Macedo, Fausto. 2011. "Manifesto ataca anistia para dinheiro repatriado." *O Estado de S. Paulo*, March 22.

Macedo, Fausto and Ricardo Brandt. 2015. "Lava Jato completa um ano com parte dos processos na etapa final." *O Estado de S. Paulo*, March 15.

Madruga, Antenor. 2012. "Origens da ENCCLA." In Ricardo Andrade Saadi, Roberto Biasoli, and Ana Paula da Cunha (eds.), *ENCCLA: Estratégia Nacional de Combate à Corrupção e à Lavagem de Dinheiro: 10 anos de organização do Estado brasileiro contra o crime organizado*. Brasília: Ministério da Justiça.

Magnin, Eric. 2018. "Research Note: Varieties of Capitalism and Sustainable Development: Institutional Complementarity Dynamics or Radical Change in the Hierarchy of Institutions." *Journal of Economic Issues LII*, 4: 1143–58.

Mahoney, James. 2000. "Path Dependence in Historical Sociology." *Theory and Society*, 29: 507–48.

Maia, João M. E. and Matthew M. Taylor. 2015. "The Brazilian Liberal Tradition and the Global Liberal Order." In Oliver Stuenkel and Matthew M. Taylor (eds.), *Brazil on the Global Stage: Power, Ideas, and the Liberal International Order*, 35–56. New York: Palgrave MacMillan.

Mainwaring, Scott. 1993. "Brazilian Party Underdevelopment in Comparative Perspective." *Political Science Quarterly*, 107: 677–708.

Mainwaring, Scott. 1995. "Brazil: Weak Parties, Feckless Democracy." In Scott Mainwaring and Timothy R. Scully (eds.), *Building Democratic Institutions: Party Systems in Latin America*, 354–98. Stanford, CA: Stanford University Press.

Mainwaring, Scott and Matthew Soberg Shugart. 1997. *Presidentialism and Democracy in Latin America*. New York: Cambridge University Press.

Mainwaring, Scott, Timothy J. Power, and Fernando Bizzarro. 2017. "The Uneven Institutionalization of a Party System: Brazil." In Scott Mainwaring (ed.), *Party Systems in Latin America: Institutionalization, Decay, and Collapse*, 164–200. Cambridge: Cambridge University Press.

References

Maisonnave, Fabiano. 2019. "Tem toda essa riqueza e vai viver só de diferença de impostos?, questiona Guedes sobre Zona Franca." *Folha de São Paulo*, July 25.

Malan, Pedro S. 1986. "Relações econômicas internacionais do Brasil (1945–1964)." In Boris Fausto (ed.), *História geral da civilização brasileira*, 51–106. São Paulo: Difel.

Malloy, James. (ed.). 1977. *Authoritarianism and Corporatism in Latin America*. Pittsburgh, PA: University of Pittsburgh Press.

Mancuso, Wagner Pralon. 2003. "Construindo leis: os construtores e as concessões de serviços." *Lua Nova*, 58: 61–87.

Mancuso, Wagner Pralon. 2004. "O lobby da indústria no Congresso Nacional: empresariado e política no Brasil contemporâneo." *Dados*, 47: 505–47.

Mancuso, Wagner Pralon. 2007. "O empresariado como ator político no Brasil: balanço da literatura e agenda de pesquisa." *Revista Sociologia e Política*, 28: 131–46.

Mancuso, Wagner Pralon. 2015. "Investimento eleitoral no Brasil: balanço da literatura (2001–2012) e agenda de pesquisa." *Revista Sociologia e Política*, 23: 155–83.

Mancuso, Wagner Pralon and Amâncio Jorge Oliveira. 2006. "Abertura econômica, empresariado e política: os planos doméstico e internacional." *Lua Nova*, 69: 147–72.

Mancuso, Wagner Pralon and Davi Cordeiro Moreira. 2013. "Benefícios tributários valem a pena? Um estudo de formulação de políticas públicas." *Revista de Sociologia e Política*, 21: 107–21.

Mancuso, Wagner Pralon and Bruno Wilhelm Speck. 2014. "Financiamento de campanhas e prestação de contas." *Cadernos Adenauer* XV, 1: 134–50.

Mancuso, Wagner Pralon and Bruno Wilhelm Speck. 2015. "Financiamento empresarial na eleição para deputado federal (2002–2010): determinantes e consequências." *Teoria & Sociedade*, 23: 1–23.

Mancuso, Wagner Pralon, Maitê Pedroso Gonçalves, and Fabrizio Mencarini. 2010. "Colcha de retalhos: a política de concessão de benefícios tributários ao empresariado no Brasil (1988–2006)." In Wagner Pralon Mancuso, Maria Antonieta Parahyba Leopoldi, and Wagner Iglecias (eds.), *Estado, empresariado e desenvolvimento no Brasil: novas teorias, novas trajetórias*, 213–37. São Paulo: Editora de Cultura.

Mancuso, Wagner Pralon, Rodrigo Rossi Horochovski, and Neilor Fermino Camargo. 2016. "Empresários e financiamento de campanhas na eleição presidencial brasileira de 2014." *Teoria e Pesquisa*, 25: 38–64.

Marchetti, Vitor. 2008. "Poder Judiciário e competição política no Brasil: uma análise das decisões do TSE e do STF sobre as regras eleitorais." Unpublished Ph.D. dissertation, Pontifícia Universidade Católica de São Paulo.

Marchetti, Vitor and Rafael Cortez. 2009. "A judicialização da competição política: o TSE e as coligações eleitorais." *Opinião Pública*, 15: 422–50.

Marenco dos Santos, André Luiz and Luciano Da Ros. 2017. "Além do presidencialismo de coalizão: agendas de pesquisa da ciência política brasileira." Unpublished working paper, Universidade Federal de Santa Caterina.

Mares, David R. and Harold A. Trinkunas. 2016. *Aspirational Power: Brazil on the Long Road to Global Influence*. Washington, DC: The Brookings Institution.

Markwald, Ricardo. 2005. "The Political Economy of Foreign Trade Policy: The Brazilian Case." In Roberto Bouzas (ed.), *Domestic Determinants of National Trade Strategies: A Comparative Analysis of Mercosur Countries, Mexico and Chile*, 85–143. Paris: Obreal-Chaire Mercosur Sciences Po.

Marques, Hugo. 2003. "Banestado: Investigacao sem recursos." *Jornal do Brasil*, June 20.

Martin, Cathie Jo and Duane Swank. 2012. *The Political Construction of Business Interests: Coordination, Growth, and Equality*. New York: Cambridge University Press.

Martins, Luciano. 1985. *Estado capitalista e burocracia no Brasil pós-64*. Rio de Janeiro: Paz e Terra.

Martone, Celso L. 1993. "O conceito brasileiro de moeda." *Braudel Papers*, 4: 1–8.

Mattei, Lauro and Anthony W. Pereira. 2015. "Dilemmas of Brazilian Economic Development in the Twenty-First Century." In Anthony Pereira, Lauro Mattei, and Amanda LaCouteur (eds.), *The Brazilian Economy Today: Toward a New Socio-Economic Model?*, 1–25. New York: Palgrave Macmillan.

Mattos, César. 2013. "O que é o Plano Brasil Maior?" *Brasil: Economia e Política*. www.brasil-economia-governo.org.br/2013/10/23/o-que-e-o-plano-brasil-maior

Máximo, Wellton. 2011. "Plano Brasil Maior deve tornar mais difícil equilíbrio fiscal em 2012, diz ex-secretário de Política Econômica." *Agência Brasil*, August 6.

Mayka, Lindsay. 2019a. *Building Participatory Institutions in Latin America: Reform Coalitions and Institutional Change*. New York: Cambridge University Press.

Mayka, Lindsay. 2019b. "The Origins of Strong Institutional Design: Policy Reform and Participatory Institutions in Brazil's Health Sector." *Comparative Politics*, 51: 275–94.

McCann, Bryan. 2008. *The Throes of Democracy: Brazil since 1989*. Nova Scotia, Canada: Fernwood Publishing.

McFarland, Andrew S. 2004. *Neopluralism: The Evolution of Political Process Theory*. Lawrence, KS: University Press of Kansas.

McGuire, James W. 2010. *Wealth, Health, and Democracy in East Asia and Latin America*. New York: Cambridge University Press.

McGuire, James W. 2012. "Social Policies in Latin America: Causes, Characteristics and Consequences." In Peter Kingstone and Deborah J. Yashar (eds.), *Routledge Handbook of Latin American Politics*, 200–23. New York: Routledge.

McKay, Ben, Sérgio Sauer, Ben Richardson, and Roman Herre. 2016. "The Political Economy of Sugarcane Flexing: Initial Insights from Brazil, Southern Africa and Cambodia." *The Journal of Peasant Studies*, 43: 195–223.

McMenamin, Iain. 2012. "If Money Talks, What Does It Say?: Varieties of Capitalism and Business Financing of Parties." *World Politics*, 64: 1–38.

References

McQuerry, Elizabeth. 2001. "Managed Care for Brazil's Banks." *Federal Reserve Bank of Atlanta Economic Review*, 86: 27–44.

Medeiros, Marcelo and Pedro Souza. 2013. "Gasto público, tributos e desigualdade de renda no Brasil." *IPEA Texto para Discussão* 1844.

Medeiros, Marcelo, Pedro Herculano Guimarães Ferreira de Souza, and Fábio Ávila de Castro. 2015. "A estabilidade da desigualdade de renda no Brasil, 2006 a 2012: estimativa com dados do imposto de renda e pesquisas domiciliares." *Ciência e Saúde Coletiva*, 20: 971–86.

Medialdea, Bibiana. 2013. "Brazil: An Economy Caught in a Financial Trap (1993–2003)." *Brazilian Journal of Political Economy*, 33: 427–45.

Mello, Eduardo and Matias Spektor. 2018. "Brazil: The Costs of Multiparty Presidentialism." *Journal of Democracy*, 29: 113–27.

Mello, Patricia Campos. 2014. "Política de Dilma está quebrando o etanol, diz presidente de entidade." *Folha de S. Paulo*, April 14.

Melo, Carlos Ranulfo. 2006. "Sistema partidário, presidencialismo e reforma política no Brasil." In Glaúcio Ary Dillon Soares and Lucio R. Rennó (eds.), *Reforma política: lições da história recente*, 157–75. Rio de Janeiro: Editora FGV.

Melo, Carlos. 2018. "Relaçoes governamentais: significado, funcionamento e problemas da democracia no Brasil." In Milton Seligman and Fernando Mello (eds.), *Lobby desvendado: democracia, políticas públicas e corrupção no Brasil contemporâneo*, 147–82. Rio de Janeiro: Record.

Melo, Carlos Ranulfo and Rafael Câmara. 2012. "Estrutura da competição pela presidência e consolidação do sistema partidário no Brasil." *Dados*, 55: 71–117.

Melo, Liana. 2019. "Economistas do Real analisam desafio de retomar crescimento." *Revista Época*, June 27.

Melo, Marcus André. 2016. "Crisis and Integrity in Brazil." *Journal of Democracy*, 27: 50–65.

Melo, Marcus Andre and Carlos Pereira. 2013. *Making Brazil Work: Checking the President in a Multiparty System*. New York: Palgrave Macmillan.

Melo, Marcus André, Armando Barrientos, and André Canuto Coelho. 2014. "Taxation, Redistribution and the Social Contract in Brazil." IRIBA Working Paper: 11.

Mendes, Marcos. 2014. *Inequality, Democracy and Growth in Brazil: A Country at the Crossroads of Economic Development*. Amsterdam: Elsevier Academic Press.

Mendonça, Ricardo. 2015. "Crise do PT ameaça trajetória de queda da desigualdade, diz pesquisadora." *Folha de S. Paulo*, June 7.

Mettenheim, Kurt Eberhart. 2005. "Commanding Heights: Para uma sociologia política dos bancos federais brasileiros." *Revista Brasileira de Ciências Sociais*, 20: 47–66.

Mettenheim, Kurt Eberhart. 2010. *Federal Banking in Brazil: Policies and Competitive Advantages*. London: Pickering & Chatto Publishers.

Mettenheim, Kurt Eberhart and Maria Fernanda Freire de Lima. 2014. "Monetary Channels of Social Inclusion: A Case Study of Basic Income and the Caixa Econômica Federal in Brazil." *Revista de Administração Pública*, 48: 1451–74.

Michaud, Etienne. 2015. "Driving up the Local Content of Brazilian Cars: Inovar-Auto and Supply Chain Strategy." Brazil Works Briefing Paper.

Michener, Greg. 2010. "The Surrender of Secrecy: The Emergence of Strong Access to Information Laws in Latin America." Unpublished Ph.D. dissertation, University of Texas – Austin.

Michener, Gregory and Michael Freitas Mohallem. 2020. "A transparência piorou no governo Bolsonaro?" *Folha de S. Paulo*, March 1.

Milanez, Bruno and Rodrigo S. P. Santos. 2015. "Topsy-Turvy Neo-Developmentalism: An Analysis of the Current Brazilian Model of Development." *Revista de Estudios Sociales*, 53: 12–28.

Minella, Ary Cesar. 2007. "Maiores bancos privados no Brasil: um perfil econômico e sociopolítico." *Sociologias*, 9: 100–25.

Ministério da Fazenda, *Secretaria de Acompanhamento Econômico*. 2017. "Efeito redistributivo da política fiscal no Brasil." Brasília. www.fazenda .gov.br/centrais-de-conteudos/publicacoes/boletim-de-avaliacao-de-politicas-publicas/arquivos/2017/efeito_redistributivo_12_2017.pdf

Ministério da Fazenda. 2018. "Dívida pública federal: Plano Anual de Financiamento 2018." Brasília: Secretaria do Tesouro Nacional, número 18 (Janeiro). https://bit.ly/2wVm2O4

Ministério da Fazenda. 2019. "3° Orçamento de Subsídios da União," Ministério da Fazenda, Secretaria de Avaliação de Políticas Públicas, Planejamento, Energia e Loteria. www.economia.gov.br/central-de-conteudos/publicacoes/ boletim-subsidios/arquivos/2019/30-orcamento-subsidios-da-uniao.pdf/view

Ministério do Planejamento. 2014. "Perfil das empresas estatais federais." www .planejamento.gov.br/assuntos/empresas-estatais/publicacoes/perfil-das-empresas-estatais/perfil-das-empresas-estatais-2013

Ministry of Health of Brazil. Secretariat for Health Surveillance. 2017. "Responding to HIV and Zika in Brazil." April. www.iasociety.org/Web/Web Content/File/EduFundBrazil_11Presentation_AdeleSchwartzBenzaken.pdf

Miranda, Rodrigo Nunes de. 2013. "Zona Franca de Manaus: desafios e vulnerabilidades." Núcleo de Estudos e Pesquisas do Senado: Textos para Discussão 126. www12.senado.leg.br/publicacoes/estudos-legislativos/tipos-de -estudos/textos-para-discussao/td-126-zona-franca-de-manaus-desafios -e-vulnerabilidades

Modenesi, André de Melo and Rui Lyrio Modenesi. 2012. "Quinze anos de rigidez monetária no Brasil pós-Plano Real: uma agenda de pesquisa." *Revista de Economia Política*, 32: 389–411.

Molina, Oscar and Martin Rhodes. 2002. "Corporatism: The Past, Present, and Future of a Concept." *Annual Review of Political Science*, 5: 305–31.

Montecinos, Verónica and John Markoff. 2009. "Epilogue: A Glance Beyond the Neoliberal Moment." In Verónica Montecinos and John Markoff (eds.), *Economists in the Americas*, 309–30. Cheltenham: Edward Elgar.

Montecinos, Verónica, John Markoff, and María José Álvarez-Rivadulla. 2009. "Economists in the Americas: Convergence, Divergence and Connection." In Verónica Montecinos and John Markoff (eds.), *Economists in the Americas*, 1–62. Cheltenham: Edward Elgar.

References

Monteiro Lobato, José Bento Renato. 1933. "O país da tavolagem." In *Antevéspera: reações mentais dum ingênuo* [Ebooks Brasil, 2003]. São Paulo: Cia. Editora Nacional. www.ebooksbrasil.org/adobeebook/antevespera.pdf

Montero, Alfred P. 1998. "State Interests and the New Industrial Policy in Brazil: The Case of the Privatization of Steel, 1990–1994." *Journal of Interamerican Studies and World Affairs*, 40: 27–62.

Montero, Alfred P. 2000. "Devolving Democracy? Political Decentralization and the New Brazilian Federalism." In Peter R. Kingstone and Timothy J. Power (eds.), *Democratic Brazil: Actors, Institutions and Processes*, 58–76. Pittsburgh, PA: University of Pittsburgh Press.

Montero, Alfred P. 2001. "Decentralizing Democracy: Spain and Brazil in Comparative Perspective." *Comparative Politics*, 33: 149–69.

Montero, Alfred P. 2014a. *Brazil: Reversal of Fortune*. Cambridge: Polity Press.

Montero, Alfred P. 2014b. "Why Developmentalism Persists in Democratic Brazil." Paper presented at the annual conference of the Latin American Studies Association.

Moraes, Márcia Azanha Ferraz Dias de and David Zilberman. 2014. *Production of Ethanol from Sugarcane in Brazil*. Switzerland: Springer International Publishing.

Moraes, Wallace dos Santos de. 2014. "Petismo e Chavismo: variedades de capitalismo e de regulação trabalhista no Brasil e na Venezuela." *Dados*, 57: 359–97.

Morais, Lecio and Alfredo Saad-Filho. 2012. "Neo-Developmentalism and the Challenges of Economic Policy-Making under Dilma Rousseff." *Critical Sociology*, 38: 789–98.

Morck, Randall, Daniel Wolfenzon, and Bernand Yeung. 2005. "Corporate Governance, Economic Entrenchment, and Growth." *Journal of Economic Literature*, XLIII: 655–720.

Moreira, Mauricio M. 2009. "Brazil's Trade Policy: Old and New Issues." IDB Working Paper Series, #IDB-WP-139.

Morgan, Glen, Richard Whitely, and Eli Moen (eds.). 2005. *Changing Capitalisms? Complementarities, Contradictions and Capability Development in an International Context*. Oxford: Oxford University Press.

Morgan, Marc. 2017. "Falling Inequality beneath Extreme and Persistent Concentration: New Evidence for Brazil Combining National Accounts, Surveys and Fiscal Data, 2001–2015." WID. world Working Paper Series No. 2017/12.

Moro, Sérgio Fernando. 2018. "Preventing Systemic Corruption in Brazil." *Daedalus*, 147: 157–68.

Movimento Brasil Competitivo. 2018. "Histórico." May 24. www.mbc.org.br/portal/historico

Mungiu-Pippidi, Alina. 2015. *The Quest for Good Governance: How Societies Develop Control of Corruption*. Cambridge: Cambridge University Press.

Musacchio, Aldo and Sérgio G. Lazzarini. 2014. *Reinventing State Capitalism: Leviathan in Business, Brazil and Beyond*. Cambridge: Harvard University Press.

Najberg, Sheila. 1989. "Privatização de recursos públicos: Os empréstimos do sistema BNDES ao setor privado nacional com correção monetária parcial." Unpublished M.A. Thesis. Rio de Janeiro: Economics Department, PUC-Rio.

References

Napolitano, Giuliana. 2018. "Banco Central autoriza compra da XP pelo Itaú, mas com restrições." *Revista Exame*, August 10.

Newman, Gray. 2016. "Was it ALL her fault? An Economist re-examines Brazil's Crisis." *Americas Quarterly*, September 30.

Nicolau, Jairo. 2002. "Como controlar o representante? Considerações sobre as eleições para a Câmara de Deputados no Brasil." *Dados*, 45: 219–36.

Nicolau, Jairo. 2017. *Representantes de quem: os (des)caminhos do seu voto da urna à Câmara dos Deputados*. Rio de Janeiro: Zahar.

Nobre, Marcos. 2010. "O fim da polarização." *Revista piauí*, 51. piaui.folha.uol.com.br/materia/o-fim-da-polarizacao

Nóbrega, Mailson da. 2005. *O futuro chegou: Instituições e desenvolvimento no Brasil*. São Paulo: Editora Globo.

Nóbrega, Mailson da and Gustavo Loyola. 2006. "The Long and Simultaneous Construction of Fiscal and Monetary Institutions." In Lourdes Sola and Laurence Whitehead (eds.), *Statecrafting Monetary Authority: Democracy and Financial Order in Brazil*, 57–84. Oxford: Centre for Brazilian Studies.

Nogueira, José Ricardo, Rozane Bezerra Siqueira, and Carlos Feitosa Luna. 2015. "Taxation, Inequality and the Illusion of the Social Contract in Brazil." *Revista Pesquisa & Debate*, 26: 190–209.

North, Douglass C. 1990. *Institutions, Institutional Change, and Economic Performance*. Cambridge: Cambridge University Press.

Nunes, Edson. 1997. *A gramática política no Brasil: clientelismo e insulamento burocrático*. 2003 ed. Rio de Janeiro: Jorge Zahar Editor.

Nunes, Rodrigo M. 2015. "The Politics of Sentencing Reform in Brazil: Autonomous Bureaucrats, Constrained Politicians and Gradual Policy Change." *Journal of Latin American Studies*, 47: 121–48.

Nunn, Amy. 2009. *The Politics and History of AIDS Treatment in Brazil*. New York: Springer.

NUPPS-ABJ (Núcleo de Estudos de Políticas Públicas da Universidade de São Paulo and Associação Brasileira de Jurimetria). 2019. "Justiça criminal, impunidade e prescrição." Brasília: Conselho Nacional de Justiça.

O Estado de S. Paulo. 2011. "Fiasco do Brasil Maior." September 7.

O Estado de S. Paulo. 2013. "Ibope: Dilma e Marina têm empate técnico no segundo turno." July 18.

O Estado de S. Paulo. 2014. "Efetivo da Polícia Federal aumentou no atual governo." September 27.

O Estado de S. Paulo. 2016. "Fórum pede para Senado resgatar projeto original." December 3.

O Globo. 2017. "Joesley pede para nomear president da Vale em troca de dinheiro a Aécio." May 23.

O Globo. 2018a. "País tem em vigor 11 leis que deveriam impedir a crise fiscal." January 15.

O Globo. 2018b. "Indústria tem menor participação no PIB desde os anos 1950." March 5.

OECD. 2016. "Programme for International Student Assessment (PISA) Results from PISA 2015 – Brazil." www.oecd.org/pisa/pisa-2015-Brazil.pdf

References

337

OECD. 2017a. "Brazil." In *Education at a Glance 2017: OECD Indicators*, OECD Publishing, Paris. doi:https://doi.org/10.1787/eag-2017-74-en

OECD. 2017b. "Brazil: Follow-up to the Phase 3 Report and Recommendations." February. www.oecd.org/corruption /anti-bribery/Brazil-Phase-3-Written-Follow-Up-Report-ENG.pdf

Oliveira, Ivan Tiago Machado. 2011. "Determinantes sistêmicos e domésticos da política comercial externa brasileira: uma análise das estratégias de negociação comercial do Brasil (1995–2010)." Unpublished Ph.D. dissertation in Administration, Universidade Federal da Bahia.

Oliveira, Ivan Tiago Machado. 2012. Author Interview with Oliveira, trade specialist and research at IPEA, Brasília, May 22.

Oliveira, Ivan, Pedro da Motta Veiga, Sandra Polónia Rios, and Fernando Ribeiro. 2019. *The Political Economy of Trade Policy in Brazil*. Brasília: IPEA.

Oliveira, Vanessa Elias de. 2009. "Poder Judiciário: árbitro dos conflitos constitucionais entre estados e União." *Lua Nova*, 78: 223–50.

Oliveira, Vanessa Elias de and Lincoln N. T. Noronha. 2011. "Judiciary-Executive Relations in Policy Making: The Case of Drug Distribution in the State of São Paulo." *Brazilian Political Science Review*, 5: 10–38.

Olivieri, Cecília. 2007. "Política, burocracia e redes sociais: as nomeações para o alto escalão do Banco do Brasil." *Revista de Sociologia e Política*, 29: 147–68.

Olivieri, Cecília. 2010. *A lógica política do controle interno: o monitoramento das políticas públicas no presidencialismo brasileiro*. São Paulo: Annablume Editora.

Onuki, Janina. 2010. "Interesses comerciais brasileiros na América do Sul." *Cadernos Adenauer*, 11: 90–6.

Paduan, Roberta. 2016. *Petrobras: uma história de orgulho e vergonha*. Rio de Janeiro: Objetiva.

Paes de Barros, Ricardo and Diana Coutinho. 2014. "As relações entre escolaridade e mercado de trabalho." *Revista Pátio*, March 20. https://loja .grupoa.com.br/revista-patio/artigo/10170/as-relacoes-entre-escolaridade-e-m ercado-de-trabalho.aspx

Palermo, Vicente. 2000. "Como se governa o Brasil? O debate sobre instituições políticas e gestão de governo." *Dados*, 43: 521–57.

Palermo, Vicente. 2016. "Brazilian Political Institutions: An Inconclusive Debate." *Brazilian Political Science Review*, 10: 1–29.

Pareto, Vilfredo. 1972 [1906]. *Manual of Political Economy*. Translated by Ann S. Schwier. London: MacMillan.

Pargendler, Mariana. 2016. "Governing State Capitalism: The Case of Brazil." In Benjamin L. Liebman and Curtis J. Milhaupt (eds.), *Regulating the Visible Hand?: The Institutional Implications of Chinese State Capitalism*, 377–402. Oxford: Oxford University Press.

Paula, Germano Mendes de and Ana Paula Avellar. 2008. "Reforms and Infrastructure Regulation in Brazil: The Experience of ANTT and ANTAQ." *The Quarterly Review of Economics and Finance*, 48: 237–51.

Pavão, Nara. 2015. "Failures of Electoral Accountability for Corruption: Brazil and Beyond." Unpublished PhD dissertation, University of Notre Dame.

References

Payne, J. Mark, Daniel Zovatto G., and Mercedes Mateo Díaz. 2007. *Democracies in Development: Politics and Reform in Latin America.* Washington, DC: Inter-American Development Bank.

Pedreira Campos, Pedro Henrique. 2014. *"Estranhas catedrais": as empreiteiras brasileiras e a ditadura civil-militar, 1964–1988.* Rio de Janeiro: Editora da UFF.

Pellegrini, Josué Alfredo. 2018. "Gastos (benefícios) tributários." Brasília: Instituição Fiscal Independente, Nota Técnica No. 17.

Pereira, Anthony W. 2016. "Is the Brazilian State 'Patrimonial'?" *Latin American Perspectives,* 43: 135–52.

Pereira, Carlos and Bernardo Mueller. 2002. "Comportamento estratégico em presidencialismo de coalizão: as relações entre Executivo e Legislativo na elaboração do orçamento Brasileiro." *Dados, 45:* 265–301.

Pereira, Carlos and Lucio Rennó. 2001. "O que é que o reeleito tem? Dinâmicas político-institucionais locais e nacionais nas eleições de 1998 para a Câmara dos Deputados." *Dados, 44:* 323–62.

Pereira da Costa, Katarina and Pedro da Motta Veiga. 2011. "O Brasil frente à emergência da África: comércio e política comercial." *Textos Cindes 24.*

Pessanha, Charles. 2009. "Controle externo: a função esquecida do Legislativo." In *O sociólogo e as políticas públicas: ensaios em homenagem a Simon Schwartzman.* Felipe F. Schwartzman, Isabel F. Schwartzman, Luisa F. Schwartzman, and Michel L. Schwartzman (eds.), 243–58. Rio de Janeiro: Fundação Getúlio Vargas.

Pessôa, Samuel. 2011. "O contrato social da redemocratização." In Edmar Lisboa Bacha and Simon Schwartzman (eds.), *Brasil: a nova agenda social,* 204–12. Rio de Janeiro: LTC.

Pessôa, Samuel. 2015. "Ainda não caiu a ficha." *Folha de São Paulo,* June 21.

Pessôa, Samuel. 2019. "O Pibinho e o conflito distributivo." *Folha de S. Paulo,* June 2.

Pierson, Paul. 2000. "Increasing Returns, Path Dependence, and the Study of Politics." *American Political Science Review,* 94: 251–67.

Pierson, Paul. 2004. *Politics in Time: History, Institutions, and Social Analysis.* Princeton, NJ: Princeton University Press.

Pires, Roberto and Gomide, Alexandre. 2014. "Burocracia, democracia e políticas públicas: arranjos institucionais de políticas de desenvolvimento." *IPEA Texto para Discussão 1940.*

Pochmann, Marcio and Anselmo Luís dos Santos. 1998. "Encargos sociais no Brasil: uma nova abordagem metodológica e seus resultados." Cadernos do CESIT (Texto para discussão n. 26). www.cesit.net.br/cesit/images/stories/26 Cadernos doCESIT.pdf

Polanyi, Karl. 1957. *The Great Transformation: The Political and Economic Origins of Our Time.* Boston, MA: Beacon Press.

Polga-Hecimovich, John. 2019. "Ideologia versus capacidade: Dilma Rousseff, as Forças Armadas e o Programa de Aceleração do Crescimento." In Luciana Santana (ed.), *Instituições, comportamento político e democracia,* 33–60. Alagoas: Editora Universidade Federal de Alagoas (UFAL).

References

Polga-Hecimovich, John and Alejandro Trelles. 2016. "The Organizational Consequences of Politics: A Research Agenda for the Study of Bureaucratic Politics in Latin America." *Latin American Politics & Society*, 58: 56–79.

Polícia Federal. 2014a. "Termo de Colaboração No. 01, Paulo Roberto Costa." Superintendência Regional no Estado do Paraná, August 29.

Polícia Federal. 2014b. "Termo de Colaboração No. 73, Paulo Roberto Costa." Superintendência Regional no Estado do Paraná, September 11.

Polícia Federal. 2017. "Estatística de Operações." July. www.pf.gov.br/imprensa/estatistica/operacoes

Pontes, Jorge and Márcio Anselmo. 2019. *Crime.gov: quando corrupção e governo se misturam*. Rio de Janeiro: Objetiva.

Portes, Alejandro. 2012. "Institutions and Development: A Conceptual Reanalysis." In Alejandro Portes and Lori D. Smith (eds.), *Institutions Count: Their Role and Significance in Latin American Development*, 1–23. Berkeley, CA: University of California Press.

Porto, Mauro P. 2011. "The Media and Political Accountability." In Timothy J. Power and Matthew M. Taylor (eds.), *Corruption and Democracy in Brazil: The Struggle for Accountability*, 103–26. Notre Dame, IN: University of Notre Dame Press.

Porzecanski, Arturo C. 2015. "Brazil's Place in the Global Economy." In Oliver Stuenkel and Matthew M. Taylor (eds.), *Brazil on the Global Stage: Power, Ideas, and the Liberal International Order*, 143–62. New York: Palgrave MacMillan.

Possebom, Vítor. 2017. "Free Trade Zone of Manaus: An Impact Evaluation using the Synthetic Control Method." *Revista Brasileira de Economia*, 71: 217–31.

Power, Timothy J. 2010. "Optimism, Pessimism, and Coalitional Presidentialism: Debating the Institutional Design of Brazilian Democracy." *Bulletin of Latin American Research*, 29: 18–33.

Power, Timothy J. and Mahrukh Doctor. 2004. "Another Century of Corporatism? Continuity and Change in Brazilian Corporatist Structures." In Howard J. Wiarda (ed.), *Authoritarianism and Corporatism in Latin America, Revisited*, 218–41. Gainesville, FL: University Press of Florida.

Power, Timothy J. and Matthew M. Taylor. 2011. *Corruption and Democracy in Brazil: The Struggle for Accountability*. Notre Dame, IN: University of Notre Dame Press.

Power, Timothy J. and Cesar Zucco. 2008. "Estimating Ideology of Brazilian Legislative Parties, 1990–2005: A Research Communication." *Latin American Research Review*, 44: 218–46.

Power, Timothy J. and Cesar Zucco. 2011. *O Congresso por ele mesmo: autopercepções da classe política brasileira*. Belo Horizonte: Editora UFMG.

Praça, Sérgio. 2013. *Corrupção e reforma orçamentária no Brasil 1987–2008*. São Paulo: Anna Blume.

Praça, Sérgio and Matthew M. Taylor. 2014. "Inching toward Accountability: The Evolution of Brazil's Anticorruption Institutions, 1985–2010." *Latin American Politics & Society*, 56: 27–48.

Praça, Sérgio, Andréa Freitas, and Bruno Hoepers. 2011. "Political Appointments and Coalition Management in Brazil, 2007–2010." *Journal of Politics in Latin America*, 3: 141–72.

Prado, Maria Clara R. M. do. 2005. *A real história do Real*. São Paulo: Record.

Prado, Mariana Mota. 2008. "Challenges and Risks of Creating Independent Regulatory Agencies: A Cautionary Tale from Brazil." *Vanderbilt Journal of Transnational Law*, 141: 435.

Prado, Mariana Mota and Michael J. Trebilcock. 2018. *Institutional Bypasses: A Strategy to Promote Reforms for Development*. New York: Cambridge University Press.

Prado, Mariana Mota, Mario G. Schapiro, and Diogo R. Coutinho. 2016. "The Dilemmas of the Developmental State: Democracy and Economic Development in Brazil." *Law and Development Review*, 9: 369–410.

Prado, Viviane Muller. 2019. "Enforcing Insider Trading Law: The Brazilian Experience." Mimeo, Fundação Getulio Vargas Law School.

Prebisch, Raúl. 1949. *The Economic Development of Latin America and Its Principal Problems*. Lake Success, NY: United Nations Economic Commission for Latin America.

Prebisch, Raúl. 1963. "Toward a Dynamic Development Policy for Latin America." New York: United Nations. repositorio.cepal.org/handle/11362/14892

Presidência da República. 2011, "Discurso da Presidenta da República, Dilma Rousseff, durante cerimônia de entrega do navio Celso Furtado." November 25. www.biblioteca.presidencia.gov.br

Prillaman, William C. 2000. *The Judiciary and Democratic Decay in Latin America: Declining Confidence in the Rule of Law*. Westport, CT: Praeger.

Puttomatti, Giulia da Cunha Fernades. 2002. "Os dois anos de implementação da lei de responsabilidade fiscal no Brasil: avanços e desafios." VII Congresso Internacional do CLAD sobre a Reforma do Estado e da Administração Pública. Painel: Ética como instrumento de gestão. October. http://unpan1.un.org/intradoc/groups/public/documents/CLAD/clad0044115.pdf

Ramos, Alberto. 2015. Presentation at the Peterson Institute for International Economics, Washington, DC, September 9.

Ramos, Pedro. 2011. "Financiamentos subsidiados e dívidas de usineiros no Brasil: uma história secular e ... atual?" *História Econômica & História de Empresas*, XIV: 7–32.

Ramos, Pedro. 2016. "Trajetória e situação atual da agroindústria canavieira do Brasil e do mercado de álcool carburante." In Gesmar Rosa dos Santos (ed.), *Quarenta anos de etanol em larga escala no Brasil: desafios, crises e perspectivas*, 47–82. Brasília: IPEA.

Rede Brasil Atual. 2011. "Dilma entrega navio Celso Furtado com defesa de distribuição de renda." November 25. http://www.redebrasilatual.com.br/econ omia/2011/11/dilma-entrega-navio-celso-furtado-com-defesa-de-distribuicao-de-renda

Reinert, Erik S. 2007. *How Rich Countries Got Rich ... and Why Poor Countries Stay Poor*. New York: Carroll & Graf Publishers.

Reis, Bruno P. W. 2018. "Um réquiem para os partidos? Sistema partidário no Brasil, daqui para o futuro." *Journal of Democracy em Português*, 7: 49–88.

References 341

Rennó, Lúcio R. and Andrea Cabello. 2010. "As bases do Lulismo: a volta do personalismo, realinhamento ideológico ou não alinhamento?" *Revista Brasileira de Ciências Sociais*, 25: 39–60.

Resende, Antônio Vieira. 2000. "A política industrial do Plano Real." Texto para Discussão. Belo Horizonte: UFMG/Cedeplar.

Reuters. 2015. "Petrobras takes $17 billion charge in wake of scandal, promises 'normality'." April 22.

Reuters. 2017. "Brazil likely to limit cuts to local content requirements in oil contracts." December 11.

Reuters. 2018. "Com apostas em etanol, usinas do Brasil ampliam investimentos em produção." December 3.

Reuters. 2019. "Brazil unlikely to privatize state power firm Eletrobras – Senate leader." September 19.

Rich, Jessica A. J. 2013. "Grassroots bureaucracy: Intergovernmental Relations and Popular Mobilization in Brazil's AIDS Policy Sector." *Latin American Politics and Society*, 55: 1–25.

Rich, Jessica A. J. 2019. *State-Sponsored Activism: Bureaucrats and Social Movements in Democratic Brazil*. Cambridge: Cambridge University Press.

Rich, Jessica A. J. and Eduardo J. Gómez. 2012. "Centralizing Decentralized Governance in Brazil." *Publius*, 42: 636–61.

Ricupero, Bernardo. 2007. *Sete lições sobre as interpretações do Brasil*. São Paulo: Alameda.

Rizzo, Alana and Joel Velasco. 2018. "As empresas conseguem migrar do crony capitalism para práticas íntegras de interação com o governo?" In Milton Seligman and Fernando Mello (eds.), *Lobby desvendado: democracia, políticas públicas e corrupção no Brasil contemporâneo*, 183–208. Rio de Janeiro: Record.

Rochabrun, Marcelo. 2019. "Boeing drops Embraer name from Brazil commercial jet division." *Reuters*, May 23.

Rochabrun, Marcelo. 2020. "Embraer and Boeing's $4.2 Billion Deal Ruled Out Pandemic as Pretext to Cancel." *Reuters*, April 30.

Rodrigues, Antonio Gustavo. 2012. "ENCCLA 10 anos." In Ricardo Andrade Saadi, Roberto Biasoli, and Ana Paula da Cunha (eds.), *ENCCLA: Estratégia Nacional de Combate à Corrupção e à Lavagem de Dinheiro: 10 anos de organização do Estado brasileiro contra o crime organizado, 69–70*. Brasília: Ministério da Justiça.

Rodrigues, Fernando. 2013. "Dilma cresce e oposição encolhe, aponta Datafolha." *Folha de S. Paulo*, November 30.

Rodriguez Neto, Eleutério, José Gomes Temporão, and Sarah Escorel. 2003. *Saúde: promessa e limites da Constituicão*. Rio de Janeiro: Editora Fiocruz.

Rodrik, Dani. 1996. "Understanding Economic Policy Reform." *Journal of Economic Literature*, 34: 9–41.

Rodrik, Dani. 2004. "Getting Institutions Right." Unpublished manuscript. http://ksghome.harvard.edu/~drodrik/papers.html

Rodrik, Dani. 2007. *One Economics, Many Recipes: Globalization, Institutions, and Economic Growth*. Princeton, NJ: Princeton University Press.

Roett, Riordan. 1978. *Brazil: Politics in a Patrimonial Society.* New York: Praeger.

Roett, Riordan. 2011. *The New Brazil.* Washington, DC: Brookings Institution.

Rohter, Larry. 2010. *Brazil on the Rise: The Story of a Country Transformed.* New York: Palgrave Macmillan.

Rojas, Shunko. 2013. "Understanding Neo-Developmentalism in Latin America: New Industrial Policies in Brazil and Colombia." In David M. Trubek, Helena Alviar Garcia, Diogo R. Coutinho, and Alvaro Santos (eds.), *Law and the New Developmental State: The Brazilian Experience in Latin American Context,* 65–113. Cambridge: Cambridge University Press.

Romero, Simon. 2012. "As Growth Ebbs, Brazil Powers Up Its Bulldozers." *New York Times,* June 22.

Rosales, Osvaldo. 2004. "Chile 's Multidimensional Trade Policy." In Vinod K. Aggarwal, Ralph Espach, and Joseph S. Tulchin (eds.), *The Strategic Dynamics of Latin American Trade,* 3–36. Stanford, CA: Stanford University Press.

Rosenn, Keith S. 2014. "Recent Important Decisions by the Brazilian Supreme Court." *The University of Miami Inter-American Law Review,* 45: 297–334.

Rosillo-Calle, Frank and Luis A.B. Cortez. 1998. "Towards ProÁlcool II—a review of the Brazilian Bioethanol Programme." *Biomass and Bioenergy,* 14: 115–24.

Rossignolo, Darío. 2012. "Estimación de la recaudación potencial del impuesto a la renta en América Latina." *CEPAL:* Série Macroeconomia del Desarrollo, 120. www.cepal.org/es/publicaciones/5353-estimacion-la-recaudacion-potencial-impuesto-la-renta-america-latina

Rotberg, Robert I. 2017. *The Corruption Cure: How Citizens and Leaders can Combat Graft.* Princeton, NJ: Princeton University Press.

Rothstein, Bo. 2011. "Anti-corruption: The Indirect 'Big Bang' Approach." *Review of International Political Economy,* 18: 228–50.

Ruggie, John Gerard. 2008. "Introduction: Embedding Global Markets." In John Gerard Ruggie (ed.), *Embedding Global Markets: An Enduring Challenge,* 1–9. Aldershot: Ashgate.

Sá e Silva, Fábio de and David Trubek. 2018. "Legal Professionals and Development Strategies: Corporate Lawyers and the Construction of the Telecoms Sector in Brazil (1980s–2010s)." *Law & Social Inquiry,* 43: 915–43.

Saadi, Ricardo Andrade. 2012. "ENCCLA: uma estratégia de Estado." In Ricardo Andrade Saadi, Roberto Biasoli, and Ana Paula da Cunha (eds.), *ENCCLA: Estratégia Nacional de Combate à Corrupção e à Lavagem de Dinheiro: 10 anos de organização do Estado brasileiro contra o crime organizado,* 15. Brasília: Ministério da Justiça.

Sabatier, Paul. 1988. "An Advocacy Coalition Framework of Policy Change and the Role of Policy-Oriented Learning Therein." *Policy Sciences,* 21: 129–68.

Sachsida, Adolfo. 2017. "Introdução." In Adolfo Sachsida (ed.), *Tributação no Brasil: estudos, ideias e propostas,* 9–10. Brasília: IPEA.

Sáez, Raúl E. 2007. "Hacia el libre comercio: treinta años de apertura comerical en Chile." In Marcos Sawaya Jank and Simão Davi Silber (eds.), *Políticas comerciais comparadas: desempenho e modelos organizacionais,* 231–72. Sao Paulo: Singular.

References

Salerno, Mario Sergio and Talita Daher. 2006. *Política Industrial, Tecnológica e de Comércio Exterior (PITCE): balanço e perspectivas.* Brasília: ABDI.

Salgado, Lucia Helena. 2003. "Agências regulatórias na experiência brasileira: um panorama do atual desenho institucional." *IPEA Texto para Discussão 941.*

Salles, Fernanda Cimini, Tulio Chiarini, Marcia Siqueira Rapini, and Leandro Alves Silva. 2017. "Domestic Businesses, Multinationals and the State: An Essay on the Dynamics Underpinning the 'Low-Innovation Trap' in Brazil." Paper presented at the 15th Globelics International Conference, Athens, Greece, October 11–13.

Samuels, David J. 1999. "Incentives to Cultivate a Party Vote in Candidate-Centric Electoral Systems: Evidence from Brazil." *Comparative Political Studies,* 32: 487–9.

Samuels, David. 2001. "Money, Elections, and Democracy in Brazil." *Latin American Politics and Society,* 43: 27–48.

Samuels, David. 2002. "Pork-Barreling Is Not Credit-Claiming or Advertising: Campaign Finance and the Sources of the Personal Vote in Brazil." *The Journal of Politics,* 64: 845–63.

Samuels, David and Scott Mainwaring. 2004. "Strong Federalism, Constraints on the Central Government, and Economic Reform in Brazil." In Edward L. Gibson (ed.), *Federalism and Democracy in Latin America,* 85–129. Baltimore, MD: The Johns Hopkins University Press.

Santana, Carlos Henrique Vieira. 2011. "Conjuntura crítica, legados institucionais e comunidades epistêmicas: limites e possibilidades de uma agenda de desenvolvimento no Brasil." In Renato Boschi (ed.), *Variedades de capitalismo, política e desenvolvimento na América Latina,* 121–63. Belo Horizonte: Editora UFMG.

Sant'Ana, Jéssica. 2019. "Governo anuncia pacotão de concessões: 59 ativos e expectative de atrair R$1.6 trilhão." *Gazeta do Povo,* May 8.

Santos, Fabiano and Márcio Grijó Vilarouca. 2008. "Political Institutions and Governability from FHC to Lula." In Peter Kingstone and Timothy Power (eds.), *Democratic Brazil Revisited,* 57–80. Pittsburgh, PA: University of Pittsburgh Press.

Santos, Gesmar Rosa dos. 2016. "Introdução." In Gesmar Rosa dos Santos (ed.), *Quarenta anos de etanol em larga escala no Brasil: desafios, crises e perspectivas,* 11–16. Brasília: IPEA.

Santos, Gesmar Rosa dos, Carlos Eduardo de Freitas Vian, Pery Francisco Assis Shikida, and Walter Belik. 2016. "Apontamentos e diretrizes para políticas públicas." In Gesmar Rosa dos Santos (ed.), *Quarenta anos de etanol em larga escala no Brasil: desafios, crises e perspectivas,* 283–304. Brasília: IPEA.

Santos, Gesmar Rosa dos, Eduardo Afonso Garcia, Pery Francisco Assis Shikida, and Darcy Jacob Rissardi Júnior. 2016. "Trajetória e situação atual da agroindústria canavieira do Brasil e do mercado de álcool carburante." In Gesmar Rosa dos Santos (ed.), *Quarenta anos de etanol em larga escala no Brasil: desafios, crises e perspectivas,* 17–46. Brasília: IPEA.

Santos, Luiz Alberto dos. 2007. "Regulamentação das atividades de lobby e seu impacto sobre as relações entre politicos, burocratas e grupos de interesse no ciclo de políticas públicas – análise comparativa dos Estados Unidos e Brasil."

Unpublished Ph.D. dissertation, Universidade de Brasília, Instituto de Ciências Sociais.

Santos, Luiz Alberto dos. 2009. "Burocracia profissional e a livre nomeação para cargos de confiança no Brasil e nos EUA." *Revista do Serviço Público*, 60: 5–28.

Santos, Rafael Liza, Alexandre di Miceli da Silveira, and Lucas Ayres Barros. 2012. "Board Interlocking in Brazil: Directors' Participation in Multiple Companies and Its Effect on Firm Value and Profitability." *Latin American Business Review*, 13: 1–28.

Santos, Wanderley Guilherme dos. 1978. *Ordem burguesa e liberalismo político*. São Paulo: Duas Cidades.

Sargent, Thomas J. and Neil Wallace. 1981. "Some Unpleasant Monetarist Arithmetic." *Federal Reserve Bank of Minneapolis Quarterly Review*, 5: 1–17.

Schapiro, Mario G. 2013a. "Ativismo estatal e industrialismo defensivo: instrumentos e capacidades na política industrial brasileira." IPEA *Texto para Discussão* 1856.

Schapiro, Mario G. 2013b. "O que a política industrial pode aprender com a política monetária?" *Novos Estudos CEBRAP*, 96: 117–30.

Schapiro, Mario G. 2016. "Discricionariedade desenvolvimentista e controles democráticos: uma tipologia dos desajustes." *Revista Direito GV*, 12: 311–44.

Schapiro, Mario G. 2017. "O estado pastor e os incentivos tributários no setor automotivo." *Revista de Economia Política*, 37: 437–55.

Schapiro, Mario G. and Matthew M. Taylor. 2020. "The Political Economy of Brazil's Enigmatic Central Bank, 1988–2018." In Mustafa Yagci (ed.), *The Political Economy of Central Banking in Emerging Economies*, 168–81. London: Routledge.

Scheffer, Mário and Lígia Bahia. 2011. "Representação política e interesses particulares na saúde: o caso do financiamento de campanhas eleitorais pelas empresas de planos de saúde no Brasil." *Interface (Botucatu)*, 15: 947–56.

Scherer, Clóvis. 2015. "Payroll Tax Reduction in Brazil: Effects on Employment and Wages." In *ISS Working Paper Series*. Erasmus University: International Institute of Social Studies.

Schick, Allen. 2018. Comments at workshop on "The Challenges of the Contemporary Administrative State: Brazil and the United States in Comparative Perspective." Workshop of the Escola Nacional de Administração Pública and Woodrow Wilson Center, Washington, DC, May 23.

Schmitt, Rogério, Leandro Piquet Carneiro, and Karina Kuschnir. 1999. "Estratégias de campanha no horário gratuito de propaganda eleitoral em eleições proporcionais." *Dados* 42, 277–301.

Schmitter, Philippe C. 1971. *Interest Conflict and Political Change in Brazil*. Stanford, CA: Stanford University Press.

Schmitter, Philippe C. 1982. "Reflections on Where the Theory of Neo-Corporatism Has Gone and Where the Praxis of Neo-Corporatism May Be Going." In Gerhard Lehmbruch and Philippe C. Schmitter (eds.), *Patterns of Corporatist Policy Making*, 259–79. London: Sage.

Schmitter, Philippe C. and Gerhard Lehmbruch. 1979. *Trends toward Corporatist Intermediation*. Beverly Hills: Sage Publications.

References   345

Schneider, Ben Ross. 1991. *Politics within the State: Elite Bureaucrats and Industrial Policy in Authoritarian Brazil.* Pittsburgh, PA: University of Pittsburgh Press.

Schneider, Ben Ross. 1999. "The Desarrollista State in Brazil and Mexico." In Meredith Woo-Cumings (ed.), *The Developmental State,* 276–305. Ithaca, NY: Cornell University Press.

Schneider, Ben Ross. 2004. *Business Politics and the State in Twentieth-Century Latin America.* Cambridge: Cambridge University Press.

Schneider, Ben Ross. 2009. "Big Business in Brazil: Leveraging National Endowments and State Support for International Expansion." In Lael Brainard and Leonardo Martínez-Diáz (eds.), *Brazil as an Economic Superpower? Understanding Brazil's Changing Role in the Global Economy,* 159–86. Washington, DC: Brookings Institution Press.

Schneider, Ben Ross. 2010. "Business Politics in Latin America: Patterns of Fragmentation and Centralization." In David Coen, Wyn Grant, and Graham Wilson (eds.), *The Oxford Handbook of Business and Government,* 307–29. Oxford: Oxford University Press.

Schneider, Ben Ross. 2013. *Hierarchical Capitalism in Latin America: Business, Labor, and the Challenges of Equitable Development.* New York: Cambridge University Press.

Schrank, Andrew and Marcus J. Kurtz. 2005. "Credit Where Credit Is Due: Open Economy Industrial Policy and Export Diversification in Latin America and the Caribbean." *Politics & Society, 33:* 671–702.

Schvarzer, Jorge. 2004. "Poder político-social, condições de mercado e mudança estrutural." In Brasilio Sallum Jr. (ed.), *Brasil e Argentina hoje: política e economia,* 15–46. Bauru, SP: Edusc.

Schwartsman, Alexandre. 2018. "Mercado se ilude com promessa de programa econômico liberal de Bolsonaro." *Folha de S. Paulo,* October 17.

Schwartsman, Hélio. 2017. "Estado capturado." *Folha de S. Paulo,* June 14.

Schwarz, Roberto. 1973. "As ideias fora do lugar." *Estudos CEBRAP, 3:* 150–61.

Secretaria do Tesouro Nacional. 2015. *Resultado do Tesouro Nacional.* June 23. www.tesouro.fazenda.gov.br/resultado-do-tesouro-nacional

Seligman, Milton and Mateus Affonso Bandeira. 2018. "O propósito das relações governamentais: principais questões e alguns dilemas." In Milton Seligman and Fernando Mello (eds.), *Lobby desvendado: democracia, políticas públicas e corrupção no Brasil contemporâneo,* 227–44. Rio de Janeiro: Record.

Shaffer, Gregory and Michelle Ratton Sanchez Badin. In press. "Building Legal Capacity and Adapting State Institutions in Brazil." In Gregory Shaffer (ed.), *Emerging Powers and the World Trading System: The Past and Future of International Economic Law.* New York: Cambridge University Press.

Shugart, Matthew Soberg and John M. Carey. 1992. *Presidents and Assemblies: Constitutional Design and Electoral Dynamics.* New York: Cambridge University Press.

Shugart, Matthew Soberg and Stephan Haggard. 2001. "Institutions and Public Policy in Presidential Systems." In Stephan Haggard and Mathew

D. McCubbins (eds.), *Presidents, Parliaments, and Policy*, 64–104. Cambridge: Cambridge University Press.

Sicsú, João. 2002. "Expectativas inflacionárias no regime de metas de inflação: uma análise preliminar do caso brasileiro." *Economia Aplicada*, 6: 703–11.

Sikkink, Kathryn. 1988. "The Influence of Raúl Prebisch on Economic Policy-Making in Argentina, 1950–1962." *Latin American Research Review*, 23: 91–114.

Sikkink, Kathryn. 1991. *Ideas and Institutions: Developmentalism in Brazil and Argentina*. Ithaca, NY: Cornell University Press.

Silva, Alexandre Manoel A. da and Rozane Bezerra Siqueira. 2012. "Existe ilusão fiscal no Brasil?" *IPEA Desafios do Desenvolvimento*, 9: 43–6.

Silva, Eliane. 2019. "Crise segue, e 23% das usinas de etanol e açúcar estão paradas nesta safra." *UOL Notícias*, April 19.

Silva, Willis Pereira da. 2012. "Estratégia consensual." In Ricardo Andrade Saadi, Roberto Biasoli, and Ana Paula da Cunha (eds.), *ENCCLA: Estratégia Nacional de Combate à Corrupção e à Lavagem de Dinheiro: 10 anos de organização do Estado brasileiro contra o crime organizado*, 80–1. Brasília: Ministério da Justiça.

Singer, Hans W. 1950. "The Distribution of Gains between Investing and Borrowing Countries." *The American Economic Review*, 40: 473–85.

Skidmore, Thomas E. 1973. "Politics and Economic Policy-making in Authoritarian Brazil, 1937–71." In Alfred Stepan (ed.), *Authoritarian Brazil*, 2–46. New Haven, CT: Yale University Press.

Skidmore, Thomas E. 1999. *Brazil: Five Centuries of Change*. New York: Oxford University Press.

Smith, Quinn and Olavo Franco Bernardes. 2013. "Mechanisms of Control on the Circulation of Foreign Capital, Products and People in Brazil." *The University of Miami Inter-American Law Review*, 44: 219–58.

Snow, Peter G. and Gary W. Wynia. 1990. (3rd ed). "Argentina: Politics in a Conflict Society." In Howard J. Wiarda and Herbert F. Kline (eds.), *Latin American Politics and Development*, 249–82. Boulder, CO: Westview Press.

Soares de Lima, Maria Regina. 1990. "A economia política da política externa brasileira: uma proposta de análise." *Contexto Internacional*, 12: 7–27.

Soares de Lima, Maria Regina. 1994. "Ejes analíticos y conflictos de paradigmas en la política externa brasileira." *America Latina/Internacional*, 1: 27–46.

Soares de Lima, Maria Regina. 2005. "A política externa brasileira e os desafios da cooperação Sul-Sul." *Revista Brasileira de Política Internacional*, 48: 24–59.

Soares de Lima, Maria Regina and Mônica Hirst. 2006. "Brazil as an Intermediate State and Regional Power: Action, Choice and Responsibilities." *International Affairs* 82: 21–40.

Soares, Sergei. 2016. "People, Productivity, and Policy: Product Growth Perspective in the Medium and Long Run in Brazil." CGD Policy Paper 088, Center for Global Development.

Soares, Sergei. 2017. "Pessoas, produtividade e políticas." *Novos Estudos Cebrap*, 107: 36.

Sodré, Antônio Carlos de Azevedo. 2002. "Lei de Responsabilidade Fiscal: condição insuficiente para o ajuste fiscal." *RAE–eletrônica*, 1. https://rae

References

.fgv.br/rae-eletronica/vol1-num2-2002/lei-responsabilidade-fiscal-condicao-insuficiente-para-ajuste-fiscal

Sola, Lourdes. 1988. "Choque heterodoxo e transição democrática sem ruptura." In Lourdes Sola (ed.), *O estado da transição*, 37–42. São Paulo: Vértice.

Sola, Lourdes. 1994. "The State, Structural Reform, and Democratization in Brazil." In William C. Smith, Carlos H. Acuña, and Eduardo A. Gamarra (eds.), *Democracy, Markets, and Structural Reform in Latin America: Argentina, Bolivia, Brazil, Chile, and Mexico*, 151–81. New Brunswick: Transaction Publishers.

Sola, Lourdes. 1998. *Idéias econômicas, decisões políticas: desenvolvimento, estabilidade e populismo*. São Paulo: Edusp.

Sola, Lourdes and Eduardo Kugelmas. 2002. "Estabilidade econômica e o Plano Real como construção política: statecraft, liberalização econômicae democratização." In Lourdes Sola, Eduardo Kugelmas, and Laurence Whitehead (eds.), *Banco Central, autoridade política e democratização: um equilíbrio delicado*, 79–110. Rio de Janeiro: Editora FGV.

Sola, Lourdes and Laurence Whitehead. 2006. *Statecrafting Monetary Authority: Democracy and Financial Order in Brazil*. Oxford: Centre for Brazilian Studies.

Sola, Lourdes, Christopher Garman, and Moisés Marques. 1998. "Central Banking, Democratic Governance and Political Authority: The Case of Brazil in a Comparative Perspective." *Revista de Economia Política*, 18: 106–31.

Souza, Amaury de. 1999. "Cardoso and the Struggle for Reform in Brazil." *Journal of Democracy*, 10: 49–63.

Souza, Celina. 2013. "Modernisation of the State and Bureaucratic Capacity-Building in the Brazilian Federal Government." In Jeni Vaitsman, José Mendes Ribeiro, and Lenaura Lobato (eds.), *Policy Analysis in Brazil*, 39–54. Bristol: Policy Press.

Souza, Maria do Carmo Campello de. 1976. *Estado e partidos políticos no Brasil (1930 a 1964)*. São Paulo: Alfa-Omega.

Speck, Bruno Wilhelm. 2010. "O dinheiro e a política no Brasil." *Le Monde Diplomatique Brasil*, May 4.

Speck, Bruno Wilhelm. 2011. "Auditing Institutions." In Timothy J. Power and Matthew M. Taylor (eds.), *Corruption and Democracy in Brazil: The Struggle for Accountability*, 127–61. Notre Dame, IN: University of Notre Dame Press.

Speck, Bruno Wilhelm. 2013. "Brazil: Crime Meets Politics." In Kevin Casas-Zamora (ed.), *Dangerous Liaisons: Organized Crime and Political Finance*, 42–75. Washington, DC: Brookings Institution Press.

Speck, Bruno W. 2016a. "Influenciar as eleições ou garantir acesso aos eleitos: o dilemma das empresas que financiam campanhas eleitorais." *Novos Estudos Cebrap*, 104: 38–59.

Speck, Bruno W. 2016b. "Game Over: duas décadas de financiamento de campanhas com doações de empresas no Brasil." *Revista de Estudios Brasileños*, 3: 125–35.

Speck, Bruno Wilhelm and Mauro Macedo Campos. 2014. "Incentivos para a fragmentação e a nacionalização do sistema partidário a partir do Horário Eleitoral Gratuito no Brasil." *Teoria e Pesquisa*, 23: 12–40.

References

Spektor, Matias. 2018. "Troca de favor e proteção pautam relação do STF e outros Poderes." *Folha de S. Paulo*, February 1.

Sreeharsha, Vinod. 2017. "Goldman Sachs Sees Big Potential for Fintech in Brazil." *New York Times*, May 15.

Stallings, Barbara. 1992. "International Influence on Economic Policy: Debt, Stabilization, and Structural Reform." In Stephan Haggard and Robert R. Kaufman (eds.), *The Politics of Economic Adjustment*, 41–88. Princeton, NJ: Princeton University Press.

Stallings, Barbara. 2016. "Innovation, Inclusion and Institutions: East Asian Lessons for Latin America?" In Alejandro Foxley and Barbara Stallings (eds.), *Innovation and Inclusion in Latin America: Strategies to Avoid the Middle Income Trap*, 1–32. New York: Palgrave Macmillan.

Stark, David and Laszlo Bruszt. 1998a. "Enabling Constraints: fontes institucionais de coerência nas políticas públicas no pós-socialismo." *Revista Brasileira de Ciencias Sociais*, *13*: 13–39.

Stark, David and Laszlo Bruszt. 1998b. *Post-Socialist Pathways: Transforming Politics and Property in Eastern Europe*. Cambridge: Cambridge University Press.

Stattman, Sarah L. 2013. "Governing Biofuels in Brazil: A Comparison of Ethanol and Biodiesel Policies." *Energy Policy*, *61*: 22–30.

Stauffer, Caroline and Jeb Blount. 2015. "Eletrobras Posts 3rd-Quarter Loss on Angra 3 Nuclear Plant Impairment." *Reuters*, November 13. https://news .trust.org/item/20151113035209-88tsd

Stein, Ernesto, Mariano Tommasi, Koldo Echebarría, Eduardo Lora, and Mark Payne. 2006. *The Politics of Policies: Economic and Social Progress in Latin America. 2006 Report*. Washington, DC: Inter-American Development Bank.

Stein, Guilherme de Queiroz and Ronaldo Herrlein Júnior. 2016. "Política industrial no Brasil: uma análise das estratégias propostas na experiência recente (2003–2014)." *Planejamento e Políticas Públicas*, *47*: 251–87.

Stepan, Alfred. 2000. "Brazil's Decentralized Federalism: Bringing Government Closer to the Citizens?" *Daedalus*, *129*: 145–69.

Stephenson, Matthew. 2020. "Corruption as a Self-Reinforcing 'Trap': Implications for Reform Strategy." *World Bank Research Observer 35*: 192–226.

Stern, Elliot. 2003. Evaluation of UNESCO Brazil's Contribution to AIDS II. UNESCO BR/ 2005/PI/H/19, 2003. http://unesdoc.unesco.org/images/0014/00 1408/140845e.pdf

Stone, Susan, James Messent, and Dorothee Flaig. 2015. "Emerging Policy Issues: Localisation Barriers to Trade." *OECD Trade Policy Papers*, No. 180. Paris: OECD Publishing, Paris.

Streeck, Wolfang. 2005. "Requirements for a Useful Concept of Complementarity." *Socio-Economic Review*, *3*: 363–6.

Streeck, Wolfgang and Kathleen Thelen. 2005. *Beyond Continuity: Institutional Change in Advanced Political Economies*. Oxford: Oxford University Press.

Streeck, Wolfgang and Kozo Yamamura. (eds.). 2001. *The Origins of Non-Liberal Capitalism: Germany and Japan in Comparison*. Ithaca, NY: Cornell University Press.

References

Sturzenegger, Adolfo C. 1990. "Trade, Exchange Rate and Agricultural Pricing Policies in Argentina." World Bank Comparative Studies. Washington, DC: World Bank.

Sugiyama, Natasha B. 2008. "Theories of Policy Diffusion: Social Sector Reform in Brazil." *Comparative Political Studies*, 41: 193–216.

Sugiyama, Natasha B. 2012. *The Diffusion of Good Government: Social Sector Reforms in Brazil*. Notre Dame, IN: University of Notre Dame Press.

Surran, Carl. 2018. "Eletrobras -12% as Bolsonaro Says He Is Unwilling to Sell Power Assets." *Seeking Alpha*, October 10.

Suzigan, Wilson and João Furtado. 2006. "Política industrial e desenvolvimento." *Revista de Economia Política*, 26: 163–85.

Tannenwald, Nina and William C. Wohlforth. 2005. "Introduction: The Role of Ideas and the End of the Cold War." *Journal of Cold War Studies*, 7: 3–12.

Tatagiba, Luciana. 2002. "Os conselhos gestores e a democratização das políticas públicas no Brasil." In Evelina Dagnino (ed.), *Sociedade civil e espaços públicos no Brasil*, 47–103. São Paulo: Paz e Terra.

Tavares, Martus. 2005. "Vinte anos de política fiscal no Brasil: dos fundamentos do novo regime à Lei de Responsabilidade Fiscal." *Revista de Economia e Relações Internacionais*, 4: 79–101.

Tavares, Martus, Álvaro Manoel, and José Roberto Afonso. 1999. "Uma proposta para um novo regime fiscal no Brasil: o da responsabilidade fiscal." *CEPAL*. https://repositorio.cepal.org/handle/11362/34662

Taylor, Matthew M. 2005. "Citizens Against the State: The Riddle of High-Impact, Low-Functionality Courts in Brazil." *Revista de Economia Política*, 25: 418–38.

Taylor, Matthew M. 2008. *Judging Policy: Courts and Policy Reform in Democratic Brazil*. Stanford, CA: Stanford University Press.

Taylor, Matthew M. 2009. "Institutional Development through Policymaking: A Case Study of the Brazilian Central Bank." *World Politics*, 61: 487–515.

Taylor, Matthew M. 2016. "The Unchanging Core of Brazilian State Capitalism, 1985–2015." Paper prepared for presentation at the meetings of the Latin American Studies Association, New York City, May 27–30.

Taylor, Matthew M. 2017. "Corruption and Accountability in Brazil." In Peter Kingstone and Timothy Power (eds.), *Democratic Brazil Divided*, 77–96. Pittsburgh, PA: University of Pittsburgh Press.

Taylor, Matthew M. 2019. "The Troubling Strength of Brazilian Institutions in the Face of Scandal." *Taiwan Journal of Democracy*, 15: 59–79.

Taylor, Matthew M. 2020. "Continuity through Change: Developmentalism and Neoliberalism in Democratic Brazil (1985–2018)." CLALS Working Paper No. 25; American University Center for Latin American and Latino Studies.

Taylor, Matthew M. and Vinicius Buranelli. 2007. "Ending up in Pizza: Accountability as a Problem of Institutional Arrangement in Brazil." *Latin American Politics and Society*, 49: 59–87.

"Ten Theses." 2011. Special edition. *Brazilian Journal of Political Economy*, 31: 844–6.

Thelen, Kathleen. 1999. "Historical Institutionalism in Comparative Politics." *Annual Review of Political Science*, 2: 369–404.

Thelen, Kathleen. 2003. "How Institutions Evolve: Insights from Comparative Historical Analysis." In James Mahoney and Dietrich Rueschemeyer (eds.), *Comparative Historical Analysis in the Social Sciences*, 208–40. Cambridge: Cambridge University Press.

Thomas, Clive S. 2009. "Understanding the Development and Operation of Latin American Interests, Power Groups and Interest Groups." In Conor McGrath (ed.), *Interest Groups and Lobbying in Latin America, Africa, the Middle East, and Asia: Essays on Drug Trafficking, Chemical Manufacture, Exchange Rates, and Women's Interests*, 3–30. Lewiston, NY: Edwin Mellen Press.

Tironi, Ernesto. 2012. Interview with Tironi, business leader, university professor and former ambassador, Santiago, Chile, June 7.

Toye, John and Richard Toye. 2003. "The Origins and Interpretation of the Prebisch-Singer Thesis." *History of Political Economy*, 35: 437–67.

Transparency International. 2015. "Brazil: Beneficial Ownership Transparency." www.transparency.org/files/content/publication/2015_BOCountryReport_Brazil.pdf

Transpetro. 2012. "Navio Celso Furtado é eleito um dos mais significativos do mundo em 2011." March 14. www.transpetro.com.br/transpetro-institucional/noticias/navio-celso-furtado-e-eleito-um-dos-mais-significativos-do-mundo-em-2011.html

Trebat, Thomas J. 1983. *Brazil's State-Owned Enterprises: A Case Study of the State as Entrepreneur*. Cambridge: Cambridge University Press.

Trubek, David M. 2013. "Law, State, and the New Developmentalism: An Introduction." In David M. Trubek, Helena Alviar Garcia, Diogo R. Coutinho, and Alvaro Santos (eds.), *Law and the New Developmental State: The Brazilian Experience in Latin American Context*, 3–27. Cambridge: Cambridge University Press.

Trubek, David M., Diogo R. Coutinho, and Mario G. Schapiro. 2013. "New State Activism and the Challenge for Law." In David M. Trubek, Helena A. Garcia, Diogo R. Coutinho, and Alvaro Santos (eds.), *Law and the New Developmental State: The Brazilian Experience in Latin American Context*, 28–62. Cambridge: Cambridge University Press.

Trubek, David M., Helena Alviar Garcia, Diogo R. Coutinho, and Alvaro Santos (eds.). 2013. *Law and the New Developmental State: The Brazilian Experience in Latin American Context*. Cambridge: Cambridge University Press.

Tsai, Kellee S. and Barry Naughton. 2015. "Introduction: State Capitalism and the Chinese Economic Miracle." In Barry Naughton and Kellee S. Tsai (eds.), *State Capitalism, Institutional Adaptation and the Chinese Miracle*, 1–26. Cambridge: Cambridge University Press.

Tsebelis, George. 2000. "Veto Players and Institutional Analysis." *Governance*, 13: 441–74.

United States District Court, Southern District of Texas, Houston Division. 2017. "United States of America v. SBM Offshore N.V., Criminal No. 17–686, Deferred Prosecution Agreement," November 29.

US Trade Representative (USTR). 2013. "2013 National Trade Estimate Report on Foreign Trade Barriers." https://ustr.gov/sites/default/files/Brazil_0.pdf

References

Vágvölgyi, Réka, Coldea Andra, Dresler, Thomas, Schrader, Josef, and Nuerk Hans-Christoph. 2016. "A Review about Functional Illiteracy: Definition, Cognitive, Linguistic, and Numerical Aspects." *Frontiers in Psychology*, 7: 1–13.

Varsano, Ricardo. 1982. "Os incentivos fiscais do imposto de renda das empresas." *Revista Brasileira de Economia*, 36: 107–27.

Vashisth, Shivam, Govind Singh, and Arun Nanda. 2012. "A Comparative Study of Regulatory Trends of Pharmaceuticals in Brazil, Russia, India and China (BRIC) countries." *Journal of Generic Medicines*, 9: 128–43.

Vasselai, Fabrício and Umberto Mignozzetti. 2014. "O efeito das emendas ao orçamento no comportamento parlamentar e a dimensão temporal: velhas teses, novos testes." *Dados*, 57: 817–53.

Vaz Ferreira, Luciano and Fabio Costa Morosini. 2013. "The Implementation of International Anticorruption Law in Business: Legal Control of Corruption Directed to Transnational Corporations." *Austral: Brazilian Journal of Strategy & International Relations*, 2: 241–60.

Veiga Filho, Lauro. 2012. "Momento crítico." *Valor Econômico*, July 24.

Veiga, Pedro da Motta. 2004. "Regional and Transregional Dimensions of Brazilian Trade Policy." In Vinod K. Aggarwal, Ralph Espach, and Joseph S. Tulchin (eds.), *The Strategic Dynamics of Latin American Trade*, 175–88. Stanford, CA: Stanford University Press.

Veiga, Pedro da Motta. 2007. "Política comercial no Brasil: características, condicionantes domésticos e policy-making." In Marcos Sawaya Jank and Simão David Silber (eds.), *Políticas comerciais comparadas: desempenho e modelos organizacionais*, 71–162. Sao Paulo: Singular.

Veiga, Pedro da Motta. 2009. "Brazil's Trade Policy: Moving Away from Old Paradigms?" In Lael Brainard and Leonardo Martinez-Diaz (eds.), *Brazil as an Economic Superpower? Understanding Brazil's Changing Role in the Global Economy*, 113–58. Washington, DC: Brookings Institution Press.

Veiga, Pedro da Motta and Vivianne Ventura-Dias. 2004. "Brazil: The Fine-Tuning of Trade Liberalization." In Miguel F. Lengyel and Vivianne Ventura-Dias (eds.), *Trade Policy Reforms in Latin America: Multilateral Rules and Domestic Institutions*, 98–124. Basingstoke: Palgrave MacMillan.

Vergara, Alberto and Daniel Encinas. 2016. "Continuity by Surprise: Explaining Institutional Stability in Contemporary Peru." *Latin American Research Review*, 51: 159–80.

Versiani, Isabel and Dimmi Amora. 2015. "Empréstimos subsidiados do BNDES custam R$184 bilhões à União." *Folha de S. Paulo*, August 9.

Vianna, Herbert. 1995. *Luís Inácio (300 Picaretas)*. Rio de Janeiro: Sony/ATV Music Publishing LLC.

Villela, André A. 2015. "Ever Wary of Liberalism: Brazilian Foreign Trade Policy from Bretton Woods to the G-20." In Oliver Stuenkel and Matthew M. Taylor (eds.), *Brazil on the Global Stage: Power, Ideas, and the Liberal International Order*, 163–80. New York: Palgrave MacMillan.

Wade, Robert. 2004 [1990]. *Governing the Market: Economic Theory and the Role of Government in East Asian Industrialization*. Princeton, NJ: Princeton University Press.

Wade, Robert. 2018. "The Role of the State in Escaping the Middle-Income Trap: The Case for Smart Industrial Policy." In Ana Célia Castro and Fernando Filgueiras (eds.), *The State in the 21st Century*, 181–208. Brasília: ENAP.

Wampler, Brian. 2009. "Following in the Footsteps of Policy Entrepreneurs: Policy Advocates and Pro Forma Adopters." *Journal of Development Studies*, 45: 572–92.

Wampler, Brian. 2015. *Activating Democracy in Brazil: Popular Participation, Social Justice, and Interlocking Institutions*. Notre Dame, IN: University of Notre Dame Press.

Wang, Daniel Wei. 2015. "Right to Health Litigation in Brazil: The Problem and the Institutional Responses." *Human Rights Law Review, 15*: 617–41.

Wang, Daniel Wei L., Natalia Pires de Vasconcelos, Vanessa Elias de Oliveira, and Fernanda Vargas Terrazas. 2014. "Os impactos da judicialização da saúde no município de São Paulo: gasto público e organização federativa." *Revista de Administracão Pública, 48*: 1191–206.

Weaver, R. Kent and Rockman, Bert A. 1993. "Assessing the Effects of Institutions: When and How Do Institutions Matter?" In R. Kent Weaver and Bert A. Rockman (eds.), *Do Institutions Matter?* Washington, DC: The Brookings Institution.

Wedeen, Lisa. 2002. "Conceptualizing Culture: Possibilities for Political Science." *American Political Science Review, 96*: 713–28.

Weir, Margaret and Theda Skocpol. 1985. "State Structures and the Possibilities For 'Keynesian' Responses to the Great Depression in Sweden, Britain, and the United States." In Peter Evans, Dietrich Rueschemeyer, and Theda Skocpol (eds.), *Bringing the State Back In*, 107–68. Cambridge: Cambridge University Press.

Werneck Vianna, Luiz. 2002. *A democracia e os três poderes no Brasil*. Belo Horizonte: Editora UFMG.

Werneck, Rogério L. Furquim. 1987. *Empresas estatais e política macroeconômica*. Rio de Janeiro: Campus.

Weyland, Kurt. 1995. "Social Movements and the State: The Politics of Health Reform in Brazil." *World Development, 23*: 1699–712.

Weyland, Kurt. 1998. "From Leviathan to Gulliver? The Decline of the Developmental State in Brazil." *Governance, 11*: 51–75.

Weyland, Kurt. 2002. *The Politics of Market Reform in Fragile Democracies: Argentina, Brazil, Peru, and Venezuela*. Princeton, NJ: Princeton University Press.

Wiarda, Howard J. 1973. "Toward a Framework for the Study of Political Change in the Iberic-Latin Tradition: The Corporative Model." *World Politics, 25*: 206–35.

Wiarda, Howard J. 1981. *Corporatism and National Development in Latin America*. Boulder, CO: Westview Press.

Wiarda, Howard J. (ed.). 2004. *Authoritarianism and Corporatism in Latin America, Revisited*. Gainesville, FL: University Press of Florida.

Williamson, John. 1990. "What Washington Means by Policy Reform." In John Williamson (ed.), *Latin American Adjustment: How Much Has Happened?*, 7–20. Washington, DC: Institute for International Economics.

References

Williamson, John. 2002. "Did the Washington Consensus Fail?" Speech at the Center for Strategic and International Studies, Washington, DC, November 6. www.piie.com/commentary/speeches-papers/did-washington-consensus-fail

Willis, Eliza J. 1986. "The State as Banker: The Expansion of the Public Sector in Brazil." Unpublished Ph.D. dissertation, University of Texas at Austin.

Wilson, James Q. 1989. *Bureaucracy: What Government Agencies Do and Why They Do It*. New York: Basic Books.

Winkler, J. T. "Corporatism." 1976. *European Journal of Sociology*, 17: 100–36.

Wiziack, Julio and Maeli Prado. 2017. "Contrapartidas de subsídio à indústria não foram cumpridas, afirma TCU." *Folha de S. Paulo*, May 29.

Wolford, Wendy. 2016. "The Casa and the Causa: Institutional Histories and Cultural Politics in Brazilian Land Reform." *Latin American Research Review*, 51: 24–42.

Woo-Cumings, Meredith. 1999. "Introduction: Chalmers Johnson and the Politics of Nationalism and Development." In Meredith Woo-Cumings (ed.), *The Developmental State*, 1–31. Ithaca, NY: Cornell University Press.

Wood, Stewart. 2001. "Business, Government, and Patterns of Labor Market Policy in Britain and the Federal Republic of Germany." In Peter Hall and David Soskice (eds.), *Varieties of Capitalism: The Institutional Foundations of Comparative Advantage*, 247–74. Oxford: Oxford University Press.

World Bank. 1984. "Brazil: Economic Memorandum." A World Bank Country Study, Washington, DC: The World Bank.

World Bank. 1987. *World Development Report 1987*. New York: Oxford University Press.

World Bank. 2004. "Project Performance Assessment Report, Brazil—First and Second AIDS and STD Control Projects." Report No. 28819.

World Bank. 2010. World Integrated Trade Solution. July 17, 2012. https://wits .worldbank.org/countrysnapshot/en/BRA

World Bank. 2013. *Doing Business 2014: Understanding Regulations for Small and Medium-Size Enterprises*. Washington, DC: World Bank Group.

World Bank. 2016. "Retaking the Path to Inclusion, Growth, and Sustainability: Brazil Systematic Country Diagnostic." Report No. 101431-BR.

World Bank. 2017a. *A Fair Adjustment: Efficiency and Equity of Public Spending in Brazil (Brazil Public Expenditure Review)*.

World Bank. 2017b. "Country Partnership Framework for the Federative Republic of Brazil for the Period FY18-FY23." Report No. 113259-BR.

World Bank. 2018a. FCI GP, "Policy Note: Improving the Efficiency of Credit Markets." August.

World Bank. 2018b. *Jobs and Growth: Brazil's Productivity Agenda*. Washington, DC: World Bank Group.

World Bank. Various Years. World Development Indicators (WDI). http://data .worldbank.org/data-catalog/world-development-indicators

Xavier, Wlamir Gonçalves, Rodrigo Bandeira-de-Mello, and Rosilene Marcon. 2014. "Institutional Environment and Business Groups' Resilience in Brazil." *Journal of Business Research*, 67: 900–7.

Yadav, Vineeta. 2011. *Political Parties, Business Groups, and Corruption in Developing Countries*. Oxford: Oxford University Press.

Zimmermann, Augusto. 2008. "How Brazilian Judges Undermine the Rule of Law: A Critical Appraisal." *International Trade and Business Law Review*, 11: 179–217.

Zockun, Maria Helena (ed.). 2007. "Simplificando o Brasil: propostas de reforma na relação econômica do governo com o setor privado." Texto para Discussão 3. São Paulo: Fundação Instituto de Pesquisas Econômicas (FIPE). www .fipe.org.br/Content/downloads/publicacoes/textos/texto_03_2007.pdf

Zucco, Cesar and Benjamin E. Lauderdale. 2011. "Distinguishing Between Influences on Brazilian Legislative Behavior." *Legislative Studies Quarterly*, 36: 363–96.

Zuvanic, Laura and Mercedes Iacoviello (with Ana Laura Rodriguez Gusta). 2010. "The Weakest Link: The Bureaucracy and Civil Service Systems in Latin America." In Carlos Scartascini, Ernesto Stein, and Mariano Tommasi (eds.), *How Democracy Works: Political Institutions, Actors, and Arenas in Latin American Policymaking*, 147–76. Washington, DC: Inter-American Development Bank.

Index

1988 Constitution, 36, 39, 41, 43, 57, 104, 107, 114, 122, 128, 133, 189, 196, 198, 203, 211, 213, 226, 233, 236, 241, 262, 280, 282, 284, 299

ABDI, Agência Brasileira de Desenvolvimento Industrial, 163, 165, 181, 186, 187, 242, 289, 343
Abreu e Lima refinery, 105
Abreu, Marcelo, 86
accountability agencies, 10, 189, 193
accountability, horizontal, 187, 236
accountability, vertical, 128, 182, 187, 236
actors, 262, 271
Afonso, José Roberto, 208
agricultural policy, 173
Alckmin, Geraldo, 240
Alcolumbre, David, 254
alternative payroll tax, 163, 165, 166
Alves, Roberto Carlos, 126
Amaral, Delcídio, 235
Ambev, 147
Amsden, Alice, 71
Andrade Gutierrez, 98, 147
ANEEL, 52, 134, 173, 270
ANFIP, National Association of Fiscal Auditors of the Revenue Service, 165
ANP, 52, 155, 173, 270
anticorruption, 20, 190, 192, 200, 216, 217, 219, 222, 226, 237, 257, 258, 263, 294, 296
ANVISA, 52, 134, 270, 279

Argentina, 40, 43, 57, 75, 76, 78, 80, 82, 83, 84, 85, 86, 87, 111, 112, 170, 172, 260, 266, 267, 272, 274, 275, 309, 310, 312, 318, 319, 325, 328, 345, 346, 347, 349
Arida, Pérsio, 20, 264
Asian tigers, 71
Associação Brasileira de Engenharia Industrial, ABEMI, 148
authoritarian rule, 10
automotive industry, 105, 169, 170, 171, 172, 178, 183, 255, 291
automotive regime, 64, 105, 169, 170, 171, 172
autonomous bureaucracy, 2, 12, 31, 197, 233, 237, 242, 244, 245, 246, 252, 259, 262, 302
  limits on, 200
Azul. See JetBlue

Bacha, Edmar, 86, 305
backward linkages, 9, 169
balance of payments crises, 36, 37, 49, 62
bancada parlamentar, 134, 182, 254, 255, 285
  evangelicals, 285
Banco do Brasil, 49, 50, 87, 94, 99, 105, 106, 130, 149, 152, 202, 211, 240, 249, 253, 269, 278, 293, 295, 300, 337
Banco Opportunity, 102
Banestado, 150, 189, 288, 332
bankruptcy, 106, 161, 174
Bastos, Márcio Thomaz, 218

Batista, Eike, 103, 156, 184, 235, 289, 321
Batista, Joesley, 121, 130, 137, 336
Bayer, 178
Belluzzo, Luiz Gonzaga, 72, 86
Bendine, Aldemir, 130
BM&FBovespa, 48, 93, 101, 277
BNDES, 29, 40, 49, 50, 60, 78, 81, 82, 86,
87, 93, 94, 96, 97, 98, 100, 101, 103,
104, 105, 141, 145, 161, 163, 164,
176, 178, 181, 187, 188, 206, 208,
209, 224, 227, 233, 238, 240, 248,
253, 254, 256, 269, 278, 279, 281,
286, 287, 291, 293, 294, 295, 299,
306, 316, 321, 324, 335, 351
BNDES credit, 80, 97, 98, 104, 170
BNDESpar, 100, 101, 102, 249, 279, 287
Boeing, 250, 254, 328
Bolsa Família, 7, 42, 44, 267, 281, 319
Bolsonaro, Jair, 12, 20, 61, 63, 81, 98, 167,
231, 232, 247, 248, 250, 251, 252,
253, 254, 255, 256, 257, 258, 259,
292, 302, 311, 316, 320, 321, 325,
329, 345, 349
as Queen of England, 254, 257
boom and bust, 5, 239
Boudou, Amado, 85
BR Distribuidora, 249
Bradesco, 50, 147, 152
Braskem, 151, 152, 286
Brazil Foods, 106, 156
Bresser stabilization plan, 203
Bresser-Pereira, Luiz Carlos, 71
bribes, 130, 147, 150, 152, 153, 241, 288,
289
BRICs, 6
BTG Pactual, 147
budget amendments, 125, 256, 283
Bulhões, Otávio Gouveia de, 86, 275
bureaucratic insulation, 10, 96, 196, 223,
294, 295

Cabral, Sérgio, 184, 230
Caixa Econômica Federal (CEF), 49, 50, 99,
149, 152, 240, 249, 269, 278, 280, 333
Camargo Corrêa, 156
campaign finance, 122, 129, 131,
134, 135, 137, 138, 141, 142, 143,
146, 147, 148, 153, 154, 192, 257,
287, 294
capital markets, 49, 61, 117, 261, 269
capital scarcity, 36

capitalismo de laços. See networked
capitalism
Cardoso administration, 101, 105, 205,
208, 240, 263, 293
Cardoso, Fernando Henrique, 12, 27, 38,
55, 63, 64, 81, 101, 138, 149, 155,
169, 170, 171, 174, 205, 227, 238,
240, 241, 248, 275, 278, 280, 288
Cavallo, Domingo, 85
CDES, 145, 146, 284, 287
CEBES, Centro Brasileiro de Estudos da
Saúde, 212
Celso Furtado, 229, 230, 231, 232
Central Bank, 19, 20, 41, 46, 47, 48, 49, 56,
82, 87, 88, 133, 198, 200, 202, 203,
205, 206, 209, 211, 217, 219, 248,
255, 263, 268, 269, 276, 349
Centro Brasileiro de Estudos da Sáude,
CEBES, 212
CEPAL, Comisión Económica para América
Latina y el Caribe, 67, 68, 86, 305,
320, 324, 342, 349
Cerveró, Nestor, 153
CGU, Federal Comptroller General, 11,
190, 198, 209, 216, 299, 303, 314
Chagas, Helena, 217, 230, 314
checks and balances, 4, 12, 25, 118, 122, 150,
151, 154, 158, 187, 190, 237, 258
weakness of, 5, 127, 128, 129, 130, 193
Chile, 6, 7, 43, 71, 75, 76, 77, 78, 80, 82, 83,
84, 85, 86, 87, 94, 127, 131, 195,
247, 267, 268, 274, 285, 297, 305,
306, 309, 318, 332, 342, 347, 350
Unidad Popular, 78
China, 6, 23, 36, 45, 48, 54, 157, 249, 254,
270, 279, 307, 323, 351
CIMA, Interministerial Council for Sugar
and Alcohol, 173, 292
civil service, 11, 26, 44, 85, 114, 115, 189,
191, 194, 195, 196, 197, 199, 202,
203, 206, 207, 210, 214, 216, 222,
223, 224, 225, 226, 227, 237, 258,
259, 296, 297, 298, 299
functional capacity, 195, 297
clientelism, 198, 222
CNDI, Conselho Nacional de
Desenvolvimento Industrial, 162, 181
CNI, National Confederation of Industry,
70, 131, 132, 133, 136
COAF, 217, 220, 299
coalition, 266, 279, 282, 283, 299, 301

Index

357

coalition bargaining
  broker, 251
  uncertainty in, 126
coalitional presidentialism, 12, 25, 26, 29,
    121, 122, 127, 130, 147, 154, 155,
    180, 187, 192, 222, 228, 229, 232,
    241, 246, 258, 259, 261, 262, 288, 289
  and developmental policies, 129
  definition of, 123
  tool kit of, 29, 123, 129
Cofins, 291
collective action problem, 61, 123, 289
collective incentives, 19
Collor, Fernando, 12, 27, 38, 63, 72, 77, 79,
    81, 101, 138, 140, 155, 169, 170,
    171, 174, 178, 204, 213, 222, 227,
    238, 278, 288, 293, 299
Colombia, 8, 268, 342
commodity boom, 5, 71, 79
comparative advantage, 8, 9, 72, 142, 172,
  178
comparative political economy, 3, 23, 24
  the role of single-country studies, 23
compulsory licenses, 299
compulsory licensing, 214, 215
Conceição Tavares, Maria da, 86
construction firms, 94, 98, 141, 147, 290
consumer electronics, 168
conta movimento, 202, 203
control, 262, 269, 270, 272, 276, 279, 280,
    282, 283, 287, 289, 292, 298
control mechanisms, 2, 4, 10, 12, 25, 26, 30,
    100, 122, 127, 158, 160, 167, 169,
    172, 177, 179, 180, 181, 184, 185,
    192, 193, 229, 232, 233, 238, 241,
    242, 244, 246, 257, 258
  definition of, 157, 158
  in neoliberal policy, 239, 251
controls
  horizontal, 160
coordination, 3, 31, 52, 65, 71, 72, 126,
    160, 177, 178, 180, 181, 185, 186,
    201, 226, 239, 261, 290, 295
coordination, problem of, 161
corporatism, 131, 132, 134, 226, 284, 334,
    339, 344, 352, 353
Correios, 99, 130, 149, 152, 231, 240, 278
corruption, 1, 128, 130, 142, 147, 148, 150,
    151, 152, 153, 154, 158, 179, 189,
    190, 191, 192, 217, 219, 220, 221,
    223, 231, 247, 251, 257, 286, 288,

289, 296, 297, 299, 300, 307, 309,
310, 312, 313, 317, 320, 327, 335,
337, 339, 342, 347, 348, 349, 351, 353
Cosan, 176, 292
Costa, Paulo Roberto, 54, 108, 147, 148,
    149, 176, 185, 231, 288, 310, 315,
    338, 339, 351
counterpart commitment. See reciprocity
counterpart reciprocity. See reciprocity
CPI, Congressional Committee of Inquiry,
    288
CPMF, 153, 205, 240, 253
credit markets, 91, 98
  cost of credit, 39, 47
  credit incentives, 186
  earmarked loans, 47, 49, 99, 269
  financing, 9, 50
  intragroup finance, 93
  preferential financing, 9
cross-shareholding, 27, 39, 51, 80, 92, 101,
    102, 227, 233, 235, 240, 287
Cruzado Plan, 37, 202, 203, 204, 222
CSAA, sectoral fund for sugar and alcohol,
    173
Cunha, Eduardo, 134, 149, 184, 296, 316
custo Brasil, 132, 133, 185
CVM securities and exchange commission,
    133, 192, 300

Dallagnol, Deltan, 221
Dantas, Daniel, 102, 184, 307
De Sanctis, Fausto, 221
debt 101
  crisis, 36, 60, 62, 70, 73, 74, 80, 97, 99,
    161, 293
  private sector, 134, 174, 179, 206, 268, 299
  public sector, 37, 40, 43, 44, 45, 47, 48, 179,
    201, 202, 203, 208, 209, 210, 211,
    267, 268, 269, 274, 275, 281, 299
  regressivity, 267
  service, 51, 248, 295, 299
  subnational, 206, 207, 209, 210
defensive parochialism, 30, 122, 123, 180,
    235, 243, 244, 258, 259
democracy, 1, 2, 3, 5, 6, 8, 10, 11, 22, 23, 24,
    25, 26, 36, 37, 38, 39, 43, 74, 76, 86,
    112, 113, 123, 131, 132, 138, 142,
    160, 186, 187, 192, 194, 200, 201,
    210, 211, 229, 232, 240, 247, 248,
    258, 266, 280, 282, 283, 293, 295, 352
demographic dividend, 6, 59, 260

Index

devaluation, 38
developmental hierarchical market economy (DHME), 2, 29, 90, 117, 122, 155, 166, 229, 232, 246, 259, 262
developmental state, 2, 3, 4, 9, 10, 12, 20, 25, 27, 30, 31, 35, 36, 37, 38, 39, 40, 48, 61, 64, 81, 89, 94, 96, 111, 121, 122, 123, 129, 130, 147, 148, 149, 155, 157, 158, 161, 162, 180, 185, 187, 192, 197, 224, 227, 228, 229, 231, 232, 233, 237, 238, 240, 242, 243, 244, 245, 246, 247, 249, 251, 253, 256, 258, 259, 260, 261, 262, 266, 276, 288, 295, 297, 302
developmentalism, 1, 3, 8, 10, 12, 26, 27, 28, 36, 46, 51, 64, 65, 69, 70, 71, 73, 76, 80, 87, 88, 89, 105, 121, 158, 169, 170, 179, 227, 238, 239, 241, 243, 258, 261, 266, 273, 274, 293
  and coordination problems, 3, 52, 72, 261
  and market failures, 72
  and natural monopolies, 72
  as national self-discovery, 72
  definition of, 65
  embeddedness of ideas, 62, 89
  from old to new, 75
  new, 27, 72, 73, 74
    role of the state in, 74
developmentalist ideas, 28, 64, 65, 66, 69, 74, 238
Dipp, Gilson, 217
Dirceu, José, 138
domestic content requirements, 9, 54, 55, 60, 61, 103, 104, 171, 183, 230, 233, 253, 279, 293
domestic industry, 9, 72, 97, 137
Dupont, 178

economic growth
  as residual, 39, 59, 180, 233
education, 3, 9, 11, 16, 27, 29, 58, 91, 108, 112, 113, 158, 183, 215, 235, 267, 273, 281, 282, 298, 300, 309
  access, 113
  outcomes, 112
  unsqueaky wheel, 113
electoral system, 121, 138, 180, 182
Eletrobras, 99, 152, 240, 253, 278, 341, 349
embedded autonomy, 157, 186
Embraer, 55, 99, 110, 250, 254, 295, 319, 328, 341

Embrapa, 176, 178, 224
Emergency Social Fund (FSE), 205
ENCCLA, National Strategy for Combating Corruption and Money Laundering, 216, 217, 218, 219, 220, 221, 222, 223, 300, 307
energy policy, 173
epistemic community, 84, 85, 195, 200, 217
equilibrium, 263, 264, 301, 302, 303
equity market, 93, 96
Estrella, Guilherme, 231
ethanol production, 172, 173, 174, 175, 176, 177, 178, 292, 305
Europe, 18, 27, 63, 323, 348
European Union, 6, 208
exchange rate, 35, 38, 45, 46, 48, 54, 56, 73, 136, 137, 162, 170, 206, 209, 266, 270, 271, 274, 291, 299
  appreciation of, 45, 56, 74, 271, 274
  floating, 61
  management, 54
exchange rate management, 274

Faria de Sá, Arnaldo, 157, 165
Faria, Lindberg, 230
Farias, P.C., 138
FAT, 60, 97, 269, 278
Federal Police, 11, 190, 198, 242, 252, 307
Fernández, Alberto, 77
Fernández, Roque Benjamin, 85
FGTS, 60, 269, 278, 280
Fibria, 106, 156
FIESP, Federation of Industries of the State of São Paulo, 132, 136, 164, 249, 253, 319
FINAME, 103, 104
financial sector, 11, 25, 29, 60, 94, 243, 268
  Basel requirements, 49
  bifurcation of, 48
  concentration of, 49
FINEP, 163, 167, 176, 212, 281
Fiocruz, 212, 319, 341
firm organization, 28, 62
  bifurcation of, 95
  capital intensive firms, 108
  commodity-producing firms, 29
  complementarities of, 116
  concentration, 95
  exporting firms, 56
    multinational corporations, 56
  foreign, 96

Index

hierarchical business groups, 92
multinational corporations, 59, 91, 183, 235
  protection of, 105
private firms, 9, 92, 94, 96, 101, 108, 113
privileges of incumbency, 30, 131, 166, 192, 193, 238, 243, 244, 245, 294
segmentation of firm life, 91
undiversified business groups, 96
fiscal
  primary expenditure, 43, 44
fiscal crisis, 62, 80, 231, 246, 268, 290
fiscal federalism, 203
fiscal imperative, 27, 36, 37, 38, 39, 40, 59, 64, 116, 117, 125, 126, 129, 186, 225, 234
fiscal policy
  fiscal constraints, 2, 10, 40, 45, 60, 246
  fiscal illusion, 60, 234, 268
fiscal reform, 37, 38, 60, 125, 194, 201, 204, 208
Foreign Corrupt Practices Act (FCPA), 36, 37, 38, 201, 208, 209, 210, 211, 290, 298, 316
fiscally opaque, 2, 27, 39, 40, 46, 60, 97, 117, 121, 129, 161, 185, 186, 234, 240, 243, 244, 294
flex car, 173, 175, 292
foreign capital, 38, 39, 56, 57, 61, 63, 209, 254
Foreign Corrupt Practices Act, 136, 152, 314
foreign investment, 39, 40, 53, 57, 60, 71, 104, 177, 234, 266, 285
foro privilegiado, 190, 237, 297
Fortes, Heráclito, 184
forward linkages, 9, 169, 172
Franco, Gustavo, 86, 205, 276
Franco, Itamar, 38, 63, 64, 204, 209, 293
Friedman, Milton, 71
Frondizi, Arturo, 76
FTAA, Free Trade Area of the Americas, 57
Funcef, 146, 278, 279, 287
Fundação Getulio Vargas, Rio de Janeiro (FGV-Rio), 85, 264, 275, 283, 308, 314, 317, 320, 340
Fundo Partidário, 139
Furnas, 152
Furtado, Celso, 68, 69, 70, 71, 72, 79, 86, 96, 170, 181, 187, 229, 230, 259, 289, 291, 293, 295, 301, 320, 321, 349

generic drugs, 214
Gerdau, 101, 156
Germany, 16, 21, 353
Gillette, 168
global financial crisis, 97, 102, 161, 167, 260
Globo, 156, 167, 210, 281, 309, 319, 336
government relations, 122, 131, 246
  pragmatism of, 182
government shareholder, 99
  majority shareholder, 99
  minority shareholder, 99
Graças Foster, Maria das, 231
Great Depression, 66, 70
Gudin, Eugenio, 79, 275, 276
Guedes, Paulo, 61, 248, 249, 250, 251, 252, 253, 256, 257, 313, 316, 331
Guerra, Lair, 216, 288

Harley Davidson, 168
hierarchical market economy (HME), 28, 90, 91, 107, 192, 234, 243, 244
  competitive advantage in commodities, 94
Hirschman, Albert, 9, 66, 71, 272, 287, 324
HIV treatment, 200
HIV/AIDS program, 194, 212, 214, 215, 216, 226
Honda, 168
horizontal accountability, 187
horse-trading, 2, 126, 241, 256
human capital, 3, 8, 9, 59, 72, 94, 111, 164, 172, 236
hyperactive paralysis, 26
  and institutional change, 26
hyperinflation, 7, 36, 37, 38, 60, 62, 80, 197, 204, 233, 266, 282, 293

IAA, Institute for Sugar and Alcohol, 175, 292
ICMS, 103
Iguatemi, 156
IMF, 64, 88, 208, 223, 295
import restrictions, 170
import substituting industrialization (ISI), 36, 50, 64, 66, 71
impunity, 147, 150, 151, 154, 189, 190, 191, 296
INAMPS, 212, 214
income inequality, 7, 59, 116

Index

incrementalism, 2, 20, 22, 26, 31, 122, 155, 195, 200, 204, 219, 222, 225, 227, 228, 237, 242, 246, 252, 254, 256, 258, 259, 262, 263, 264, 266, 267, 302, 303
indexation, 37, 46, 47, 268, 302
  and inertial inflation, 47
India, 6, 23, 50, 135, 270, 279, 351
indigenous industry, 8, 9, 63, 105
Indonesia, 23, 48, 55
industrial policy, 39, 53, 64, 79, 103, 179
  vertical targeting, 103
industrialization, 3, 66, 68, 72, 273, 275, 327
inflation, 11, 37, 38, 39, 43, 46, 47, 48, 49, 56, 60, 67, 74, 77, 88, 105, 177, 178, 202, 203, 205, 209, 266, 268, 276, 277, 278, 280, 298
inflation stabilization, 20, 27, 37, 40, 54, 56, 64, 75, 81, 202, 203, 204, 207, 222, 282, 293
influence peddling, 152, 189, 252, 283
informality, 39, 58, 107, 218, 254
Informatics Law, 104
infrastructure, 48, 52, 129, 158, 176, 189, 224, 231, 248
  investment, 11, 44, 51, 97, 162, 230, 233
  SOE predominance, 96
innovation, 2, 74, 96, 105, 116, 117, 158, 160, 162, 163, 164, 166, 170, 171, 172, 176, 195, 237, 260, 281, 293, 294, 343
  financing, 281
  Schumpeterian, 167, 181, 293, 294
innovation financing, 167
Inovar Auto, 169, 170, 255, 291, 313, 334
institutional change, 14
  big push, 20
  incrementalism, 20, 21, 31
  subway car example, 15
institutional complementarities, 1, 2, 4, 5, 12, 15, 16, 17, 18, 19, 20, 21, 22, 23, 24, 25, 26, 27, 30, 31, 32, 35, 59, 61, 65, 91, 114, 147, 161, 162, 195, 223, 227, 231, 237, 242, 248, 258, 261, 302
  and institutional change, 26
  and varieties of capitalism, 16
  emergent properties, 17
  hierarchically superior institutions, 246
  within the macroeconomic domain, 40
institutional domains, 4, 13, 21, 26, 239, 252, 258, 303

institutional equilibrium, 1, 4, 5, 6, 18, 19, 20, 22, 25, 26, 29, 30, 31, 59, 91, 121, 122, 131, 153, 158, 161, 184, 185, 192, 195, 228, 229, 231, 232, 236, 238, 239, 242, 246, 252, 258
  and intent, 18
  as dynamic state, 19
  Bolsonaro, 247
  checks and balances, 130
  decadent developmentalism, 258
  ideas as ballast for, 65
  multiple equilibria, 246
  reversion to, 240, 241, 252
  shift, 18, 31
  strategies, 16
institutional multiplicity, 161
institutions
  collective incentives, 13
  recurring patterns of behavior, 13
  rules of the game, 13
interest group
  capture, 22, 71, 88, 158, 222
interest group perspective, 22
international financial institutions
  conditionalities, 55, 89
International Monetary Fund, 81, 326
investment, 2, 3, 6, 9, 10, 11, 27, 39, 45, 48, 50, 51, 53, 60, 61, 66, 67, 72, 73, 91, 93, 94, 97, 99, 100, 111, 129, 158, 163, 165, 170, 171, 178, 225, 233, 234, 236, 238, 256, 260, 267, 269, 271, 274, 278, 279, 285, 292
IPI, 103, 105, 163, 178, 291, 293
Ipiranga, 176, 292
ISEB, 86
Itamaraty, 271, 295, 299
Itaú Unibanco, 50, 92, 106

J&F, 110, 151
Janene, José, 138, 147
Japan, 8, 21, 23, 157, 168, 239, 307
JBS, 92, 106, 130, 137, 147, 156, 184, 250, 287
  purchase of Swift and Pilgrim's Pride, 106
Jefferson, Roberto, 138
Jereissati, Tasso, 235
JetBlue, 279
Johnson, Chalmers, 71
Joint Stock Company Law, 279
Jucá, Romero, 184
judicial irresolution, 191, 257

Index

judiciary, 10, 20, 23, 43, 47, 76, 101, 107, 122, 128, 133, 141, 150, 151, 152, 160, 161, 162, 189, 190, 191, 192, 200, 206, 207, 209, 210, 215, 216, 217, 218, 219, 220, 223, 226, 229, 237, 241, 257, 258, 280, 281, 288, 296, 297, 299, 300, 305
Jurong, 230

Keynesian policies, 66, 272, 314, 324
Kirchner, Néstor and Cristina Fernández de, 77
Korea. See South Korea
Krueger, Anne, 71

labor
  taxes, 280
labor force productivity, 109
labor market, 59
  CLT, Consolidation of Labor Laws, 58
  duality of, 58
  informality, 109
  labor force productivity, 111
  segmentation, 90, 95, 107, 109, 131
  segmentation of, 29, 108
  skilled labor, 9, 16, 96, 113, 183
labor policy, 58, 107, 173, 280
labor unions, 108, 164, 226, 231, 280, 285
Lacerda, Guilherme, 279
Lava Jato, 99, 142, 147, 148, 149, 150, 152, 185, 189, 190, 191, 231, 232, 242, 249, 250, 251, 257, 283, 288, 289, 296, 330
Lessa, Carlos, 86
Levy, Joaquim, 79
Lewis, Arthur, 71
liberalism
  as an out of place idea, 70
  ascendant in Brazil, 79
  institutional fetishism of, 69, 70
Lobão, Edson, 90, 230
local content requirements, 270, See domestic content requirements
lost decade, 70
Loyola, Gustavo, 206
Luiz Inácio Lula da Silva, 63, 90, 102, 106, 129, 138, 147, 149, 150, 156, 175, 177, 181, 184, 190, 198, 231, 235, 238, 240, 241, 266, 268, 269, 279, 281, 292, 293, 296, 305, 306, 310, 323, 328, 330, 343

Machado, Sérgio, 231
Macri, Maurício, 77
Madruga
  Antenor, 218
Madruga, Antenor, 218
Maggi, 156
Malan, Pedro, 70, 87, 88, 157, 331
Manaus Free Trade Zone, 167, 168, 169, 172, 257
Mantega, Guido, 35, 77, 87, 88, 97, 149, 266, 276
Marco Polo, 110
Mariel port, 105
market credibility, 46, 84, 135, 204, 205, 209, 210
market failures, 3, 8, 9
Martínez de Hoz, José Alfredo, 85
Mattar, Salim, 249
Meirelles, Henrique, 276
Mendes Júnior, 152
Mendonça de Barros, Luiz Carlos, 206
Menem, Carlos, 77, 85
Mercosur, 57, 248, 270, 271, 332
merit hiring, 10, 37, 142, 190, 195, 196, 198, 288, 297
Mexican Peso crisis, 37
Mexico, 23, 36, 43, 87, 111, 131, 260, 267, 270, 285, 332, 345, 347
middle-income trap, 158, 352
military, 266, 275, 278, 295
military regime, 2, 36, 40, 53, 64, 77, 80, 85, 86, 96, 104, 123, 133, 140, 142, 167, 195, 204, 212, 240, 266, 275, 283
Minha Casa, Minha Vida, 224
minimum wage, 58, 74, 268
mining, 95, 100, 102, 108, 110, 130, 147, 166, 169, 184, 235
Ministério Público, 189, 198, 217, 303, 307, 309
minority shareholding, 60, 100, 101, 102, 180, 287
monetary authority, 27, 36, 46, 47, 49, 50, 266, 282
monetary policy
  ineffectiveness of, 46
  interest rates
    and financialization, 18, 48
  real interest rates, 47, 49, 74, 97, 98, 105, 206, 253
  SELIC rate, 98
Monsanto, 178

moral hazard, 206, 210
Moro, Sérgio, 189, 221, 251, 257, 297, 335
Motta, Sérgio, 138
Myrdal, Gunnar, 71

national development plan, 98
national preferences, 61, 64, 90, 105
neoliberal, 10, 11, 12, 27, 38, 45, 63, 73, 74, 78, 79, 83, 85, 86, 87, 89, 105, 118, 169, 170, 174, 227, 232, 238, 239, 247, 248, 251, 259, 273, 274, 275, 276
neoliberalism, 76, 80, 241, 274, 293
  as emergency response to crisis, 63
Net, 106, 267, 277
networked capitalism, 5, 102
Neves, Aécio, 121, 130, 149, 150, 184
new social contract, 43, 115
New Zealand, 208
Nigeria, 53
Nóbrega, Mailson da, 202

O'Donnell, Guillermo, 160
OAS, 147, 150, 151, 156, 300
Odebrecht, 92, 98, 99, 130, 147, 151, 152, 153, 156, 237, 286, 289
OECD, 6, 16, 40, 42, 55, 112, 225, 271, 279, 294, 300
OGX, 237
Oi, 106, 279
open-list proportional representation (OLPR), 123, 128, 139, 145, 182, 192
Organic Law of Health, 213

Palocci, Antonio, 87, 138
Pan-American Health Organization, 212
Parente, Pedro, 253
party fragmentation, 282
party system
  effective number of parties, 123, 255
  fragmentation, 29, 30, 121, 123, 124, 126, 129, 131, 135, 155, 181, 182, 192, 235, 236, 237, 251, 255
path dependence, 17, 21, 22, 284
patrimonialism, 5, 195
patronage, 87, 195, 196, 296
PDP, Política de Desenvolvimento Produtivo, 162, 163, 167, 176, 291, 323
pension funds, 30, 100, 101, 102, 106, 129, 146, 152, 184, 188, 233, 240, 253, 278, 287

pension reform. See social security reform
Perdigão, 106
personal vote, 139, 182
Peru, 7, 268, 298
Petrobras, 52, 81, 99, 105, 106, 110, 130, 147, 148, 149, 150, 152, 153, 155, 176, 178, 185, 230, 231, 234, 240, 249, 253, 270, 278, 288, 289, 292, 306, 308, 310, 314, 328, 341
Petros, 146, 278, 279, 287
Pezão, Luiz, 230
Philips, 237
pilot agency, absence of, 186, 187, 188, 242
Pinheiro, Wagner, 231, 279
Pinochet, Augusto, 71, 77
PIS, 60, 97, 269, 291
PIS-PASEP, 60
PITCE, Política Industrial, Tecnológica e de Comércio Exterior, 162, 163, 166, 167, 176, 181, 281, 343
Plano Brasil Maior, 64, 162, 163, 164, 165, 166, 167, 170, 176, 183, 186, 229, 242, 290, 309, 332
plea bargaining, 130, 220, 257
PMDB, Partido do Movimento Democrático Brasileiro, 127, 144, 148, 149, 184, 230, 279, 283, 288, 296
Pochmann, Márcio, 86, 280, 338
policy resoluteness, 75, 76, 77, 89, 122, 180, 181
Policy resoluteness and decisiveness, 274
Política Industrial, Tecnológica e de Comércio Exterior (PITCE), 343
political appointments, 152
political influence, 107, 161, 192, 250
Pontifícia Universidade Católica, Rio de Janeiro, 64, 85, 86, 88, 275, 304, 335
Postalis, 278
Pou, Pedro, 85
Prebisch, Raúl, 35, 67, 68, 70, 71, 272, 273, 340, 346, 350
pre-salt oil, 36, 55, 104, 148, 231
presidential power, 123
  agenda-setting, 124
  appointments, 129, 188
  budgetary powers, 125
  cabinet powers, 126
  dirty secret, 233
  partisan powers, 124
Previ, 102, 146, 278, 279, 287
price controls, 177

Index

privatization, 11, 18, 38, 51, 53, 60, 63, 64, 73, 80, 81, 97, 99, 100, 101, 184, 208, 209, 227, 248, 253, 255, 269, 274, 275, 278
  public support for, 81
Proálcool, 173, 174, 291, 292
productivity, 6, 9, 11, 50, 67, 73, 106, 107, 109, 111, 114, 158, 169, 174, 175, 179, 235, 237, 285, 353
productivity trap, 113
PROER, Programa de Estímulo à Reestruturação e ao Fortalecimento do Sistema Financeiro Nacional, 207
PROES, Programa de Incentivo à Redução do Setor Público na Atividade Bancária, 207, 282
PROFARMA, 279
Proinfa, Incentive Program for Alternative Energy Sources, 173
PROMEF, Programa de Modernização e Expansão da Frota, 230
PRONATEC, 163, 164, 281
protectionism, 53, 56, 164, 271
protests, 8, 231
PSDB, Partido da Social Democracia Brasileira, 63, 80, 87, 127, 130, 144, 147, 148, 149, 150, 180, 182, 231, 240, 251, 276, 283, 288, 315
PT, Partido dos Trabalhadores, 63, 80, 87, 113, 127, 144, 147, 148, 149, 150, 158, 162, 174, 176, 180, 182, 230, 250, 276, 279, 283, 288, 296, 315, 333

Queiroz Galvão, 147

R&D, 158, 162, 163, 168, 171, 176, 184, 290, 291, 293, 294
Reagan, Ronald, 71
Real Plan, 7, 37, 43, 56, 58, 64, 81, 88, 133, 175, 203, 204, 205, 206, 209, 266, 302
reciprocity, x, 30, 141, 157, 159, 161, 163, 166, 167, 169, 178, 187, 237, 256, 280
reform, 2, 5, 8, 10, 11, 12, 20, 22, 23, 31, 41, 52, 61, 64, 79, 83, 108, 117, 126, 155, 163, 183, 186, 195, 200, 201, 202, 205, 207, 208, 209, 211, 214, 216, 219, 220, 221, 222, 226, 227, 232, 236, 237, 238, 239, 246, 247, 248, 251, 253, 254, 255, 256, 257, 259, 267, 274, 284, 296, 297, 298

parametric not paradigmatic, 12, 44, 122, 155, 181
reactive to short-term crisis, 122
smuggled, 185
regressivity, 5
  civil service spending, 225
  inflation, 74
  pensions, 116, 226
  public sector wages, 225
  social policy, 2, 27, 61, 114, 115
  spending, 59
  taxation, 39, 41, 42, 60, 115, 234, 290
  taxes, 267
regulatory agencies, 12, 51, 52, 53, 160, 173, 188, 239, 251, 254, 257, 270, 293
regulatory bodies, 51, 52, 104, 155, 269, 300
regulatory uncertainty, 162
Reintegra, 103
rent-seeking, 9, 72, 134, 146, 159, 160, 179, 190, 193, 226
resoluteness of policy, 274
Ricardian models of trade, 71
Rodrigues, Roberto, 177
Rodriguez Neto, Eleutério, 213, 341
Rosa, Sérgio, 279, 314, 340, 343
Rose-Ackerman, Susan, 160
Rousseff, Dilma, 49, 62, 63, 64, 81, 105, 124, 138, 142, 147, 149, 158, 167, 169, 170, 171, 178, 184, 201, 210, 229, 230, 231, 235, 238, 241, 248, 252, 266, 268, 280, 281, 292, 301, 335, 338, 340
Russia, 23, 208, 351
Rwanda, 21

S system, 112, 250, 313
  vocational training, 112, 113
Sadia, 103, 106
sanitarista movement, 211, 212, 213, 214, 216
Santander, 50, 151, 287
Sarney, José, 55, 126, 167, 235, 278, 293
savings, 6, 10, 59, 60, 61, 66, 68, 97, 99, 111, 158, 163, 248, 260, 269, 278, 280
SBM, 237, 288, 289, 350
sectoral incentives, 165, 181, 183, 184, 193, 235
sectoral policy, 29, 61, 64, 169, 293
sectoral privileges, 129
selectivity, 179
Serra, José, 208, 214, 240

shipbuilding, 9, 104, 229, 230, 231
shoe producers, 170
SIAFI, 202
Siderbrás, 101
Simples regime, 109
Singer, Hans, 71
slush funds, 129
social policy
  segmented, 114
social security, 11, 20, 30, 43, 58, 59, 60, 61,
  100, 102, 106, 109, 115, 122, 129,
  145, 163, 165, 184, 226, 233, 240,
  248, 251, 253, 256, 267, 278, 279,
  280, 287, 290
social security reform, 251, 256
social spending, 39, 59, 60, 114
SOEs, state-owned enterprises, 45, 53, 73,
  81, 92, 99, 100, 105, 107, 116, 131,
  132, 149, 151, 153, 155, 184, 188,
  206, 241, 246, 249, 253, 278, 279,
  290, 295, 298
  census of, 99
soft budget constraint, 70
South Africa, 23
South Korea, 8, 48, 79, 110, 157, 236, 239,
  247, 294
special interests, 61, 253, 257
spillover effects, 72, 169
state
  size of, 40
state dominance
  legal foundations, 96
state-owned banks, 11, 48, 49, 73, 94, 129,
  173, 174, 180, 184, 187, 188, 206,
  207, 211, 217, 224, 234, 246, 248,
  249, 269, 278, 282, 300
statute of limitations, 191, 297
stock market, 155
strategic control, 10, 158, 162, 226
strategic planning, 4, 10, 159,
  294, 295
strategic review, 193, 294
structuralism, 66, 67, 68, 69, 86,
  272, 273
Sudan, 53
SUFRAMA, 251, 257
SUMOC, 86, 87, 295
sunset provisions, 164, 179, 290
SUS, Sistema Único de Sáude, 104, 211, 213,
  214, 319
Syngenta, 178

Taiwan, 8, 239, 349
Tavares, Martus, 208
tax breaks, 30, 139, 164, 165, 171, 176, 182,
  183, 184, 185, 186, 235, 290, 291, 293
tax exemptions, 42, 103, 104, 168, 179
tax incentives, 55, 60, 103, 104, 107, 170,
  172, 179, 233, 255, 291
tax rebates, 168
tax reform, 12, 41, 183, 248, 256, 267
Taxa de Juros de Longo Prazo (TJLP), 98
taxation, 27, 40, 42, 43, 44, 60, 61, 76, 109,
  203, 268, 282
  CIDE, 177
  indirect, 42
  regressivity of, 40, 42
TCU, 104, 106, 152, 154, 160, 172, 188,
  190, 300, 321, 353
technology, 8, 9, 68, 91, 94, 106, 107, 159,
  163, 164, 166, 169, 171, 172, 178,
  255, 281, 291
Tele Norte Leste, 106
Temer, Michel, 20, 27, 75, 79, 108, 125,
  155, 184, 190, 231, 238, 246, 250,
  251, 252, 253, 254, 257, 281, 284,
  298, 303, 329
terms of trade, 8, 66, 67, 68, 72
textile industry, 144, 165, 170
Thatcher, Margaret, 71
total factor productivity, 6
trade opening, 274, 293
trade policy
  export finance, 103, 104, 293
  export subsidies, 60, 73, 103
  external constraints, 54
  non-tariff barriers, 54, 55, 64
  PROEX, 54
  selective opening, 73
  tariff protections, 60, 103, 105, 253, 292
  tariffs, 9, 54, 76, 77, 103, 185, 271, 276,
    291, 293
  trade integration, 57
  trade liberalization, 12, 53, 55, 56, 57, 73,
    75, 77, 81, 132, 274, 285
    discriminatory, 170
  trade opening
    purposes of, 56
transparency, 20, 37, 127, 188, 204, 205, 209,
  211, 216, 233, 234, 266, 299, 350
Transpetro, 229, 230, 231, 237, 350
tripé, 36, 38, 209
Trubek, David, 160

UERJ, 212, 312
UFRJ, Universidade Federal do Rio de Janeiro, 86
UNICA sugar producer association, 175
UNICAMP, Universidade Estadual de Campinas, 86
unions, private sector, 108
unions, public sector, 108
United States, ix, 6, 7, 16, 23, 48, 50, 52, 55, 57, 82, 83, 84, 85, 86, 97, 98, 99, 103, 106, 136, 137, 138, 139, 152, 168, 169, 172, 174, 208, 248, 257, 271, 278, 286, 289, 292, 311, 312, 317, 324, 325, 328, 350
upgrading coalition, 31, 180, 182, 184, 213
Uruguay, 6, 271, 321
usineiros, 175, 305, 320, 340
UTC, 147

Vale, 63, 99, 100, 101, 102, 106, 110, 121, 130, 147, 235, 253, 279, 289, 336
varieties of capitalism, 3, 16, 17, 25, 26, 35, 91
Venezuela, 105, 260, 318
veto player, 2, 5, 22, 31, 121, 122, 145, 181, 198, 199, 200, 201, 212, 220, 222, 225, 226, 235, 237, 244, 258, 261
Vicunha, 101
Votorantim, 106, 277

Wade, Robert, 71
Washington Consensus, 4, 23, 27, 38, 63, 71, 73, 87, 273, 274, 353
Worker Productivity, 110
World Bank, 10, 48, 97, 216
World Economic Forum (WEF), 51, 112, 226
World Trade Organization, 55, 271, 291, 299
WTO, 270, 271

XP Investimentos, 255

Lightning Source UK Ltd.
Milton Keynes UK
UKHW010814101120
373118UK00004B/10